CW01657673

Germany Divided

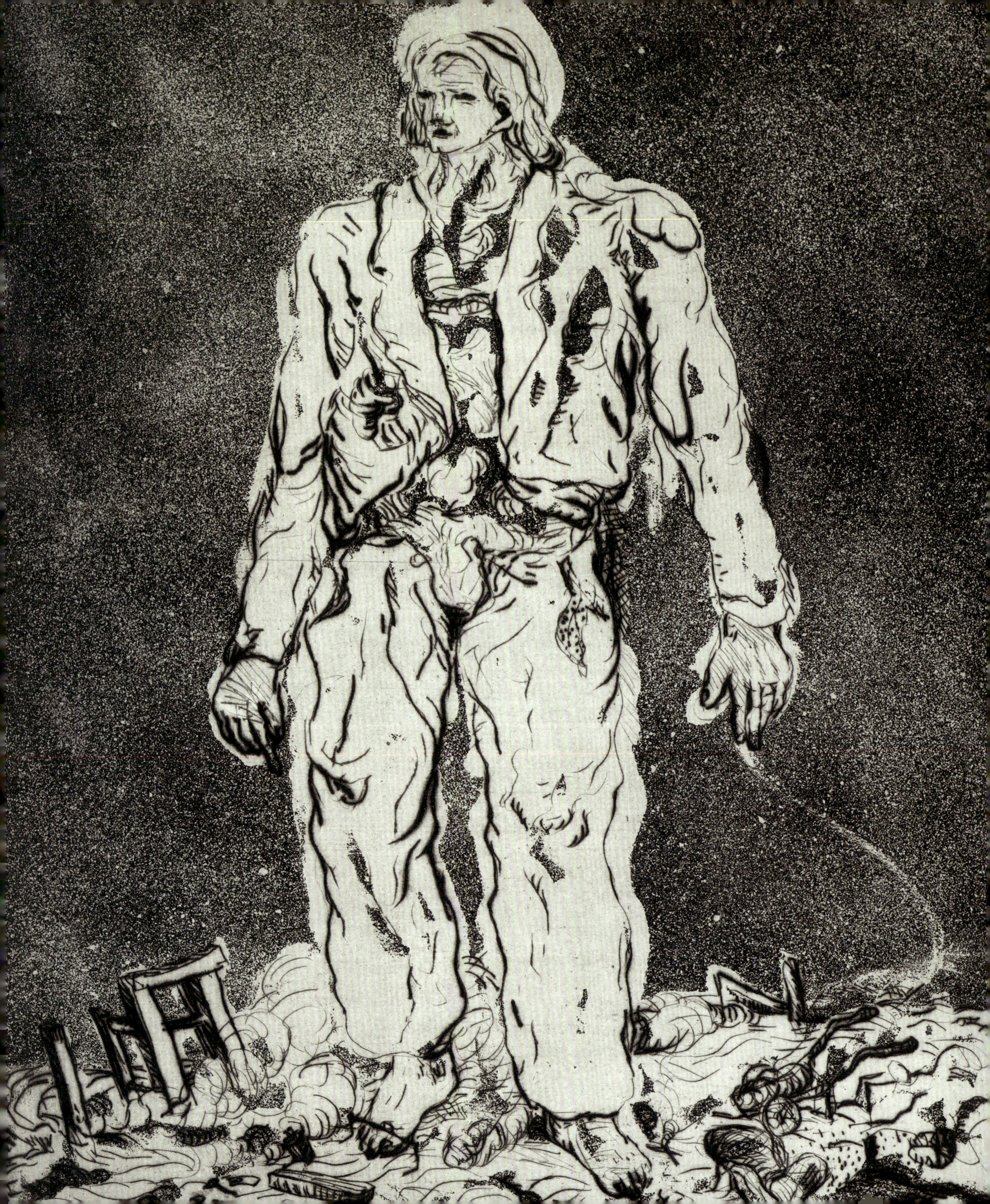

The British Museum

Germany Divided

Baselitz and his generation

From the Duerckheim Collection

John-Paul Stonard

Published to accompany the exhibition *Germany divided: Baselitz and his generation* at the British Museum from 6 February to 31 August 2014.

This exhibition has been made possible by the provision of insurance through the Government Indemnity Scheme. The British Museum would like to thank the Department for Culture, Media and Sport, and Arts Council England for providing and arranging this indemnity.

© 2014 The Trustees of the British Museum

John-Paul Stonard has asserted the right to be identified as the author of this work.

First published in 2014 by The British Museum Press
A division of The British Museum Company Ltd
38 Russell Square, London WC1B 3QQ
britishmuseum.org/publishing

A catalogue reference for this book is available from the British Library

ISBN 978-0-7141-2690-6

Designed by Thomas Manss & Company
Printed in Italy by Graphicom srl

Papers used by The British Museum Press are recyclable products made from wood grown in well-managed forests and other controlled sources. The manufacturing processes conform to the environmental regulations of the country of origin.

FSC
www.fsc.org
MIX
Paper from responsible sources
FSC® C013123

Many of the works illustrated in this book are from the collection of the British Museum. Museum registration numbers and provenance details can be found in the catalogue listing on pages 168–77 and the illustration credits on page 189. Further information about the Museum and its collection can be found at britishmuseum.org.

Frontispiece: *Der Hirte* ('Herdsman'), 1965 (detail).
Georg Baselitz, see cat. 10, p. 52

Contents

Director's Foreword

The present exhibition, with the accompanying gift by Count Christian Duerckheim of thirty-four works on paper by Baselitz and his contemporaries, is a transformative moment in the British Museum's long-standing collecting of German prints and drawings. This tradition can be traced back to the Museum's beginnings in 1753 when an album of drawings by Albrecht Dürer was one of the great treasures of the founding collection of the Anglo-Irish doctor and Enlightenment man of science, Hans Sloane. The album contained studies that fitted Sloane's natural history interests, such as Dürer's beguilingly fantastical drawing of a rhinoceros, but it seems certain that the learned doctor also marvelled at Dürer's dazzling originality and creative range in watercolour, pen and chalk.

Around this original nucleus successive generations of curators, like Campbell Dodgson, and donors such as William Mitchell gathered prints and drawings that reflect the rich regional diversity of the German-speaking world, from the Swiss Alps traversed by countless German artists from Dürer to Baselitz on their way to Italy, to the shores of the Baltic that inspired Caspar David Friedrich as well as Ernst Ludwig Kirchner. The scholarly rigour and professionalism that guided the acquisition and cataloguing of this material in the Department of Prints and Drawings in the late 19th and early 20th centuries owed much to the inspiration of its counterparts in Berlin, Dresden and Munich. These close ties were loosened by two world wars but they were never severed entirely, not least because the rise of National Socialism brought a brilliant crop of art historians to Britain: such as the Vienna-university-trained Hungarian, Johannes Wilde, whose catalogue of the Museum's Michelangelo drawings remains indispensable.

Throughout the last century the appreciation of German Old Master prints and drawings remained high at the British Museum, but the same could not be said of contemporary graphic art. With a few exceptions, such as the fine group of Käthe Kollwitz prints in Campbell Dodgson's Bequest in 1949, this was too radically experimental for curatorial tastes in London. It was not until the latter part of the 1970s that the newly appointed Frances Carey and Antony Griffiths began to repair this gap by acquiring Expressionist prints for the exhibition, *The Print in Germany 1880–1933*, in 1984.

At much the same time Count Christian Duerckheim was beginning to form his outstanding collection of German contemporary art, a selection of which he has generously allowed us to show in this exhibition, *Germany Divided: Baselitz and his generation*. His offer to donate around a third of the works to the British Museum, as well as funding the present publication written by John-Paul Stonard, means that the legacy of the exhibition is hugely significant. The gift of such major works by Baselitz, Lüpertz, Palermo, Penck, Polke and Richter from the 1960s and 1970s, the seminal period for these key artists, allows their contribution to be added to the long historical sweep of German graphic art represented at the British Museum. The thoughtful, informed selection from the wealth of Count Duerckheim's collection by the exhibition's curator, Stephen Coppel, is highlighted by the fascinating evolution it traces of the fracturing and inversion of motifs that can be observed in Baselitz's work.

The fact that all the artists in *Germany Divided*, in common with Count Duerckheim himself, were born in East Germany but at different times moved to the West makes it the ideal starting point to begin the examination of the country's complex history and culture. This story will be explored further in the exhibition opening in autumn 2014 to mark the twenty-fifth anniversary of the fall of the Berlin Wall. It is thanks to Christian Duerckheim that we can bring this narrative to the present era with Baselitz and his contemporaries' widely different reactions to Germany's long fractured, now reunited, state.

Neil MacGregor
Director, British Museum, London

Introduction: Go West Young Man!

Late in the afternoon of Sunday, 3 August 1980, the artist A.R. Penck (Ralf Winkler; b. 1939) was driven by a friend from his home in Dresden to a small town on the border between East and West Germany. With nothing but a few notebooks and music cassettes, he set out on foot to cross to the West. After many years of opposition to the East German state, Penck had earlier that day been given permission to leave the country by midnight – he was, by his own choice, *Ausgebürgert* – 'denaturalized'. Crossing the border, he was stopped by guards, who questioned him and listened to his cassettes, but let him pass. It was a long walk, about ten miles, to the border town of Bebra on the western side. His whole life, he later recalled, seemed split in two: 'Still in the East, yet in the West. Us in the East, them in the West; us in the West, them in the East, from one system to another. Is it another system? How so? Why have I come here? There's no way back! Time stands still and yet continues. This is a new identity. I seem back in my childhood, and at the same time in a world of science fiction.'[1]

All of the artists in this selection of prints and drawings from the collection of Count Christian Duerckheim had their origins in eastern Germany, but moved and made their careers in the West. This journey seems to have been a rite of passage for success as an artist in West Germany after 1961, the year in which the borders were closed and work began on constructing the Berlin Wall. Penck remained in the East longer than the others, but made his name in the West thanks to the dealer Michael Werner, and others who were supporting and showing his work. Markus Lüpertz (b. 1941) and Sigmar Polke (1941–2010) had both moved during childhood with their families as part of the forced expulsion of some eight million Germans from the eastern territories lost at the end of the Second World War (fig. 1).[2] For others, the journey was less dramatic; Blinky Palermo (born as Peter Schwarze; later Peter Heisterkamp; 1943–77) moved west with his foster family at the age of nine for the sake of his father's career. Others stayed and trained in the East, but soon realized that it would be impossible for them to follow an 'official' career as an artist in East Germany. Georg Baselitz (b. 1938) was obliged to move to West Berlin after being expelled from the Art Academy in East Berlin. Gerhard Richter (b. 1932) spent time living and working in Dresden as a Socialist artist before deciding that life would be better on the other side of the Wall.

Cultural reconstruction

In his memoirs, the German statesman Konrad Adenauer described the sense of utter destitution and loss that faced Germans in the wake of the War (fig. 2): 'Every day thousands of citizens streamed back into Cologne, on foot or by whatever transport was later available on goods trains. I can still see those open freight cars, jammed with people who wanted to get home again, no matter what hardships were involved. Pale, tired, haggard, they carried the few belongings they still had, and usually found nothing but their destroyed homes.'[3] Those born during the 1940s grew up among ruins, with 'brick dust between one's teeth', as the writer Günter Grass put it, in a situation of profound political instability.[4] The division of Germany into four military zones of occupation – Soviet, American, British and French – was agreed at the Potsdam Conference in the summer of 1945. The Conference also ratified the dramatic redefinition of the eastern border of Germany, leading to the expulsion of the German population from territories ceded to Poland, Hungary and Czechoslovakia. Many of the refugees witnessed by Adenauer entering Cologne were those expelled from the former eastern territories.

1. Map of Germany in 1961 indicating the interzonal borders of West Germany of 1945 and the territories ceded to Poland and the USSR in 1949

2. *Fronleichnamsprozession 1946* ('Corpus Christi Procession 1946'), published in *Gesang im Feuerofen* ('Songs of the Furnace'), 1947
Hermann Claasen

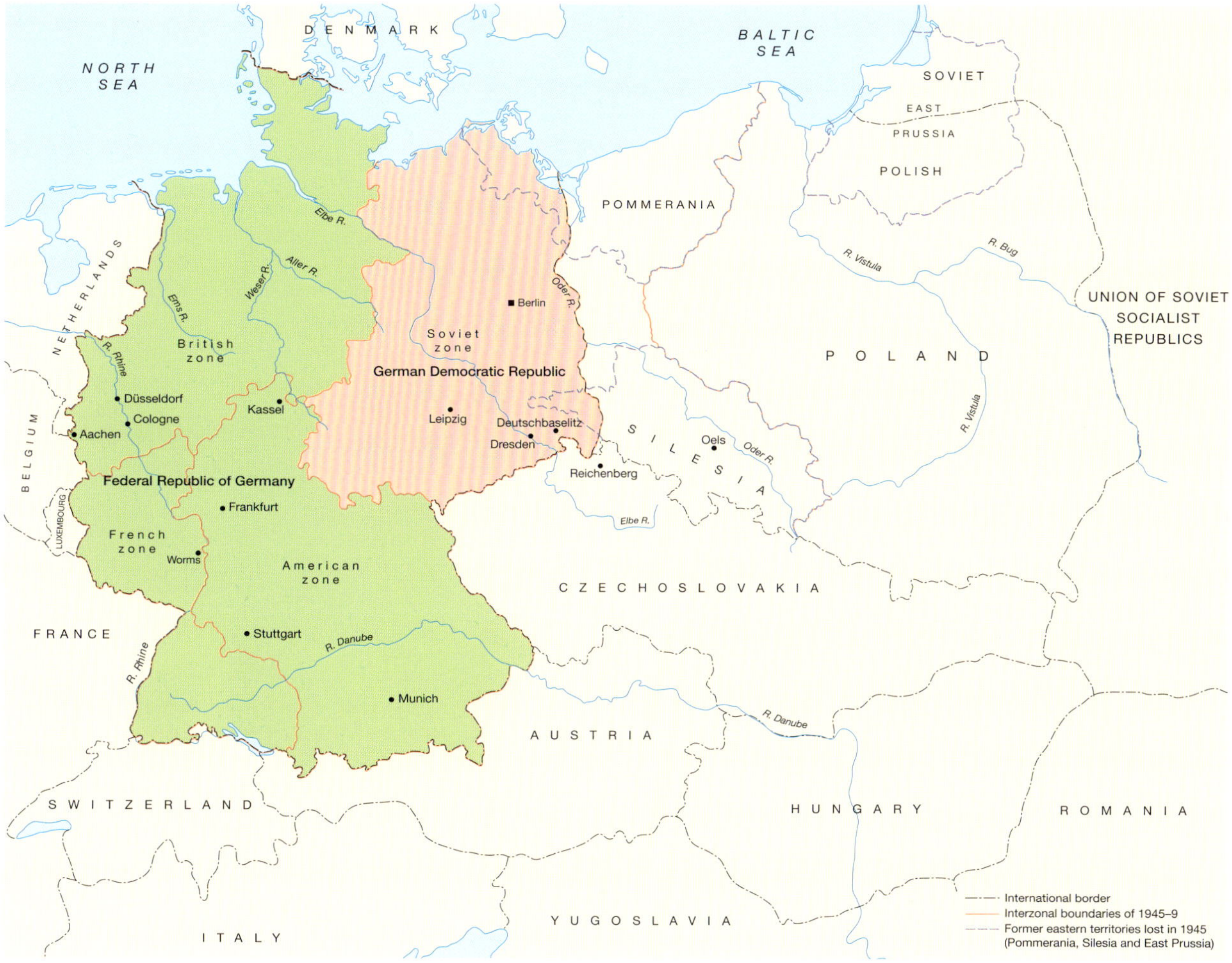

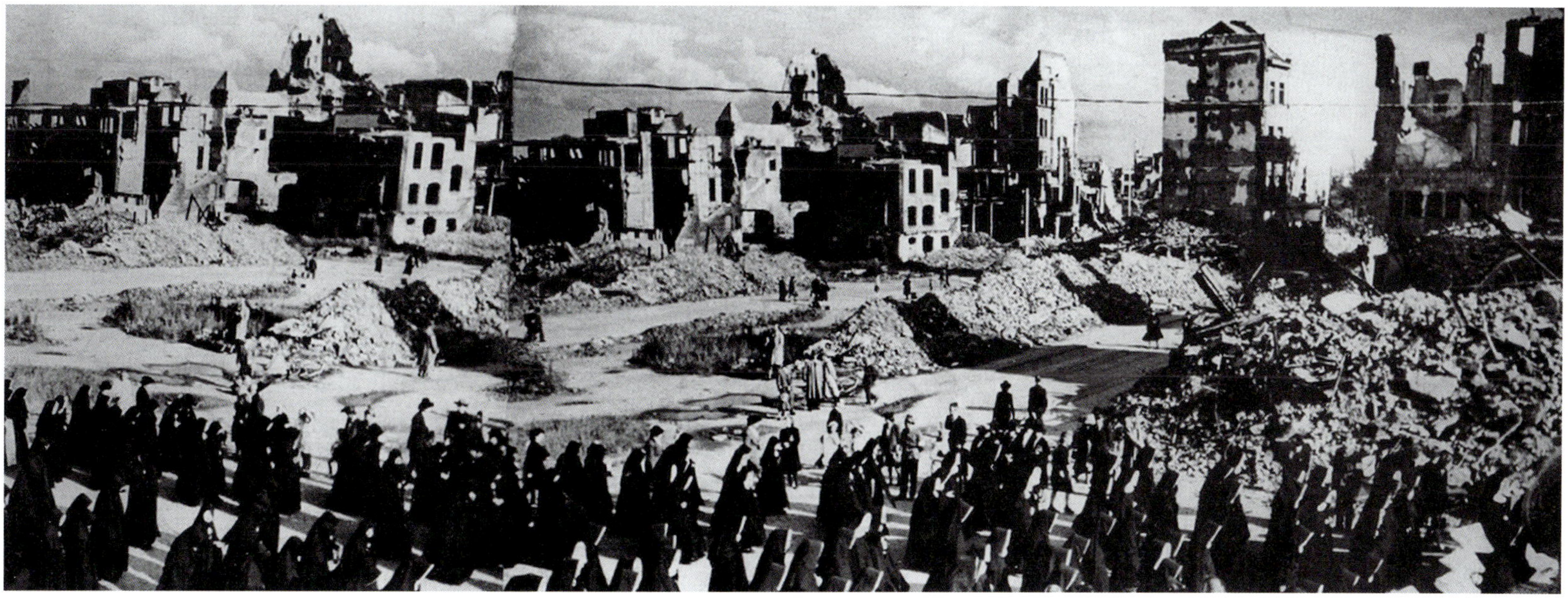

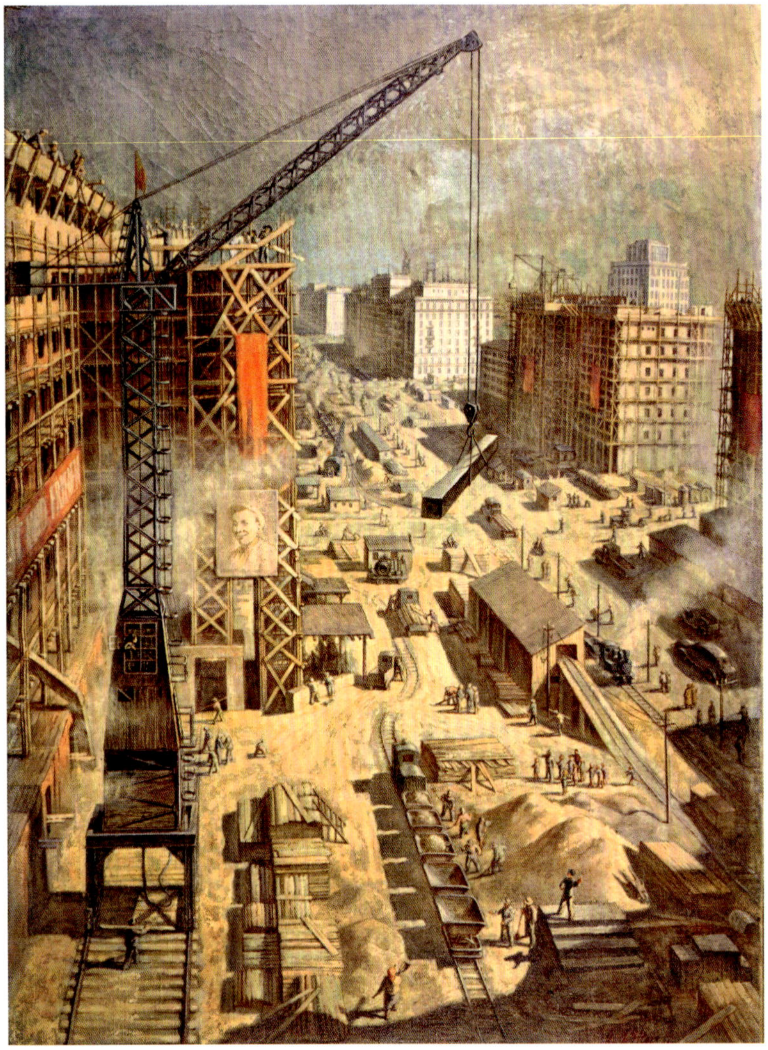

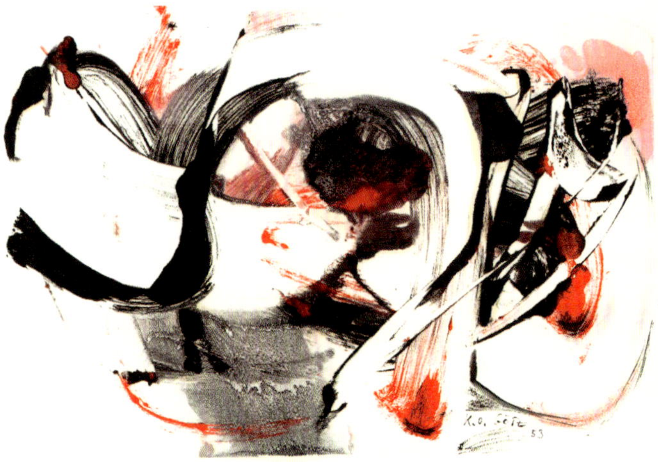

Allied policies also turned towards 're-education' and rebuilding civilian life. The arts played a vital role in cultural reconstruction, particularly in the Soviet Zone, initially the most active in promoting cultural activity.[5] For many artists, the first few years after the Second World War were a golden age of freedom and exchange, following their experience under the Third Reich. The division of Germany into two separate States in late 1949, however, threw up new barriers and ideological demands. The 'style wars' that took place in the visual arts, and which quietly raged in criticism and interpretation throughout the 1950s, are well known; the adoption of Socialist Realism as the official style of painting in East Germany was countered by the promotion of abstraction as the emblem of freedom in the West. In his 1954 *Malerei im 20. Jahrhundert* ('Painting in the Twentieth Century'), Werner Haftmann (1912–99) presented an influential statement of this vision of abstract painting as a product of the 'free' politics of Western Europe (figs 3–4). It was a case of politics by other means; style as the expression of competing ideologies reduced to their most basic terms. How much the 'style wars' determined what artists were making and thinking is another question.

Throughout the 1950s, cultural reconstruction in the West was buoyed by an astounding economic boom; the 'Economic Miracle', or *Wirtschaftswunder*. Optimism about the future was accompanied by a feeling that the past was recoverable – however much this meant ignoring certain aspects of recent history. The first *Documenta* exhibition held in 1955 in the West German town of Kassel, only twenty miles from the border with the East, was a direct expression of this newfound confidence. Held in the ruins of the Fridericianum, the oldest public museum in Germany, *Documenta* combined paintings and sculpture made before and after the War, suggesting a direct continuity and effectively discounting the legacy of the Third Reich. The displays also placed German art back into a broader European context, after years of isolation. The photographic pantheon of modern German artists at the entrance was a bold statement of pride in a tradition that the National Socialists had tried to sever (fig. 5). The point was made forcibly by the confrontation, in one of the main galleries, of a large painting by Fritz Winter (1905–76) *Komposition in Blau und Gelb* ('Composition in Blue and Yellow', 1955), opposite *Girl in Front of a Mirror* (1932) by Pablo Picasso (1881–1973).

The personal freedoms of life in West Germany, symbolized by *Documenta*, and the relatively higher standard of living, created a strong allure for those living on the other side of the inter-German border. Migration and escape from East Germany to the West was so common that the authorities had a word for it: *Republikflucht* ('desertion from the Republic'). Artists and writers left East Germany in increasing numbers following the 1959 *Bitterfeld Weg* ('Bitterfeld Path') policy of Walter Ulbricht, the East German leader, reinforcing Socialist Realism and the duty of artists to participate in forging a Socialist nation – making it virtually impossible to create works of art or literature devoted to any other goal. By 1961, when the East–West border was closed and construction on the Berlin Wall had begun, around three and a half million people had left for the West, of whom, according to an exhibition staged in Dresden in 1990, some 665 were professional artists.[6] Few made the return journey.

At the centre of this dramatic political and cultural confrontation stood the city of Berlin. From the beginning of the century it had risen swiftly to become an emblem of Germany as a modern, cosmopolitan nation; after 1945 it was relegated to the isolated stage upon which the Cold War was played out. Yet throughout the post-War period Berlin remained an object of fascination, just as Paris had been in the second half of the nineteenth century, if for contrasting reasons: the laid-back Baudelairean *flâneur* found no counterpart in the frenetic 'wall-jumpers', photographed in mid-flight trying to cross the barricade to the West, or tangled in barbed wire, described by Peter Schneider in his novel *Der Mauerspringer* ('The Wall Jumper').[7]

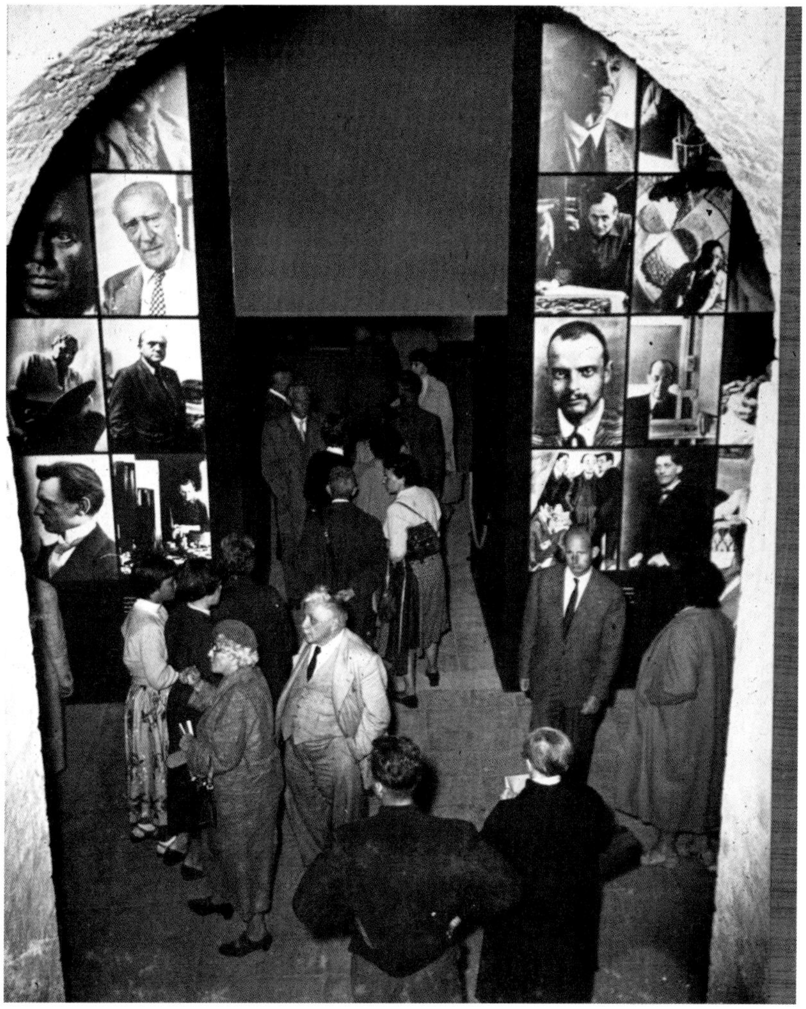

Printmaking

Printmaking in Germany had boomed after 1919, in the early years of the Weimar Republic. Hyperinflation had resulted, perhaps perversely, in a large expansion in the market for prints, and artists were willing to oblige.[8] The situation after 1945 was very different, not least as the result of a complete collapse in the market for art, and shortages, if not of subject matter, then certainly of artists and materials. The series of woodcuts and drawings produced by Wilhelm Rudolph (1889–1982) of the ruins of Dresden, or Werner Heldt's (1904–54) drawings of Berlin, and works by Hans Uhlmann (1900–75) and Fritz Winter remain isolated examples.[9] Photography offered a more direct

3. *Aufbau der Stalinallee* ('Construction of the Stalinallee'), 1953
Heinz Löffler
Oil on canvas, 1405 x 1005 mm
Stadtmuseum, Berlin

4. *Untitled*, 1953
Karl Otto Götz
Monotype on paper, 299 x 455 mm
Tate, London

5. Photograph of the entrance to *Documenta*, Kassel, 1955
Günther Becker

and practical way of recording the often surreal spectacle of ruins, notably in the case of Hermann Claasen's (1889–1987) photographs of the ruins of Cologne, published as the picture book *Gesang im Feuerofen* ('Songs of the Furnace'), in 1947 (see fig. 1).

This situation remained largely unchanged throughout the 1950s. Older figures dominated: on his death in 1955 Willi Baumeister (1889–1955) gave way to Ernst Wilhelm Nay (1902–68), who had begun his career in the late 1920s, as the leading figure in German painting. Nay produced a significant body of drawings and watercolours, and was a pioneer of abstract painting in post-War Europe, but was far less active as a printmaker.[10] Above all, the dominant nature of abstract painting and a notion of art, epitomized by the work of Nay, as a realm above, or beyond, the physical world, meant that artists rarely engaged with the physical facts of the world around them.

It was against this background that the early works of Georg Baselitz presented a direct challenge to the 'official' art of the West. In the years around 1960 he began making works that launched a critical attack on contemporary society, while reaching back and reviving traditional ways of making art, in particular in the field of printmaking. His elaboration of a range of techniques in many traditional forms of printmaking, particularly etching and woodcut, place him among the foremost printmakers of the twentieth century.

The 1961 *Pandemonium Manifesto*, written with the artist Eugen Schönebeck (b. 1936), echoes a spirit of militant existentialism and absurdist nihilism that Baselitz had encountered in the work of Antonin Artaud (1896–1948) and Samuel Beckett (1906–89): 'The poets lay in the gutter, their bodies in the morass. The whole nation's spittle, floating on their soup', Baselitz wrote.[11] His paintings and drawings of the time show strange malformed creatures in desolate landscapes, nightmarish visions culminating in the painting *Die große Nacht im Eimer* ('Big Night Down the Drain'; see fig. 2, p. 35), depicting a stunted figure masturbating in a darkened space. The painting became the subject of a public scandal when it was confiscated from Baselitz's first exhibition, in October 1963 at the Galerie Werner & Katz, Berlin, on the grounds of public indecency.[12]

Baselitz's first attempts at printmaking were made the following year, using soft ground, a simple technique of tracing the design through paper onto a waxed etching plate. The drawing *Hunde* ('Dogs'), of 1964 (cat. 4), was the result of this process, and was used to create the 1964 etching *Heulende Hunde*.[13] An early portfolio of twelve of these etchings was published by Michael Werner during the same year (fig. 6), but was not a commercial success (only one portfolio sold, to the dealer Rudolph Zwirner).

Heroes

It was with his *Helden* ('Heroes') series, including around forty paintings and over one hundred drawings and prints, that Baselitz produced his first major body of printmaking. The motif dominating the series, a single 'heroic' figure in a landscape, can be traced back to a drawing made while Baselitz was on a scholarship in Florence in 1965 (cat. 7). In the works that followed, the *Helden* (the title is decidedly ironic) emerge as battle-scarred figures in a war-torn landscape, barefoot, bedraggled, surrounded by symbolic objects evoking the ruins of war and the post-War condition of displacement and homelessness (fig. 7). They take on a variety of guises: shepherd, soldier, artist, all like avatars, or incarnations of a deity (cats 8, 11). Above all, these 'heroes' represent the broken male psyche – the 'humiliated, diminished status of German males – reduced from the supermen of Hitler's burnished armies to a ragged troupe of belatedly returning prisoners…'.[14] The emotional states of Baselitz's troupe range from the pathos of defeat to a sense of delirious joy at liberation.

Baselitz has described the origins of his *Helden*, at least in part, as being inspired by Russian literature of the Revolutionary and post-Revolutionary period, the only books that were available in East Germany in the first post-War years.[15] Many of his figures are shown with frozen gestures, evoking the harsh conditions of battle on the Eastern front; we might even compare them to the grotesque impromptu sculptures of dead German soldiers described by the Russian writer and war correspondent Vasily Grossman. 'Practical jokers', he wrote in his war diaries, 'put the

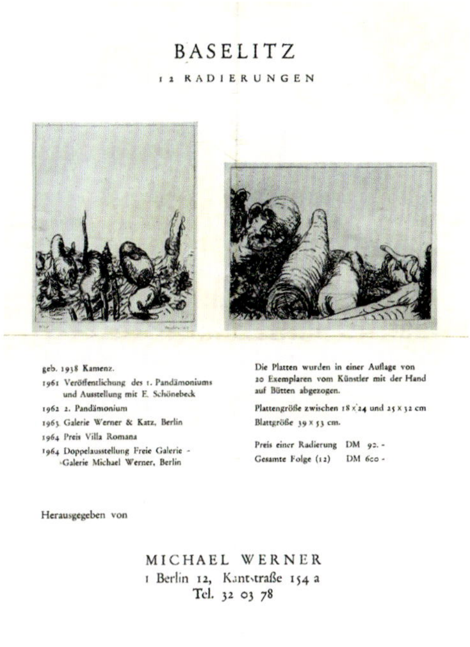

BASELITZ

12 RADIERUNGEN

geb. 1938 Kamenz.

1961 Veröffentlichung des 1. Pandämoniums und Ausstellung mit E. Schönebeck

1962 2. Pandämonium

1963 Galerie Werner & Katz, Berlin

1964 Preis Villa Romana

1964 Doppelausstellung Freie Galerie - Galerie Michael Werner, Berlin

Die Platten wurden in einer Auflage von 20 Exemplaren vom Künstler mit der Hand auf Bütten abgezogen.

Plattengröße zwischen 18 x 24 und 25 x 32 cm

Blattgröße 39 x 53 cm.

Preis einer Radierung DM 92.-

Gesamte Folge (12) DM 600.-

Herausgegeben von

MICHAEL WERNER
1 Berlin 12, Kantstraße 154 a
Tel. 32 03 78

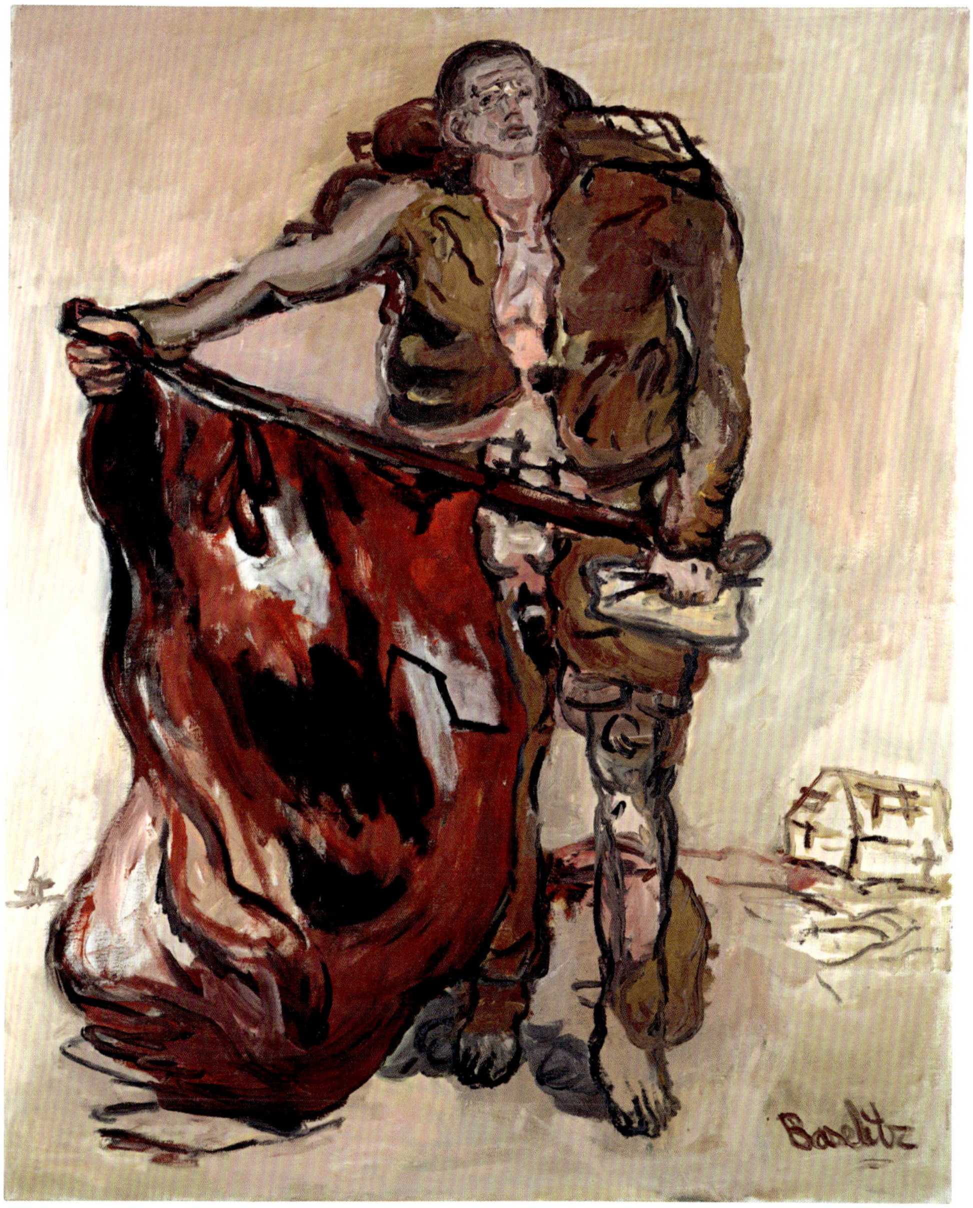

6. Flyer for portfolio of twelve etchings by Georg Baselitz, 1964

7. *Mit roter Fahne* ('With a Red Flag'), 1965
Georg Baselitz
Oil on canvas, 1620 x 1300 mm
Private collection, Germany

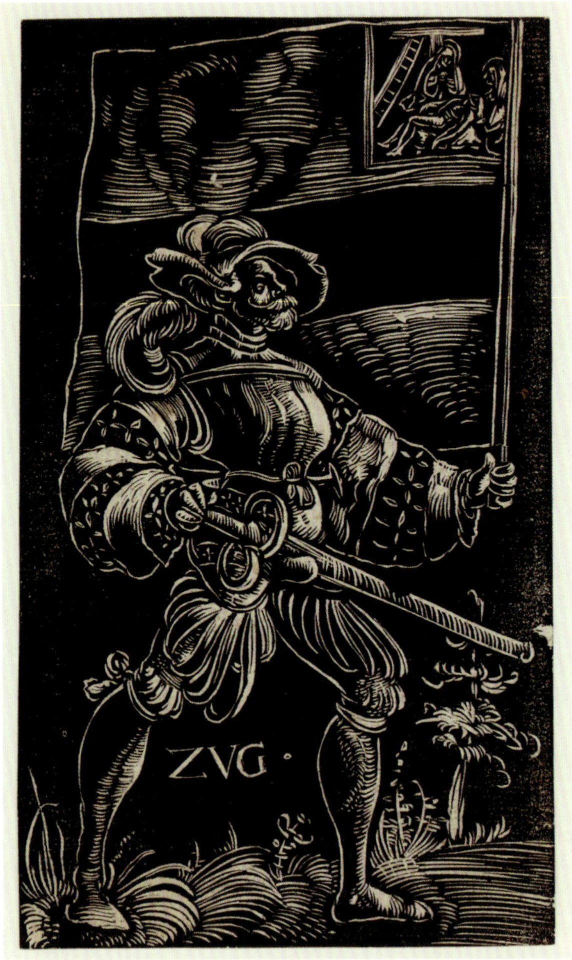

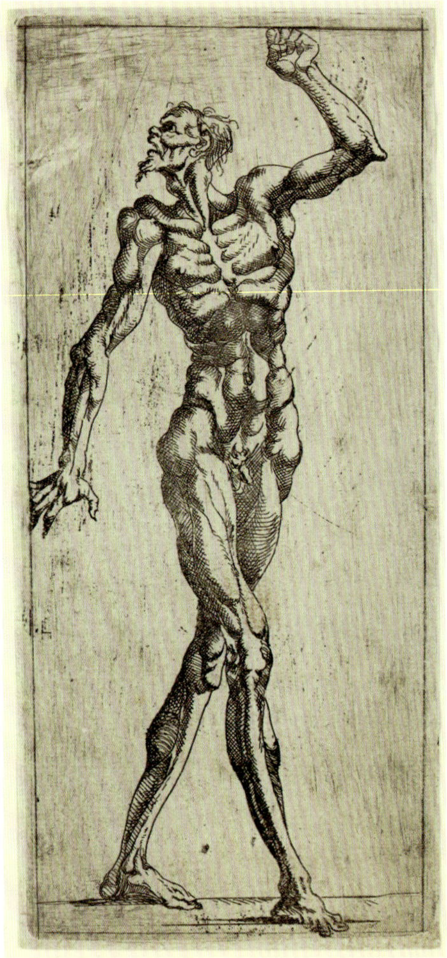

8. *Zug: Standard-bearers of the Swiss Confederation*, 1521
Urs Graf
Woodcut on paper, 191 x 110 mm
British Museum, London

9. *Naked Man*, *c.* 1543
Juste de Juste
Etching on paper, 202 x 90 mm
British Museum, London

frozen Germans on their feet, or on their hands and knees, making intricate, fanciful sculpture groups. Frozen Germans stand with their fists raised, or with their fingers spread wide. Some of them look as if they are running, their heads pulled into the shoulders. They are wearing torn boots, thin *shinelishki* (greatcoats), paper undershirts that don't hold the warmth. At night the fields of snow seem blue under the bright moon, and the dark bodies of frozen German soldiers stand in the blue snow [...].'[16]

Another point of reference, alongside literary sources, came from the sixteenth-century Mannerist prints that Baselitz began to study and collect while in Florence. The Mannerist depiction of the human body is echoed in Baselitz's figure types, in particular the elongation of the body set against a small head and exaggerated musculature, for example in the strange sinewy figures etched by the French artist Juste de Juste (*c.* 1505–*c.* 1559; fig. 9), or the proud martial figures of Urs Graf (*c.* 1485–*c.* 1528; fig. 8) and Hendrick Goltzius (*c.* 1558–*c.* 1617; fig. 10), works by whom Baselitz owned.[17]

Baselitz combines these diverse sources to create a cast of powerful poetic symbols. They are on the one hand self-portraits, or impersonations perhaps, made by an artist whose work was largely unknown, identifying with similarly beleaguered or forgotten types. More generally they offer a view on the pathos of victimhood and suffering, an important theme in Germany during the 1950s. Many Germans felt that the trauma experienced by ordinary people, particularly those victims of the expulsions from the eastern territories, had been ignored, overshadowed by the notion of 'collective guilt' and the sense that the German population somehow deserved what they had endured. In 1953 the vast historical publication, *Die Vertreibung der deutschen Bevölkerung aus den Gebieten östlich der Oder-Neisse* ('The expulsion of the German populations from the regions east of the Oder-Neisse'), documented over two million deaths through starvation, murder and suicide as a result of the expulsions, recorded by countless interviews and eyewitness accounts.[18] In such publications, and in the minds of the millions of expellees,

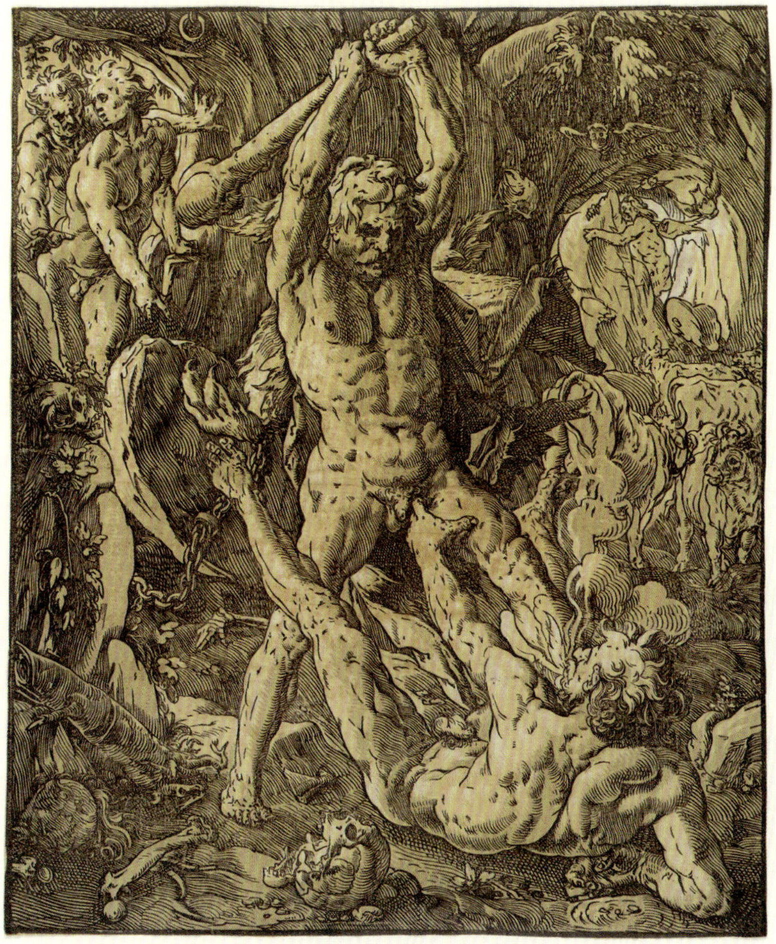

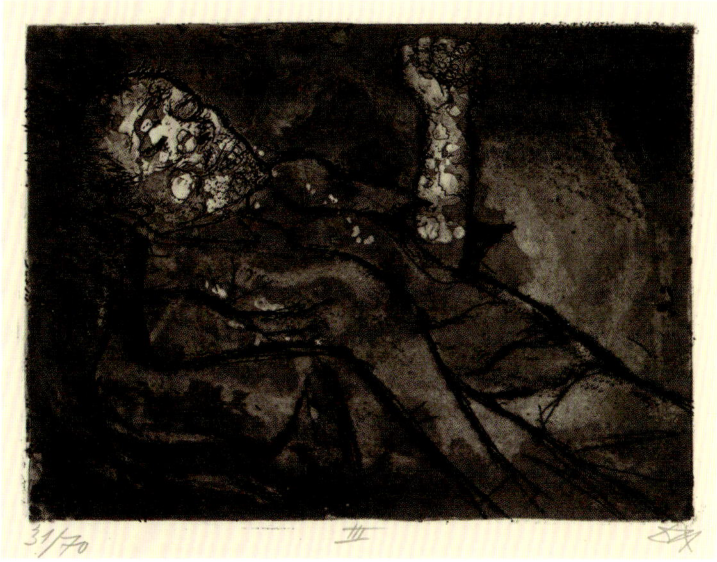

the image of German suffering was an important counter to the culture of collective war guilt and part of an emotive argument for the return to Germany of the former eastern territories.

Baselitz's *Helden* echo these suppressed themes of German suffering. They are, of course, retrospective in this sense. Just as Otto Dix (1891–1969) waited almost a decade before memorializing the horror and absurdity of the First World War in his epic 1924 print cycle of fifty etchings, *Der Krieg* ('War'; fig. 11), Baselitz's *Helden* look back almost two decades to the *Stunde Null* ('Zero Hour') of 1945. This time lag was important: only in the 1960s was it possible for a younger generation of artists, who had not been implicated in the Third Reich, to take a critical look at the legacy of the Second World War. The 'historical turn', as it might be called, in art of this moment, involved the resurgence of the past both as subject matter and in terms of techniques with strong national associations. Where Baselitz's use of etching has been compared with the rediscovery of the medium by nineteenth-century artists, leading to the 'etching

10. *Hercules and Cacus*, 1588
Hendrik Goltzius
Chiaroscuro woodcut from three blocks on paper, 405 x 330 mm
British Museum, London

11. *Dead Man in the Mud* from the portfolio *Der Krieg* ('War'), 1924
Otto Dix
Etching and aquatint,
207 x 265 mm
British Museum, London

revival', his use of the woodcut brings to mind the revival of the technique by Expressionist artists in Germany earlier in the twentieth century (fig. 12). His chiaroscuro woodcuts are among his most powerful graphic works, reinventing an old and deeply unfashionable technique from the sixteenth century. Baselitz's appeal to national traditions was to find its echo in the work of Anselm Kiefer (b. 1945), an artist not represented in this exhibition, but whose large painted woodcut, *Wege der Weltweisheit: die Hermannsschlacht* ('The Paths of World Wisdom: Hermann's Battle'), reflects also this strong, and distinctly German, engagement with national history (fig. 13).

Fracturing and inversion

Following his *Heroes* series, Baselitz turned to subjects suggestive of nature and rural life (he had moved with his family to the countryside in 1966): cows, dogs and woodsmen. Baselitz's new device of 'fracturing', by which both the subject and the space around it are divided, as if sliced in sections, gives these images of nature an artificially constructed appearance. Even when it looks like nature, Baselitz seems to say, art is not 'naturalistic', or 'realistic' – it is always, before anything else, an abstract configuration of colours and forms. How in this situation can one make art that reflects the contemporary world, while remaining interesting as a work of art? A few years later Baselitz arrived at a beguilingly simple solution. The ink and watercolour drawing *Landstraße* ('Country Road'; cat. 30) shows a country scene, upside down. During the same period, Baselitz made his first inverted painting, *The Wood on its Head* (1969; see fig. 5, p. 37). The technique of inverting the motif, making a painting upside down, has the effect of emptying the image of content – focusing attention on 'abstract' pictorial values of colour and form, and in this case, vigorous brushwork – without doing away entirely with content and 'going abstract'. It is a visual double-think; both figurative and abstract. With his inverted paintings, drawings and prints, which have defined his work since *The Wood on its Head*, Baselitz created the most ingeniously simple negotiation between the demands of abstraction and naturalism that defined the visual arts in the post-War era.

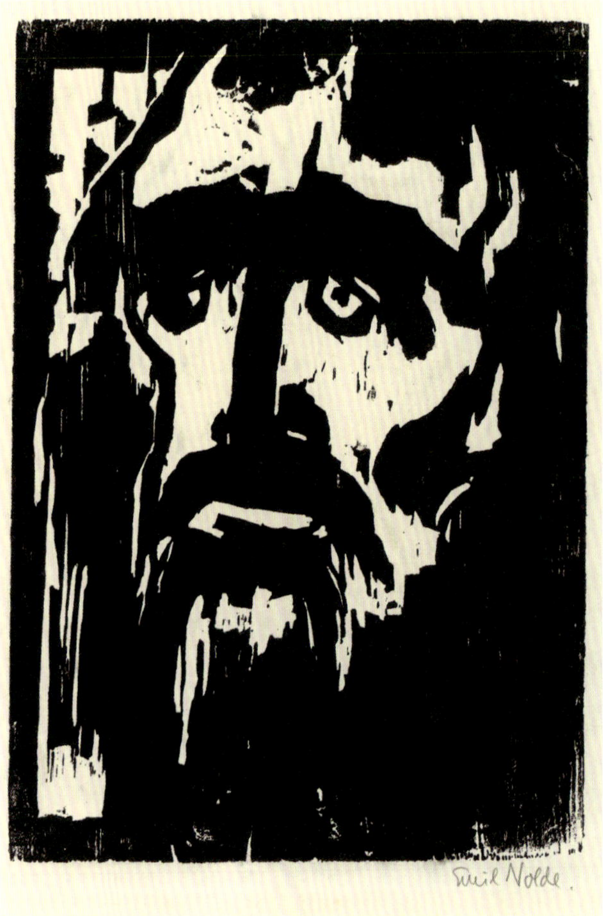

12. *Prophet*, 1912
Emil Nolde
Woodcut on paper, 323 x 220 mm
British Museum, London

13. *Wege der Weltweisheit: die Hermannsschlacht* ('The Paths of World Wisdom: Hermann's Battle'), 1982–93
Anselm Kiefer
Woodcut, emulsion, oil and collage on paper on canvas,
4900 x 6120 mm
Guggenheim Museum, Bilbao

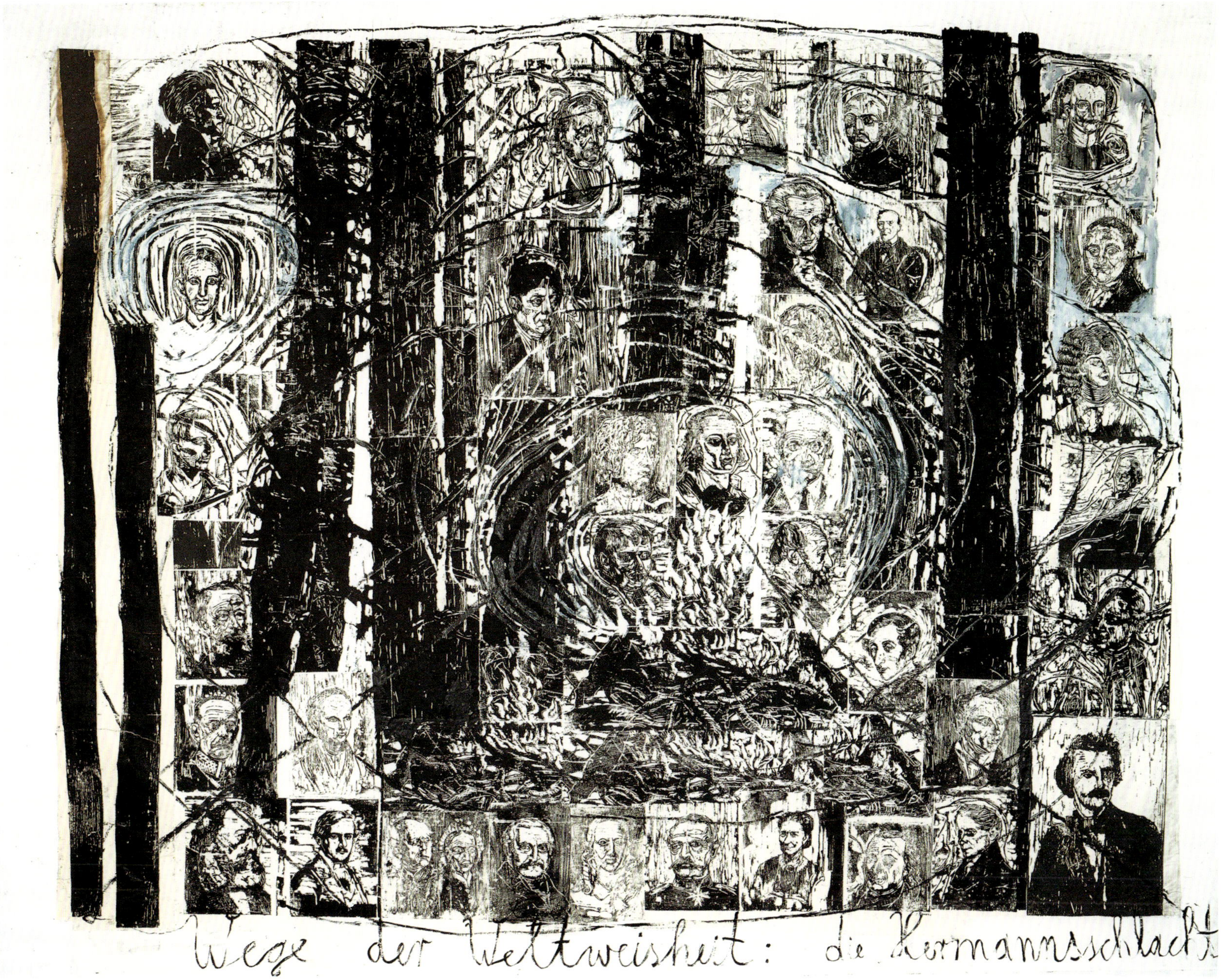
Wege der Weltweisheit: die Hermannsschlacht

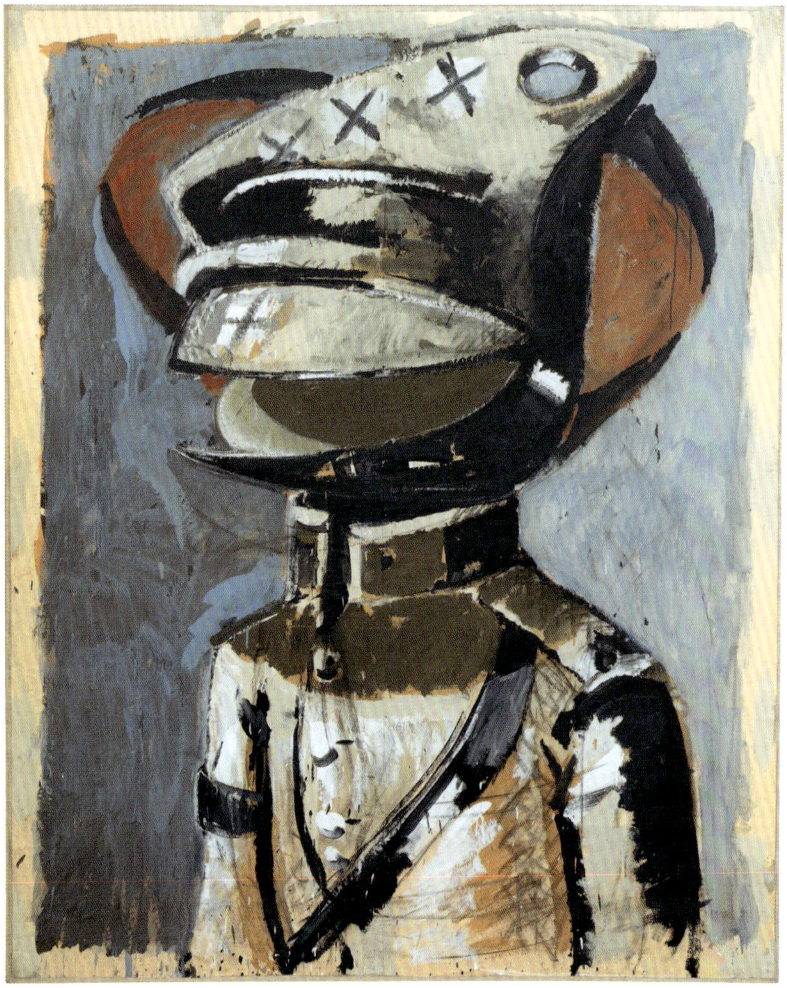

14. *Cyclops H Dithyrambic*, 1973
Markus Lüpertz
Gouache on kraft paper laid on canvas, 2400 x 1900 mm
Albertina, Vienna

East–West

In 1962, having finished his studies and having spent a period working in a coalmine, Markus Lüpertz (b. 1941) moved from the Rhineland to West Berlin. He was one of the many young men who went to Berlin to avoid the military draft – part of a West German government scheme to encourage young people to relocate to the isolated city. Soon after arriving, Lüpertz co-founded an artists' cooperative, centred around the Galerie Großgörschen 35, a support group for artists at the beginning of their careers, most of whom had studied at the Hochschule der Künste in West Berlin. Lüpertz later described Berlin as a Protestant city that had never welcomed painters, even during the 1920s, the reason nevertheless why painting, 'is at its most aggressive there'.[19]

Lüpertz's first exhibited works were large abstract paintings that he termed 'Dithyrambic', and which signalled his ambitions as an artist making energetic, lyrical abstract paintings – although with none of the historical or political references present in Baselitz's work of his Berlin period. It was in a subsequent series, the *Motif* paintings, begun in 1972, that more recognizable historical imagery appeared, particularly German military helmets, and other items connected with war (fig. 14). A series of small drawings of heads wearing helmets with visors shows how Lüpertz developed this particular motif (cats 42, 43). He was the first artist to use German military imagery in such a direct manner – although Gerhard Richter had used war imagery a few years previously, it had always been filtered by his use of photographic sources, and thus held at arm's length. For Lüpertz it was a matter of direct address. He consciously used Nazi imagery as a way of forcing recognition of the horrors of the recent past. He developed the motifs and compositions for his paintings in numerous drawings (his output as a printmaker is by contrast relatively small), using a range of media and materials, whatever was closest to hand, making little distinction between the preparatory sketch and the finished work. 'Drawings are

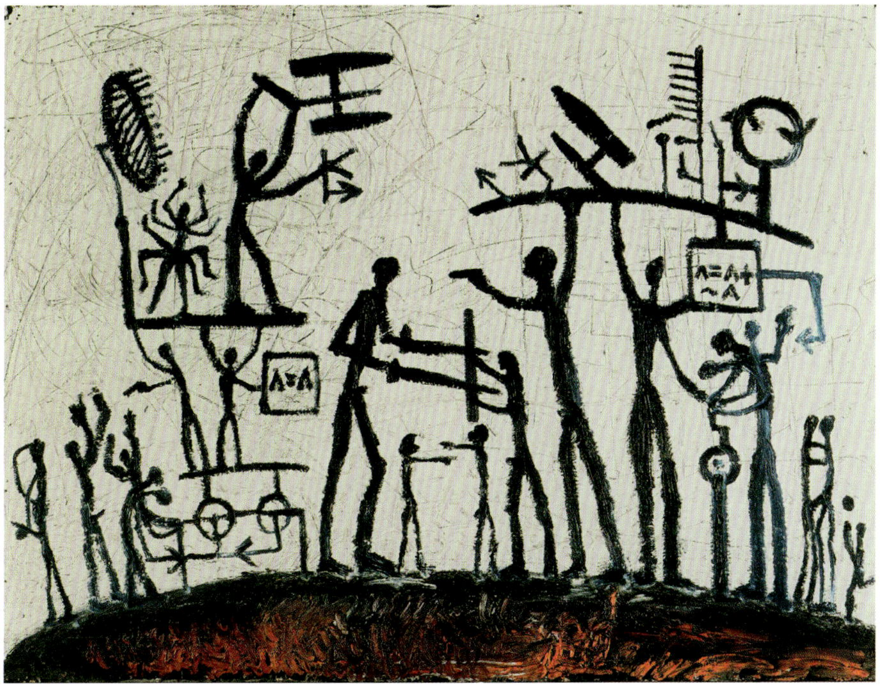

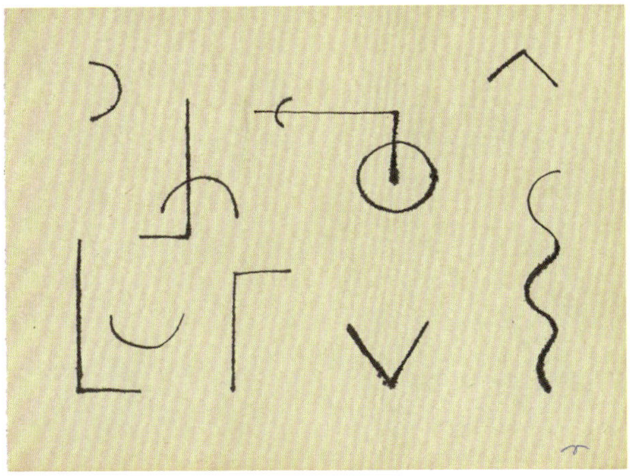

15. *Weltbild I* ('World-picture I'), 1961
A.R. Penck
Oil on fibreboard, 1220 x 1600 mm
Kunsthaus, Zürich

16. *Ohne Titel* ('Untitled'), *c.* 1969
A.R. Penck
Ink on paper, 1480 x 1990 mm
Duerckheim collection

different. There I play, try out different things. Drawings are so easily corrected. There are no technical difficulties. One can work through one subject, work on ten drawings at the same time.'[20]

The serial nature of Baselitz's and Lüpertz's work suggests a stream or an outpouring of imagery. This drive to improvise endlessly on the basis of a single motif is characteristic of many artists of their generation in Germany. Picasso offered the most immediate model for the prolix oeuvre, structured in terms of theme and variation. In Germany, after 1945, such an overwhelming flow of imagery might also be seen as a form of compensation for the art lost and destroyed during the Second World War, and for the disappearance of an entire generation of artists, who would otherwise have completed their training in the 1940s.

Alongside Baselitz and Lüpertz, A.R. Penck was one of the most prolific artists of his generation, producing a vast amount of work, largely uncatalogued.[21] Such an outpouring, in his case, might be considered as a form of protest, like the endless discourse of a political obsessive, a type of aesthetic filibustering. Penck's decisive journey from East to West, described at the beginning of this essay, came after working for two decades as a dissident artist in East Germany, in opposition to the East German State. His attempt to forge an alternative to the 'official' art of Socialist Realism was a result of his conviction that art could serve both society and the individual. He was more politicized than Baselitz and Lüpertz, yet also more strongly invested in an esoteric world of symbolism and oblique language.

Where Baselitz had his heroes, Penck generated a symbol for contemporary man in the unlikely form of the stick-figure. These figures populate his works from the 1960s, enacting primal social situations, making love and war by turns, creating a primitive picture of human life. They derive from prehistoric art (born Ralf Winkler, Penck took his pseudonym from the geologist and Ice Age specialist, Albrecht Penck (1858–1945)), as well as from his interest in contemporary communication and information theory (fig. 15). They appear both prehistoric and post-modern, and even extraterrestrial, for example in the case of an untitled drawing from 1967, showing a single standing figure in the act of communication (cat. 57). Penck's symbolic drawings, which he made according to his notion of 'Standart', referring to art as a form of basic communication but also as political comment, are made with an extraordinary economy, always fizzing with a sense of vivid life and a burning need to communicate (fig. 16).

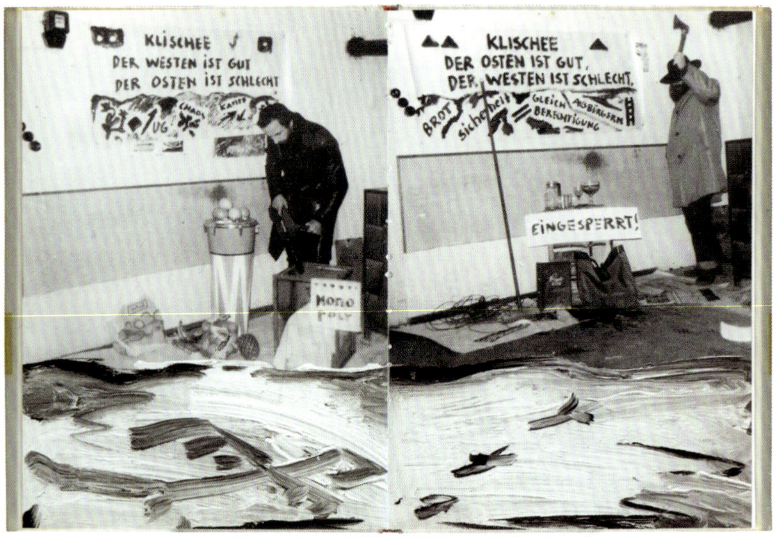

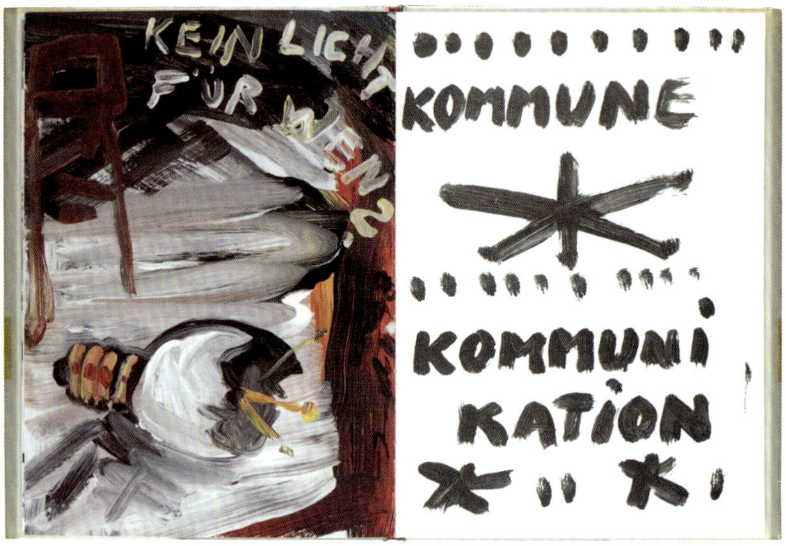

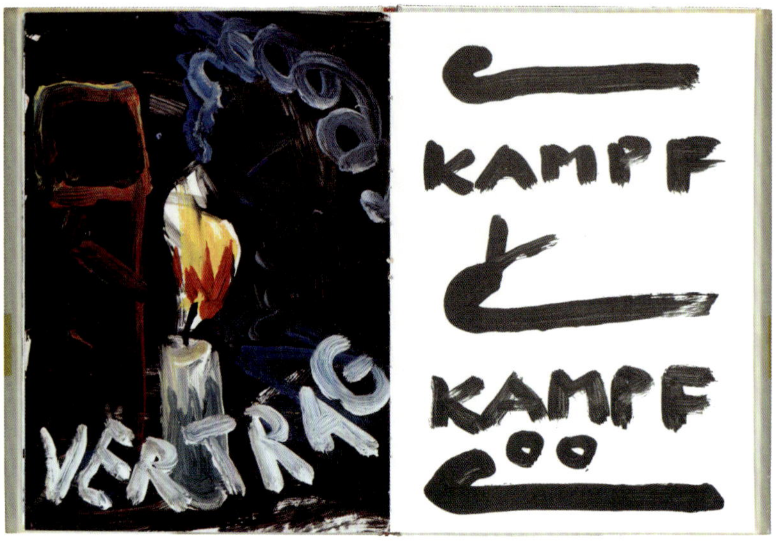

Penck's contact with artists and dealers in West Berlin and West Germany was crucial to his survival as an artist working 'underground' in the East. Michael Werner was the key figure in organizing Penck's move to the West, and had been instrumental in arranging Penck's 1976 meeting with the West German painter Jörg Immendorff (1945–2007), resulting in an exhibition at Werner's gallery in Cologne the following year: *Immendorff mal Penck, Penck mal Immendorff*.[22] In 1979, in the absence of a catalogue from this first exhibition, the two artists produced a book, *Immendorff besucht Y* (Penck was at this time using the pseudonym 'Ypsilon'), documenting Immendorff's visit to Penck in January of that year, and showing a sequence of drawings made by the two artists in reaction to each other (fig. 17).[23]

The meetings between Penck and Immendorff were less a collaboration, more a meeting of irreconcilable opposites; yet ironically it was the West German artist, Immendorff, who was the ultra-left radical, a member of the political group 'ML' that aimed for a reunited Socialist Germany, and Penck who was the 'radical individualist'.[24] Immendorff wrote in his own account of their first meeting: 'I said that we must make paintings for Stalin and Mao Tse Tung, and he answered in the language of science fiction.'[25] Immendorff's *Café Deutschland* paintings and prints (begun in 1977 and continued throughout the 1980s) depict an idealistic café where he and Penck could meet to overcome East–West division through artistic collaboration (fig. 18).[26]

The myth of their 'collaboration' arose largely through these paintings, and has otherwise been described more as a mismatch, and one that was of less significance for Penck.[27] Penck's politics, however informed by opposition to the East German State, were geared towards an individualism based on a strong aesthetic premise. His 1975 pointillist self-portrait was reportedly made as a direct response to the famous claim by Andy Warhol (1928–87) that an artist should operate 'like a machine' – a sentiment that would have appalled Immendorff. Penck had read the quote in a catalogue for an exhibition of Pop Art in Düsseldorf given to him by Michael Werner on

17. Page spreads from *Immendorff besucht Y*, 1979
A.R. Penck and Jörg Immendorff

18. *Wir Kommen* ('We're Coming'), from the series *Café Deutschland*, 1983
Jörg Immendorff
Linocut on paper, 1803 x 2294 mm
Tate, London

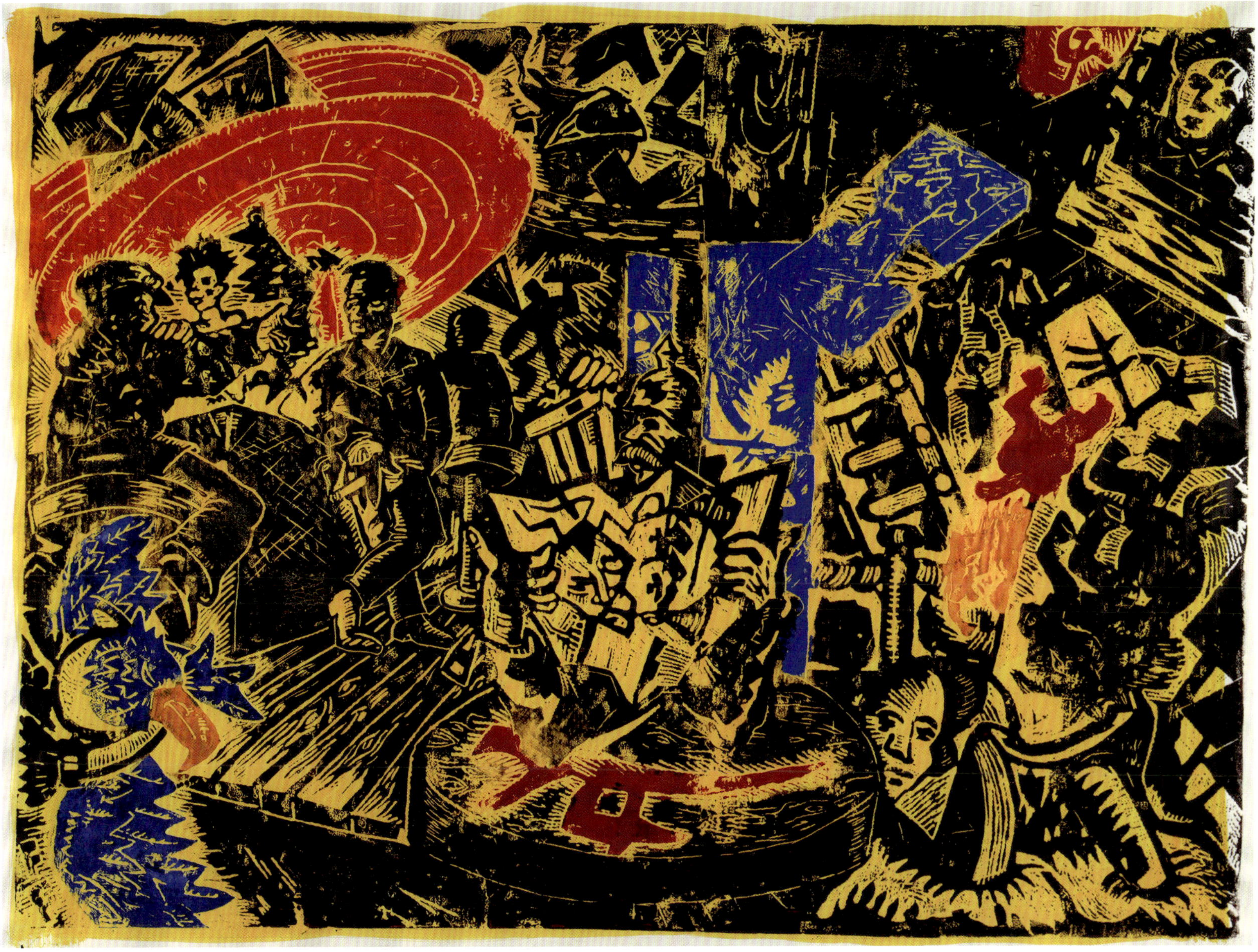

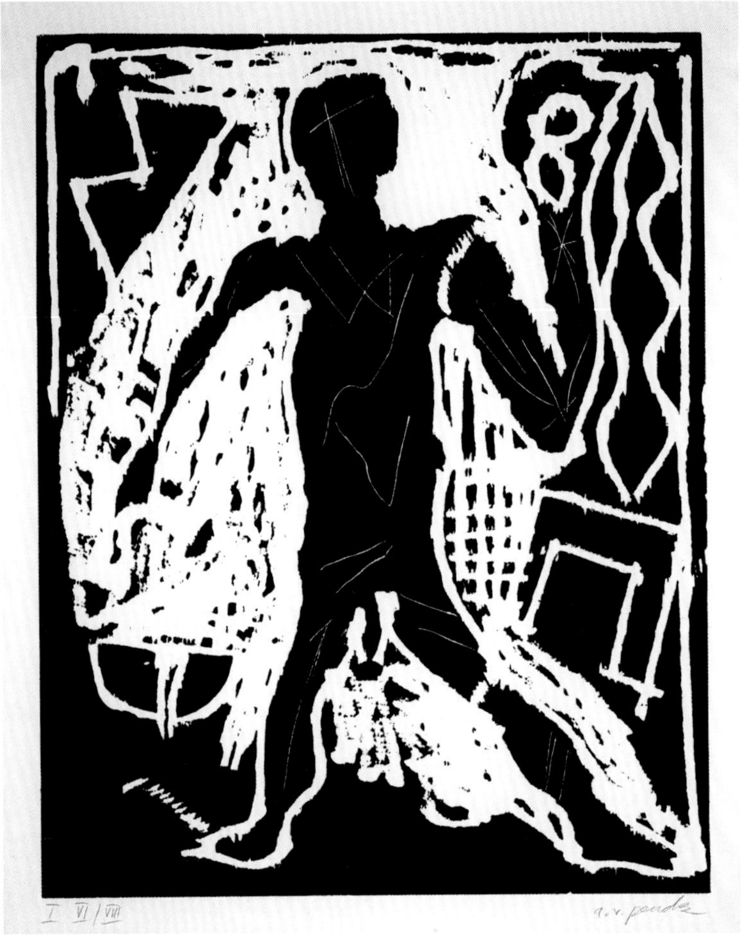

19. *Die Arbeit geht weiter*
('The Work Continues'), from the portfolio *Erste Konzentration I*
(First Concentration I), 1982
A.R. Penck
Woodcut on paper, 895 x 695 mm
British Museum, London
Presented by Count Christian Duerckheim

20. *Braunkreuz*, 1962
Joseph Beuys
Five works on paper, oil paint, upper left: 169 x 178 mm; upper right: 125 x 179 mm; lower left: 115 x 179 mm; lower centre: 177 x 178 mm; lower right: 120 x 179 mm
Tate, London

21. Blinky Palermo installing his wall painting at the Hamburger Kunstverein, 1972
Angelika Platen

one of his trips to the East.[28] Penck related to Werner that he began in the top left-hand corner, and proceeded from left to right until he reached the bottom of the sheet. Of the six prints that he contributed to the important tripartite portfolio *Erste Konzentration* ('First Concentration' or 'First Convolute'), published by Maximilian Verlag in Munich in 1982, the two large woodcuts *Die Arbeit Geht Weiter* ('The Work Continues'; fig. 19) and *Nachtvision* ('Night Vision'; cat. 68) show his ability to create vivid, universalizing symbols that are more lyrical than political, in contrast to the propagandistic nature of Immendorff's work.[29]

Art and Society

Considered together, Baselitz, Lüpertz and Penck show the extent to which, by 1964, it was no longer possible to speak in terms of a stylistic confrontation between East and West. The confrontation was now not a matter of geography, but of generations. A new cohort of artists was emerging for whom the primary goal was to contest 'official' culture, be it Socialist Realism in the East, or the 'official' nature of abstract painting in West Germany. For artists working in Berlin it was a matter of reinventing figurative painting as part of a recovery of national tradition.[30]

A different situation can be traced in Düsseldorf, the centre of artistic life in the wealthy industrial region of the Rhineland. Whereas in Berlin discussions focused on the place of the individual (one thinks of Baselitz's *Helden*, or Penck's highly esoteric symbolic language), in Düsseldorf it was a matter of examining the role of art in society in a wider sense. At the heart of this conversation was the milieu around the famous Kunstakademie and the most notorious and influential artist and teacher of the post-War period, Joseph Beuys (1921–86).[31] Beuys's influence as a teacher was less a question of style than of attitude, and in particular the notion of an 'expanded' art, moving beyond the stylistic categories and genres that had become so suffocating during the 1950s. Beuys was motivated in large part by the need to lift German art out of a sense of provincialism that had hung over the decade. He created the

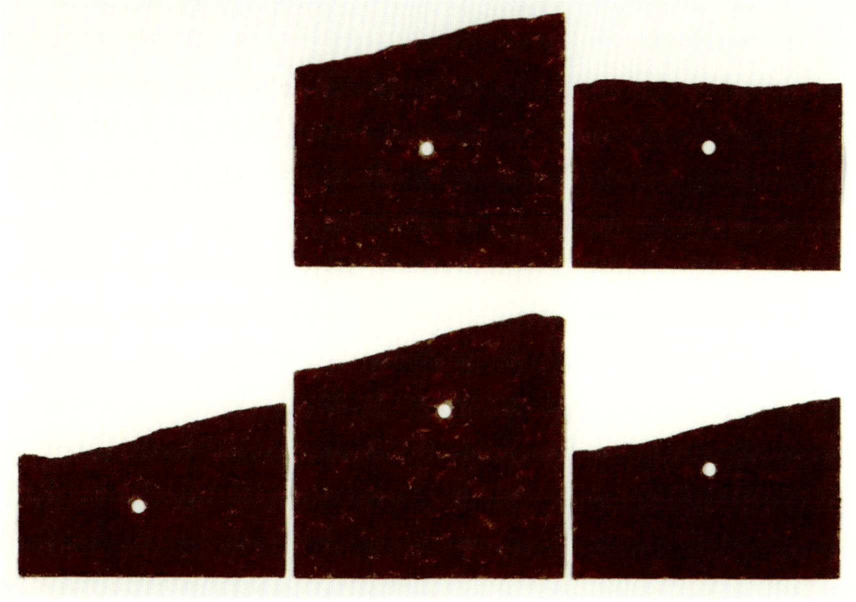

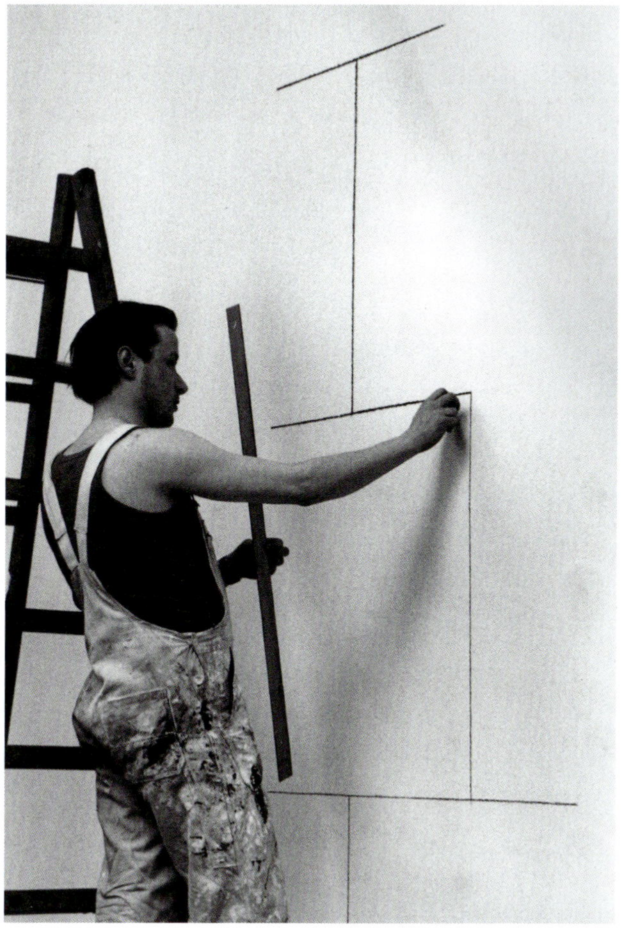

model for a German artist fully connected with an international avant-garde, without losing any sense of arising out of a national tradition, and of remaining resolutely German. Beuys's example also pointed to a new sense of spirituality, or mysticism, that might be attached to the role of the artist: in his case it was the mystique of a shaman, who might explain paintings to a dead hare or converse symbolically with a coyote.[32]

As one of Beuys's most celebrated students, Blinky Palermo took this sense of poetic mysticism and with it created a visually simple, yet extraordinarily elusive, body of abstract work, including sculptures, wall paintings and many works on paper.[33] The rust-coloured pigment in the monochrome screenprint from a 1973 portfolio, comprising two lithographs and one screenprint (cats 54–56), for example, appears to derive directly from the *Braunkreuz* used by Beuys from the late 1950s – an earthy, dark-red pigment consisting of different types of paint and symbolic substances such as blood (fig. 20).[34] The three prints in Palermo's portfolio act as a record of a wall painting installed at the Kunstverein, Hamburg, from one week during March 1973, consisting of a series of monochrome red walls and a single linear drawing on a white wall (fig. 21).

Where many of Palermo's prints and drawings act as records of temporary wall paintings and installations, others document the forms he developed as a sculptor. The portfolio *4 Prototypes* (1970) gathers together a series of shapes frequently used by Palermo in his wall-mounted sculptures, known as *Objekte* ('Objects'). The four 'prototypic' shapes – a green scalene triangle, a blue isosceles triangle, a black square and a grey ovoid shape, like a fingerprint – are presented without title or explanation (cats 50–53). Only when seen in the context of Palermo's work as a whole do they begin to take on meaning. The grey ovoid shape is repeated in several drawings (cats 48, 49), and produced as sculptures, existing in a number of variants. The blue triangle appeared as a sculpture in 1966, and three years later as an edition: a stencil, brush and blue paint, complete with instructions to paint the triangle above a door.[35] Palermo used a highly refined method of theme and variation on a set of abstract motifs, producing objects that can seem like strange, romantic fragments from another world. Nowhere is this more evident than in a mysterious untitled drawing from 1969 (cat. 47), suggestive of a darkened veil revealing a glimpse of an illuminated architectural interior. Here, meaning seems too precious to be fully revealed, as if making and appreciating art should remain ultimately a private act. Palermo's own career took on the shape of a romantic fragment following his accidental death at the age of thirty-three, on an island in the Maldives.

Reinvention

A close friend and collaborator of Palermo, Gerhard Richter emerged as the dominant figure in German art in the last three decades of the twentieth century. Where Palermo worked with quiet fragments, like incomplete refrains of chamber music, Richter worked on a symphonic scale. His virtual reinvention of painting through a spectacular 'photographic' look provided the model for a generation of younger artists, equally fascinated by the confrontation of the painted and the photographed image. Richter was in this sense the heir to Picasso, who defined the 'look' of painting in the first half of the century. But where Picasso can be considered as a master printmaker alongside Baselitz, Richter's work in traditional printmaking techniques – etching, engraving, woodcuts – is virtually non-existent. True to the spirit of the 1960s, he has produced instead numerous editions, or 'multiples', using photographic and commercial processes marked by their anonymous manufacture and uniform appearance, particularly offset printing, an inexpensive method of reproducing identical high-quality images. Richter has often used offset printing and photography to make limited edition reproductions of paintings, such as his 1991 offset print *Betty*, reproducing a 1988 oil painting, itself based on a photograph, the whole process apparently undermining any fine-art notions that might be attached either to the original painting or the 'original', that is, handmade, print.

Drawing plays a larger role in Richter's work, although in the 1960s his attitude towards the medium remained circumspect. In his early 'Pop' period, for which Richter took imagery from illustrated magazines and created paintings using his famous 'photographic' technique, he made drawings by tracing from his source imagery – a typical 'Pop' procedure (fig. 22). The purpose of the traced drawings often appears technical – to isolate a motif, and to establish composition and basic tonal areas. The drawing *Hotel oder Haus Hutter* ('Hotel or Hutter House'; cat. 82) from 1965 was used to such effect in advance of the painting *Grau Haus* ('Grey House'; 1966) yet, as with all of Richter's drawings, the relationship is not necessarily sequential; the drawing is as much a chance to explore the subject in a different medium.

Richter's works in the 'quieter' medium of drawing sustain a remarkable level of complexity and drama compared to his larger oil paintings. This is certainly true of the series of abstract drawings that he began in 1978, each made with graphite on A4 'typewriter' paper. Richter's exploration of the range of marks possible with a pencil, on such a limited scale, is the occasion for a series of virtuoso performances, as if to say that, in the end, the medium is always subservient to the creative presence of the artist. As such, these drawings appear as private works, their scale and intimacy of expression suggesting working drawings, or the result of a concentration and absorption on Richter's part; only the addition of evocative titles to certain sheets, such as *Waldbrand* ('Forest Fire') and *Adorno?*, the latter referring to the post-War German philosopher and theorist Theodor Adorno (1903–69), suggest a release of the works into the sphere of contemporary history (cats 86, 87).

Richter's watercolours are similar exercises in abstract image-making; he once described his approach to the medium, in relation to oil painting, as the 'same problem different medium'. The group of eight small sheets made on 2 January 1978, in a hotel room in Davos (cats 88–91), are among his first works in the medium. These jewel-like works show Richter's masterly

22. *Schwestern* ('Sisters'), 1967
Gerhard Richter
Oil on canvas, 650 x 750 mm
Formerly Duerckheim collection

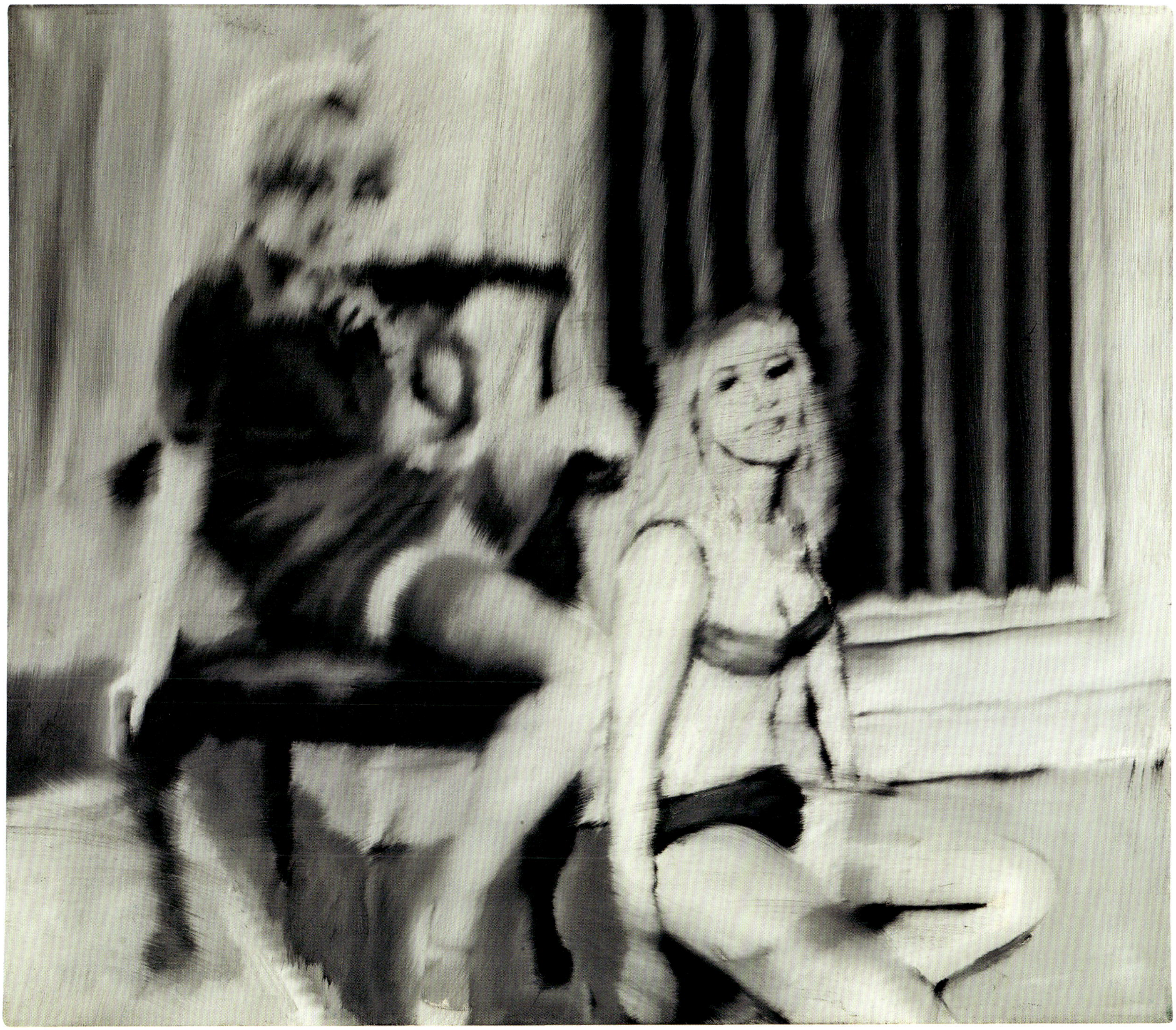

control of mark-making and colour, creating compelling but entirely abstract pictorial spaces. Like Palermo, Richter remains in the final count a highly aesthetic artist, for whom the politics of post-War life was always viewed through the filter of art and, certainly in Richter's case, searching questions of the possibilities and limits of artistic representation.

Richter included photographs of these watercolours on one of the sheets of his ongoing image archive, *Atlas*, alongside other abstract paintings (cat. 92). *Atlas* collects together source images, photographs and drawings (although many of these, as Christian Duerckheim has suggested in his interview for this catalogue, were removed by the artist), and offers an overview of his work and a sense of the way in which he transforms his source material into finished works. Many of the sheets of *Atlas* comprise photographs of the subject matter Richter has treated in painting – clouds, seascapes, landscapes – but also photographs of family and friends, often juxtaposed with found photographs. A sheet of photographs of Norwegian fjords, for example, is completed with a newspaper photograph of the same subject (cat. 94). Behind the vast archive of images is no discernible theory, apart from what appears useful or interesting. As a whole, *Atlas* functions like a vast photograph album, but defines the border of where such a private repertoire of images meets a social realm of vision.

Capitalist realism

The third 'Düsseldorf' artist to be considered is also the most elusive; his art the hardest to describe. Sigmar Polke (1941–2010) was born in Lower Silesia, one of the territories lost to Germany at the end of the Second World War. He moved as a child with his parents to West Germany and was raised around Düsseldorf, where he later became a student at the Kunstakademie. His early collaborations with Gerhard Richter and two other students, Konrad Lueg (1939–96) and Manfred Kuttner (1937–2007) under the slogan 'Capitalist Realism', were conducted in an offbeat spirit of satire that he never quite renounced; his militant humour and disregard for moral boundaries made him the most avant-garde of post-War German artists, with the exception only of Martin Kippenberger (1953–97).

In a long sequence of satirical drawings made while still a student, Polke launched his first attack on the materialism of German life in the 1950s and the frailty of contemporary consumer desires. 'Why can't I give up smoking?' one drawing asks; in another, a small man is chased by a giant pair of pliers (cat. 69). They are made in a deliberately awkward cartoon style, most with a ballpoint pen, and mimic the language and visual economy of advertising. Penck, in a text accompanying a catalogue from 1983 of Polke's drawings, describes both their 'melancholy irony' and striking economy of means, refining an idea until it becomes a form of 'magic information', suggesting a not-too distant relation with the symbolic language of Penck's *Standart* works.[36] Polke's ballpoint pen drawings were made alongside a series of paintings that show him filtering the language of American Pop Art, particularly that of Andy Warhol and Roy Lichtenstein (1923–97), through the experience of life in West Germany (fig. 23).

Polke's fascination with advertising and the printed image led him to develop a style of painting using enlarged 'raster dots' – the dots used to form images reproduced in newsprint. These dots (inevitably referred to as 'Polke dots') came to define the look of Polke's work and his obsession with confusion and interference as qualities of images, particularly those that had been put through multiple processes of mediation – from camera, to print, to screen, and so on. One of his first editioned works, the offset lithograph *Freundinnen*, published in 1967 by Galerie h, Hannover, was based on a photograph of two girls, posing innocently; the complex pattern of dots obscures and disrupts the image. Polke's use of dots contrasts with

23. *Hemden* ('Shirts'), 1964
Sigmar Polke
Lacquer on canvas, 935 x 1170 mm
Formerly Duerckheim collection

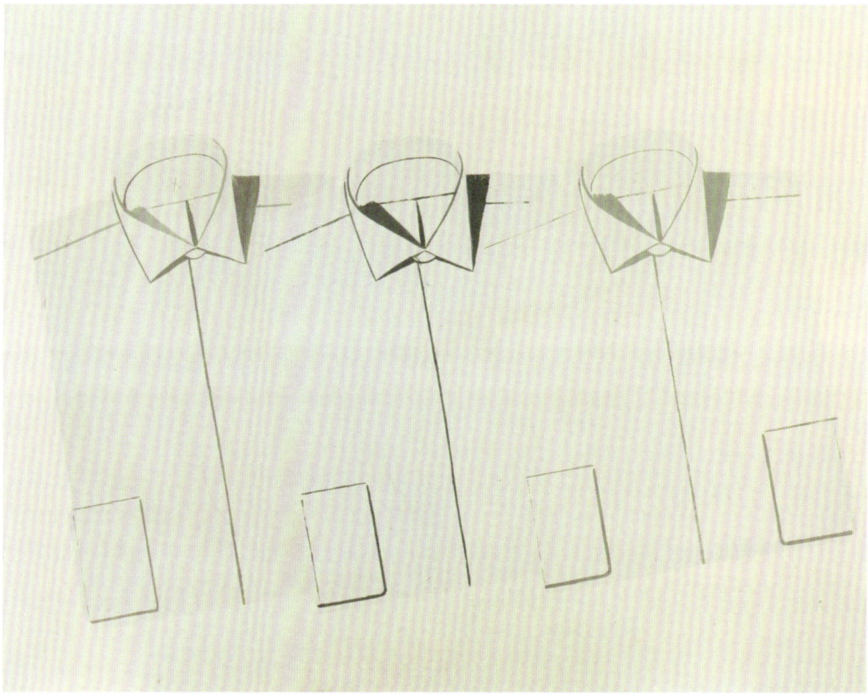

Lichtenstein's use of Ben-Day dots in his paintings of the 1960s, which mimic both the technical means but also the clarity and simplicity of advertising and commercial printing.

In the late 1960s, Polke's work evolved away from satire into the exotic, inscrutable realm of drug-induced imagery. From 1968 to 1971, Polke filled a series of sketchbooks (in fact lined students' exercise books) with drawings and collaged elements showing figures in strange postures, imagery that can best be described as dream-like, or drug-induced (cats 72, 73). They show the same combination of economy of line and a rich imaginative resource, although the element of satire, Polke's principal means of engaging his audience, has dissolved into a narcotic haze. Polke went on to make many drawings that, like those of Palermo, exist in an elusive, poetic realm, never however losing a sense of opposition that marks the works of all the artists discussed in this catalogue.

Divided Germany

These artists are all now international names. They are all also, it should be remembered, West German artists, with the partial exception of Penck, and are all male. To what extent they can be held as representative of art in post-War Germany is an open question. Their stories are very different from those being played out in the East. For many critics and historians of the art of this period it is no longer possible to discuss the creative products of one German State without acknowledging what was happening over the border, the implication being that, despite political division, some sense of cultural unity remained.[37] As the work of Polke and Palermo shows, however, 'divided Germany' was not always important, or even relevant, for artists making work in the West. The question that might be asked instead is: how did artists avoid their work being constantly overshadowed by the symbolism of political division? From the point of view of the history of art, focusing attention on individual works, as much as individual biographies, is one way of providing a more nuanced view.

These biographies are not always easy to reconstruct, yet it is at least worth recalling that throughout the 1960s and 1970s there were still only a very small group of supporters in Germany for the younger avant-garde – the generation of Baselitz and Richter. They were working without the benefit of a wide public or the types of opportunity for international exposure seen since. Dealers including Heiner Friedrich, Fred Jahn, Franz Dahlem, René Block and Michael Werner played an essential role, as did the collectors Prinz Franz von Bayern, Walter Bareiss and, of course, Count Christian Duerckheim himself. Those working in museums who offered support included Dieter Koepplin, who gave Baselitz his first museum exhibition of drawings at the Kunstmuseum in Basel in 1970, and other important figures such as Johannes Gachnang, Rudi Fuchs and Siegfried Gohr.

It was of course also the collaborations and friendships between artists that ensured their survival and success, and that

24. *Hotel Diana*, 1967
Included in René Block's portfolio
Grafik des Kapitalistischen Realismus
('Graphic Art of Capitalist Realism'),
1968
Gerhard Richter
Screenprint with varnish on
lightweight card, 594 x 800 mm
Gerhard Richter Archive

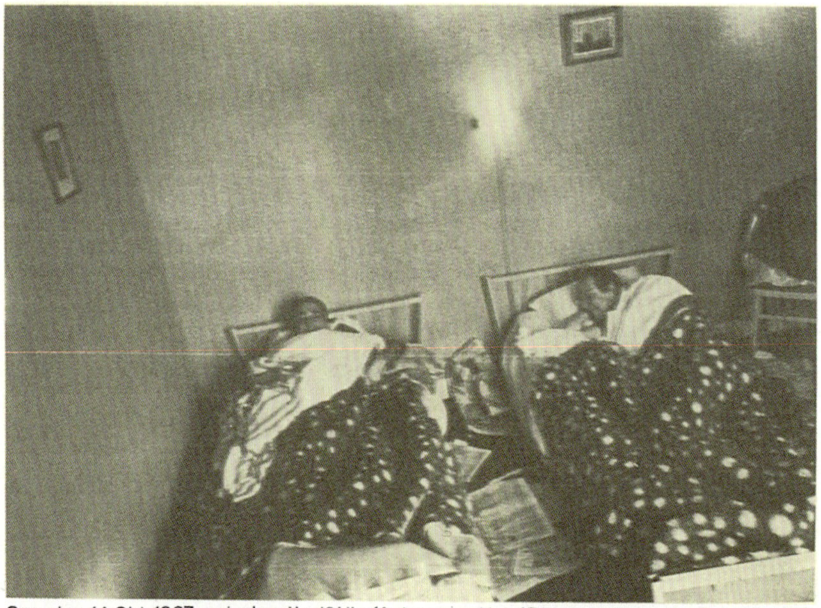

Samstag,14.Okt.1967, zwischen 11 u. 12 Uhr (Antwerpen,Hotel Diana ;rechts Polke, links Richter)

eventually propelled German art from relatively provincial status in the 1950s onto the international stage it occupied during the last two decades of the twentieth century. Collaborations were one way to re-create some sense of a whole at a time when daily life was marked by division, even if these collaborations, as in the case of Penck and Immendorff, were more a matter of confrontation and difference, rather than dialogue.

The graphic arts played a crucial role in these dialogues. Two important print portfolios in particular helped to cement generational connections between artists. René Block's 1968 portfolio, *Grafik des Kapitalistichen Realismus* ('Graphics of Capitalist Realism'), contains prints by six artists: K.P. Brehmer (1938–97), Karl-Horst Hödicke (b. 1938), Konrad Lueg, Sigmar Polke, Gerhard Richter (fig. 24) and Wolf Vostell (1932–98), all associated with the 'Düsseldorf School' (although published in West Berlin).[38] The three-part portfolio *Erste Konzentration* ('First Concentration'), published in Munich by Sabine Knust in 1982, contained prints by Baselitz, Antonius Höckelmann (1937–2000), Immendorff, Per Kirkeby (b. 1938), Lüpertz and Penck, a group of artists associated with the gallery of Michael Werner.

Drawing played an equally fundamental role. For Penck and Immendorff, drawing and working in gouache offered a way to make works as part of a live conversation. Baselitz and Eugen Schönebeck's *Pandemonium Manifesto* was based on a combination of drawings reproduced as a blueprint. Richter and Palermo marked their friendship by exchanging watercolours; for example Palermo's 1971 *Untitled (Wvz 570)*, which he gave to Richter in the final year of their collaboration.[39] Polke's early ballpoint pen drawings frequently mention Richter as part of an ongoing private joke: '*RICHTER ab September ständig in Kino*' ('Richter, in a cinema near you from September'), one of these announces. The list goes on. From today's perspective it appears that the historical legacy and political realities of post-War Germany led not only to a 'New Spirit' in painting, as the title of one important exhibition suggested, but also to a New Spirit in the making of graphic art.[40]

1. L. Grisebach (ed.), *A.R. Penck*, exh. cat., Berlin (Nationalgalerie), Zürich (Kunsthaus), 1988, p. 55.
2. East Prussia was ceded to the Soviets, and the German territories east of a natural border formed by the Oder and Lusatian Neisse rivers to Poland. See: Andrew Demshuk, *The Lost German East. Forced Migration and the Politics of Memory, 1945–1970*, Cambridge, 2012, p. 1.
3. K. Adenauer, *Memoirs 1945–53*, trans. B. Ruhm von Oppen, London, 1966, p. 22.
4. Günter Grass, 'Writing after Auschwitz', in G. Grass, *Two States, One Nation*, trans. K. Winston with A.S. Wensinger, London, 1990, pp. 104–5.
5. See: J.P. Stonard, *Fault Lines. Art in Germany 1945–1955*, London, 2007, pp. 89–201.
6. W. Schmidt (ed.), *Ausgebürgert. Künstler aus der DDR und aus dem Sowjetischen Sektor Berlins 1949–1989*, exh. cat., Dresden (Albertinum), 1990; Hamburg (Kleine Deichtorhalle), 1991.
7. Peter Schneider, *Der Mauerspringer, Darmstadt, 1982*; trans. L. Hafrey, *The Wall Jumper*, London, 1984.
8. The rise of printmaking in the first quarter of the twentieth century – the use of the woodcut by Expressionist artists, for example – was coupled with an expanding market for prints at a time when works in other media had become too expensive for many collectors. Print rooms, or *Kupferstichkabinette*, were established in museums. Most successful artists made prints. See: F. Carey and A. Griffiths, *The Print in Germany 1880–1933. The Age of Expressionism*, London, 1984. Also: R. Heller, 'Two and one: observations on the graphic arts in the two Germanies, 1945–1990', in A. Chávez and R. Heller, *Two and One. Printmaking in Germany 1945–1990*, exh. cat., Wellesley (Davis Museum and Cultural Center), 2003; Kiel (University Art Museum), 2004, pp. 3–35, here p. 5.
9. W. Rudolph, *Das Zerstörte Dresden*, Leipzig, 1988; *Werner Heldt. Zeichnungen,* with an essay by Gert H. Theunissen, Berlin, 1948. Mention might also be made of Joseph Beuys's early woodcuts, such as *Doe* (1948) and *Mudflats* (1949), and Willi Baumeister's screenprints of the early 1950s; see: A. Kren, 'Aspects of German prints after 1945', *The Print Collector's Newsletter*, vol. XIV, 1 (March–April 1983), pp. 5–8.
10. See: *Willi Baumeister. Zeichnungen*, exh. cat., Dresden (Kupferstichkabinett), 1995; Munich (Staatliche Graphische Sammlung), 1996; and M. Claesges, *Ernst Wilhelm Nay. Werkverzeichnis – Aquarelle, Gouachen, Zeichnungen*, Ostfildern, 2012.
11. English translation from R. Calvocoressi (ed.), *Georg Baselitz*, exh. cat., London (Whitechapel Gallery), 1983, pp. 23–4. Baselitz saw Artaud's work on a visit to Paris in 1959.
12. Herbert Read was asked to write the preface by the journalist Martin G. Buttig, who contributed the catalogue essay, and was allegedly instrumental in arranging the 'scandal' following a front-page article (which he had placed) in the *Berliner Zeitung* (3 October 1963) condemning the paintings as obscene. Information from Michael Werner.
13. Baselitz made these etchings at the *Druckwerkstatt* (Print Workshop) in the Schloss Wolfsburg, Wolfsburg, which had been opened in the summer of 1961, and offered grants to young artists to stay and learn printmaking. See: C. Haase, *760914 cm2 Druck. 50 Jahre Druckwerkstatt im Schloss Wolfsburg*, exh. cat., Wolfsburg (Städtische Galerie), 2011.
14. T. Judt, *Postwar*, London, 2005, p. 19.
15. R.M. Mason, *Georg Baselitz*, exh. cat., Lugano (Museo d'Arte Moderna), 2007, p. 161.
16. A. Beevor and L. Vinogradova (eds), *A Writer at War. Vasily Grossman with the Red Army 1941–1945*, London, 2005, p. 86.
17. See: *La Bella Maniera, la collection d'estampes maniéristes de Georg Baselitz*, exh. cat., Paris (École nationale supérieure des beaux-arts), 2002. For an important contemporary publication on Baselitz's appreciation of Mannerism, see: Gustav René Hocke, *Die Welt als Labyrinth*, Hamburg, 1957. A selection of five Mannerist prints, by Bartholomäus Spranger, Urs Graf, Peter Flötner, Jakob de Gheyn the Elder and Hendrick Goltzius, was included in the catalogue of one of the first exhibitions of the *Helden* works, at the Galerie Neuendorf, Hamburg, in 1973. See: *Georg Baselitz. Ein neuer Typ. Bilder 1965–66*, exh. cat., Hamburg (Galerie Neuendorf), 1973, unpaginated.
18. 'In the memories of Adenauer and most West Germans, the past to be overcome in the 1950s, the past to be incorporated systematically as part of the present, was not the past of German crimes but the past of German suffering.' Robert G. Moeller, *War Stories. The Search for a Usable Past in the Federal Republic of Germany*, Berkeley, Los Angeles, London, 2001, p. 85.
19. D. Dietrich, 'A conversation with Markus Lüpertz', *The Print Collector's Newsletter*, vol. XIV, 1 (March–April 1983), pp. 9–12, here p. 9.
20. Ibid., p. 11.
21. Penck's prolific production of drawings led him to destroy large amounts of work, once shovelling heaps of drawings out of the window of his Dresden studio, according to Michael Werner. The confused nature of Penck's production, and the manner in which his drawings were transported to the West, often en masse, has led to numerous problems with dating and chronological sequence.
22. I. Graw, *Immendorff X Penck, Penck X Immendorff. Rekonstruktion einer Ausstellung*, exh. cat., Cologne, New York (Michael Werner), 2000, unpaginated.
23. A.R. Penck and J. Immendorff, *Immendorff besucht Y*, Munich, 1979.
24. Graw, op. cit. (note 22), unpaginated.
25. J. Immendorff, *Jörg Immendorff im Gespräch mit Pamela Kort*, Kunst Heute, no. 11, Cologne, 1993, p. 64.
26. They have been described as a 'potent metaphor not only of the divisions within ourselves but also of the precariousness of our times.' D. Elliott, 'The last café', in D. Elliott, *Jörg Immendorff. Café Deutschland and Related Works*, exh. cat., Oxford (Museum of Modern Art), 1984.
27. Isabelle Graw has described Immendorff's predominant role in historicizing their meetings, and the lack of fit between Immendorff's radical left-wing political views, and Penck's less militant, more symbolic, approach. See: Graw, op. cit. (note 22), unpaginated.
28. The catalogue is *Sammlung 1968 Karl Ströher*, Berlin (Neue Nationalgalerie) and Düsseldorf (Kunsthalle), 1969. The quote from Warhol appears at the beginning of the catalogue essay by Jürgen Wissmann.
29. See: S. Knust, *Erste Konzentration. Georg Baselitz, Antonious Höckelmann, Jörg Immendorf, Per Kirkeby, Markus Lüpertz, A.R. Penck*, Munich (Maximilian Verlag), 1982; and for a discussion of their work, see: S. Coppel, "Zeitgeist' art – neo-Expressionist prints from Germany and Italy', *Art and Australia*, vol. 23, no. 4 (Winter 1986), pp. 501–6.
30. See: C. Mesch, *Modern Art at the Berlin Wall. Demarcating Culture in the Cold War Germanys*, London and New York, 2008, p. 106.
31. See: *Brennpunkt Düsseldorf 1962–1987*, exh. cat., Düsseldorf (Kunstmuseum), 1987.
32. Beuys performed *Wie Man dem toten Hasen die Bilder erklärt* ('How to Explain Pictures to a Dead Hare) on 26 November 1965 at the Galerie

Schmela in Düsseldorf, covering his head in honey and gold leaf, holding and talking to a dead hare. For his 1974 performance at the René Block Gallery, New York, *I like America and America likes me*, Beuys shared a space with a live coyote, engaging in a symbolic and mysterious communication with the animal.

33. He adopted his name while in Beuys's class at the Kunstakademie, after a fellow student likened him to the American boxing promoter Blinky Palermo.
34. Beuys's drawings were known from the early 1960s, from exhibitions of work in the collection of the brothers Hans and Franz Joseph van der Grinten, in their house in Kranenburg on the Lower Rhine.
35. C. Mehring, *Blinky Palermo. Abstraction of an Era*, New Haven and London, 2008, pp. 73–4.
36. A.R. Penck, 'Für Sigmar Polke', in *Sigmar Polke*, exh. cat., with a text by A.R. Penck, Cologne (Michael Werner), 1983, unpaginated.
37. For a survey, see: S. Barron and S. Eckmann (eds), *Art of Two Germanys: Cold War Cultures*, exh. cat., Los Angeles (County Museum of Art); Nuremberg (Germanisches Nationalmuseum), 2009; Berlin (Deutsches Historisches Museum), 2010. Claudia Mesch, for example, has argued that the possibilities for opposition were much greater in the East, and the 'freedom' of the West was banal compared to the real-life struggles of artists in the East. Underlying the art of both States, she argues, was a concern with a painterly Realism that acted as an 'ideological bridge' between the two. Those artists, such as Gerhard Richter, who developed a form of Realism based on experiences both of the East and West, she describes as marked by a 'defector dialectic'. See: Mesch, op. cit. (note 30).
38. The young gallerist René Block launched his Edition Block in West Berlin in 1966, publishing works by artists such as Joseph Beuys, Wolf Vostell, Sigmar Polke and Dieter Roth (1930–98). Block's gallery became the centre for the publication of prints and multiples in Germany.
39. See Mehring, op. cit. (note 35), p. 185.
40. The exhibition *A New Spirit in Painting*, held in 1981 at the Royal Academy in London, organized chiefly by Norman Rosenthal, was followed the next year by the exhibition *Zeitgeist*, held at the Martin-Gropius-Bau, Berlin. Both exhibitions played a key role in revitalizing painting as a medium internationally.

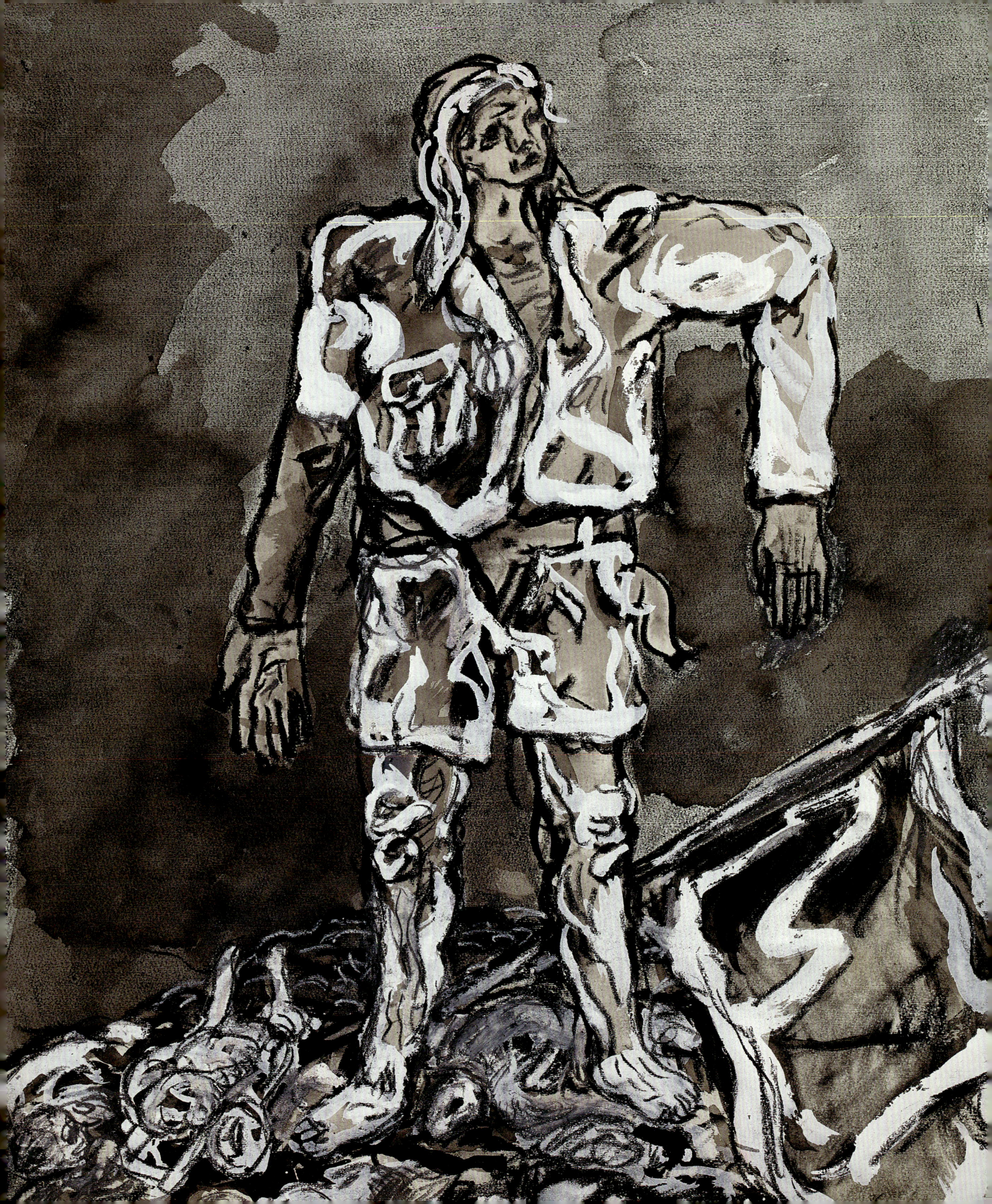

Georg Baselitz

Although best known for his upside-down paintings, Georg Baselitz has also created masterly prints and drawings and, since the late 1970s, a large body of sculpture in wood and bronze. Where his subject matter is often traditional, his artistic language is one of provocation, and his work is frequently inspired by examples of art in his extensive personal collection, ranging from Mannerist prints to African sculpture.

Baselitz was born Hans-Georg Bruno Kern in 1938, in the small Saxon village of Deutschbaselitz, in the countryside north-east of Dresden. His father was a primary school teacher and also a member of the Nazi party. Having survived the War and the Soviet invasion, the family settled in Kamenz, in the Soviet Zone, which in 1949 had become the East German State.

Following an unsuccessful application to the Hochschule für Bildende Künste (Art Academy) in Dresden, in 1955 Baselitz went to study at the Hochschule für Bildende und Angewandte Kunst (Academy of Fine and Applied Art) in East Berlin, where he was a pupil of Walter Womacka (1925–2010) and Herbert Behrens-Hangler (1898–1981). He was expelled the following year for an attitude to the East German system of art education that was deemed, as Baselitz later recalled, 'socio-politically immature'. During this time Baselitz became friends with his fellow students A.R. Penck and Peter Graf (b. 1938). Accepted into the class of the abstract painter Hann Trier (1915–99), Baselitz transferred to the Hochschule für Bildende Kunst in West Berlin. He moved permanently to West Berlin in 1958, living on Holtzendorffplatz on a grant for GDR refugees, and began painting his first serious works, under a range of influences, all led, he recalled, by 'a sense of the avant garde'.[1] He later described being 'thrown out' of the GDR: 'I believed that a Socialist society was the right thing. And then in the West there was a lot that disgusted me. Superficial things like the compulsive cleaning and the addiction to consumption.'[2]

His earliest works show a strong antipathy to the official art of East Germany, Socialist Realism, but also suggest Baselitz's doubts about the dominance of abstract painting in the West. The touring exhibition *The New American Painting*, staged in Berlin at the Art Academy in 1958, was for many young artists a revelation, particularly for the display of paintings by Jackson Pollock (1912–56), at a time when it remained difficult to see modern or contemporary painting, even in reproduction.[3] Despite the compelling work of American artists, specifically Philip Guston (1913–80), Baselitz saw that his task was to forge his own type of painting, within a German context.

A series of paintings titled the *Rayski Porträts*, begun in November 1960, shows how this early ambition was based on a combination of Expressionism and older figurative sources. The title refers to the nineteenth-century Saxon painter Louis Ferdinand von Rayski (1806–90), but the portraits are closer in style to the visceral paintings of Chaim Soutine (1893–1943), whose work Baselitz had seen in Amsterdam earlier that year. His references to Rayski were the first of many connections Baselitz would make with less well-known figures from the history of art, perhaps out of perversity, but also in the case of Rayski, from a strong sense of attachment to artistic traditions in Saxony.

Travelling to Paris in 1961, Baselitz discovered paintings by the Informel artists Wols (1913–51), Jean Fautrier (1898–1964) and Jean Dubuffet (1901–85), and also works by Antonin Artaud at the Galerie Pierre Loeb. He came across the publication *Bildnerei der Geisteskranken* ('Artistry of the Mentally Ill'; 1921) by the German psychiatrist and art historian Hans Prinzhorn (1886–1933), an illustration from which he used for his 1960 painting *G. Kopf* ('G. Head'; 1960–61). Artaud's aesthetic of violence and outrage, looking in on the 'cruel' theatre of life, provided a model for Baselitz's own strong sense of art as a provocation and the artist as provocateur. With his friend Eugen Schönebeck, also a refugee from the GDR, Baselitz staged an exhibition in an abandoned house and wrote the *Pandämonisches Manifest I* ('Pandemonium Manifesto I'), published in two versions as broadsheets announcing the exhibition (fig. 1). The text is an ecstatic, visceral, poetic evocation of the works and a rebuff to any programmatic notion of what art should be – either as realism or abstraction. The search for renewal on the basis of 'outsider' visions led Baselitz to take the Russian painter Mikhail Vrubel (1856–1910) as one subject, in the work *Hommage à Wrubel* ('Homage to Vrubel'; 1963), showing an artist who spent his final years in a mental asylum.

In 1963, Baselitz had his first solo show of early paintings, watercolours and drawings at a new gallery in Berlin established by Michael Werner and Benjamin Katz. Two of the paintings, *Die große Nacht im Eimer* ('Big Night Down the Drain'; 1962–3) and *Der nackte Mann* ('The Naked Man'; 1962), were confiscated by the district attorney. The artist and dealer were eventually fined on a charge of public indecency. *Die große Nacht im Eimer* shows a deformed, ugly figure masturbating; a deliberate 'act of aggression' as Baselitz later noted (fig. 2). No paintings sold from the first exhibition, and Baselitz continued to live in straitened circumstances in Berlin with his wife, Elke, whom he had married the previous year, and their son, Daniel.

With the painting *Oberon* (1963–4), showing four ghostly heads against a dark red background, a new poetic impulse appeared in Baselitz's work, which he pursued in a series of paintings titled *Idole* ('Idol'). In Spring 1964 he began making prints, initially in etching, during a period spent at Wolfsburg Castle; these were exhibited by Michael Werner later in the year.

In 1965, to his surprise, Baselitz was awarded a scholarship for six months at the Villa Romana in Florence, on the strength

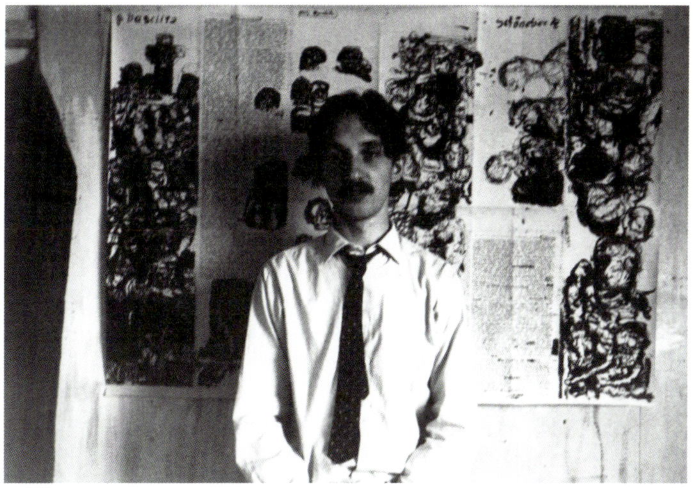

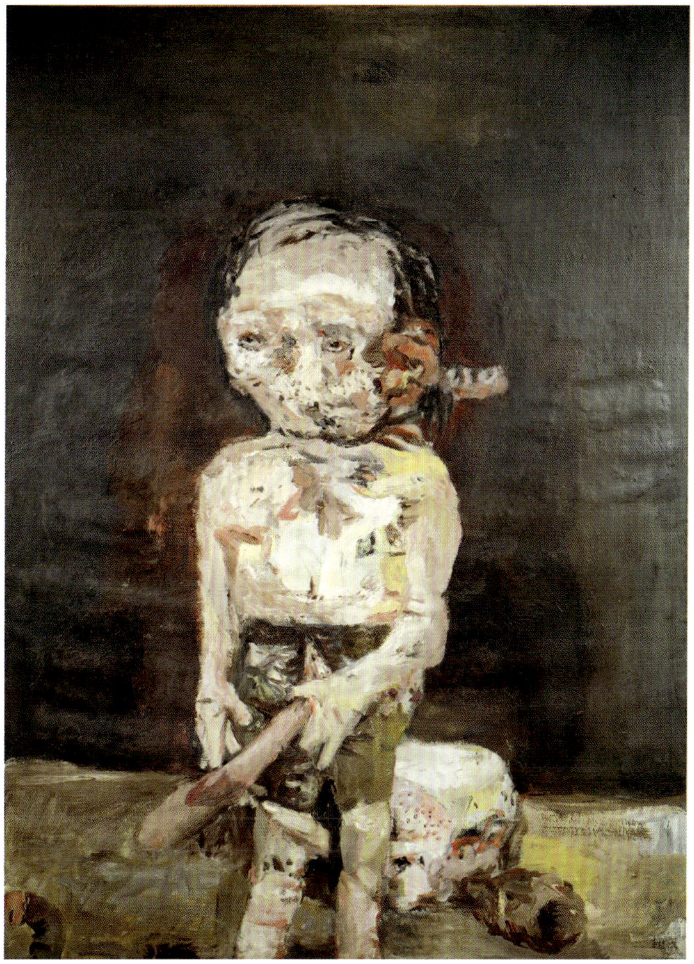

1. Georg Baselitz standing in front of *Pandemonium Manifesto II*, 1962

2. *Die große Nacht im Eimer* ('Big Night Down the Drain'), 1962–3
Georg Baselitz
Oil on canvas, 2500 x 1800 mm
Museum Ludwig, Cologne

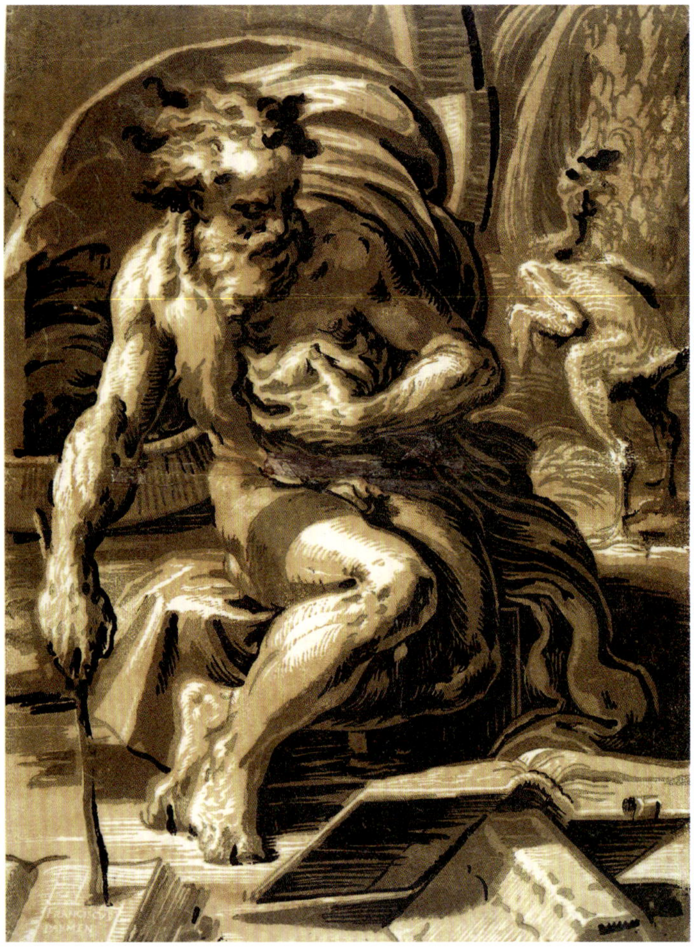

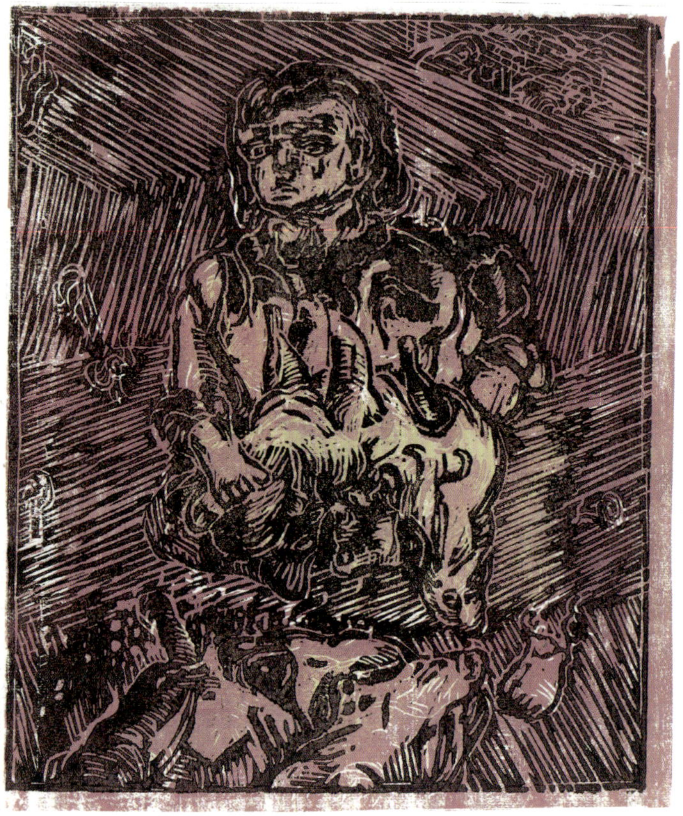

3. *Diogenes,* 1520–30
Ugo da Carpi
Chiaroscuro woodcut from three blocks, 484 x 356 mm
British Museum, London

4. *Ohne Titel,* ('Untitled), 1966
Georg Baselitz
Chiraoscuro woodcut from three blocks, 360 x 300 mm
Duerckheim collection

of a painting that he had submitted to the thirteenth annual exhibition of the Deutscher Künstlerbund in Berlin. His discovery in Florence of the Mannerist paintings and prints of artists such as Parmigianino (1503–40), Rosso Fiorentino (1494–1540) and Pontormo (1494–1557) became a crucial influence, due to the elongated, emotionally charged figure types, but also through the importance of printmaking for sixteenth-century artists. The chiaroscuro woodcuts of Ugo da Carpi (*c.* 1480–1520/32; fig. 3) and Antonio da Trento (1508–50), made on different coloured papers and developed through a number of variant states, became an important model for the woodcuts Baselitz made within the large series of *Helden* ('Heroes') works, begun on his return to Berlin (fig. 4). The motif that he explored in these works, the single heroic figure in a desolate landscape, was inspired in part by the image of the Red Army soldier in the literature of the Russian Revolution and post-Revolutionary period, in particular by Mikhail Sholokhov's patriotic saga, *And Quiet Flows the Don* (1925–40). In some forty paintings and over a hundred prints and drawings in the *Helden* series, Baselitz created a variety of poetic identities for the hero, including shepherd, soldier and artist (fig. 5). The largest painting in this series, *Die Großen Freunde* ('The Great Friends'; 1965), was shown at the Galerie Springer in Berlin, in 1966, accompanied by a mock-serious manifesto, 'Warum das Bild "Die Großen Freunde" ein gutes Bild ist' ('Why the painting "The Great Friends" is a good picture').

In 1966 Baselitz moved with his wife and two sons, Daniel and Anton, to a large rural house in Osthofen, near Worms, in south-west Germany. He later described this as a move into isolation, as a result of the scandal surrounding his first exhibition at the Galerie Werner & Katz and a wish to avoid art world politics.[4] The works he made in Osthofen treat rural subject

5. *Large Head,* 1966
Georg Baselitz
Relief print on paper, 435 x 405 mm
Tate, London

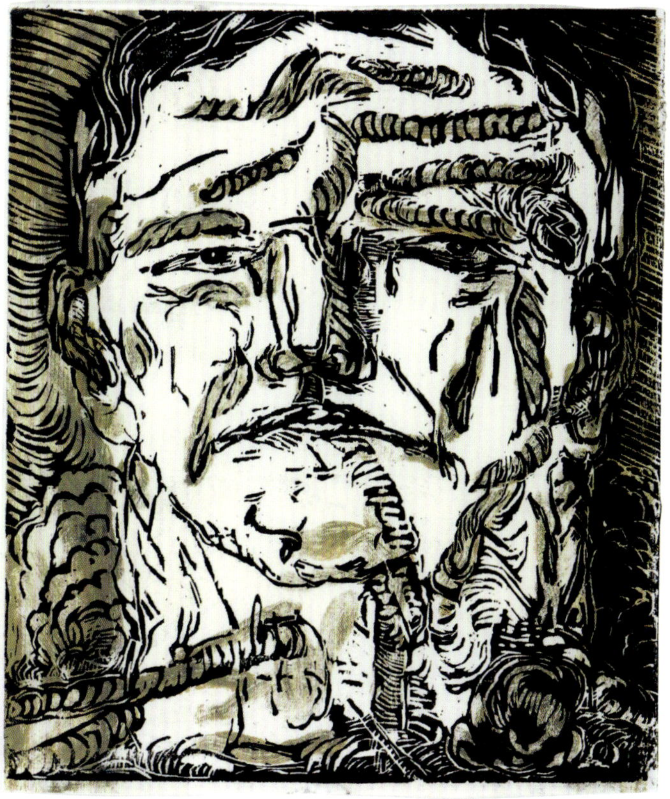

6. *Der Wald auf dem Kopf*
('The Wood on its Head'), 1969
Georg Baselitz
Oil on canvas, 2500 x 1900 mm
Museum Ludwig, Cologne

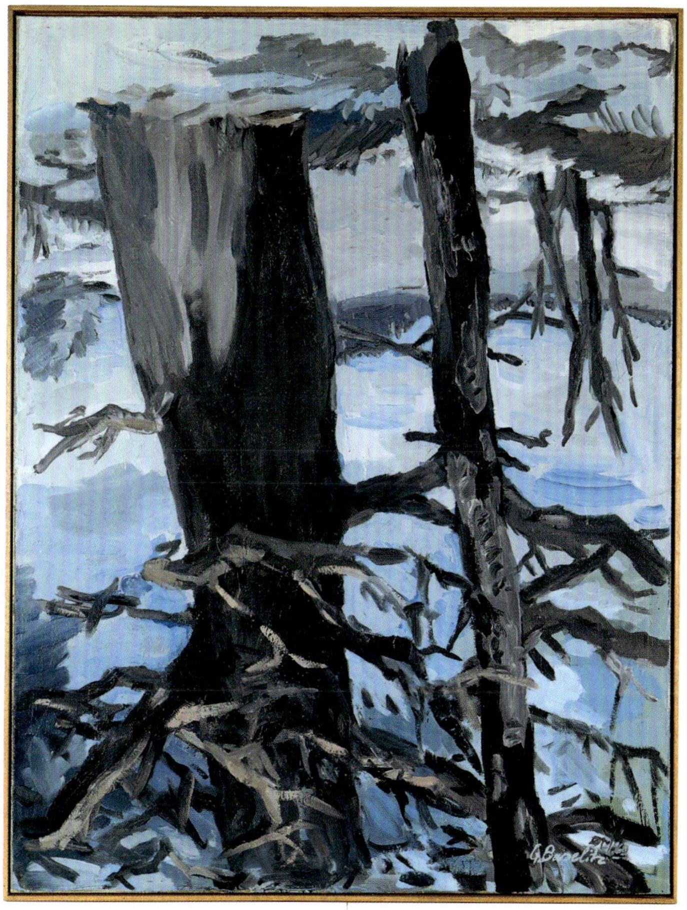

matter – hunters, dogs, cows and woodsmen – using a pictorial technique of 'fracturing': creating breaks in the naturalistic space of the painting, for example with *Erstes Frakturbild – Der neue Typ (Maler im Mantel)* ('First Fracture Painting – The New Type (Painter wearing a Coat)'; 1966). Fracturing was one method of taking the focus away from the subject matter, without making any concessions to abstract painting. The fractured painting also inevitably appears as a metaphor for the geo-political division of Germany in the post-War period. At this time Baselitz also began producing woodcuts, using a chiaroscuro technique inspired by the sixteenth-century Mannerist prints that he had begun collecting while in Florence.

Baselitz later remarked that up to 1968 he had produced 'a body of work that fills up a biography', but in that year had reached a point where he could change direction, and 'launch' himself 'into painting'.[5] The following year he made his first inverted painting, *Der Wald auf dem Kopf* ('The Wood on its Head'; fig. 6), derived from a reproduction of a painting by Rayski, *Welmsdorfer Wald* ('Welmsdorfer Forest'; *c.* 1859). The upside-down motif, which came to dominate Baselitz's work, can be seen as another method of 'abstracting' the image, without losing subject matter; it has also been linked to the tradition in Western painting of depicting the Martyrdom of St Peter, who was crucified upside down. In 1969 Baselitz made two drawings in the Gemäldegalerie (Picture Gallery), then in West Berlin, of Masaccio's (1401–28) depiction of the subject in a predella panel for the Pisa Altarpiece. As well as being, quite literally, a revolutionary format, inversion was a means by which Baselitz could focus on abstract qualities; the inverted image is like an upended glass, emptied of its contents, concentrating attention on the vessel itself – as well as on the techniques and language of painting.

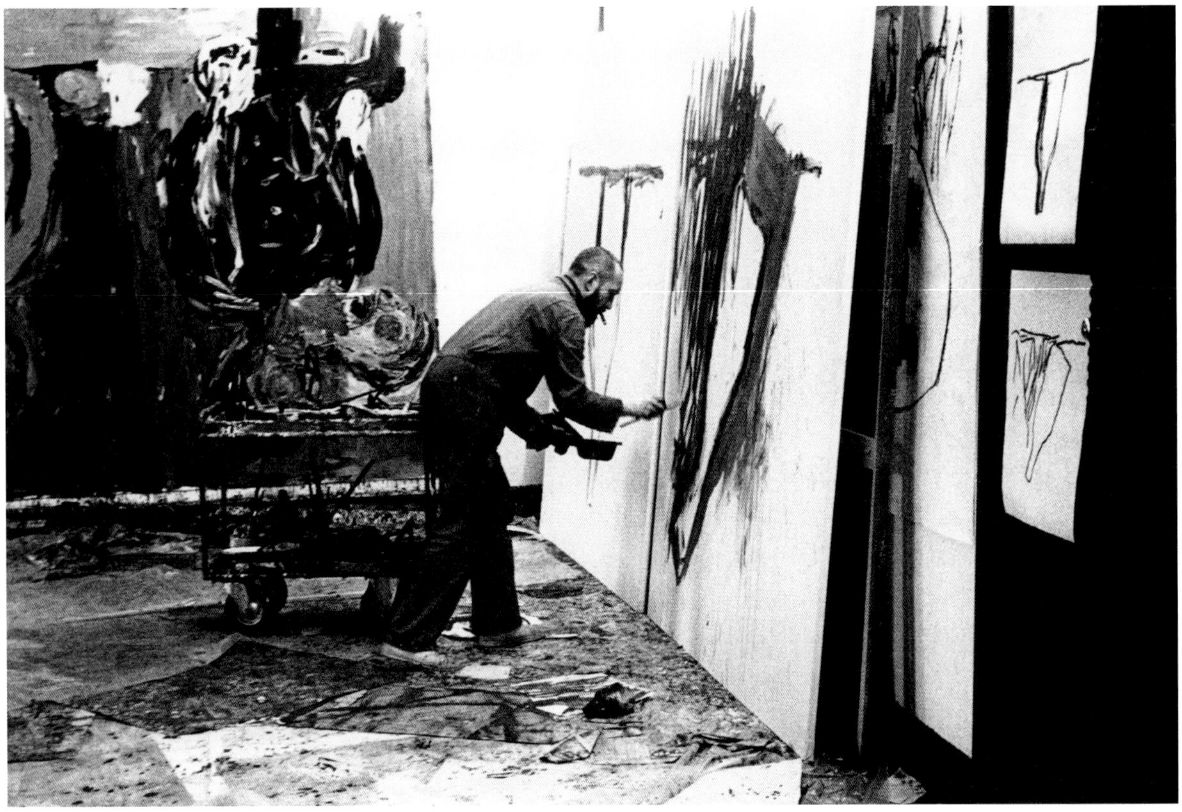

The inverted paintings were exhibited for the first time by the art dealer Franz Dahlem at a temporary gallery in Cologne in 1970. During the same year, Dieter Koepplin organized the first retrospective of Baselitz's drawings at the Kupferstichkabinett at the Kunstmuseum in Basel. Baselitz continued working on his series of inverted landscapes, as well as a series of portraits of friends, including A.R. Penck, and of his wife, Elke, and himself.

In 1971 he moved with his family to Forst an der Weinstraße in Rhineland-Palatinate, south-west Germany, and set up a studio in an old village school. Here he began painting ornithological subjects, based on photographs by the Saxon nature photographer Helmut Drechsler (1931–92), who he had assisted when a teenager. In keeping with his rejection of academic techniques or finish, and his development of a direct 'primitive' mode of painting, in 1972 Baselitz began using a technique of finger painting – literally dragging paint with his fingers – producing images of eagles, an increasingly frequent motif, portraits of his wife and of himself, all inverted. He also began working on a series titled *Fahnen* ('Flags'), for which he painted on strips of canvas mounted on the wall, and subsequently remounted on canvas.

The first retrospective of Baselitz as a printmaker was held in Leverkusen in 1974; it was accompanied by the first complete catalogue of his etchings and woodcuts, compiled by Fred Jahn and Sigrid Friedrich. The following year he moved to Derneburg Castle, near Hildesheim, where he set up a studio (fig. 7). His first teaching position came in 1977, when he was appointed as a Professor to the Staatliche Akademie der Bildenden Künste in Karlsruhe, a position he held until transferring to Berlin in 1983. He continued to experiment with different media, working on a series of large linocuts throughout 1979, and the next year on large, multi-panelled paintings using egg tempera, often combined with oil. From March of that year to the following February he worked on the eighteen panels of the major painting *Strassenbild* ('Street Painting'; 1979–80).

One of Baselitz's most striking inventions came with the creation of his first major sculpture, *Modelle für eine Skulptur* ('Model for a Sculpture'; 1979–80), a large recumbent figure with a raised arm cut from a single piece of wood and roughly painted with tempera. Displayed in the German Pavilion at the 1981 Venice Biennale, the raised-hand gesture of the figure led to heated debate about its disturbing similarity to the Nazi 'Heil Hitler' salute.

Baselitz's self-identification as a German artist was spurred on by his international success and through the exposure of his works to an Anglo–American public.[6] His first exhibition

7. Baselitz painting in his studio at Derneburg Castle, 1983

8. Panel from *'45 (Forty-five)*, 1989
Georg Baselitz
Oil and tempera on twenty wooden panels, each panel 200 x 162 cm
Kunsthaus, Zürich

in New York was held at the gallery of Xavier Fourcade in 1981, and during the same year his works were included in the historic exhibition, *A New Spirit in Painting*, organized by Norman Rosenthal for the Royal Academy of Arts, London. Rosenthal's exhibition focused on traditions of painting at a time when minimalism and conceptual art were dominant trends. Particularly in America, the combination of figurative imagery and nationalist subject matter in Baselitz's work proved controversial, and provoked a debate about the possibility of aggression as a German aesthetic tendency.[7]

Alongside his new sculptural work, Baselitz began painting in a more 'primitive' way, for example with *Orangenesser I* ('Orange Eater I'; 1981), an inverted image of a figure eating an orange, painted in a broad, expressive style. Alongside this much looser, vigorous style, an interest in religious subject matter appeared, notably with the painting *Nachtessen in Dresden* ('Supper in Dresden'; 1983), showing, up-ended, the Brücke painters Erich Heckel (1883–1970), Karl Schmidt-Rottluff (1884–1976) and Ernst Ludwig Kirchner (1880–1938) seated at a table around the Norwegian painter Edvard Munch (1863–1944). Both in subject matter and style, the painting pays further homage to the German Expressionist painter Emil Nolde (1867–1956).

Since his early scholarship to Florence, Italy remained an important source of inspiration for Baselitz, and for most of the 1980s he kept up a studio at Castiglion Fiorentino, near Arezzo, before opening a studio at Imperia on the Italian Riviera in 1987.

Baselitz's graphic works, which he continued to produce during the 1980s, were the subjects of touring retrospectives opening in 1984 at the Kunstmuseum in Basel (drawings) and the Staatliche Graphische Sammlung in Munich (prints), the latter organized by Rainer Michael Mason of the Cabinet des estampes du Musée d'art et d'histoire, Geneva. At the same time, the Munich-based dealer Sabine Knust took on the responsibility for the distribution of his graphic works. An exhibition on Baselitz as a printmaker was held at the Museum of Modern Art in New York. In his 1985 manifesto *Das Rustzeug der Maler* ('Painter's Equipment'), which he presented several times as a lecture, including a version given at the Royal Academy of Arts, London, in December 1987, Baselitz describes in allusive language the variety of experiences that it is possible to capture in painting, and asks whether contemporary artists 'are still those painters who are painting the great cave?'[8] The sense of a combination of a wide range of sources can be seen in many of his paintings of the 1980s, including the important work *Die Nacht* ('The Night'; 1985), and also the series *Das Malerbild* ('Painter's Picture'), made from 1987–8.

The fall of the Berlin Wall in 1989, and German Reunification the following year, prompted Baselitz to reflect on the period after the Second World War – another period of release and renewal. The twenty-panelled *'45* (fig. 8) was produced during an intensive period of work over four months in 1989, and was shown at the Michael Werner Gallery in Cologne the following

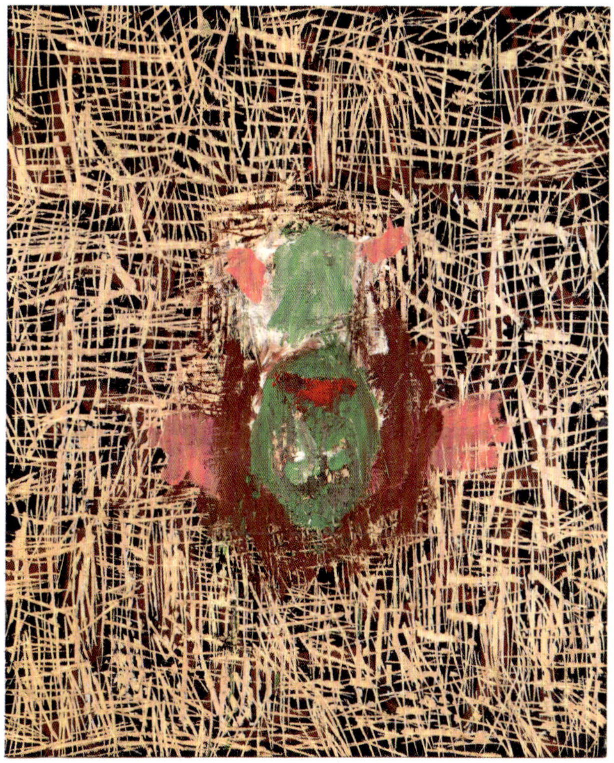

year. Most panels feature a roughly drawn inverted head of a woman, and evoke, through the title, Baselitz's memories of his childhood in and around Dresden during the war, and of the firebombing of the city in 1945. His use of oil and tempera on wooden panels covered with incisions recalls both painting and woodcut blocks. Baselitz returned to the idea in a series of eleven large sculptures in 1990, *Women of Dresden*: single large heads made of ash and covered with bright yellow tempera paint.

History and national identity emerged with renewed strength as themes in Baselitz's work in the wake of the reunification of Germany. *Der Hintergrund Geschichte* ('History as Background'; 1996) shows an inverted ghostly image of the Three Graces, overlaid by a grinning portrait of a child that might also be interpreted as an image of Adolf Hitler, whose face appears often in Baselitz's painting. During this period the colour palette of his paintings became considerably lighter, often combining bright pinks, yellows and greens, and a loose, linear drawing style. Colour became increasingly important for his sculpture, and in 1994 he produced his first fabric-covered piece, *Ding Kariert* ('Checkered Thing'). A further sculpture, *Armalamor* (a portmanteau word combining the names 'Arp', 'Maillol', 'Laurens' and 'Moore', all sculptors whose work he admired), was placed at the entrance of the newly built Deutsche Bibliothek in Frankfurt two years later.

In 1995 the first American retrospective of Baselitz's work opened at the Guggenheim Museum, New York, and toured to Los Angeles and Washington, D.C., before travelling to the Nationalgalerie in Berlin. The following year a substantial retrospective took place at the Musée d'Art Moderne de la Ville de Paris, and in 1999 a retrospective of his large prints, *Gravures Monumentales 1977–1999*, was held at the Musée Rath, Geneva.

Baselitz's 'Remix' paintings, begun in 2005, took up many of the motifs from his earlier work, including figures from the *Helden* series, redeploying them in a loose, graphic style. Sculpture came to occupy an increasingly important role in his work, with the completion of an over life-size seated figure, *Meine neue Mütze* ('My New Hat'), in 2003, and a portrait of his wife, Elke, the next year, entitled *Frau Ultramarin* ('Wife Ultramarine'). A retrospective of his sculpture was held at the Musée d'Art Moderne de la Ville de Paris in 2011, beginning with *Modelle für Eine Skulptur* and concluding with his most recent standing figures carved in wood. He began casting his wooden sculptures in bronze in 2003. In 2012 he completed a monumental bronze sculpture *BDM Gruppe* ('BDM Group'; fig. 9), based on a memory from his childhood in Deutschbaselitz of three girls, members of the Nazi youth organization *Bund Deutscher Mädel* (League of German Girls).[9]

Baselitz lives and works on Lake Ammersee, Bavaria, where he moved in 2007, and keeps a studio at Imperia on the Italian Riviera.

1. 'Georg Baselitz in conversation with Heinz Peter Schwerfel', 1988; trans. Fiona Elliott and reprinted in D. Gretenkort (ed.), *Georg Baselitz. Collected Writings and Interviews*, London, 2010, p. 179.
2. Ibid., p. 160.
3. See: G. Baselitz, 'Wenn Maler nicht rechtzeitig aus dem Fenster springen, werden sie einfach alt…', in G. Adriani (ed.), *Baselitz. 50 Jahre Malerei*, exh. cat., Baden-Baden (Museum Frieder Burda), 2009, pp. 179–83.
4. 'Georg Baselitz in conversation with Jean-Louis Froment and Jean-Marc Poinsot', in D. Gretenkort (ed.), *Georg Baselitz. Collected Writings and Interviews*, London, 2010, pp. 61–79, here p. 66.
5. Ibid., p. 65.
6. S. Behr, in N. Rosenthal, *Georg Baselitz*, London (Royal Academy), 2007, p. 135.
7. B. Buchloh, 'Figures of authority, ciphers of aggression: notes on the return of representation in European painting', *October*, 16, 1981, pp. 39–68.
8. G. Baselitz, 'Das Rustzeug der Maler', trans. Norbert Messler as 'Painter's equipment' and printed in *The Burlington Magazine*, 1021, April 1988, pp. 283–6.
9. See: J.P. Stonard, 'Baselitz black or history as background', in *Georg Baselitz. Le côté sombre*, exh. cat., Paris (Galerie Thaddeus Ropac), 2013, pp. 27–30.

9. *BDM Gruppe* ('BDM Group'), 2012
Georg Baselitz
Patinated bronze, H. 3660 mm

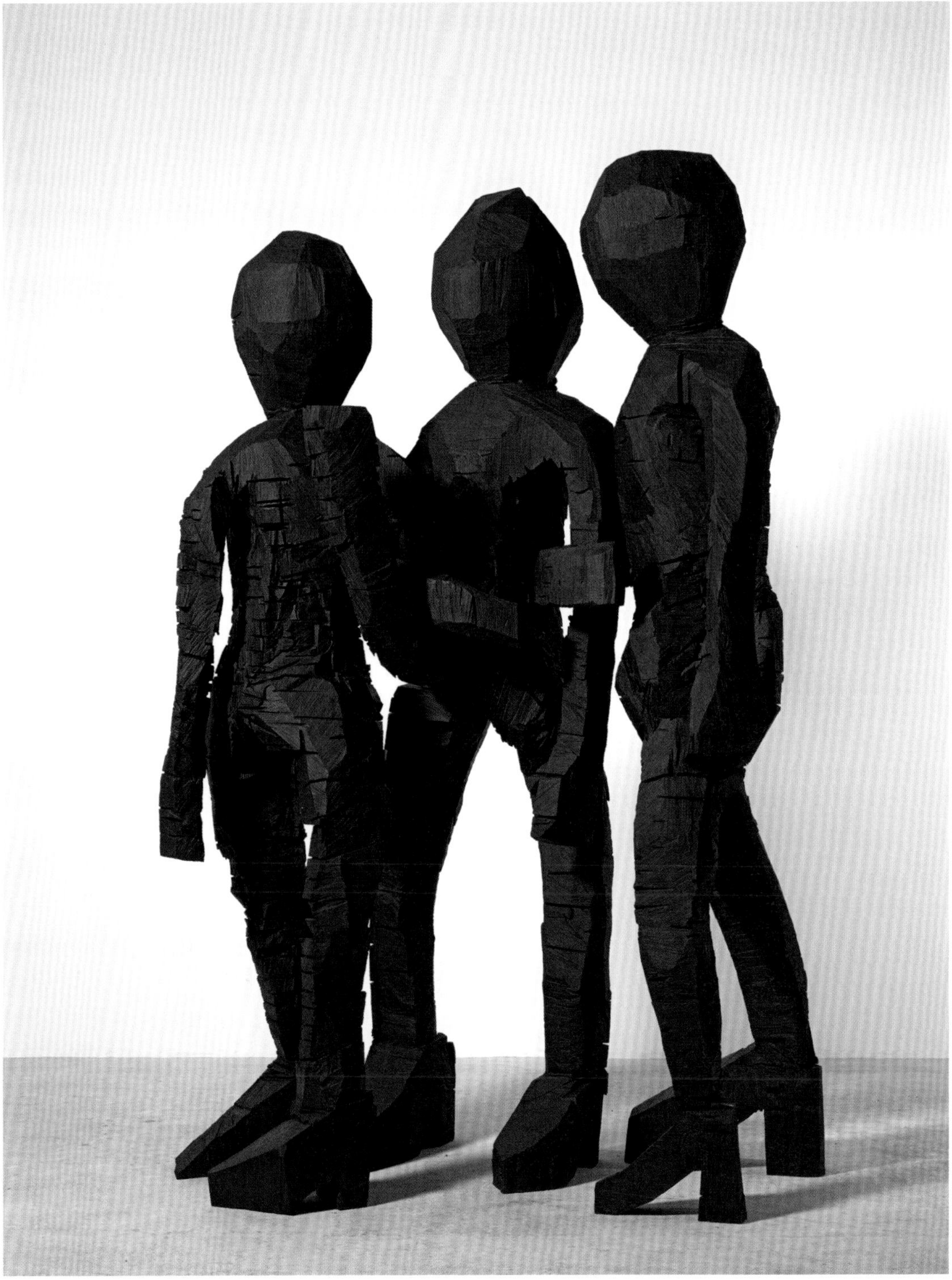

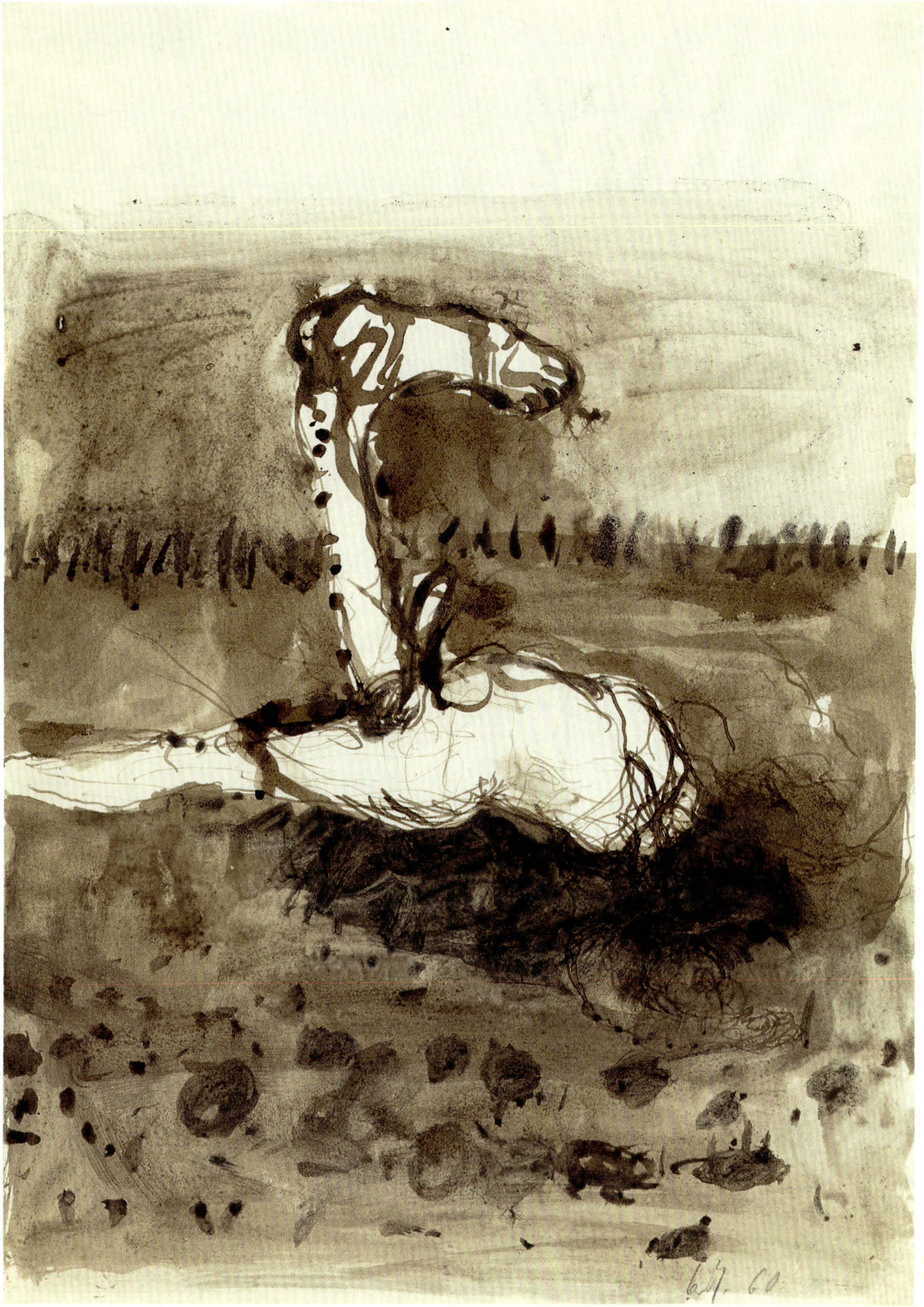

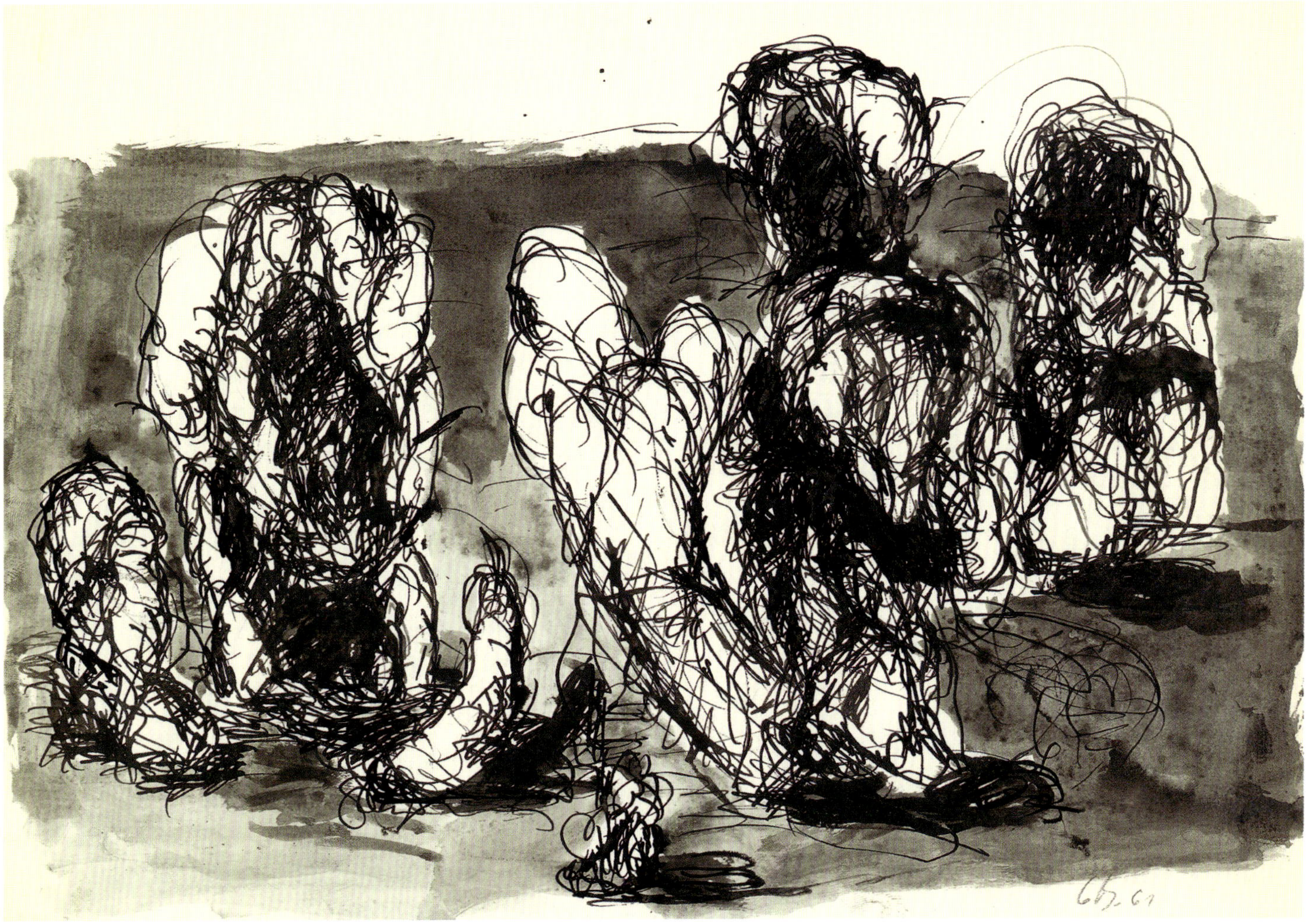

1
Der Acker ('Field'), 1960
Georg Baselitz
Ink and wash
295 x 207 mm
Presented by Count Christian
Duerckheim to the British Museum

2
Ohne Title ('Untitled'), 1961
Georg Baselitz
Pen and ink and wash
210 x 296 mm

3
Pandämonisches Manifest II
('Pandemonium Manifesto II'), 1962
Georg Baselitz and Eugen Schönebeck
Blueprint
901 x 1278 mm

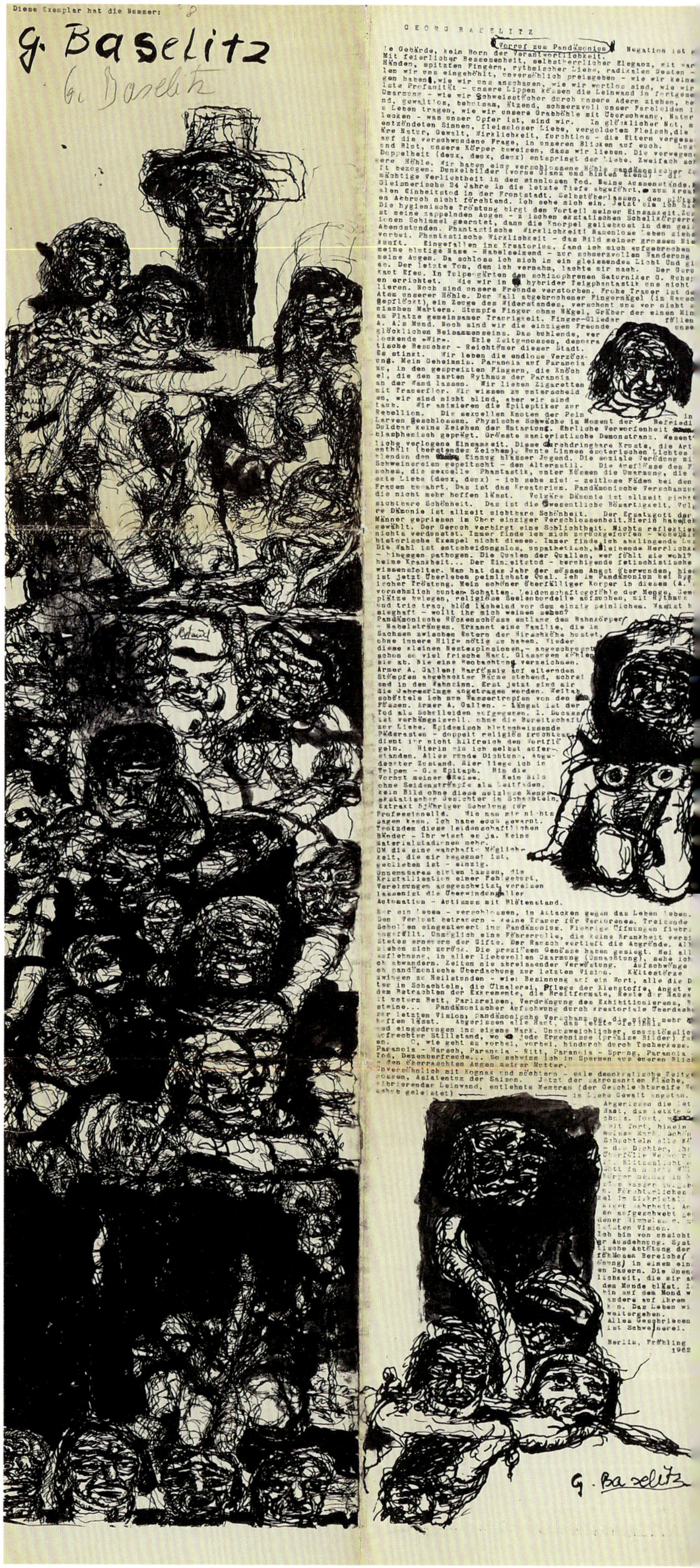

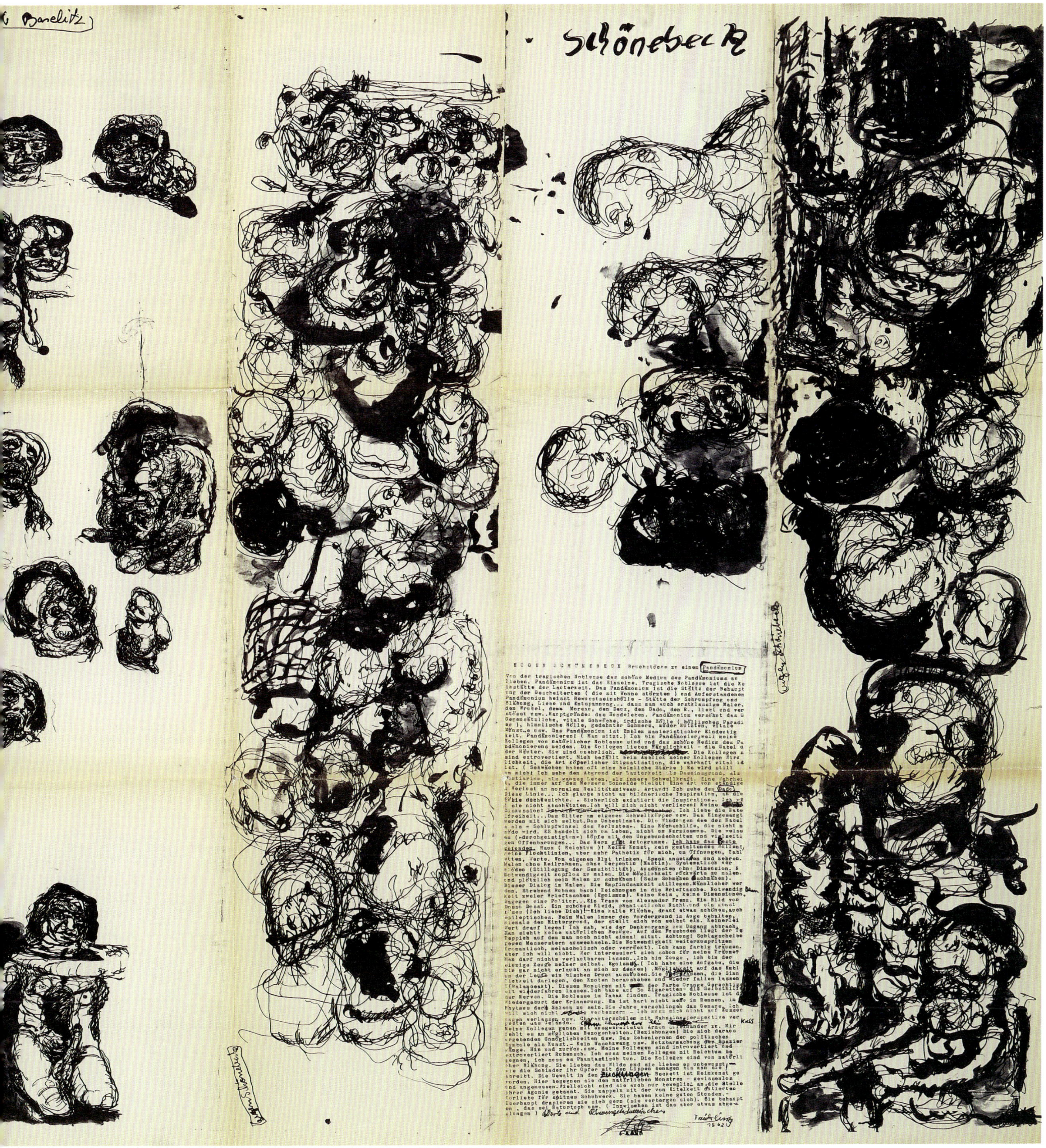
Schönebeck

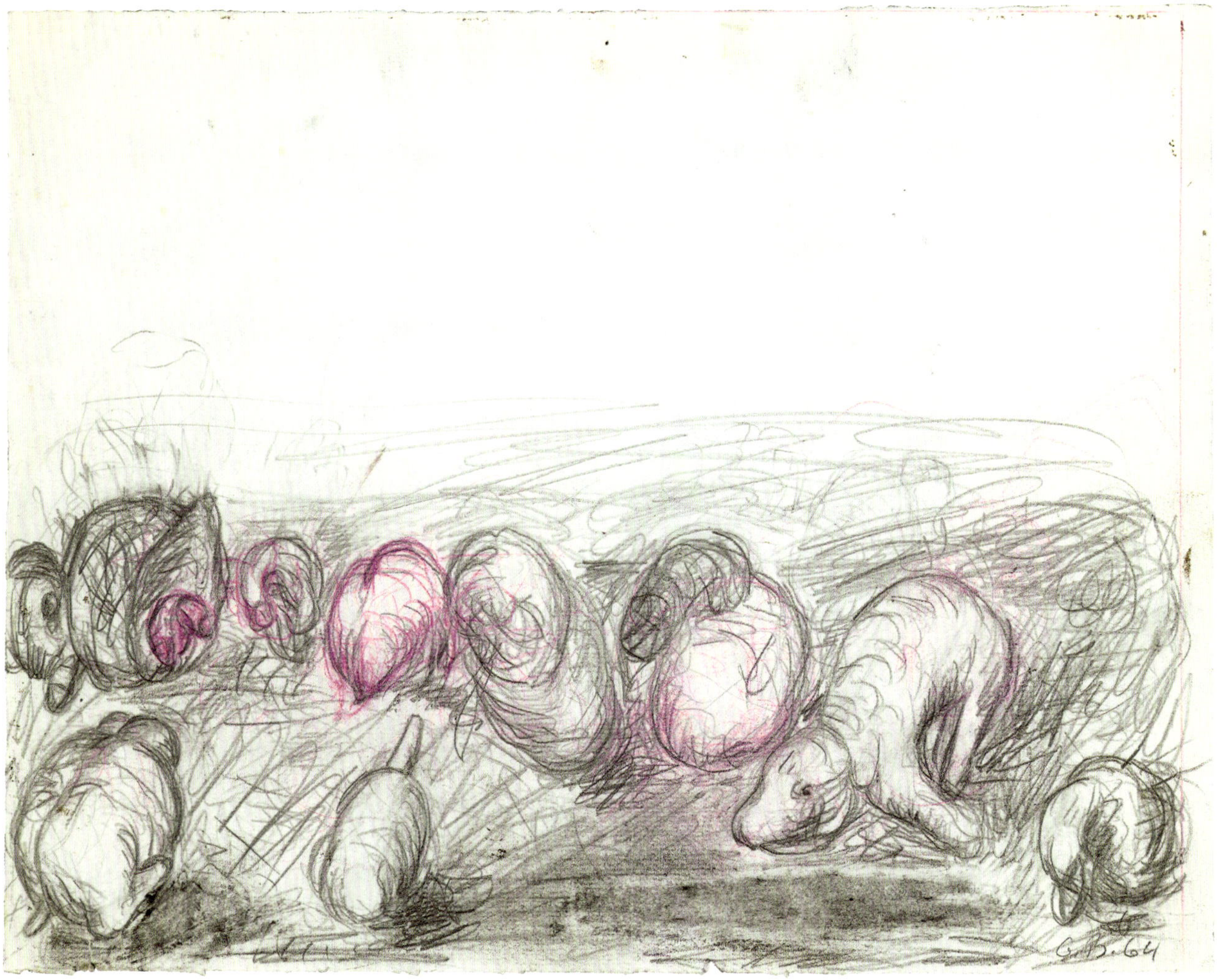

4
Hunde ('Dogs'), 1964
Georg Baselitz
Graphite and crayon
253 x 317 mm
Presented by Count Christian Duerckheim to the British Museum

5
Ohne Titel ('Untitled') *c.* 1965
Georg Baselitz
Pen and ink and wash
649 x 500 mm

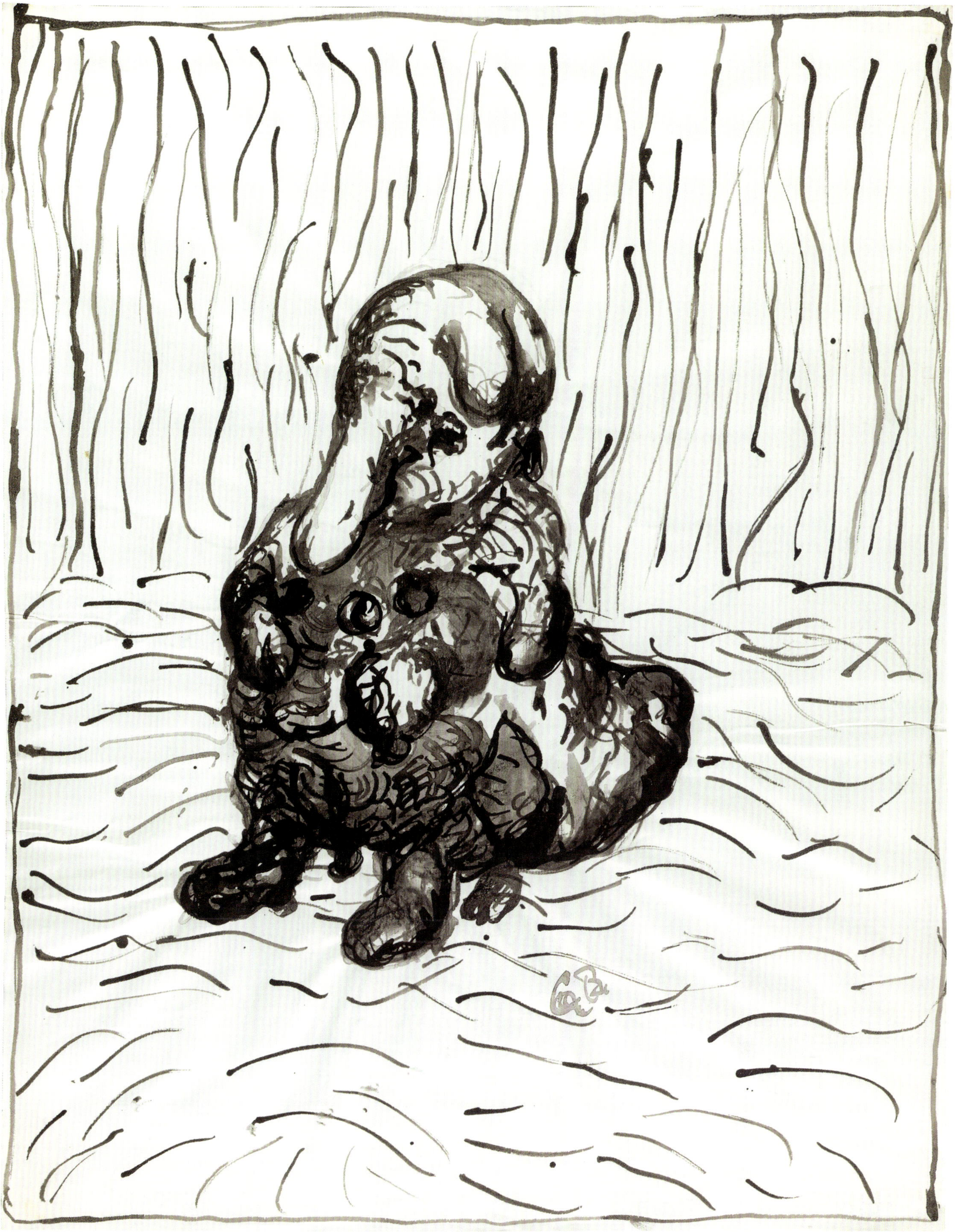

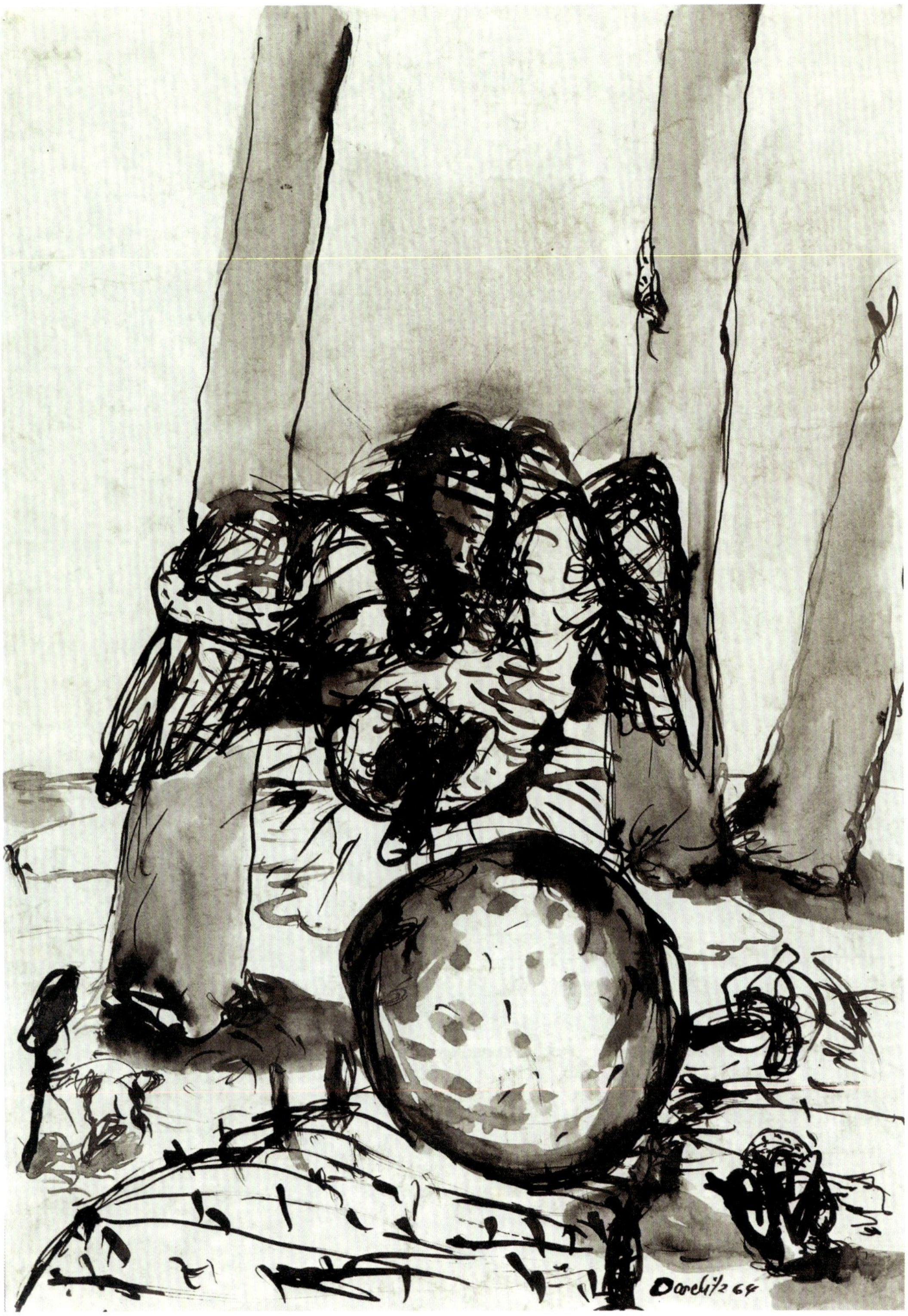

6
Ohne Titel ('Untitled'), 1964
Georg Baselitz
Pen and ink, brush and wash
498 x 345 mm
Presented by Count Christian
Duerckheim to the British Museum

7
Ohne Titel ('Untitled'), 1965
Georg Baselitz
Charcoal
495 x 376 mm
Presented by Count Christian
Duerckheim to the British Museum

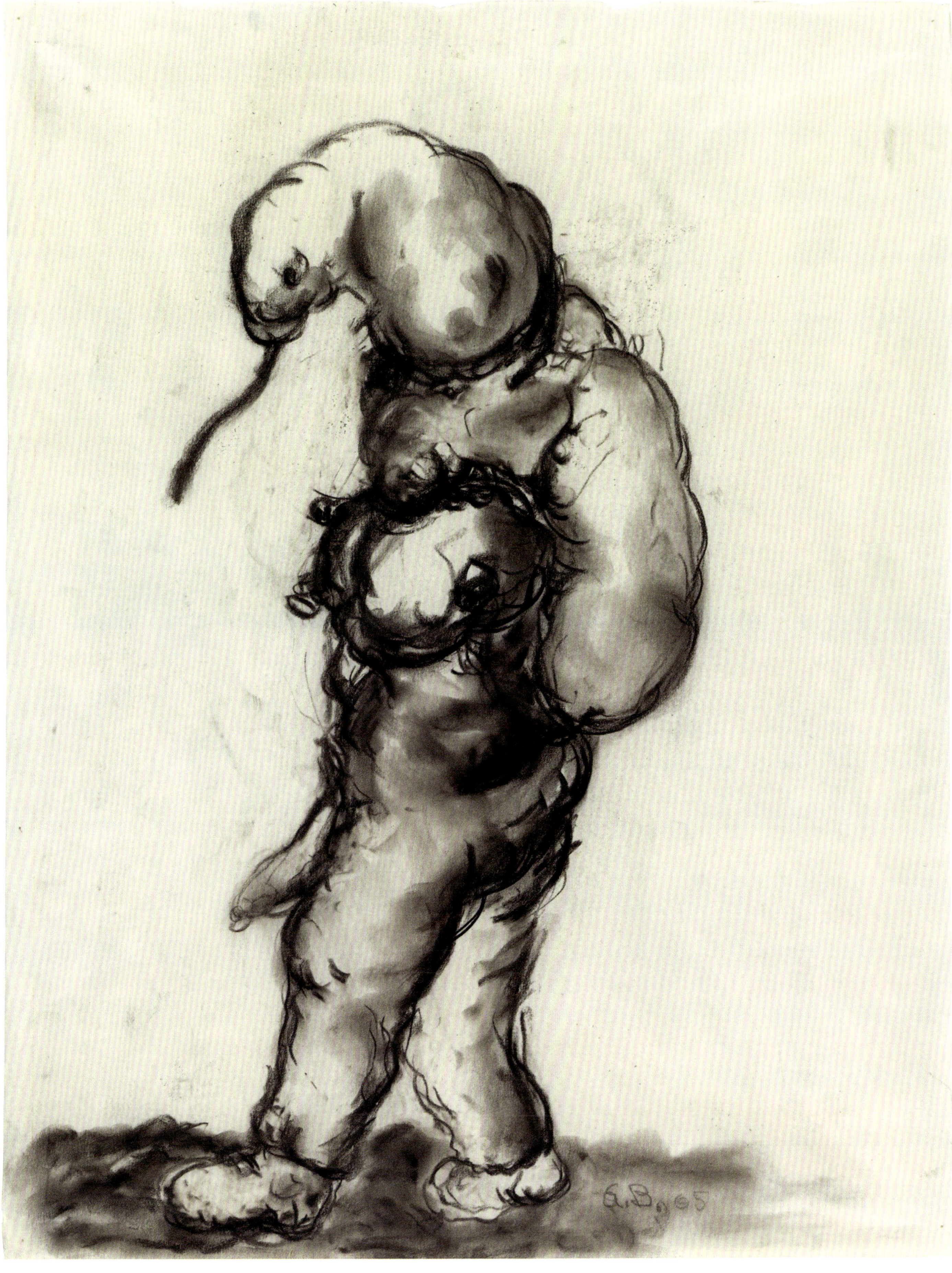

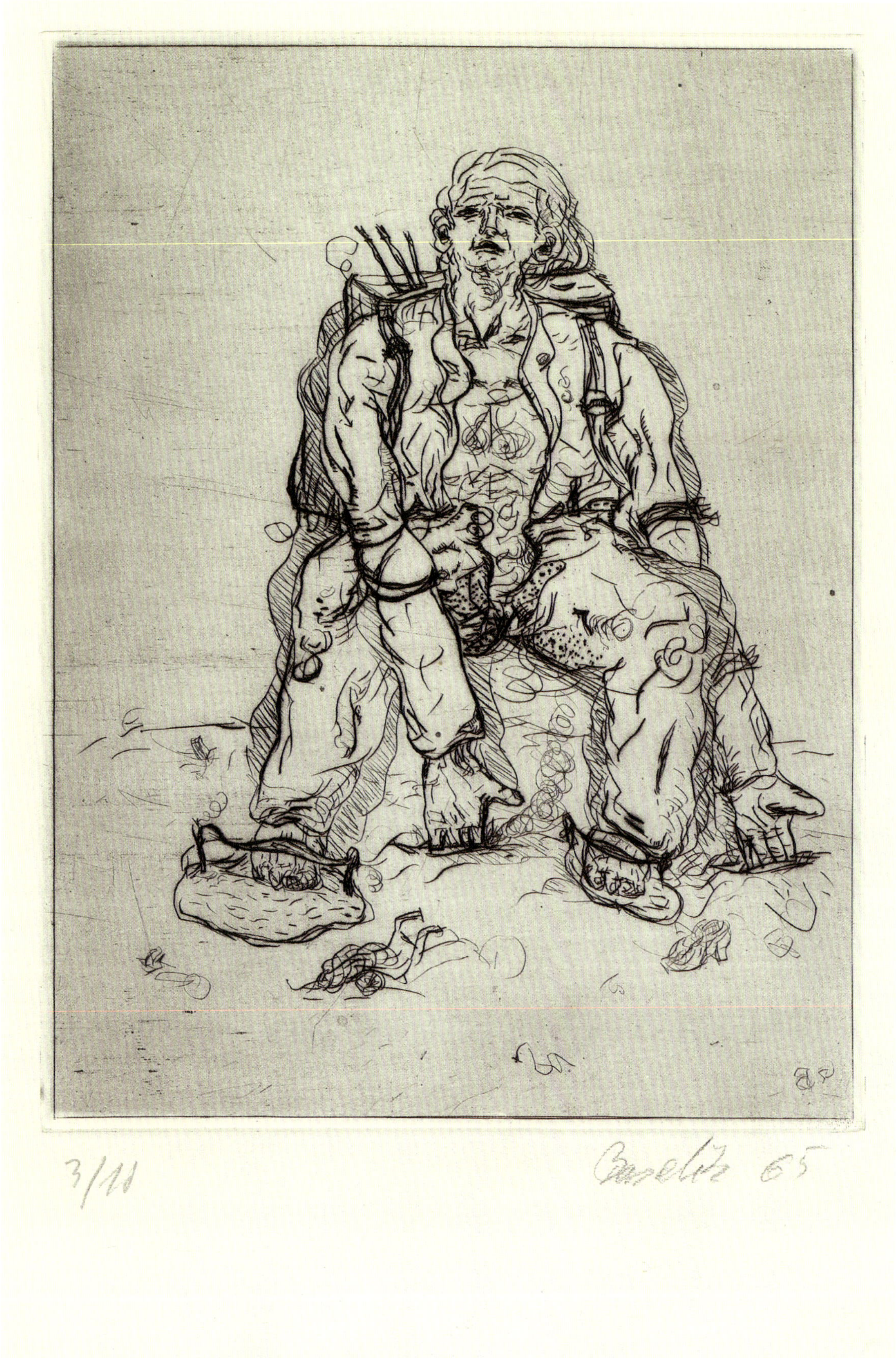

8
Die Falle ('Trap'), 1965
Georg Baselitz
Etching and drypoint with
plate-tone
315 x 235 mm
Presented by Count Christian
Duerckheim to the British Museum

9
Ohne Titel ('Untitled'), 1965
Georg Baselitz
Etching and drypoint
338 x 243mm

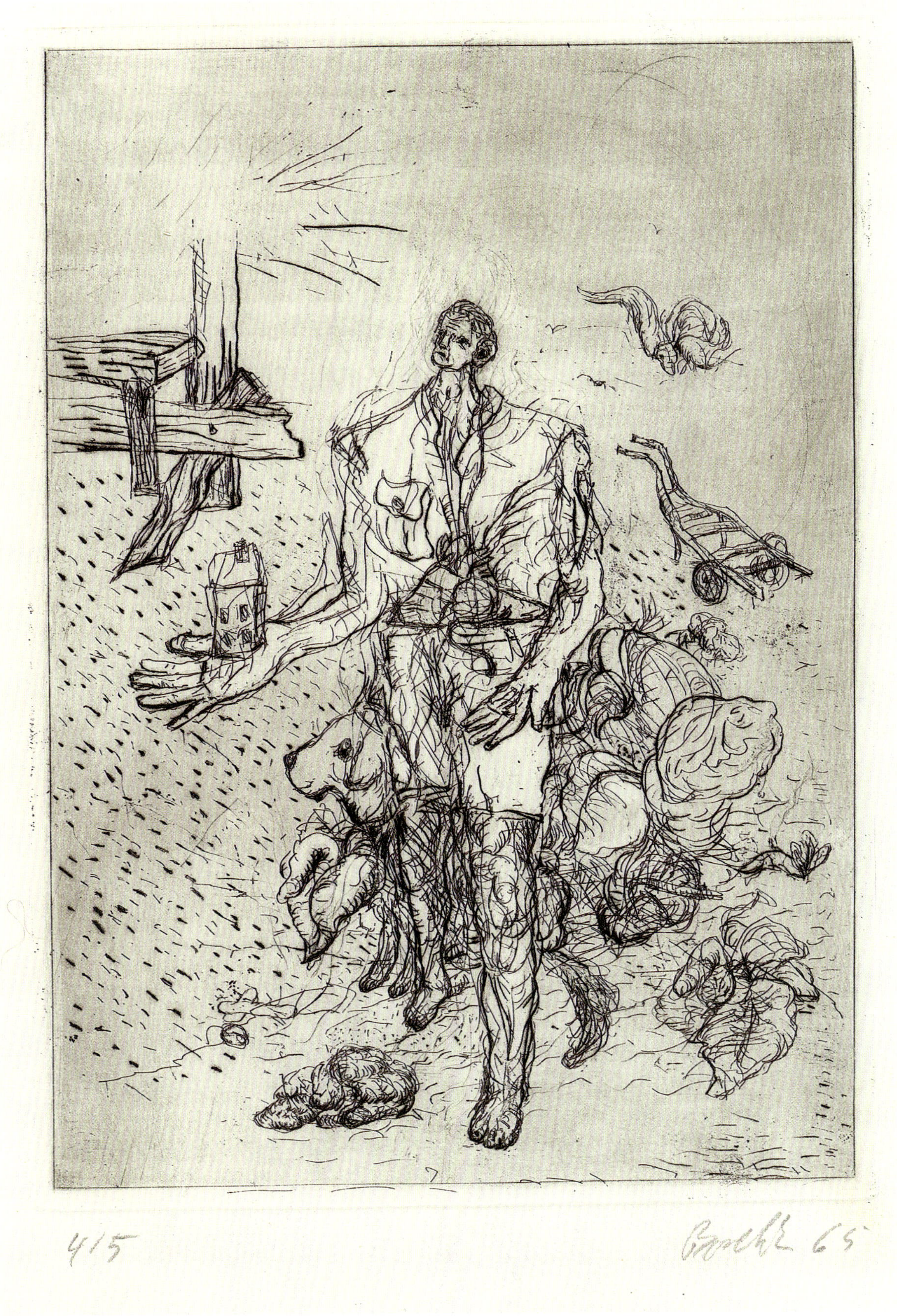

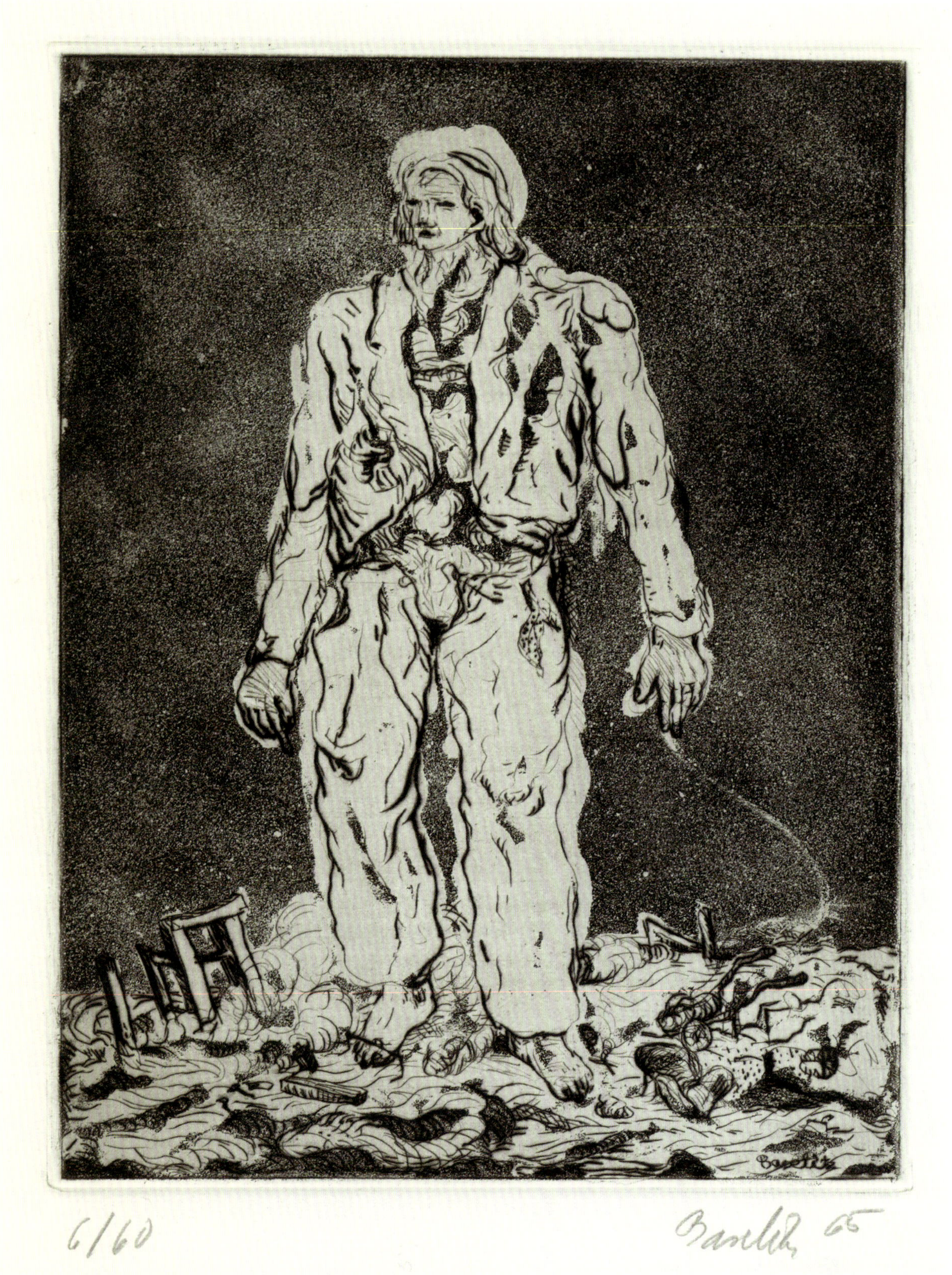

10
Der Hirte ('Herdsman'), 1965
Georg Baselitz
Etching, drypoint and aquatint
313 x 237 mm

11
Hirte ('Herdsman'), 1966
Georg Baselitz
Etching and drypoint
319 x 235 mm
Presented by Count Christian
Duerckheim to the British Museum

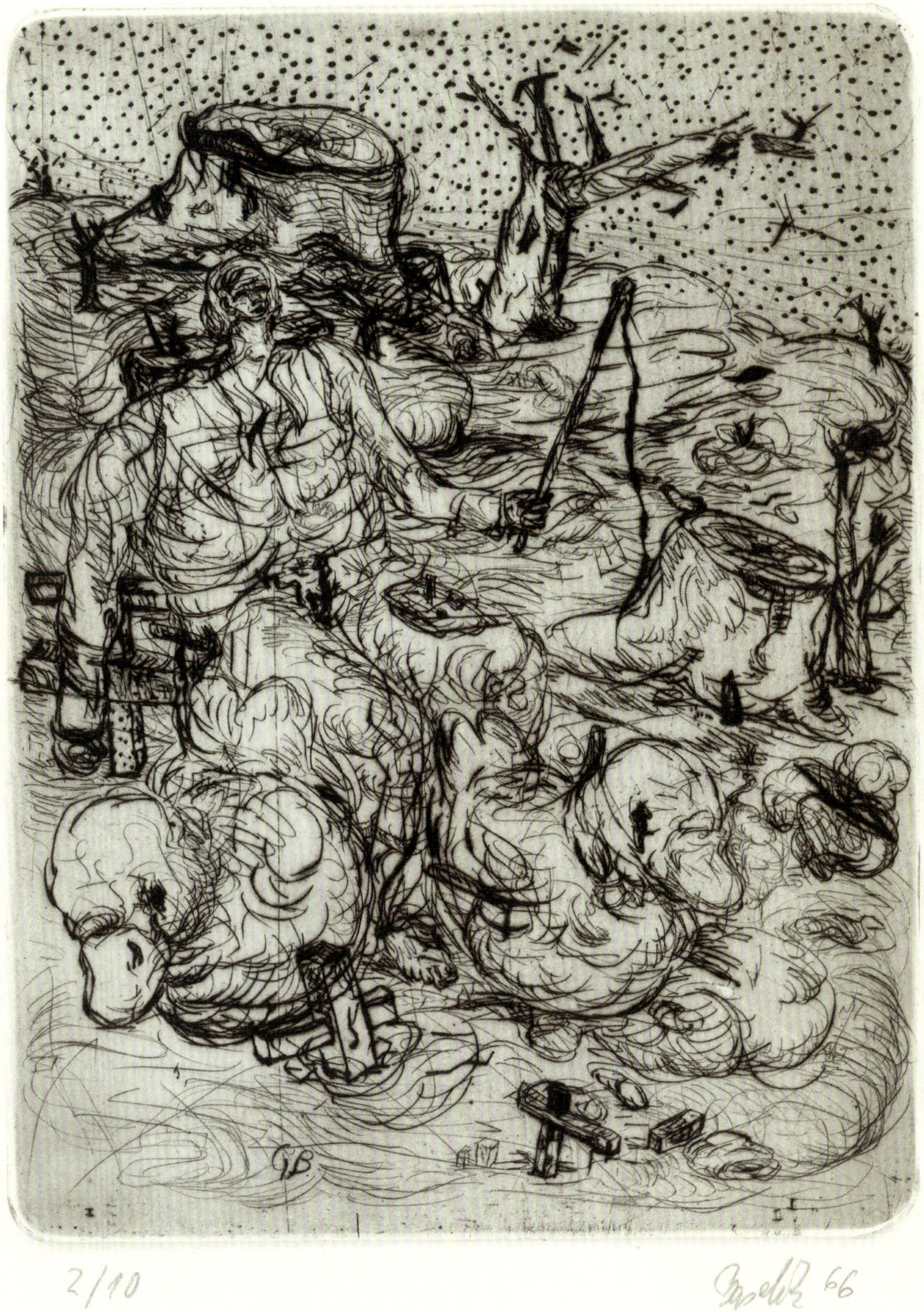

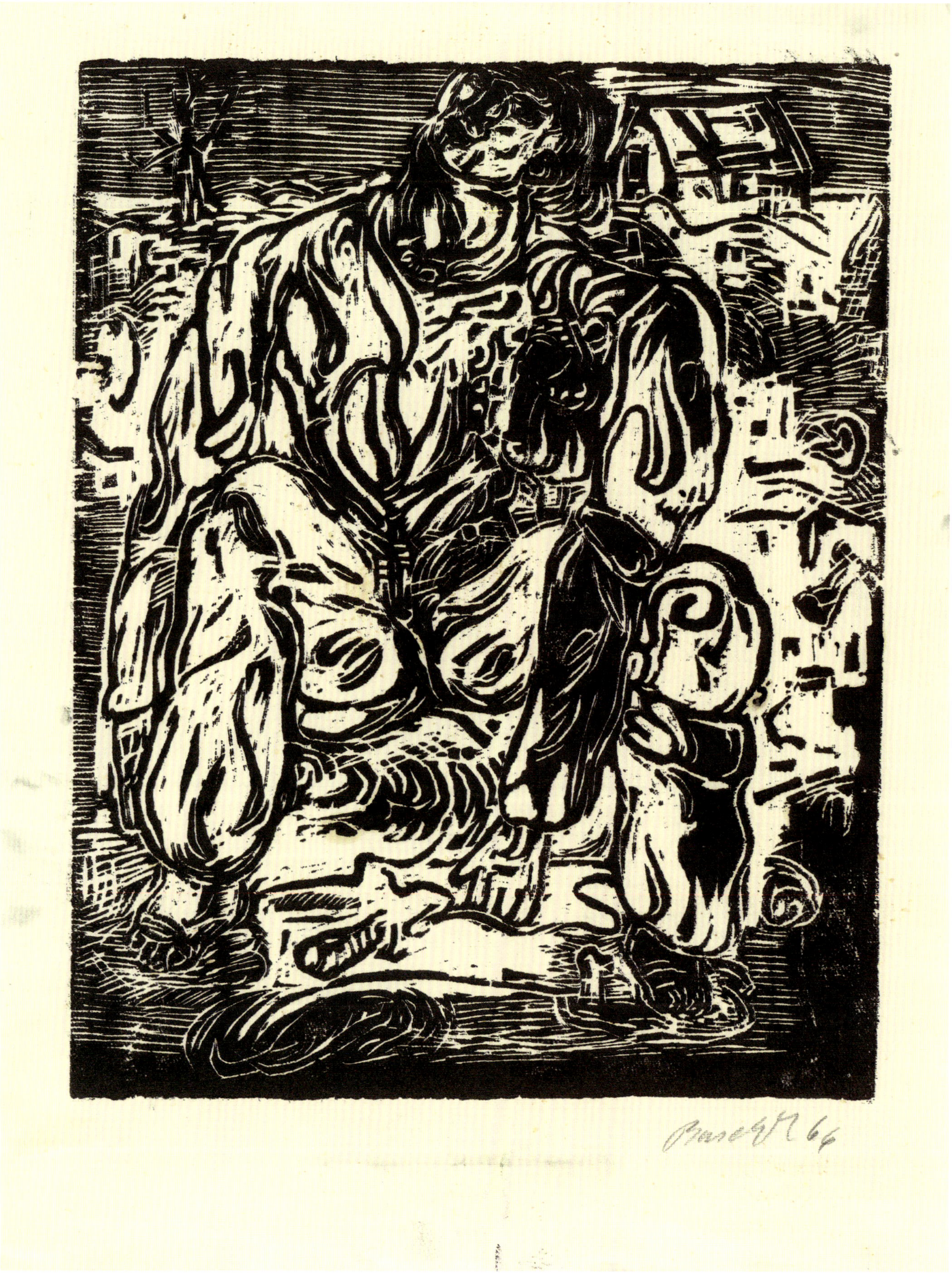

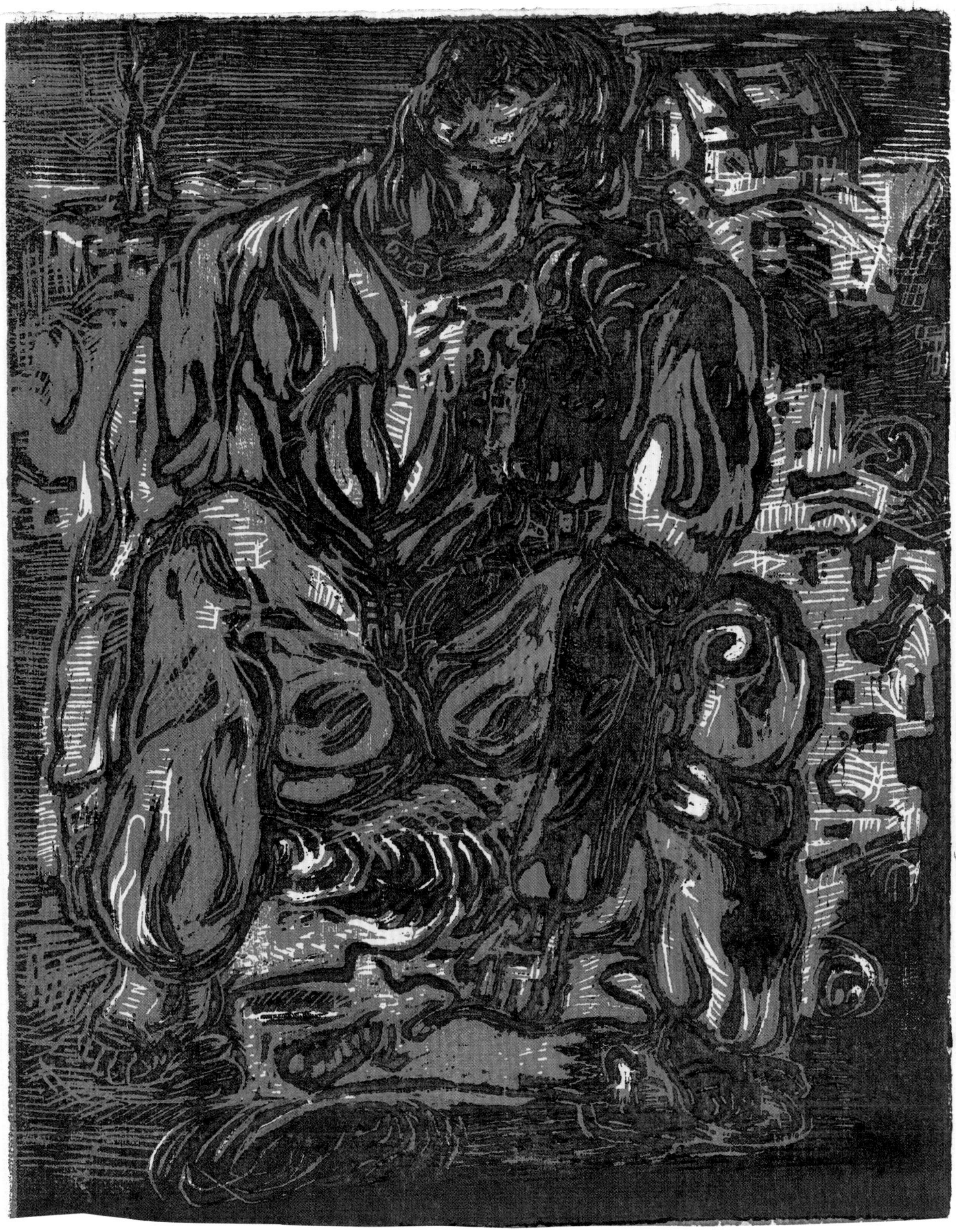

12
Ohne Titel ('Untitled'), 1966
Georg Baselitz
Woodcut
418 x 325 mm

13
Ohne Titel ('Untitled'), 1966
Georg Baselitz
Woodcut
420 x 330 mm
Presented by Count Christian
Duerckheim to the British Museum

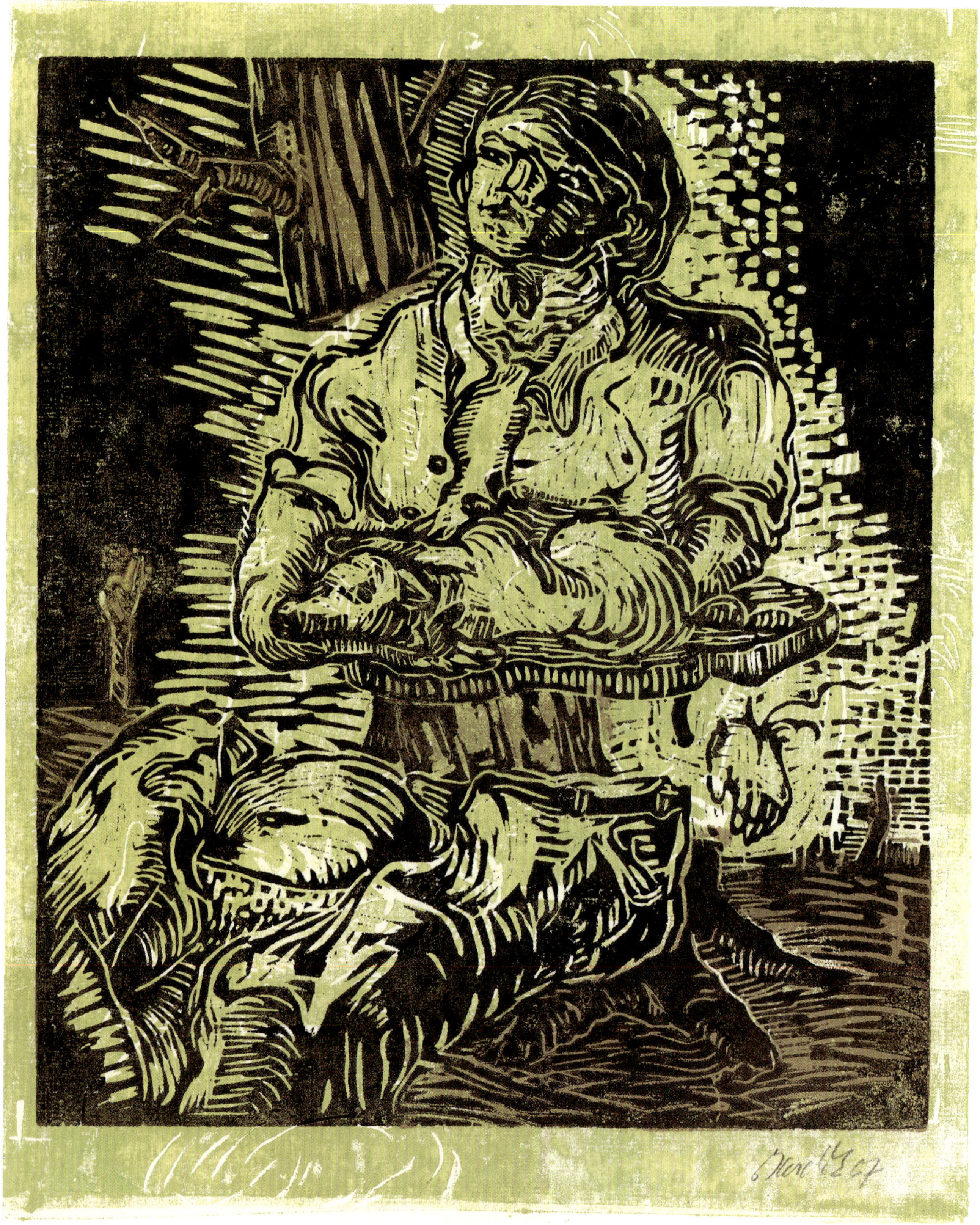

14
Ohne Titel ('Untitled'), 1967
Georg Baselitz
Woodcut
360 x 300 mm

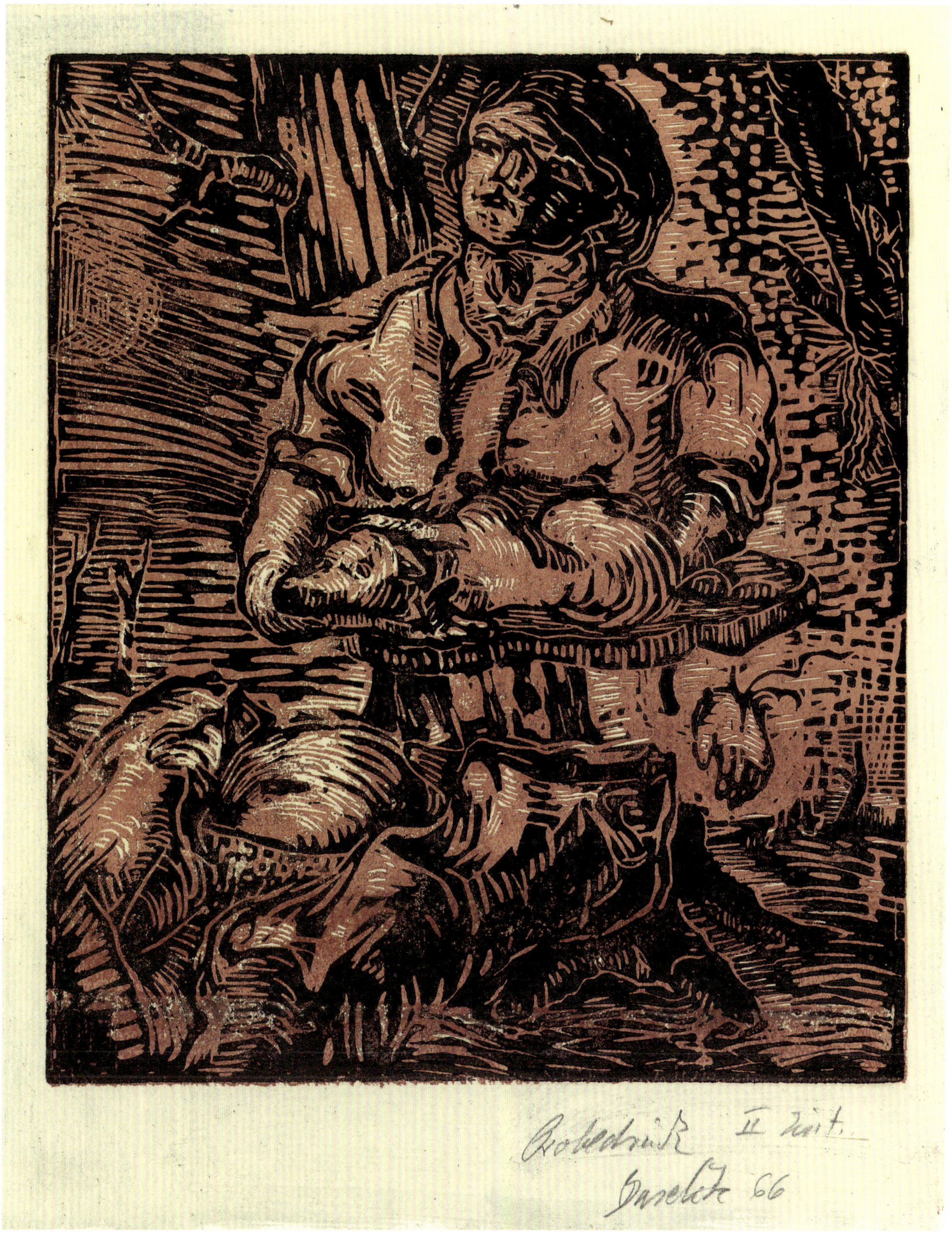

15
Ohne Titel ('Untitled'), 1966
Georg Baselitz
Woodcut
360 x 300 mm

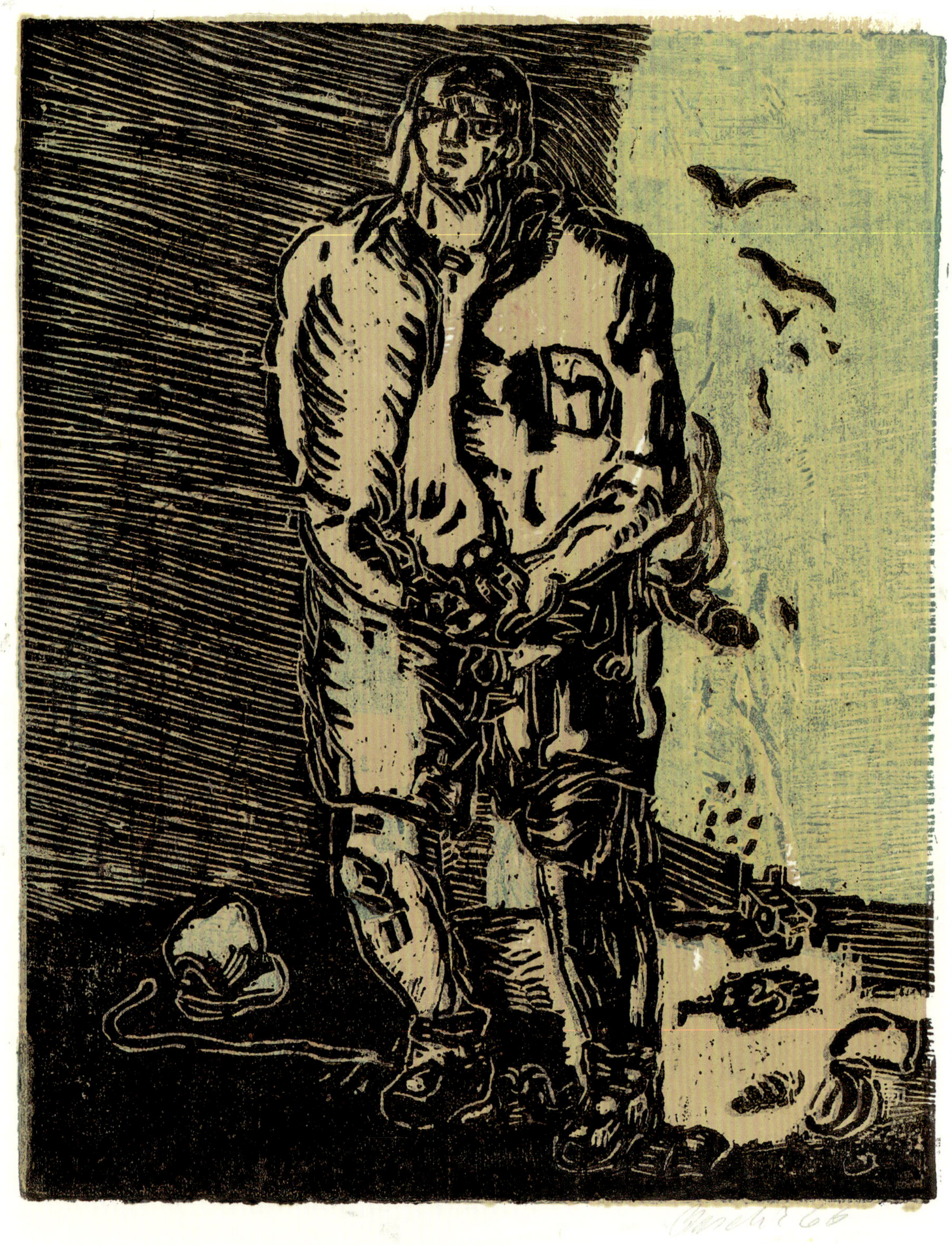

16
LR, 1966
Georg Baselitz
Woodcut
420 x 330 mm

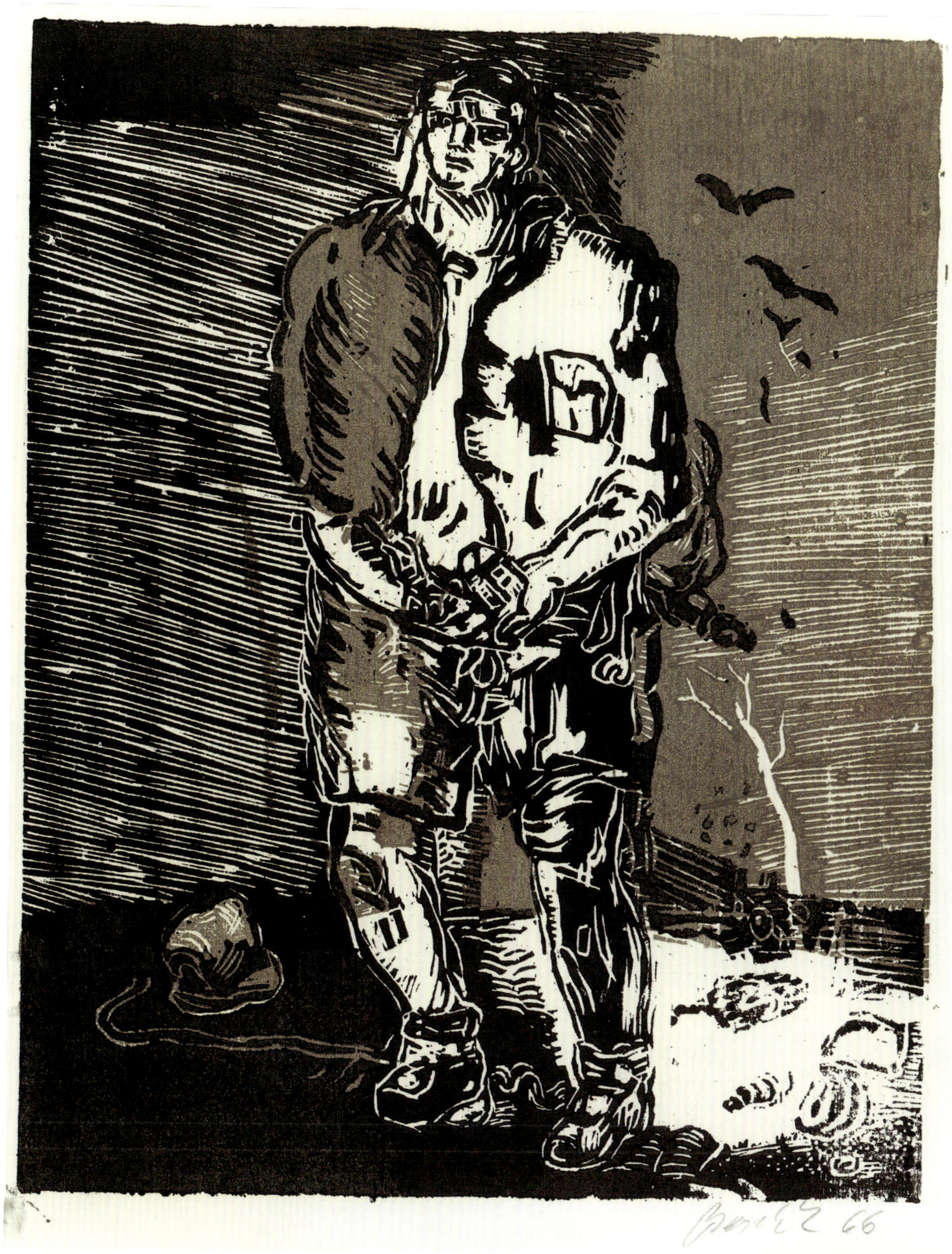

17
LR, 1966
Georg Baselitz
Woodcut
420 x 328 mm

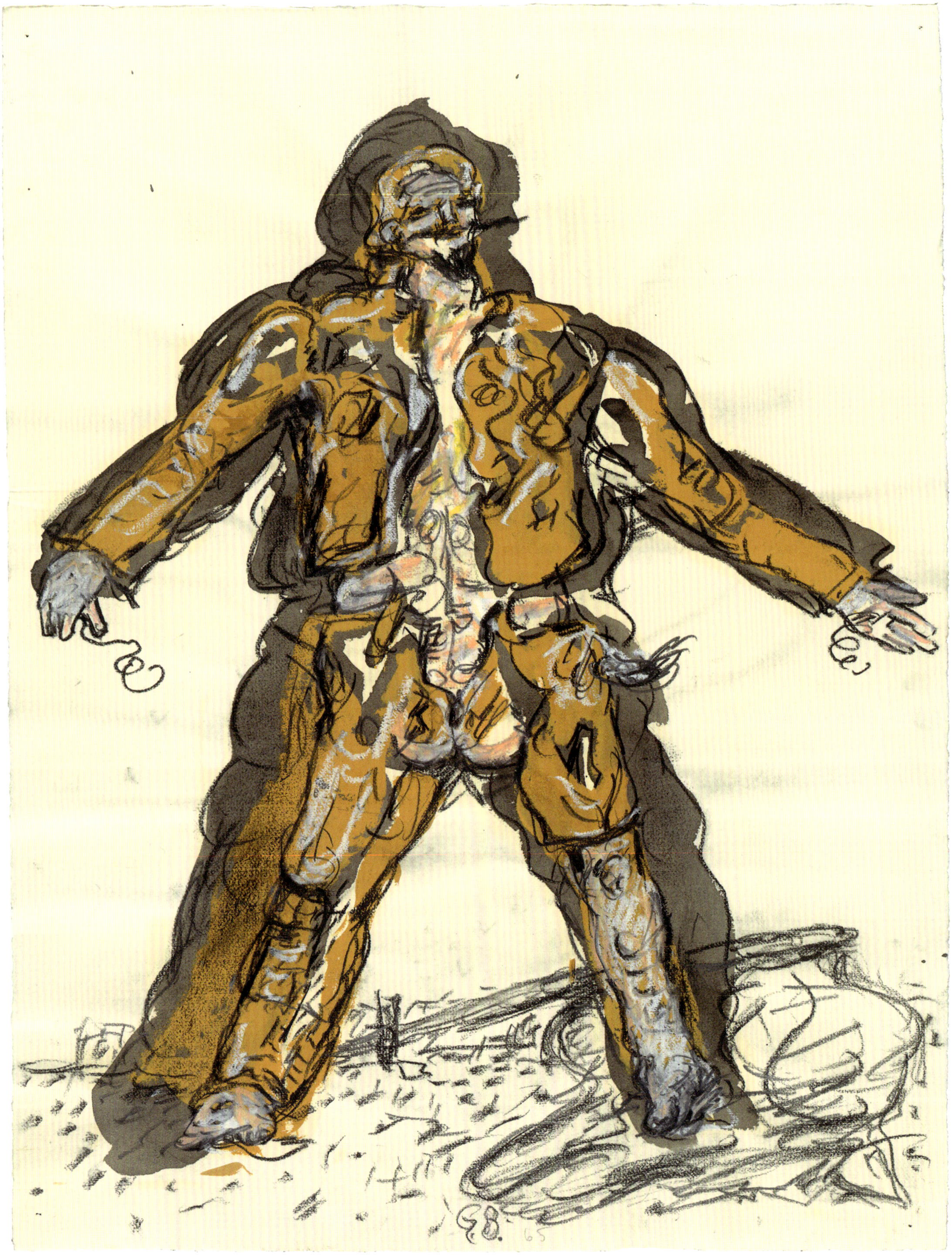

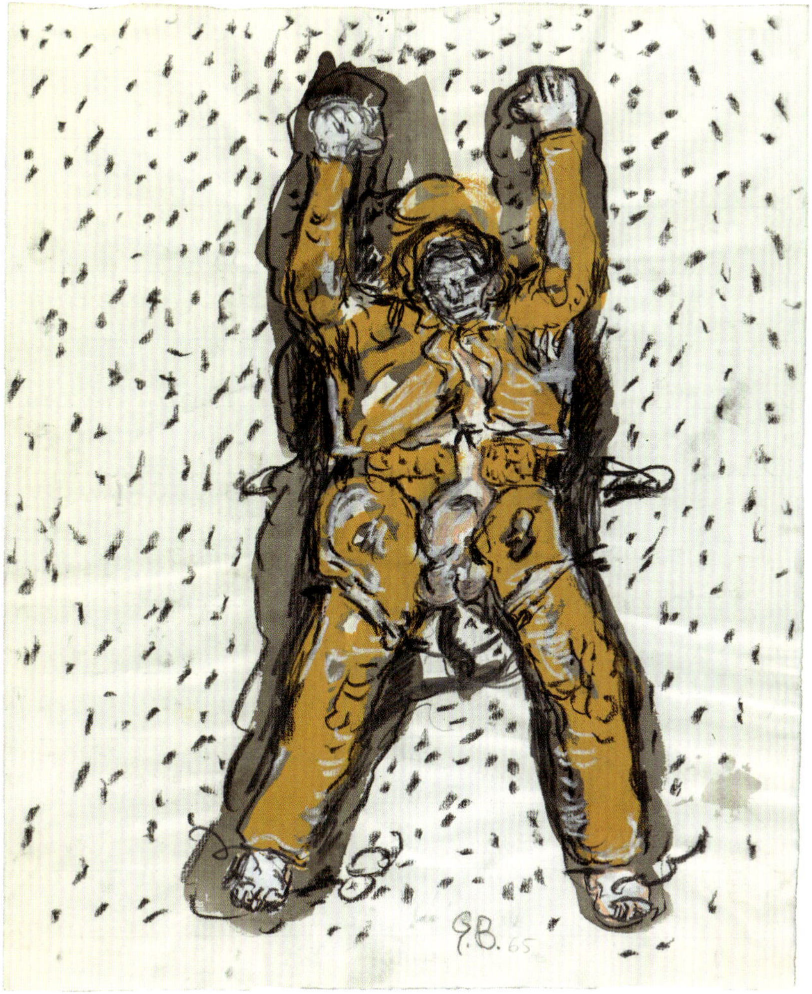

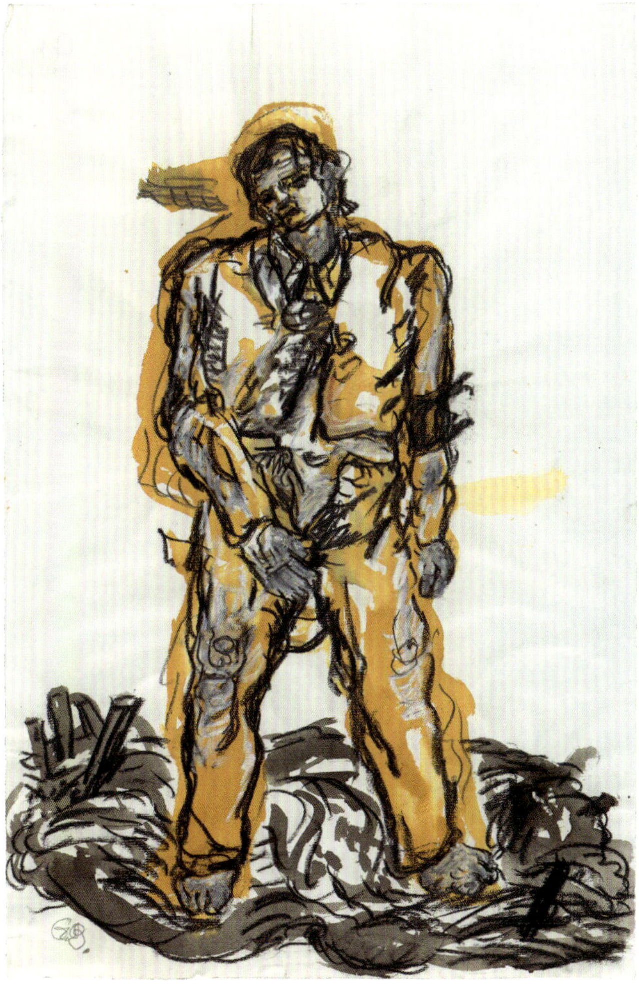

18
Partisan ('Partisan'), 1965
Georg Baselitz
Yellow ochre gouache, grey wash, charcoal, graphite, white and pink pastel
520 x 390 mm
Presented by Count Christian Duerckheim to the British Museum

19
Ein neuer Typ ('A New Type'), 1965
Georg Baselitz
Yellow ochre gouache, grey wash, charcoal, graphite, white and pink pastel
523 x 421 mm
Presented by Count Christian Duerckheim to the British Museum

20
Ein neuer Typ ('A New Type'), 1965
Georg Baselitz
Grey and yellow ochre watercolour, charcoal, graphite and white pastel
485 x 314 mm
Presented by Count Christian Duerckheim to the British Museum

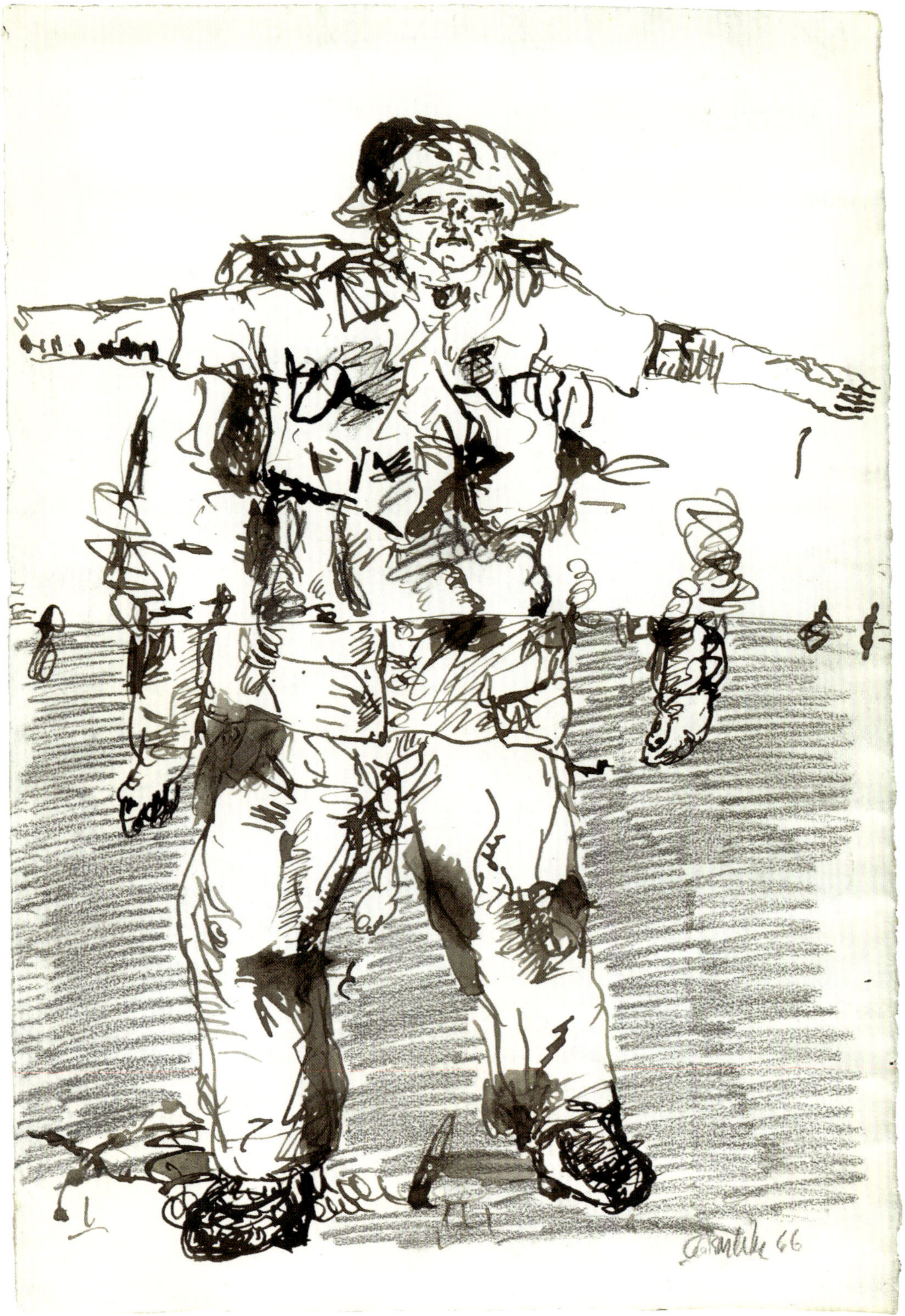

21
Zweigeteilter, mit ausgebreiteten Armen
('Divided Figure with Outstretched Arms')
1966
Georg Baselitz
Ink wash and graphite
502 x 341 mm

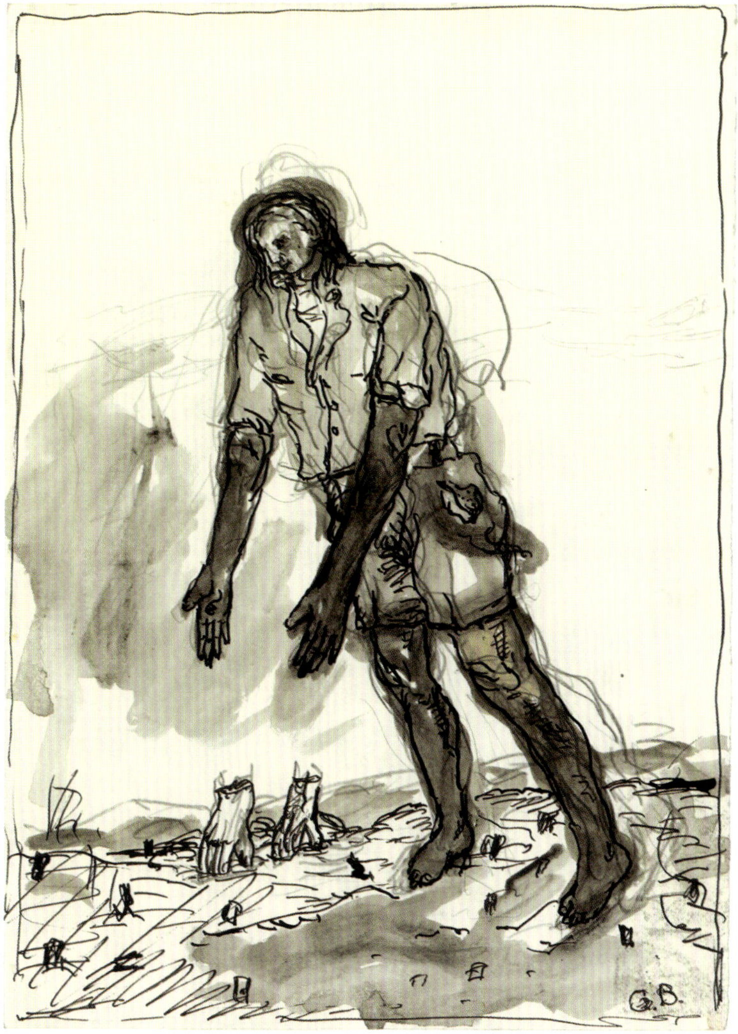

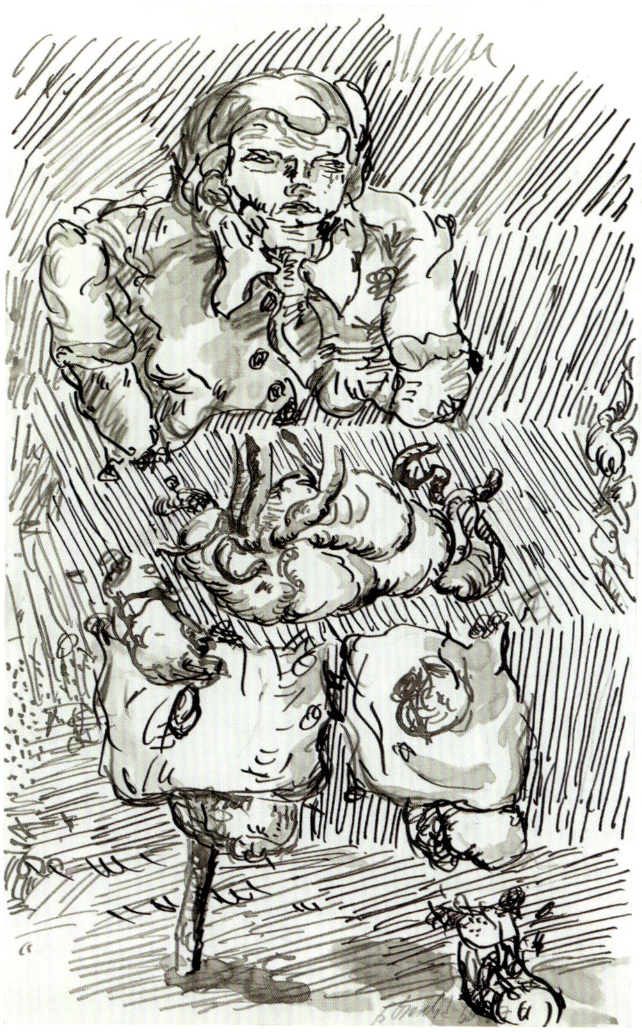

22
L(udwig) R(ichter) auf dem Wege zur Arbeit (Halt suchend), ('L(udwig) R(ichter) on the Way to Work (Getting a Grip)'), 1965
Georg Baselitz
Graphite, ink and wash
430 x 304 mm

23
Fünf Streifen – Der Hirte ('Five Stripes – The Herdsman'), 1966/67
Georg Baselitz
Ink wash and graphite
430 x 266 mm

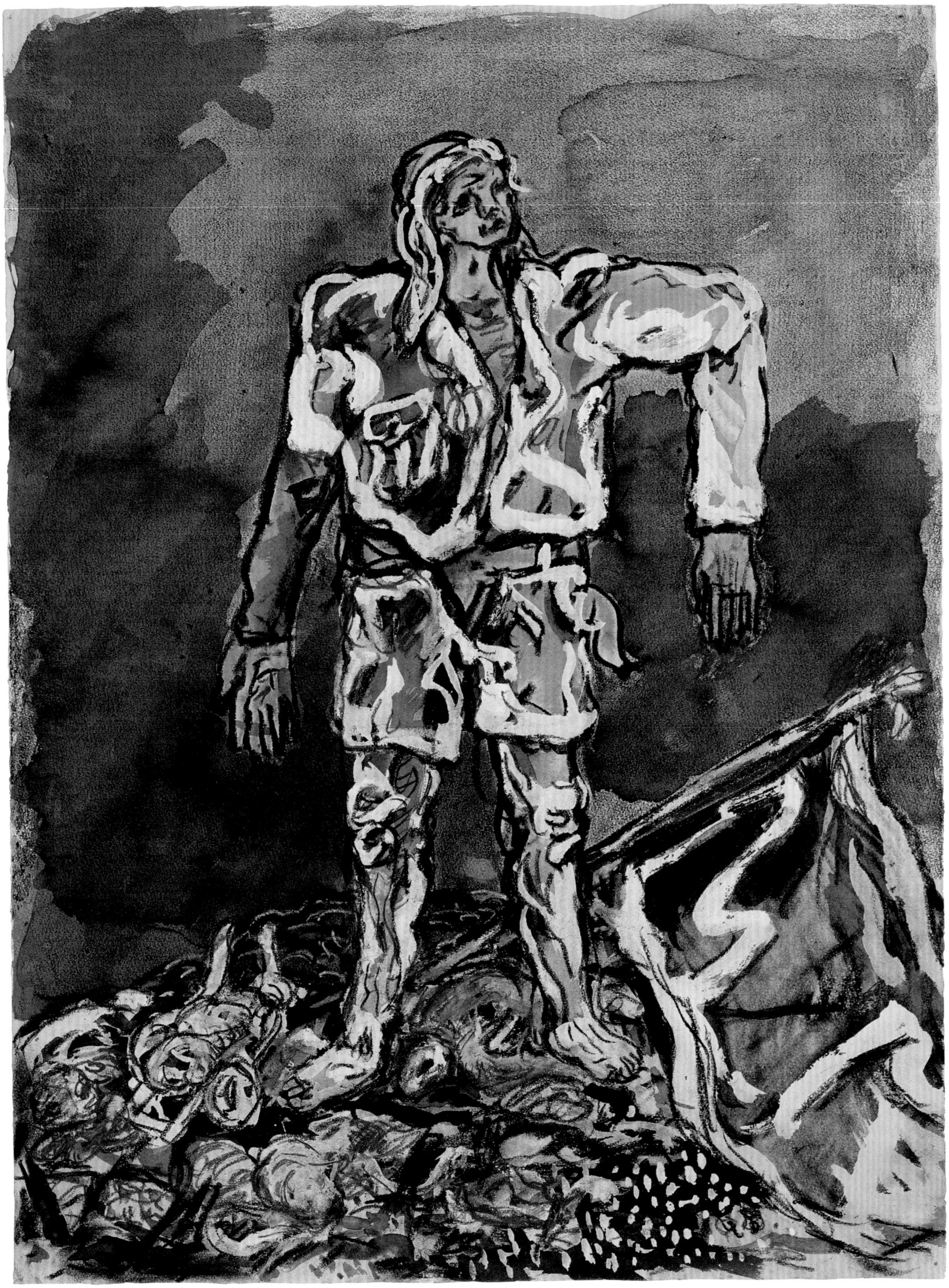

24
Ein neuer Typ ('A New Type',
c. 1965)
Georg Baselitz
Charcoal, grey wash, ink, white paint
and graphite
656 x 483 cm

25
Zwei Streifen ('Two Stripes'), 1966
Georg Baselitz
Charcoal, watercolour and graphite
500 x 295 mm
Presented by Count Christian
Duerckheim to the British Museum

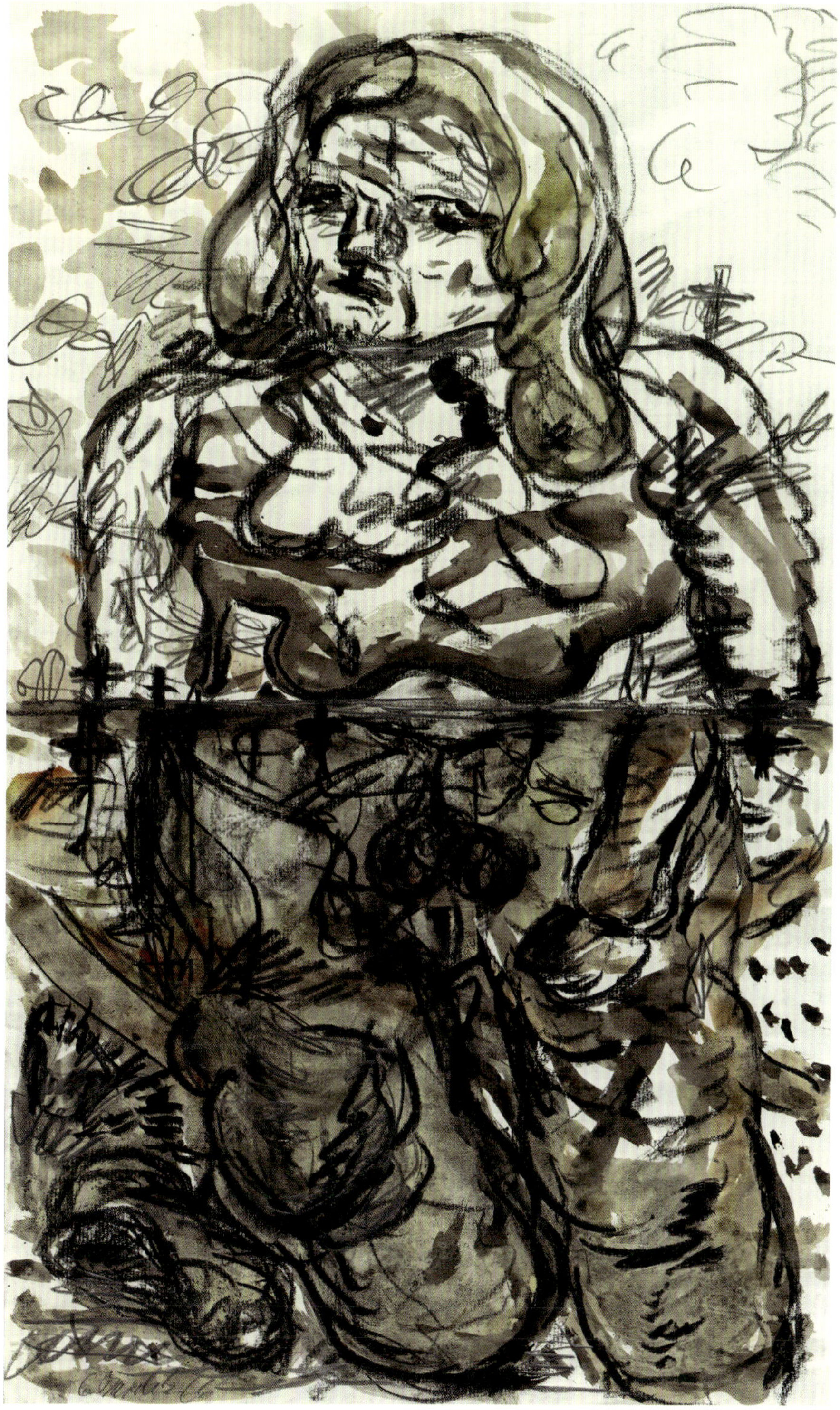

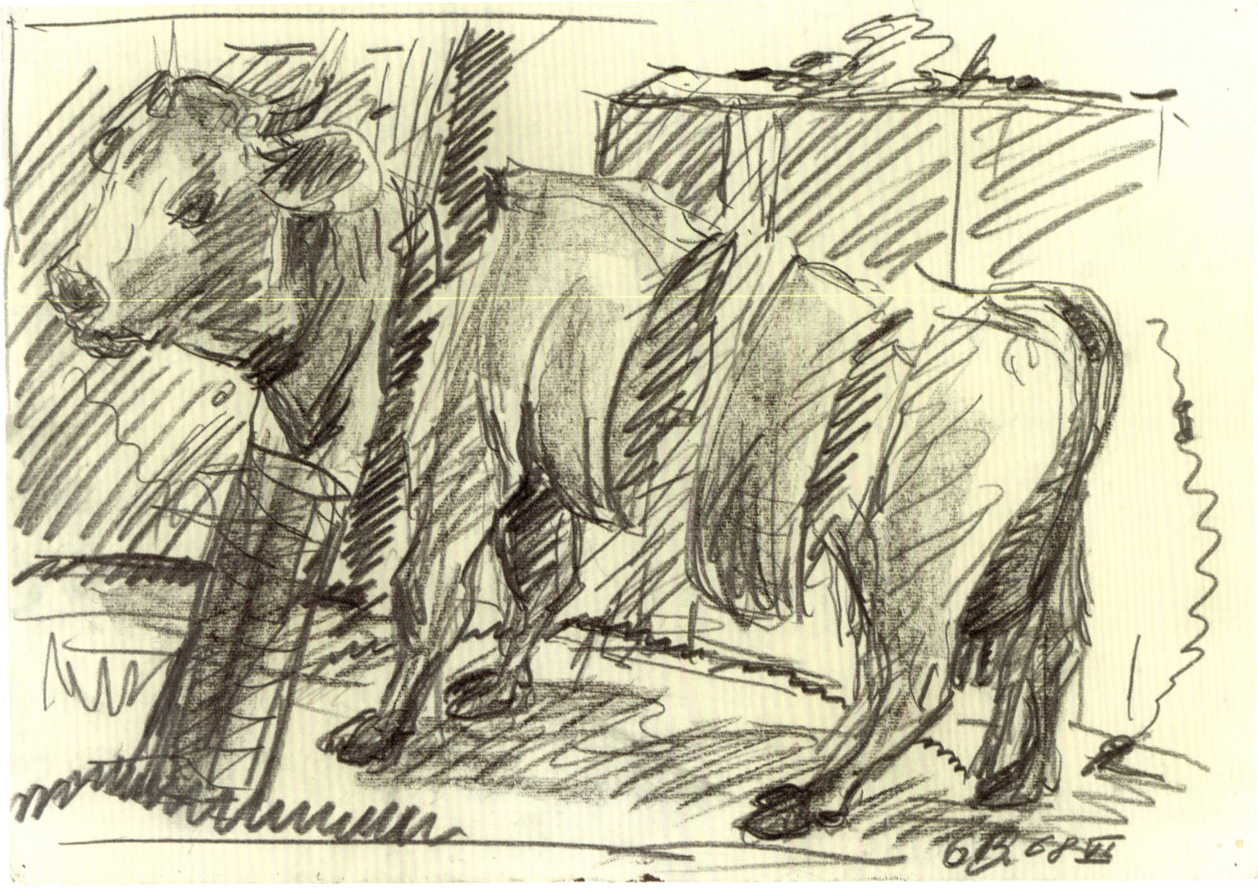

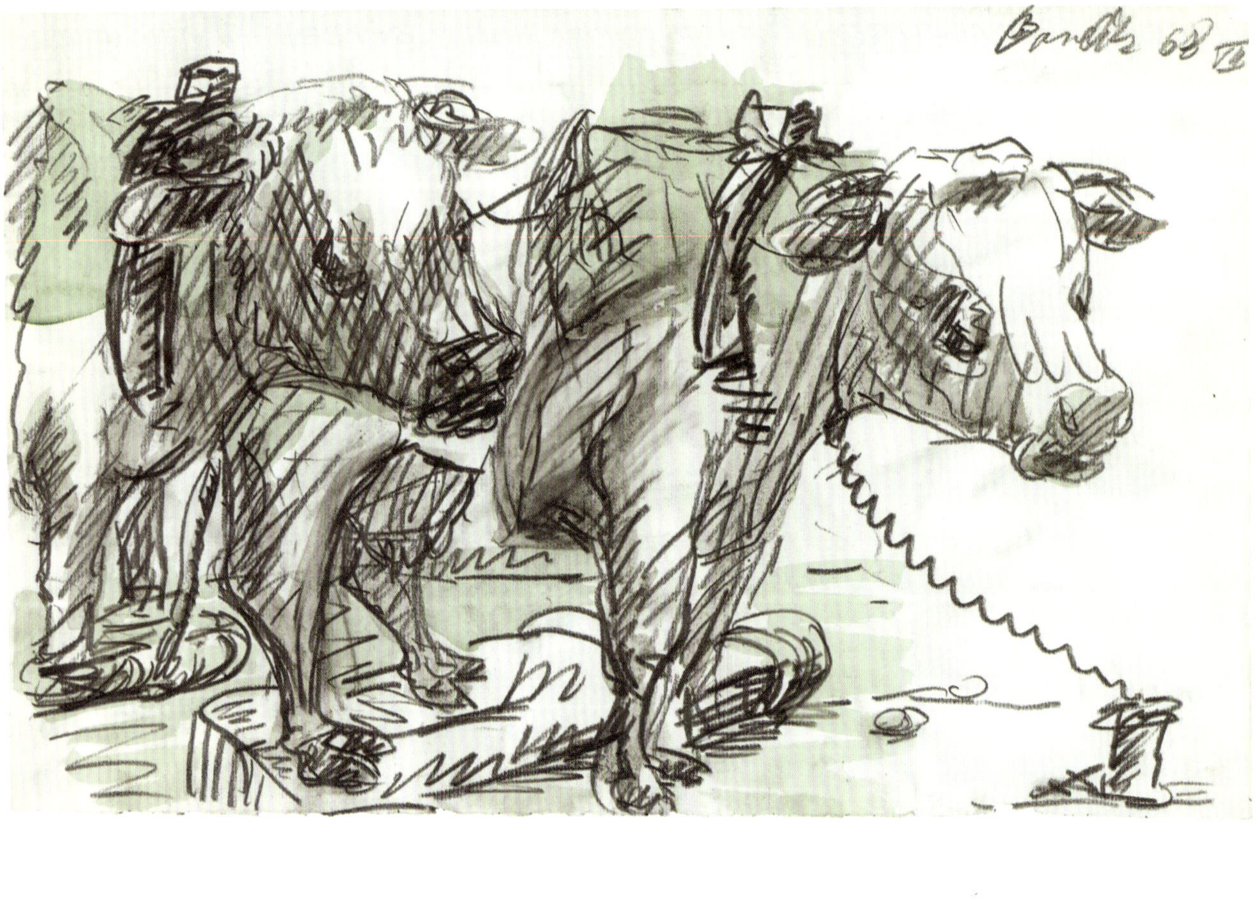

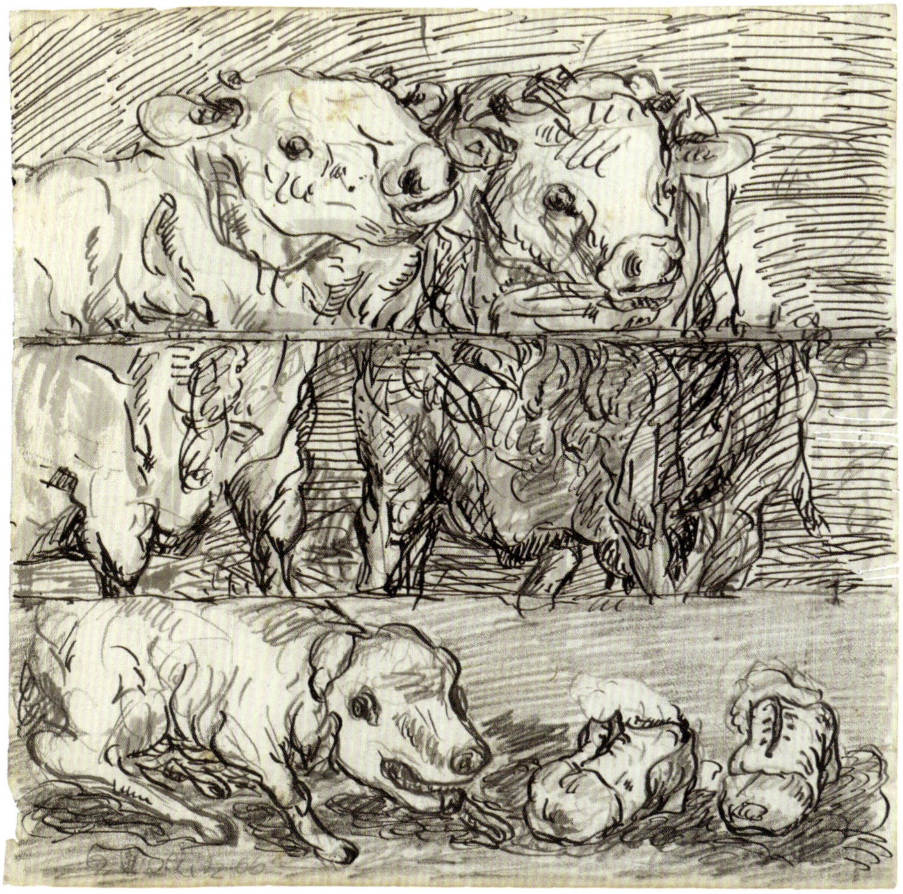

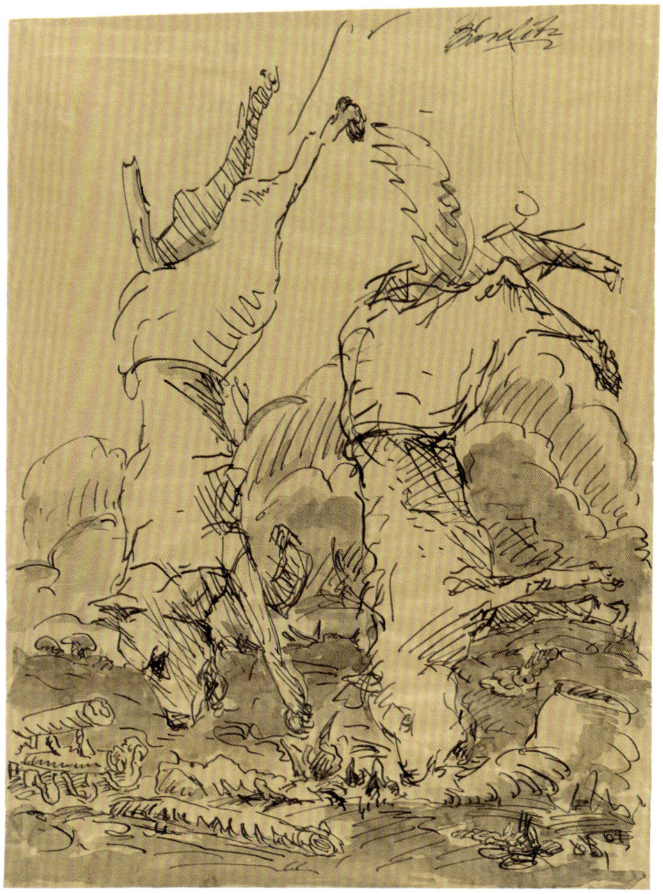

26
Ohne Titel ('Untitled'), 1968
Georg Baselitz
Charcoal and graphite
353 x 500 mm

27
Ohne Titel ('Untitled'), 1968
Georg Baselitz
Green watercolour, grey wash and graphite
325 x 498 mm
Presented by Count Christian Duerckheim to the British Museum

28
Drei Streifen Kühe ('Three Strips Cows'), 1966
Georg Baselitz
Ink, graphite and grey wash
368 x 370 mm

29
Zwei Hunde abwärts ('Two Dogs Downwards'), 1967
Georg Baselitz
Ink and wash
520 x 380 mm

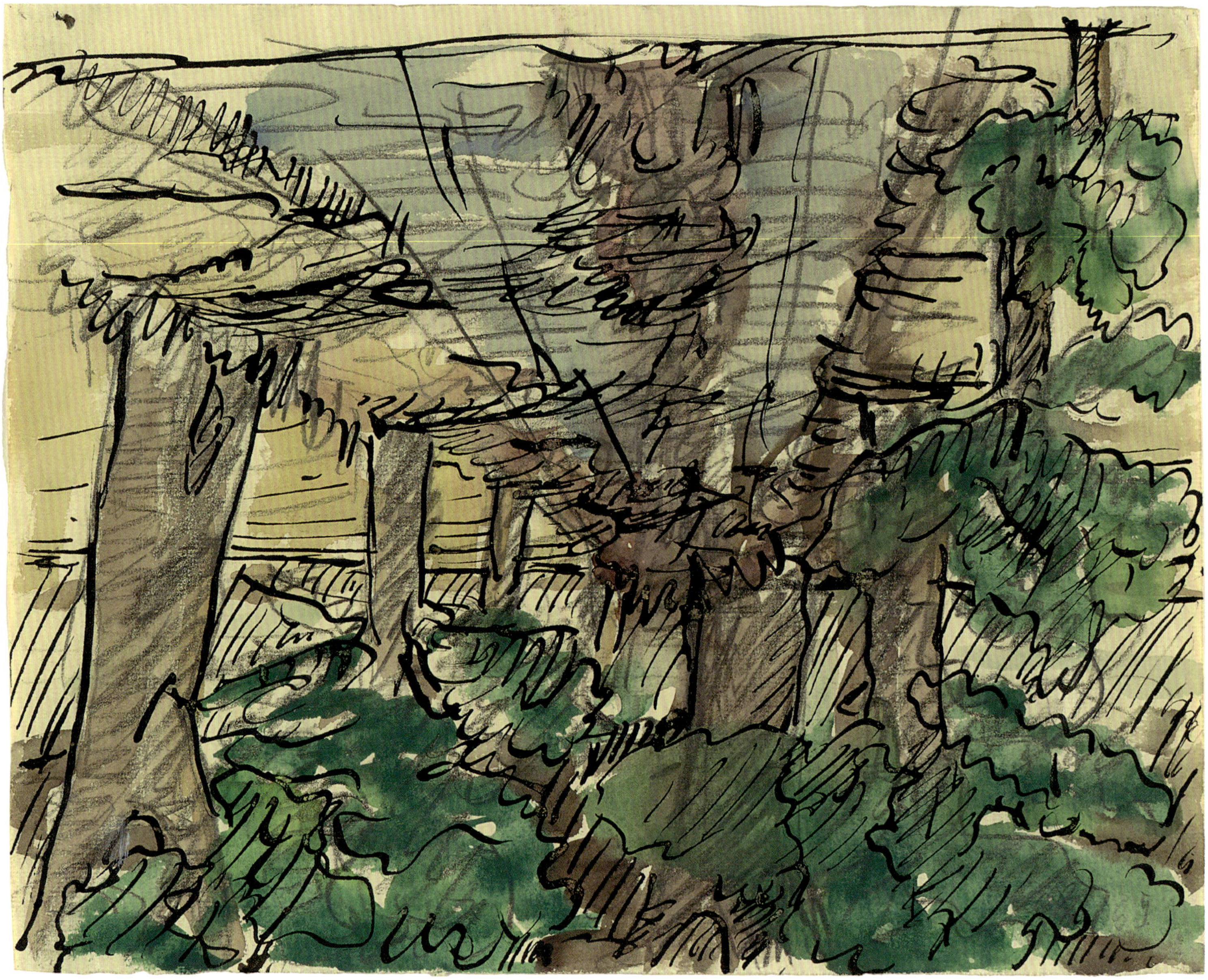

30
Landstraße ('Country Road'), 1969
Georg Baselitz
Ink, watercolour and pencil
246 x 303 mm

31
Birken (Paysage) ('Birch Trees (Paysage)'), 1972
Georg Baselitz
Ink and watercolour
577 x 435 mm
Presented by Count Christian Duerckheim to the British Museum

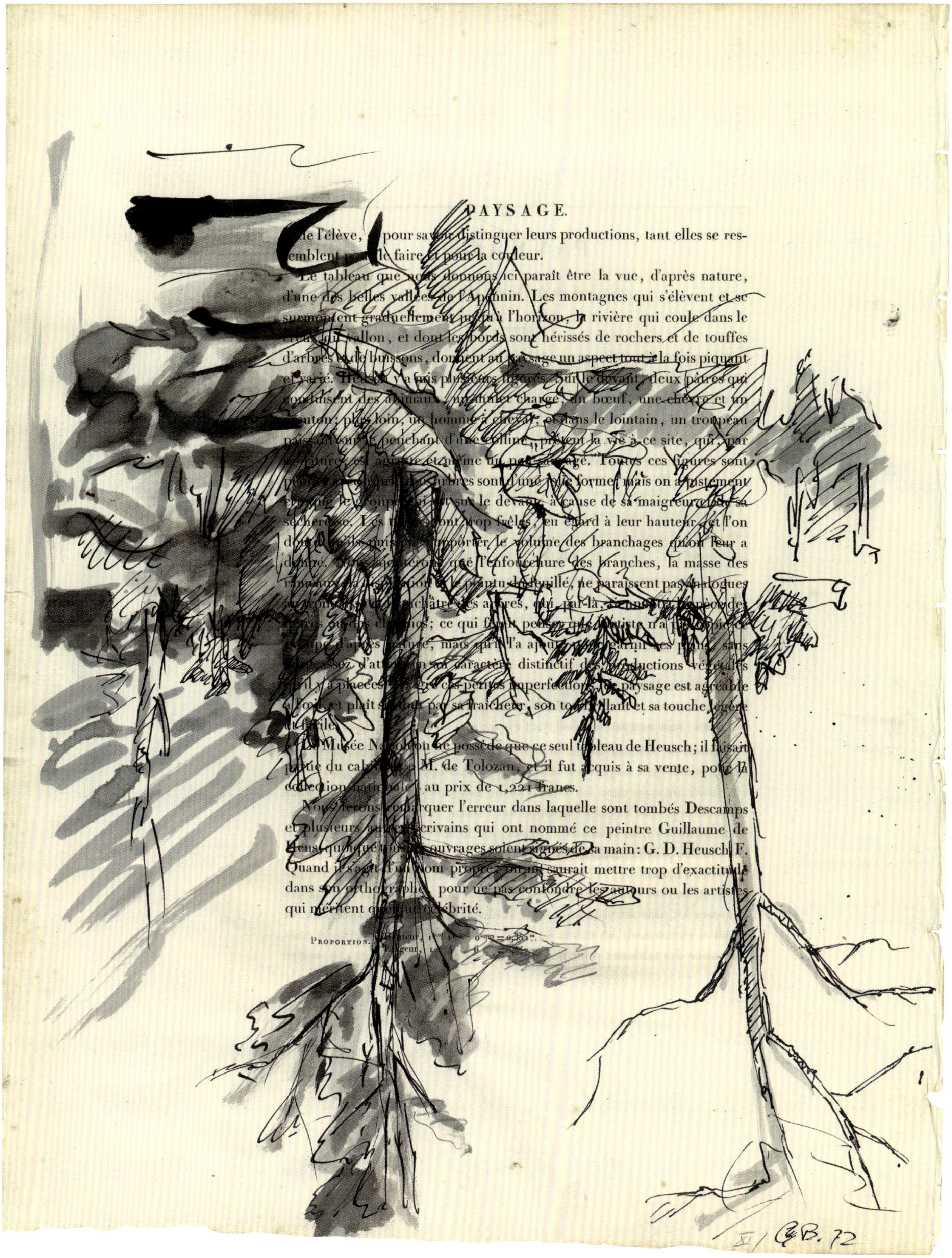
PAYSAGE.

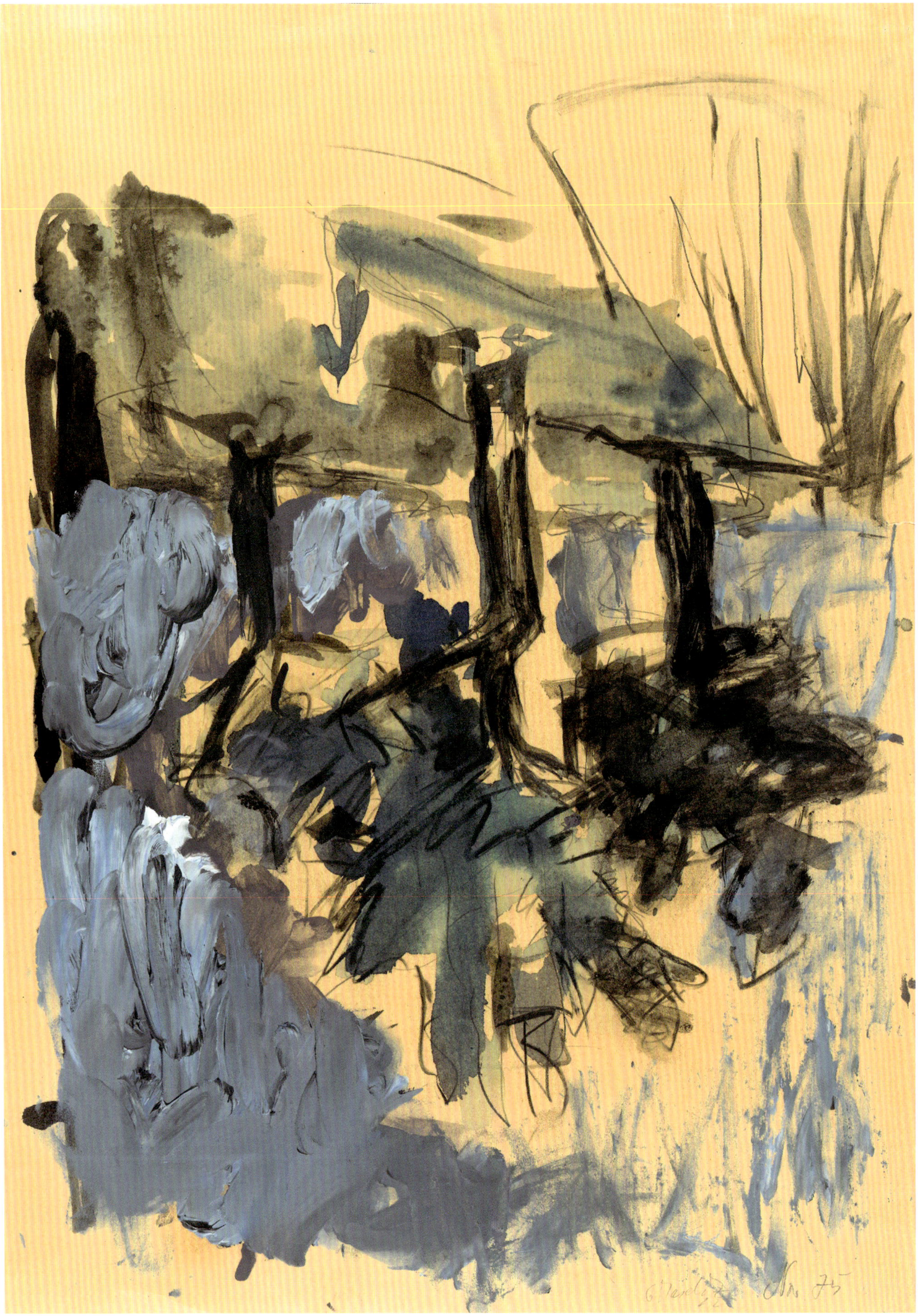

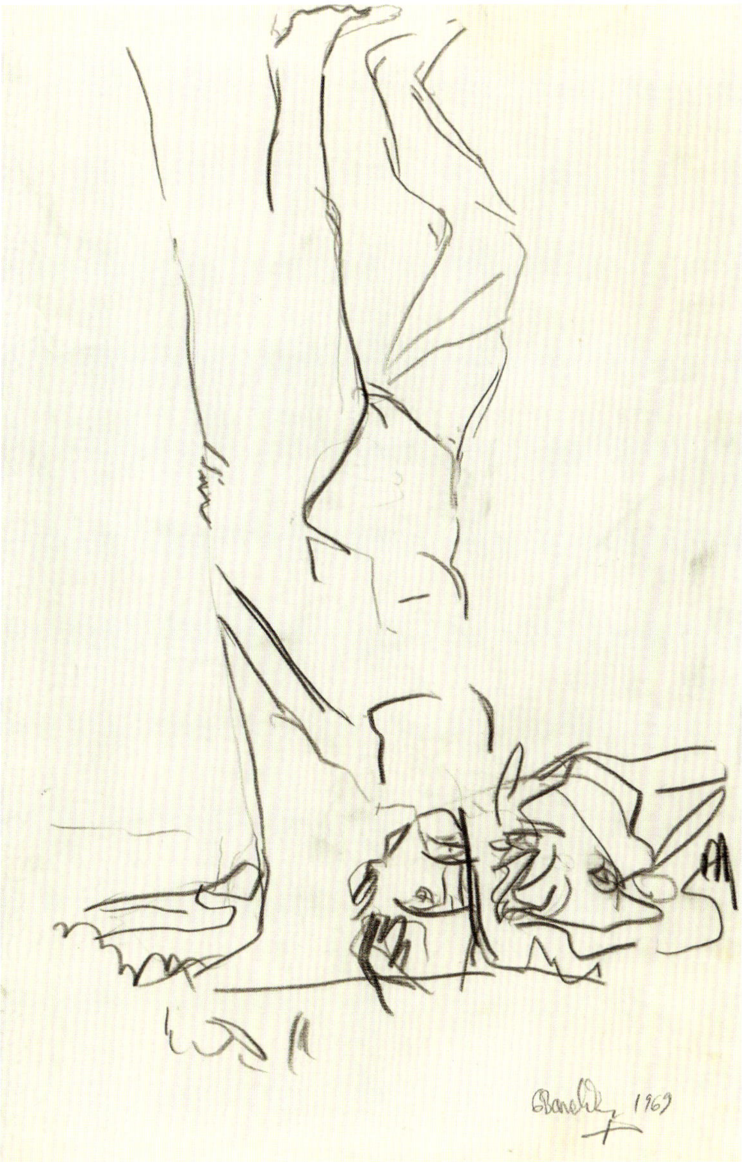

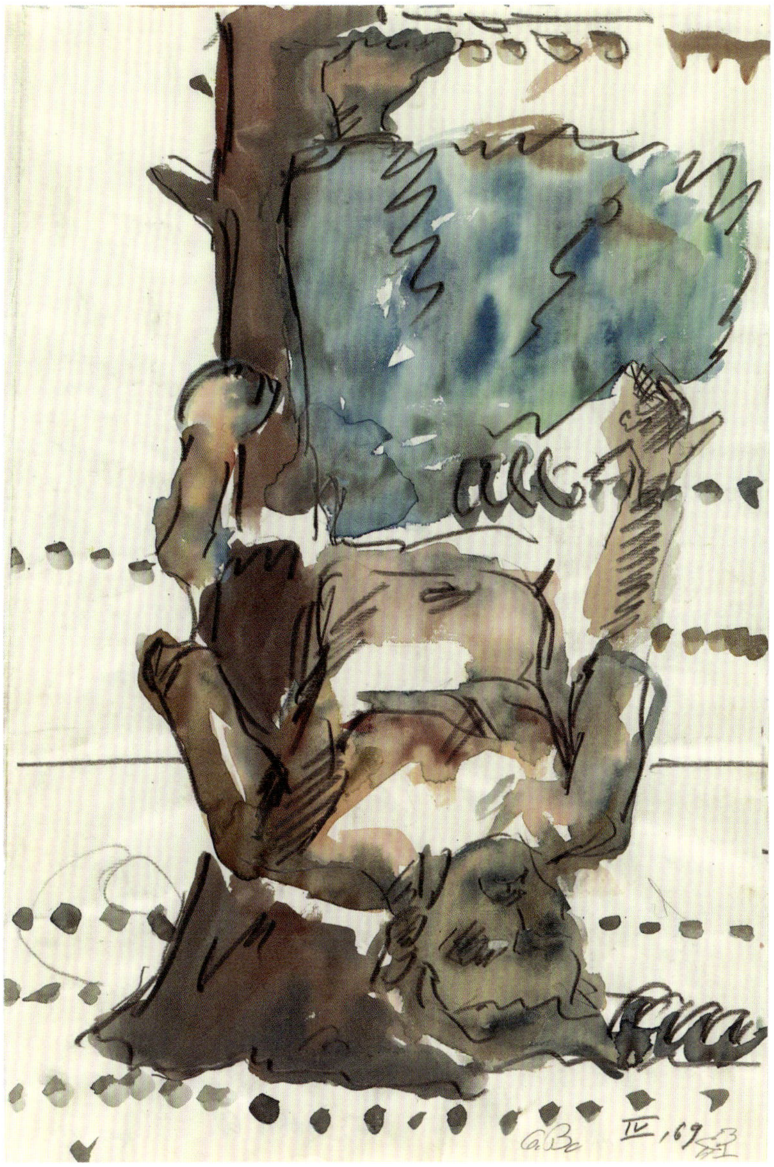

32
Apfelbäume ('Apple Trees'), 1975
Georg Baselitz
Oil, watercolour and charcoal
613 x 429 mm

33
Mann am Baum abwärts ('Man on a Tree Downwards'), 1968/69
Georg Baselitz
Charcoal
500 x 324 mm
Presented by Count Christian Duerckheim to the British Museum

34
Am Baum abwärts ('Downwards by a Tree'), 1969
Georg Baselitz
Graphite and watercolour
499 x 330 mm

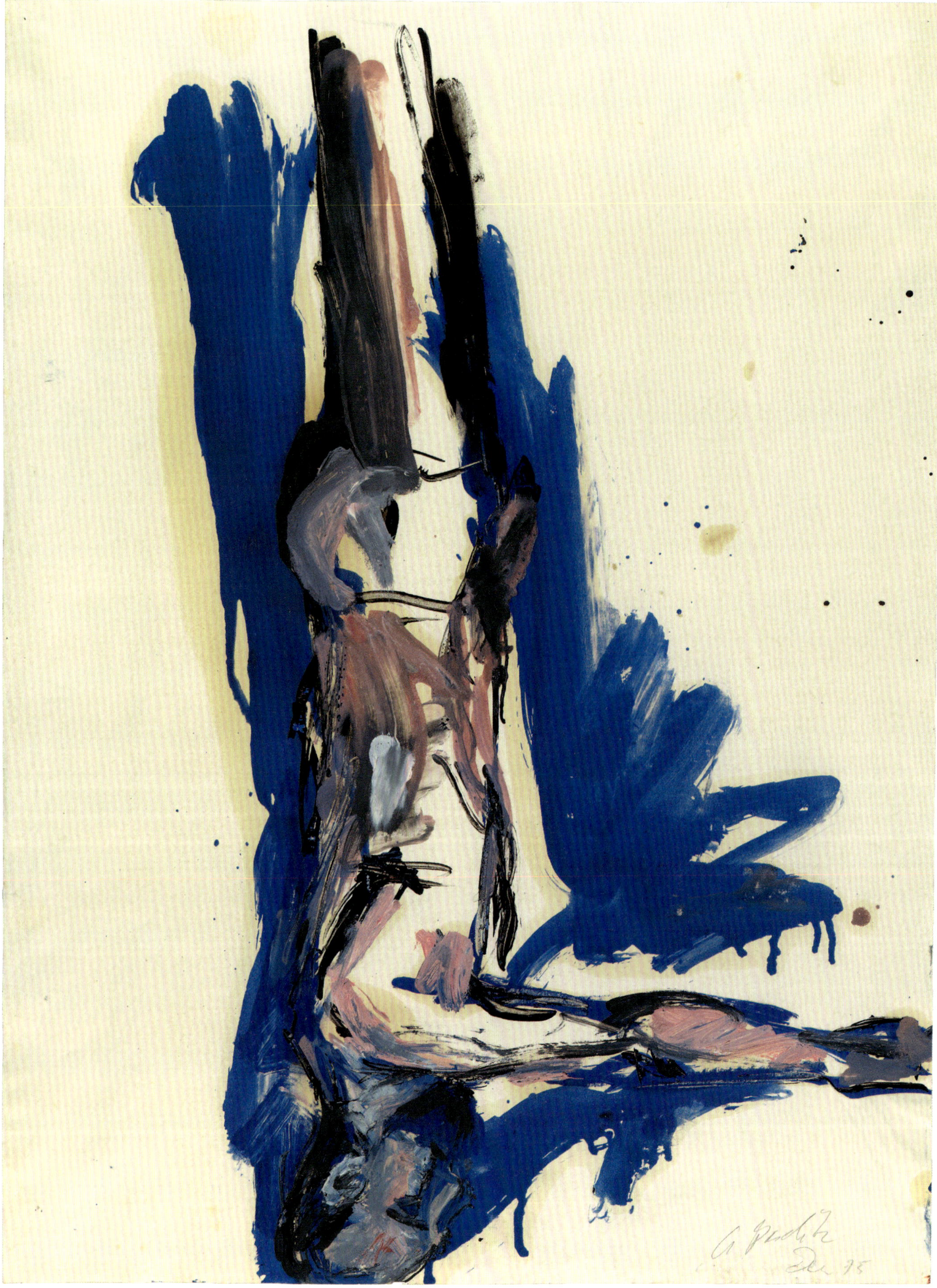

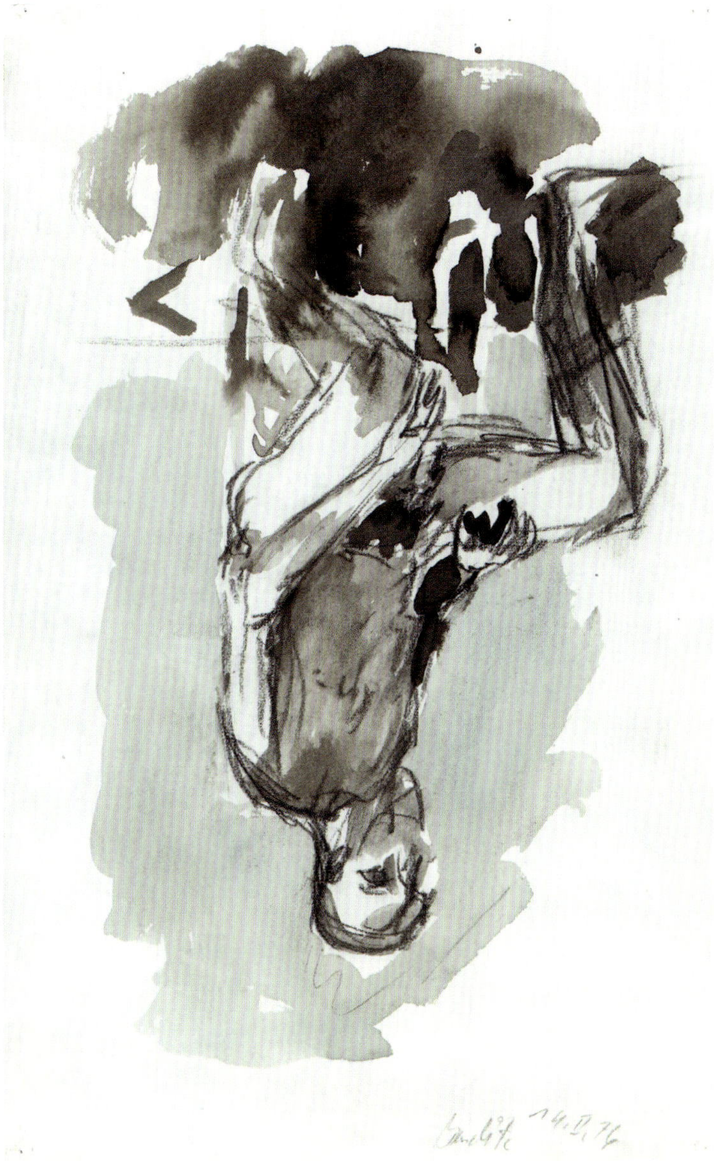

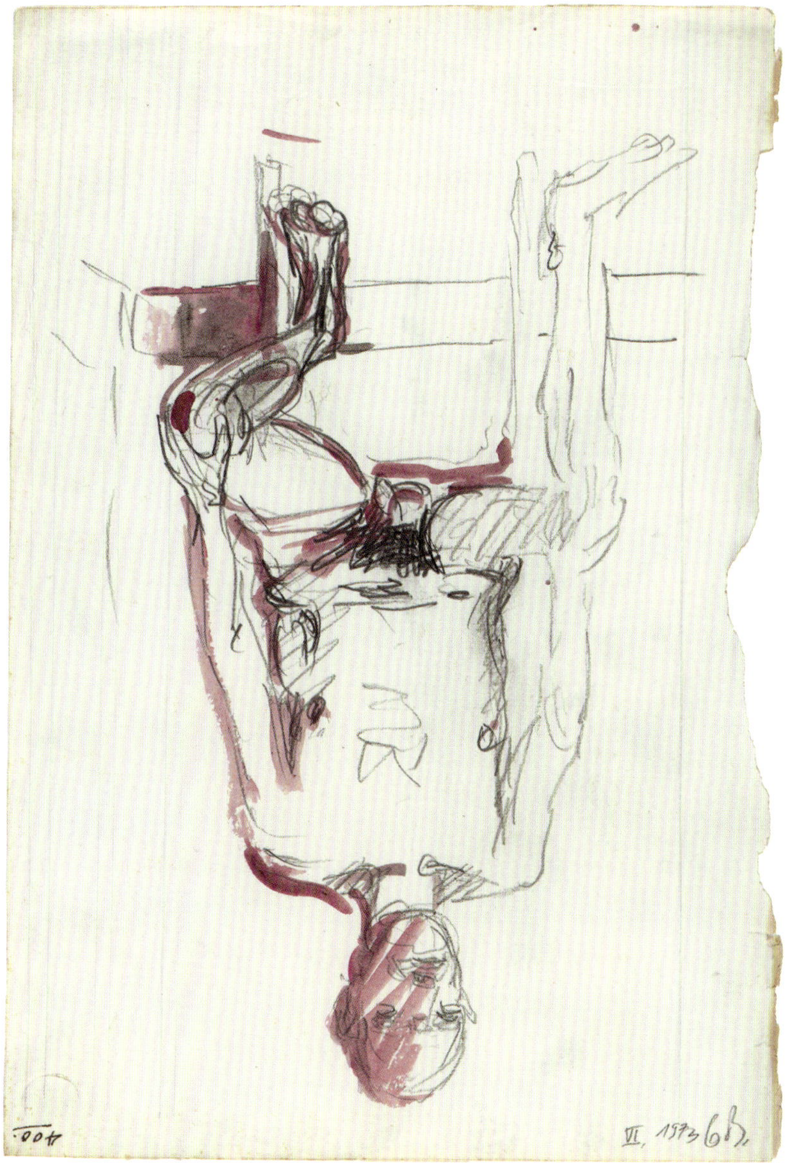

35
Akt mit Flügel ('Nude with Wings'),
1975
Georg Baselitz
Oil paint
558 x 407 mm

36
Sitzender männlicher Akt
('Seated Male Nude') 1976
Georg Baselitz
Charcoal with grey, green
and black wash
487 x 300 mm

37
Sitzender männlicher Akt ('Seated
Male Nude'), 1973
Georg Baselitz
Graphite and red watercolour
427 x 290 mm

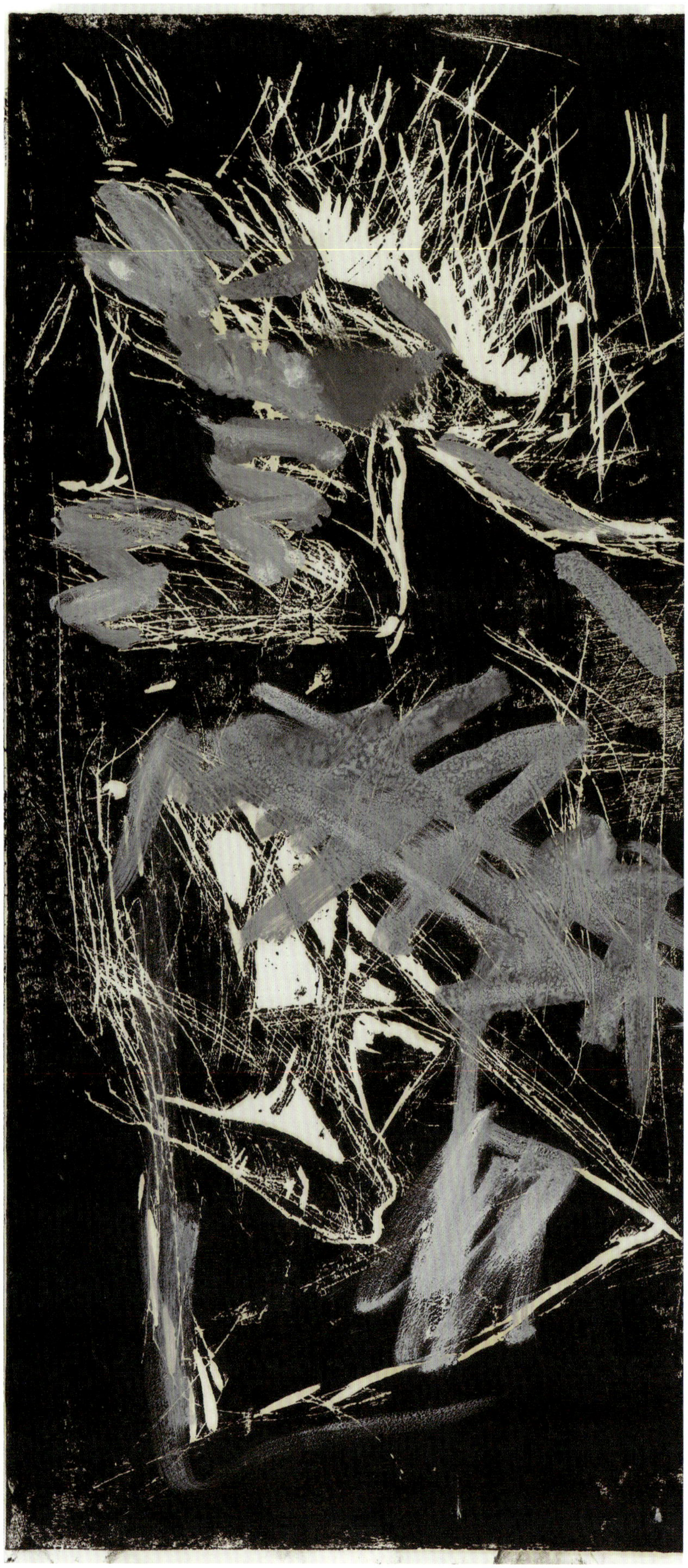

38
Adler im Gebirge ('Eagle in the Mountains'), 1977
Georg Baselitz
Linocut with overpainting
612 x 270 mm

39
Fliegender Adler ('Flying Eagle'), 1977
Georg Baselitz
Linocut with additions in grey, red
and yellow oil paint
308 x 276 mm
Presented by Count Christian
Duerckheim to the British Museum

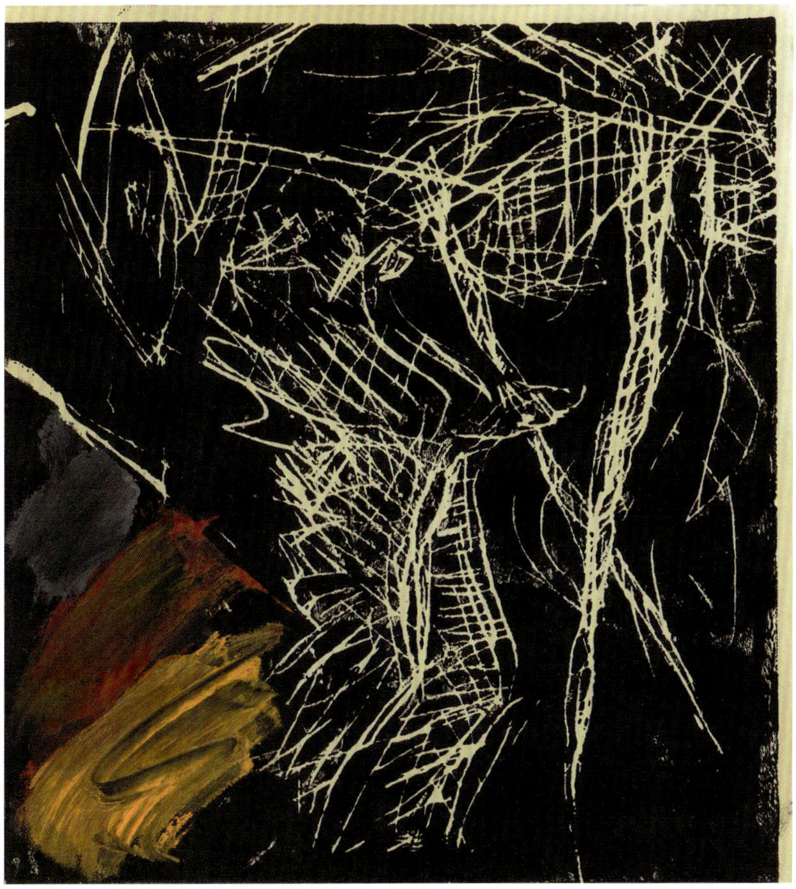

40
Adler ('Eagle') 1977
Georg Baselitz
Linocut with oil paint
300 x 270 mm
Presented by Count Christian
Duerckheim to the British Museum

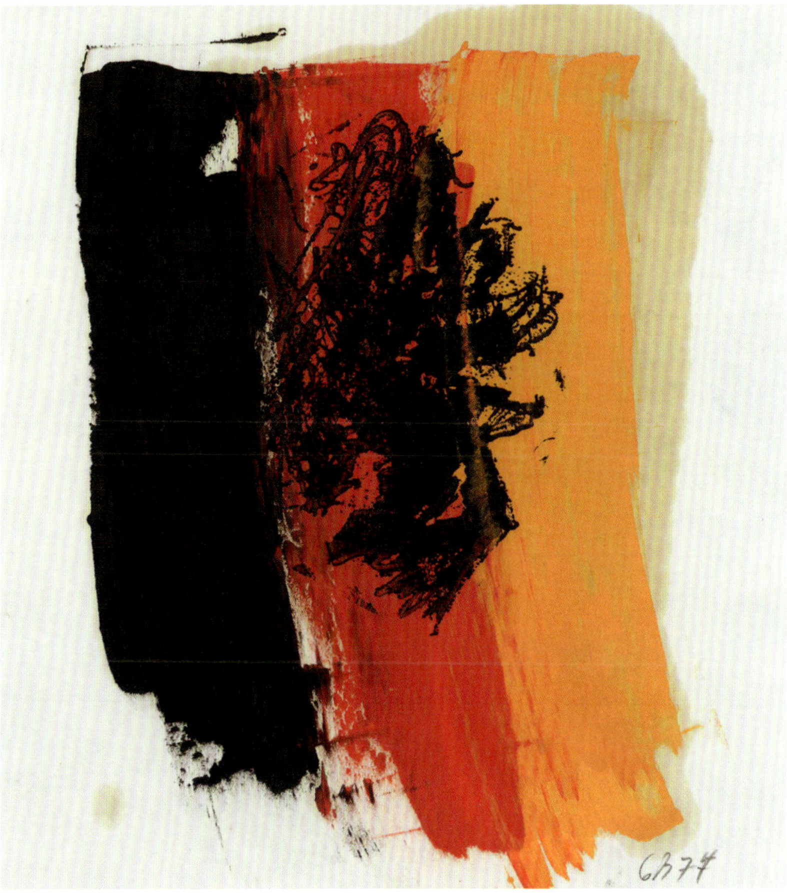

41
Adler ('Eagle'), from the portfolio
Erste Konzentration I, 1981/82
Georg Baselitz
Woodcut with oil-based ink
997 x 794 mm
Presented by Count Christian
Duerckheim to the British Museum

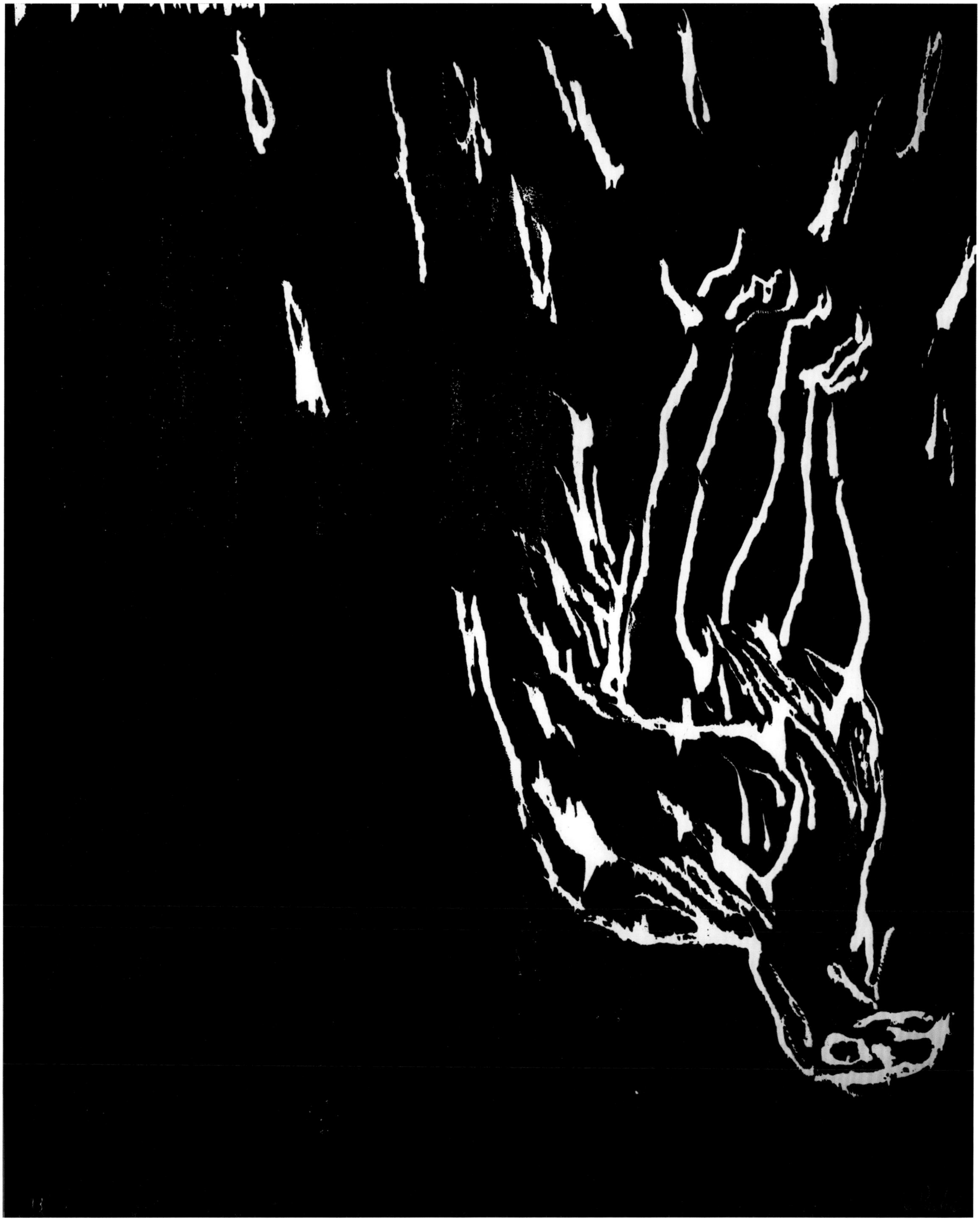

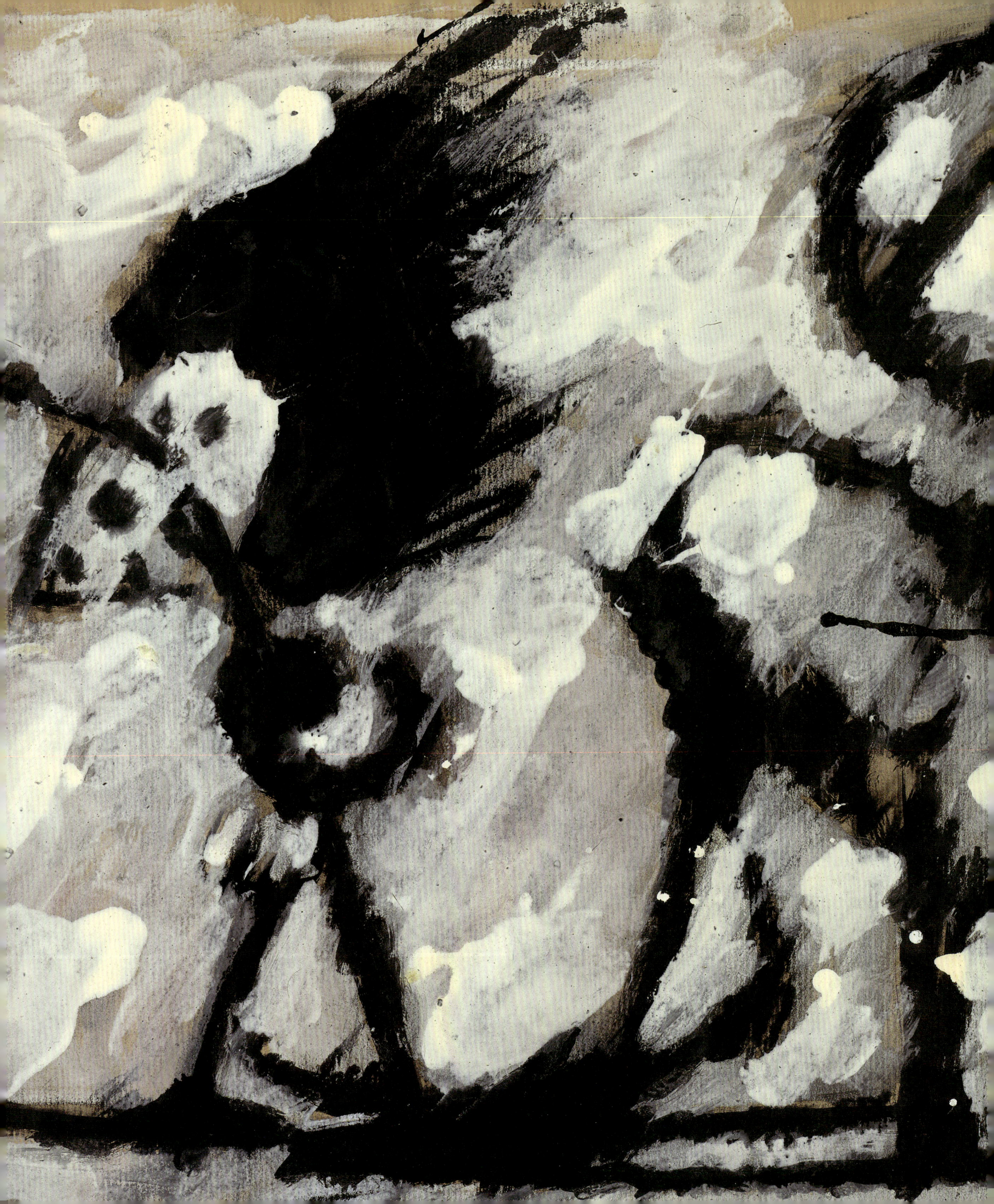

Markus Lüpertz

Markus Lüpertz is best known for his large, semi-abstract paintings using historically charged motifs and, more recently, sculptures of figures based on classical mythology.

Lüpertz was born on 25 April 1941 in Reichenberg, Bohemia (now Liberec, in the Czech Republic), to German parents. Following the mass expulsion of the German population from the newly formed Czechoslovak State in 1948, the family were forced to move west, settling in the city of Rheydt in the Rhineland. From 1956 Lüpertz attended the Werkkunstschule (Arts and Crafts School) in Krefeld, studying mural and decorative painting with Laurens Goossens (1898–1979). Around this period Lüpertz spent time studying and working at the Benedictine Maria Laach Abbey, south of Cologne, an experience he later described as formative. Although Catholicism has played an important part in Lüpertz's life, and religious themes appear often in his work, only very rarely has he made work that is explicitly devotional, for example his stained-glass windows for the church of St Andreas in Cologne, unveiled in 2008. During his early years Lüpertz also spent a semester studying at the Kunstakademie (Art Academy) in Düsseldorf, where he was later to serve as the Rector. On completing his studies in 1961, and after a short period in the French Foreign Legion, he embarked on a career as an artist.

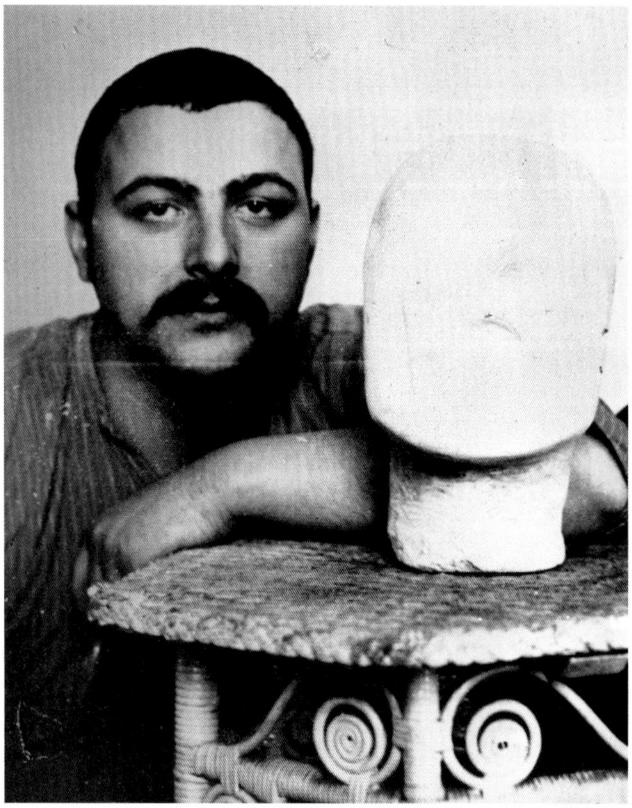

In 1962 Lüpertz moved to West Berlin, thanks to a scheme offering exemption from military service for those relocating to the marooned city (fig. 1). The title of his first works, the *Donald Duck Series*, might suggest a connection with Pop Art, although the abstract painterly style reveals a stronger relationship to the paintings of the COBRA group, particularly Asger Jorn (1914–73), and also with the Abstract Expressionism of Willem de Kooning (1904–97). He soon began making works under the title 'Dithyrambic', after Greek hymns to Dionysus, god of wine and song (fig. 2).

The bulky forms and ungainly aesthetic of these paintings were typical of much of his subsequent work – an idiom of '*brutal volgare*', as the Austrian art historian Werner Hofmann put it – but also the broad range of reference, from contemporary popular culture to the stories of antiquity.[1] The forms of his 'Dithyrambic' paintings from the early 1960s derived, in part, from the logo used by the Twentieth Century Fox Film Corporation, a motif transformed by Lüpertz into heavy three-dimensional forms rendered in a thick 'dionysiac' painting style.

These paintings were first shown in 1964 at the Gallery Großgörschen 35, the centre of an artists' cooperative founded earlier that year in West Berlin by Lüpertz and a number of other artists and students, which occupied the floor of an abandoned factory in the Schöneberg quarter. Lüpertz accompanied his paintings with short manifesto texts, *Kunst, die im Wege steht. Dithyrambisches Manifest* ('Art that Gets in the Way. Dithyrambic Manifesto'), followed two years later by a further text, *Die Anmut des 20. Jahrhunderts wird durch die von mir erfundene Dithyrambe sichtbar gemacht* ('The charm of the twentieth century is made visible through the dithyramb I invented'). In the same year, 1964, Lüpertz had his first exhibition at the Michael Werner Gallery in Cologne.

It was during a scholarship year in Florence in 1970 that Lüpertz began painting historical subjects, using imagery that obviously refers to the history of Nazism and to the Second World War. During this year, Lüpertz began working on a series, the *Motif Paintings*, developing the heavy abstract forms of the *Dithyrambic* works into recognizable imagery, including corn sheaves, military helmets (fig. 3), shovels and acorns, and the painter's palette, all painted with a loosely brushed, flat style that can be compared to the abstracted naturalism underlying Baselitz's painting at this time. It was with these pieces, still made under the larger notion of 'Dithyrambic', that Lüpertz achieved his first success, and for which he became best known.

Following these works, in the mid-1970s Lüpertz developed a further series of paintings, which he termed *Stil*, or 'Style', paintings, on the basis of a range of flat, expressive imagery, largely abstract, taking 'style' self-consciously as a subject. In the mid-1980s, he became increasingly interested in classicism and antiquity, making paintings after Camille Corot (1796–1875) and, from 1989, a series after Nicolas Poussin (1594–1665) comprising fifty-one paintings. Following the Poussin series, Lüpertz began his most extensive, and best-known series of

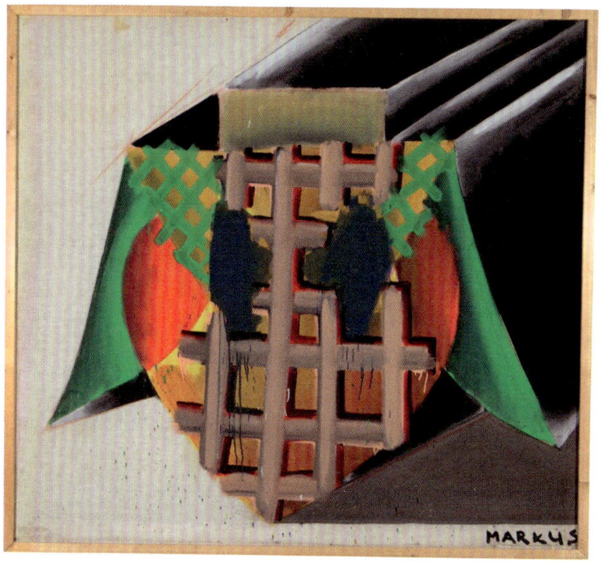

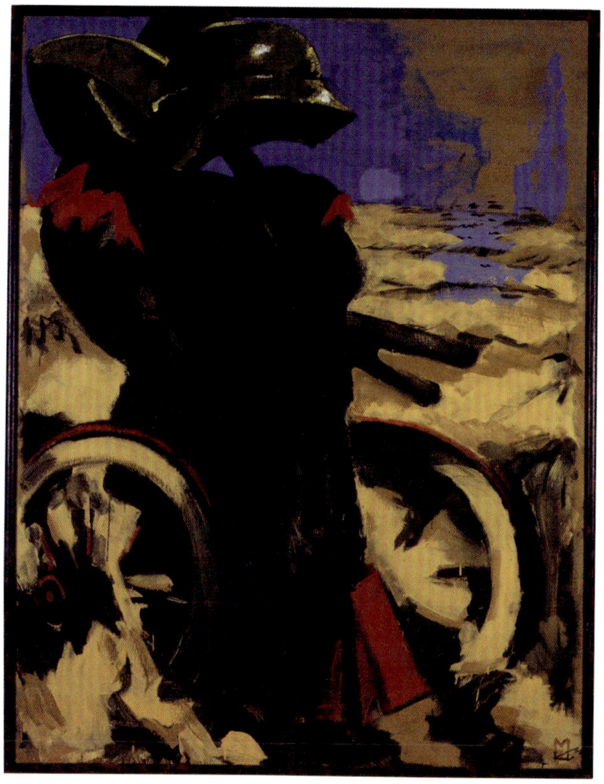

1. *Markus Lüpertz,* 1962

2. *Dithyrambe,* 1964
Markus Lüpertz
Distemper on canvas, 1450 x 1560 mm

3. *Schwarz Rot Gold I – Dithyrambisch*, 1974
Markus Lüpertz
Distemper on canvas, 2600 x 2000 mm

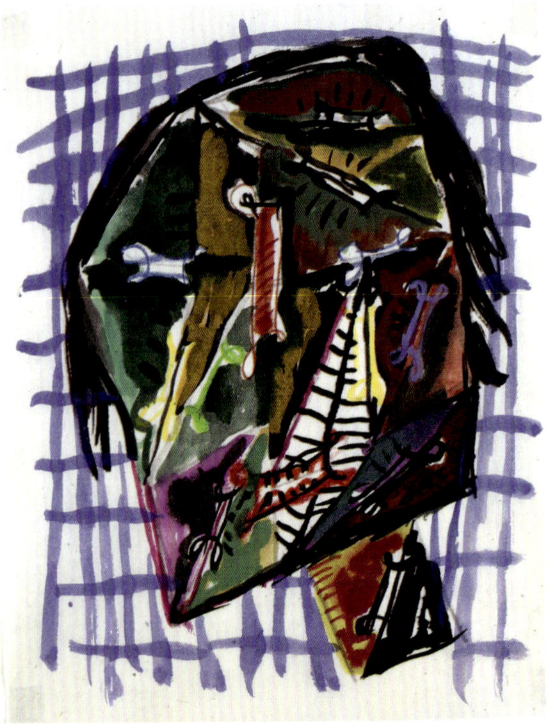

paintings to date, *Männer ohne Frauen – Parsifal* ('Men Without Women – Parsifal'; fig. 4), which takes as its central subject the figure of Parsifal, the hero of Richard Wagner's last opera. The series comprises hundreds of paintings and works on paper, all focused on a single frontal view of a male face, as well as three sculptures.

The scale and ambition of his paintings naturally led Lüpertz to create large cast sculpture in the 1980s. He worked in bronze, often painting his works, and from the middle of the decade began to create sculptures based on figures from classical mythology, for example a painted bronze figure of Apollo, created in 1989 for the Alte Oper in Frankfurt (fig. 5). Lüpertz's flamboyant personality, the source of many anecdotes, also found a natural outlet in producing set designs, beginning in 1982 with Rainer Kunad's opera *Vincent*, at the Staatstheater in Kassel. He went on to design for a number of operas, including Jules Massenet's *Werther* (Ulm, 1983; the stage set was not however used); Frank Martin's version of *The Tempest* (Bremen, 1991); and Giuseppe Verdi's *Il Trovatore* (Duisburg and Düsseldorf, 1996).

Alongside the expansion of his work into sculpture and set design, Lüpertz took up printmaking at the beginning of the 1980s, initially producing experimental, abstract drypoints, then using etching and aquatint to create more ambitious designs, most of which were printed in single examples (monoprints). He subsequently worked in woodcut and linocut, as well as lithography. Printmaking has offered Lüpertz the opportunity to explore ideas and images in a different medium, often resulting in single impressions of each state, rather than as a means of producing large marketable editions.

Lüpertz taught at the Staatliche Akademie der Bildende Künste (State Academy of Art), Karlsruhe, from 1974, and at the Kunstakademie Düsseldorf from 1986, where from 1988 to 2009 he was the Director (fig. 6). His work has been the subject of numerous retrospectives from the early 1990s, in Madrid, Bonn, Vienna, Düsseldorf and Amsterdam. In 2009 a retrospective of his paintings and sculptures made since 1963 was held at the Kunst und Ausstellungshalle in Bonn. The combination of avant-garde styles with historical and classical subjects in his painting and sculpture has led to many official commissions. These include a wall painting, *The Six Virtues*, for the entrance to the Federal Chancery in Berlin (2001), the sculpture, *Eagle*, for the Federal High Court in Karlsruhe (2005), and another, *Mercurius*, for the Post Tower in Bonn (2007).

1. W. Hofmann, 'The compact painter', in *Markus Lüpertz. Highways and Byways. A Retrospective. Paintings and Sculptures from 1963 until 2009*, exh. cat., Bonn (Kunst- und Ausstellungshalle der Bundesrepublik Deutschland), 2009, pp. 186–95.

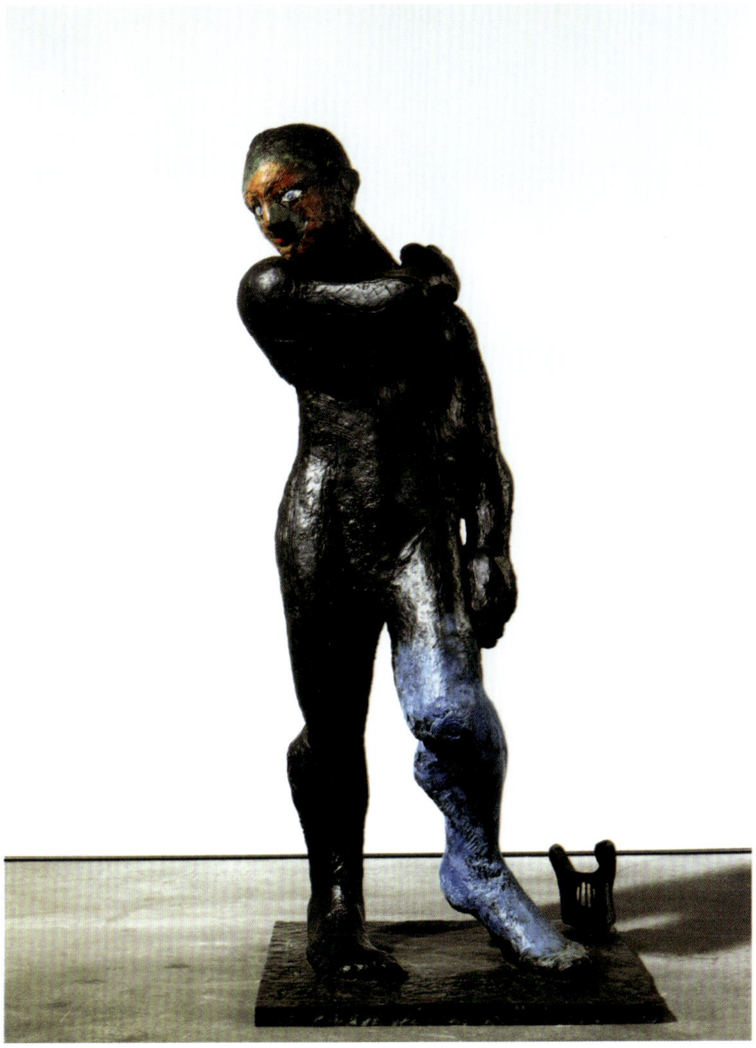

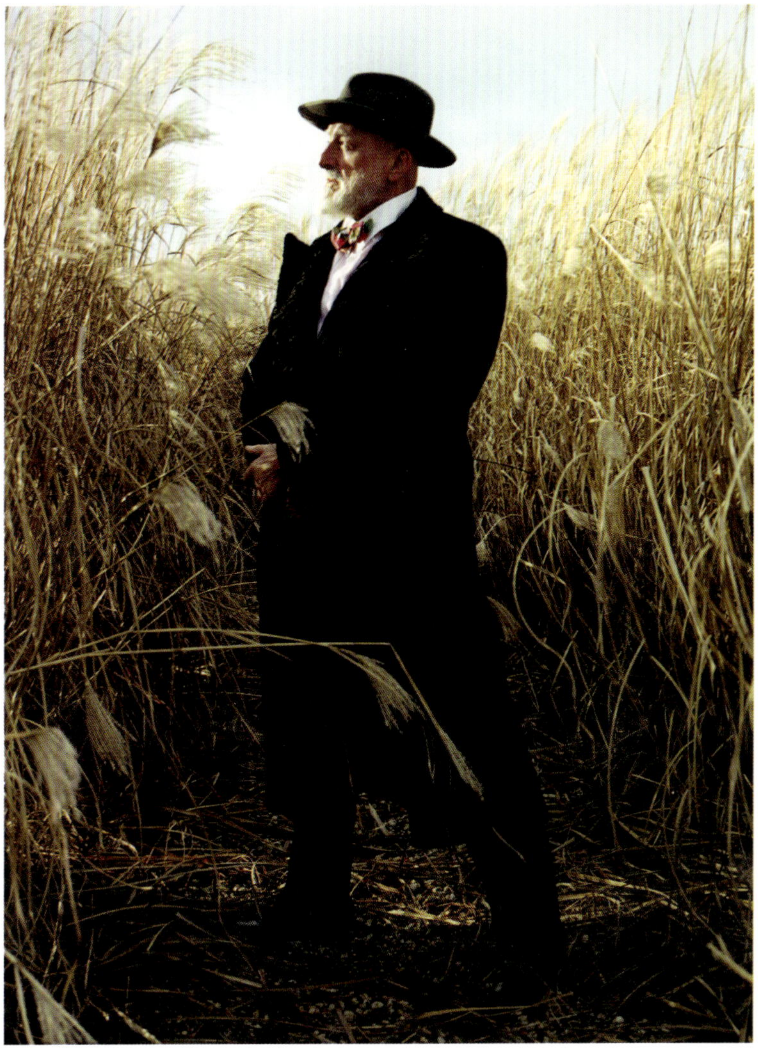

4. Drawing from series *Männer ohne Frauen – Parsifal* ('Men Without Women – Parsifal'), 1995
Markus Lüpertz
Gouache and India ink on paper, 315 x 240 mm

5. *Apollo,* 1989
Markus Lüpertz
Painted bronze, H. 1880 mm

6. *Markus Lüpertz,* 2006
Andrea Stappert

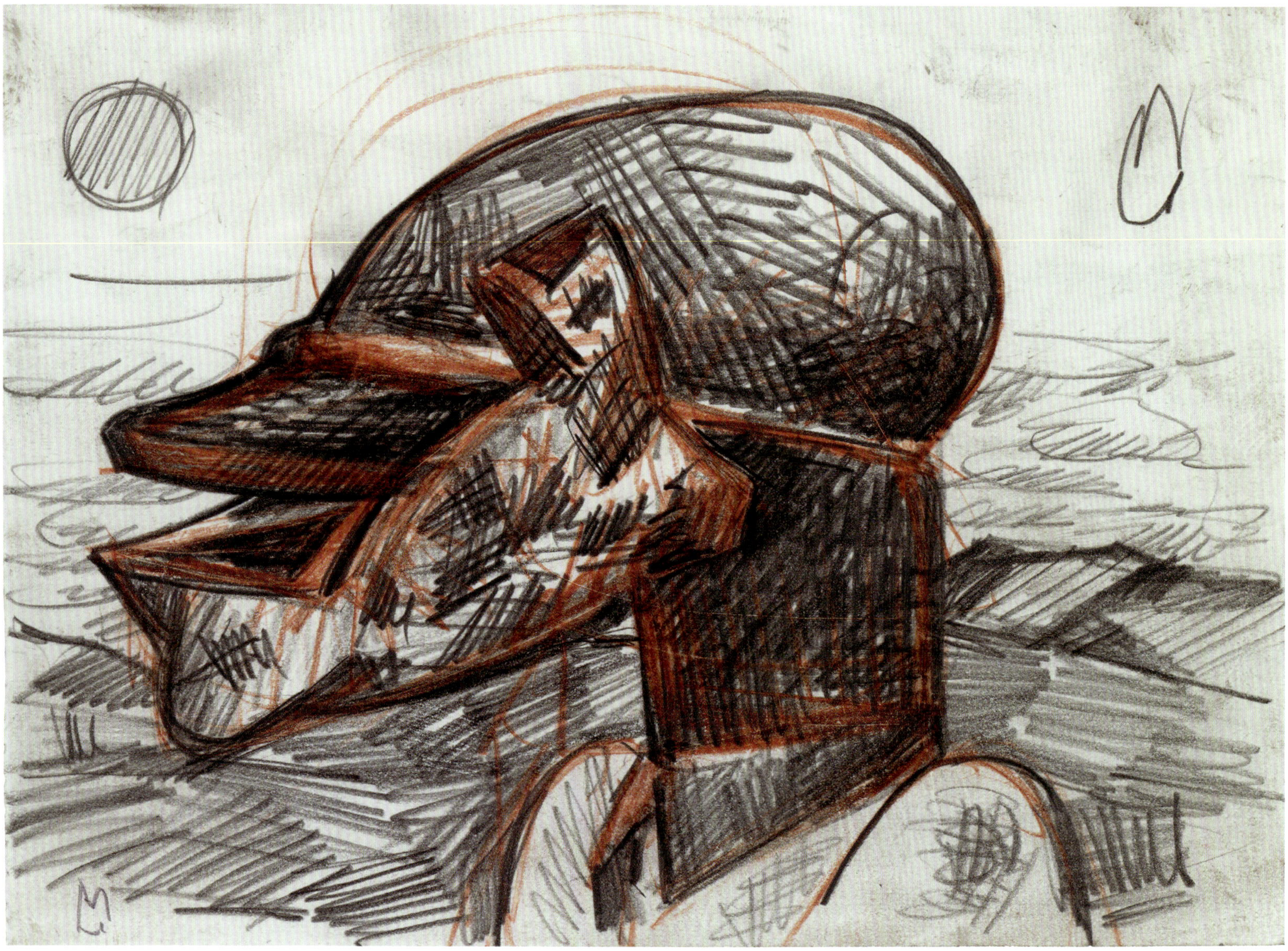

42
Ohne Titel ('Untitled'), 1972
Markus Lüpertz
Graphite and coloured pencil
150 x 205 mm

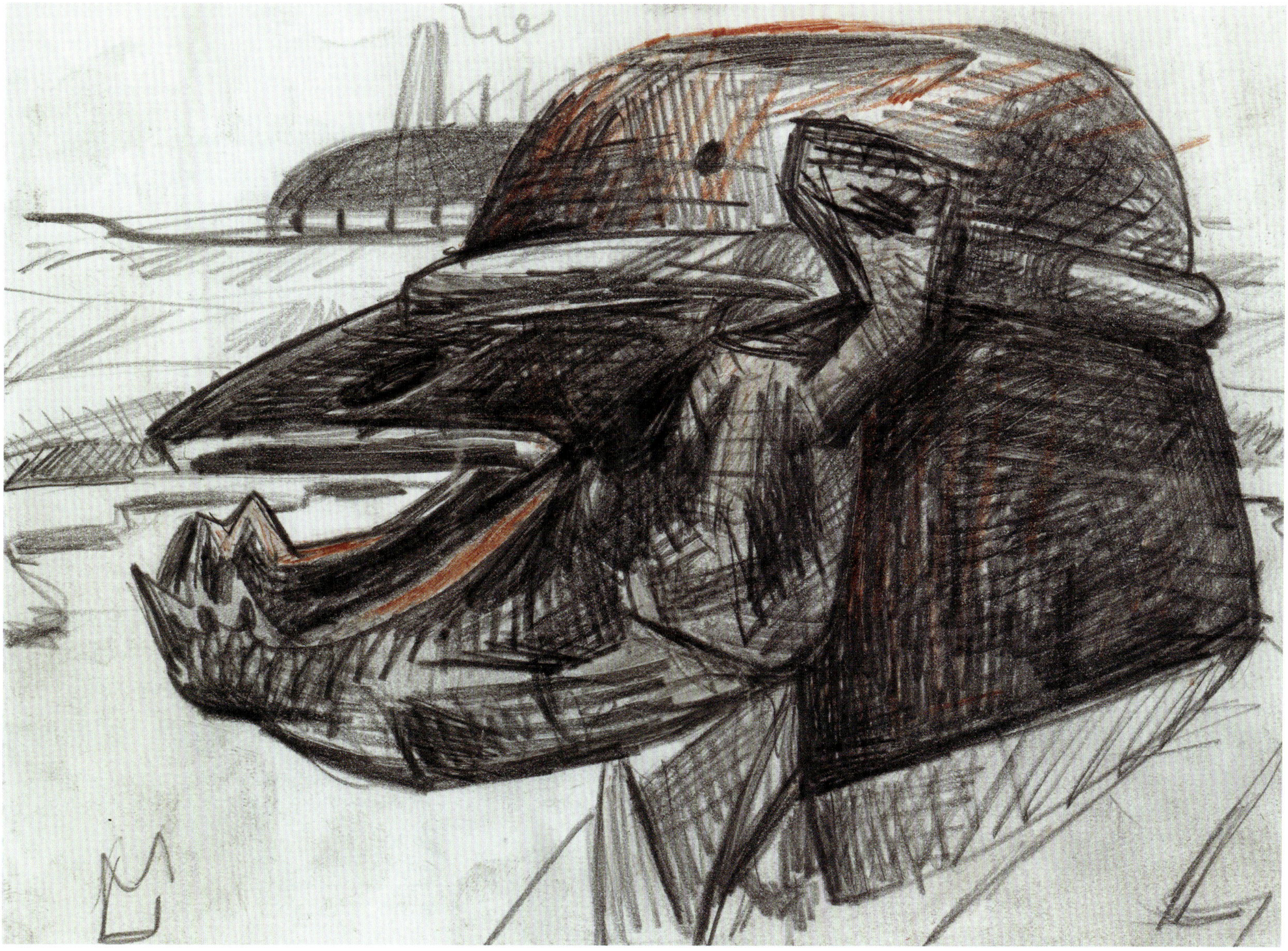

43
Ohne Titel ('Untitled'), 1972
Markus Lüpertz
Graphite and coloured pencil
150 x 205 mm

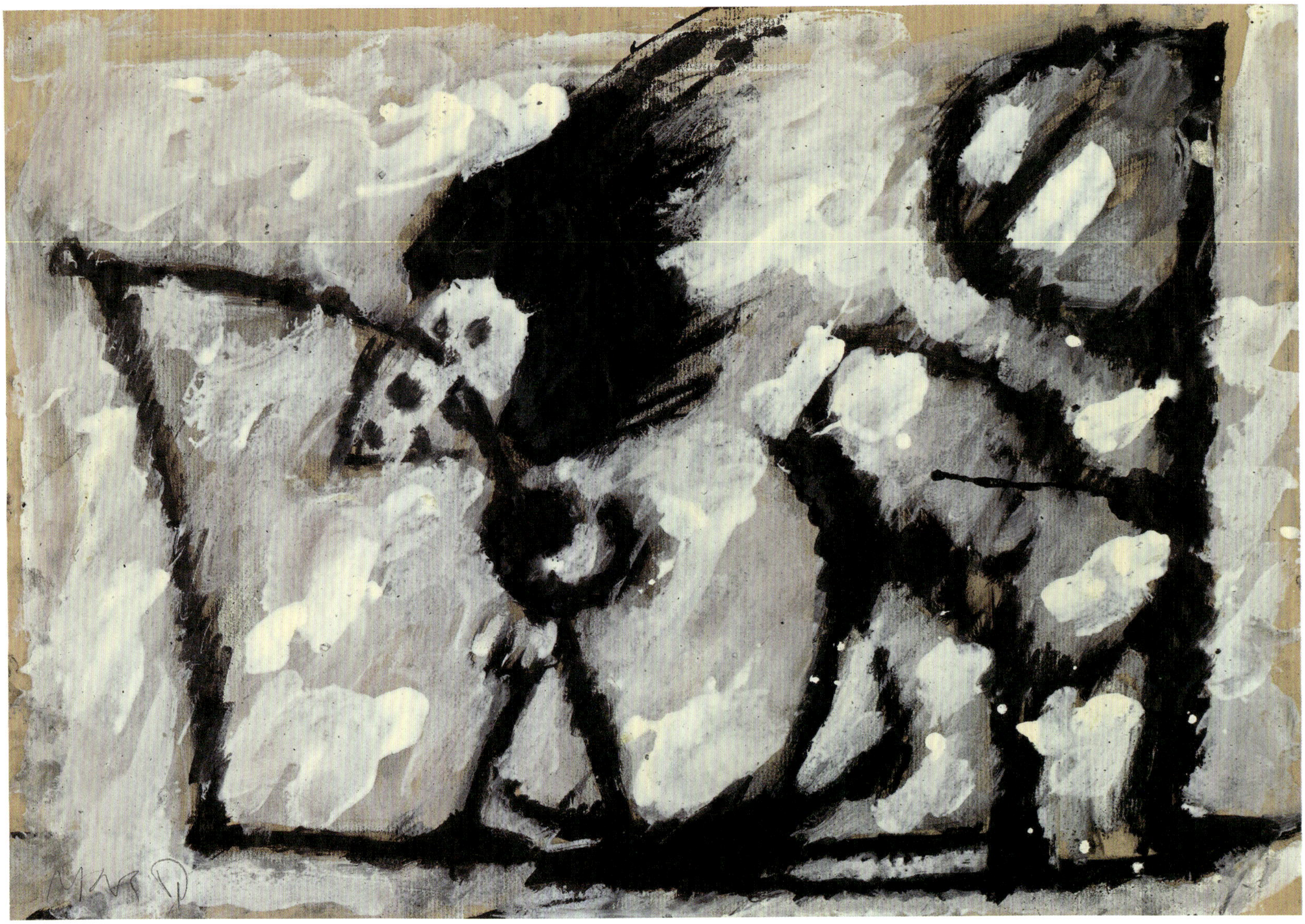

44
MONUMENT – dithyrambisch
('MONUMENT – dithyrambic'), 1976
Markus Lüpertz
Gouache and ink
447 x 626 mm
Presented by Count Christian Duerckheim
to the British Museum

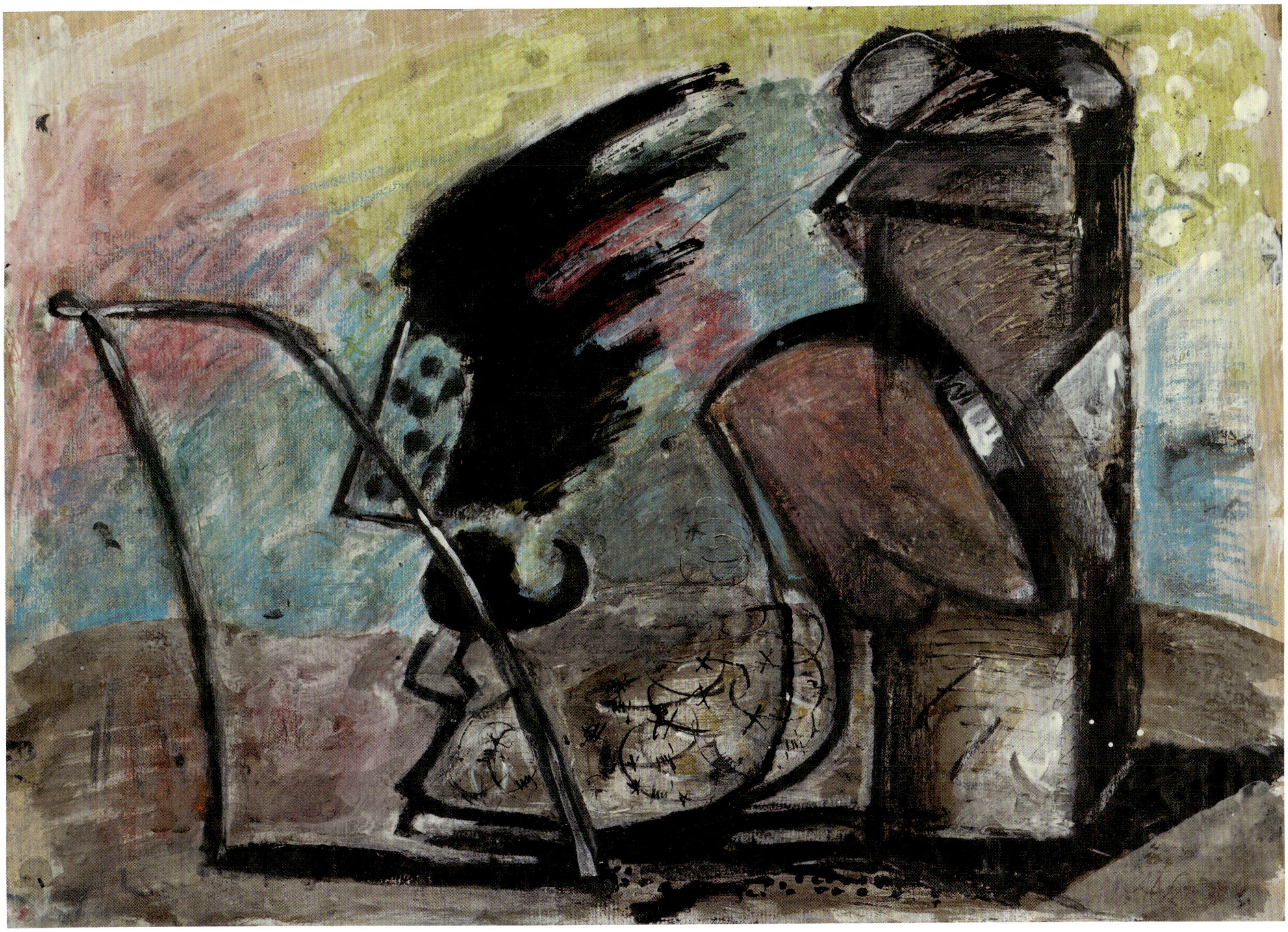

45
MONUMENT – dithyrambisch
('MONUMENT – dithyrambic'), 1976
Markus Lüpertz
Gouache, ink and oil pastel
447 x 625 mm
Presented by Count Christian Duerckheim
to the British Museum

46
Ohne Titel ('Untitled'), *c.* 1977
Markus Lüpertz
Ink wash and coloured crayon
652 x 499 mm
Presented by Count Christian
Duerckheim to the British Museum

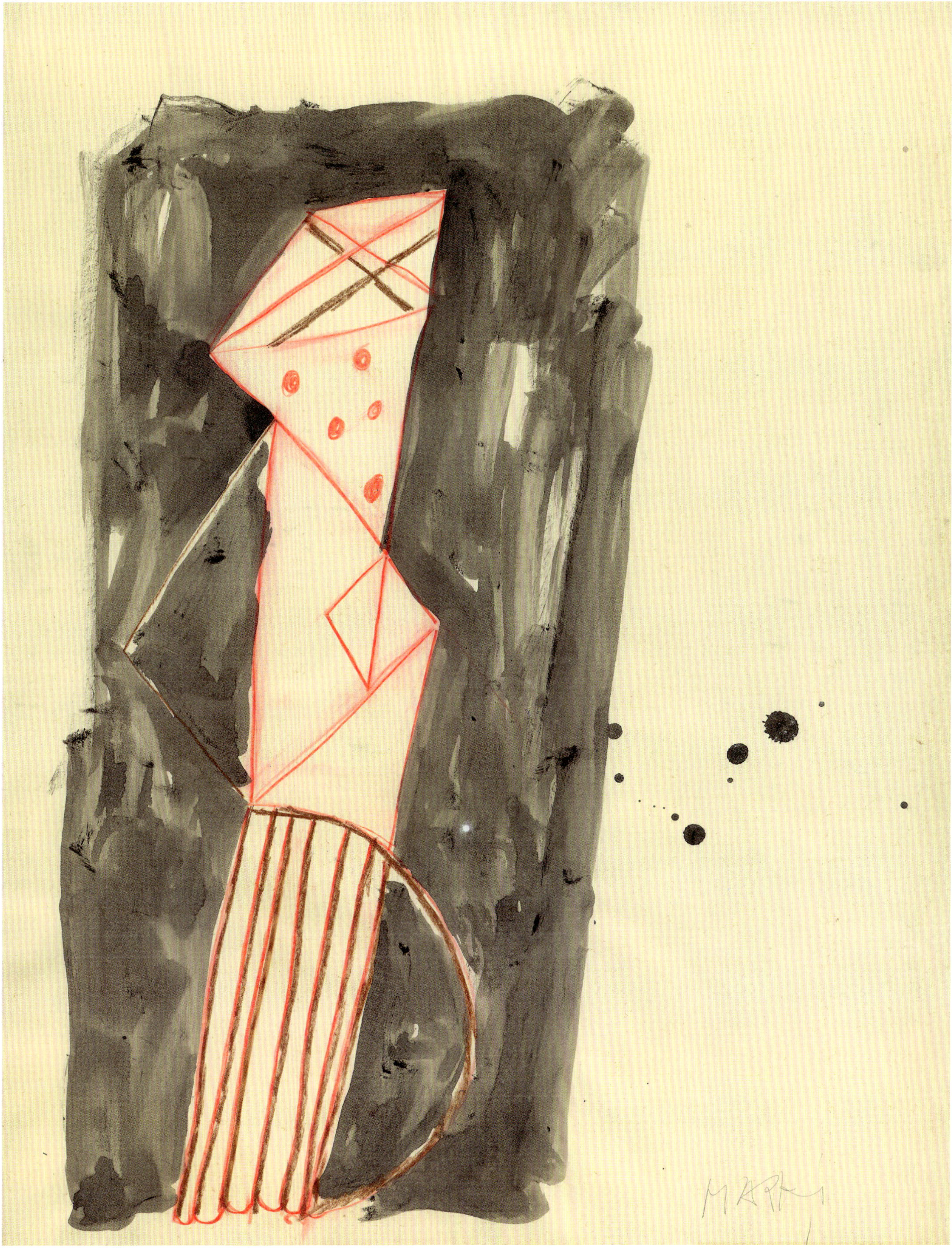

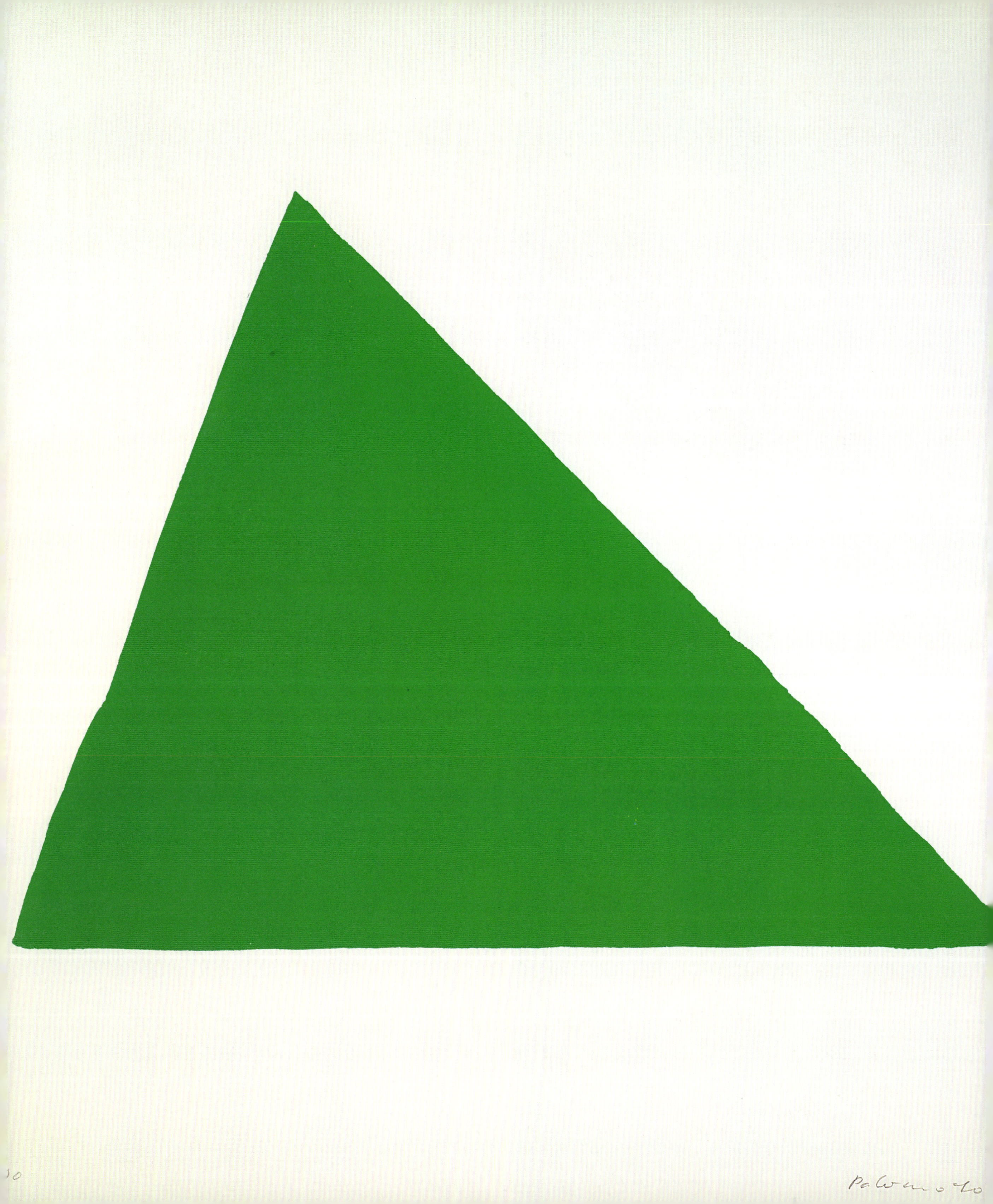

Blinky Palermo

Blinky Palermo emerged in the 1960s from the Düsseldorf Kunstakademie to create a unique body of abstract and minimal paintings, sculptures and works on paper, often made in response to architectural settings. His early death at the age of thirty-three became the basis for many myths surrounding his life and work.

Palermo was born as Peter Stolle in Leipzig on 2 June 1943, but took his mother's name, Schwarze, in the absence of his father (whose name, he learned later, was actually Eichelmann). He was adopted shortly after birth (a fact he and his twin brother learnt only at the age of eighteen) and his name changed to Heisterkamp.[1] In 1952 he moved with his adoptive family to Münster in West Germany. His foster mother, Erika Heisterkamp, died in 1958, and her husband, Wilhelm, remarried two years later.

Where Palermo's short life was unsettled and fraught, his work evolved steadily from a set of simple, clearly articulated ideas. His earliest catalogued works are a series of abstract paintings on cardboard made around 1959 to 1961 in the Informel, abstract style that dominated painting in West Germany at the time. In 1961 Heisterkamp (as he was then called) enrolled at the Werkkunstschule (Design School) in Münster to study graphic design and sculpture, and worked part-time as a window dresser for local shops. The next year, at the age of eighteen, he enrolled at the Kunstakademie, Düsseldorf, studying in the 'Free Painting Department', run by the painter Bruno Goller (1901–98). He became friends with his fellow students Sigmar Polke, Konrad Lueg and Gerhard Richter, who were soon to make their mark as part of a new avant-garde group of artists emerging from the Kunstakademie. The work of all four was marked by a scepticism, by turns comic and mystical, with the possibilities of painting and sculpture in their time.

Palermo's third rechristening occurred in 1964, after enrolling in Joseph Beuys's class at the Kunstakademie, when he adopted the name Blinky Palermo, at the suggestion of a fellow student, after Frank 'Blinky' Palermo, an American boxing manager and gangster. Different theories have been put forward for this choice, although it was most likely because of its exotic, mysterious and, above all, American sound. Beuys, who had taught sculpture at the Academy since 1961, became an important influence and supporter of Palermo's career (fig. 1). Under Beuys's tutelage, Palermo began to use simple shapes and forms, creating works that he classified as 'Objects', often little more than shaped, stretched canvases and monochrome, painted wood. *Untitled (Wvz 14)* (1964), one of the first of these objects, consists of a length of wood wrapped in Nessel (a type of thin fabric) and coloured with oil paint.

Palermo studied with Beuys as an 'ordinary' student until late 1966, and then for a year as a Meisterschüler (Master Student; fig. 2). His work had already been included in the exhibition *Weiss/Weiss* at the Alfred Schmela Gallery, Düsseldorf; his first solo exhibition took place at the Galerie Friedrich + Dahlem in Munich in May 1966. Although the latter exhibition was a

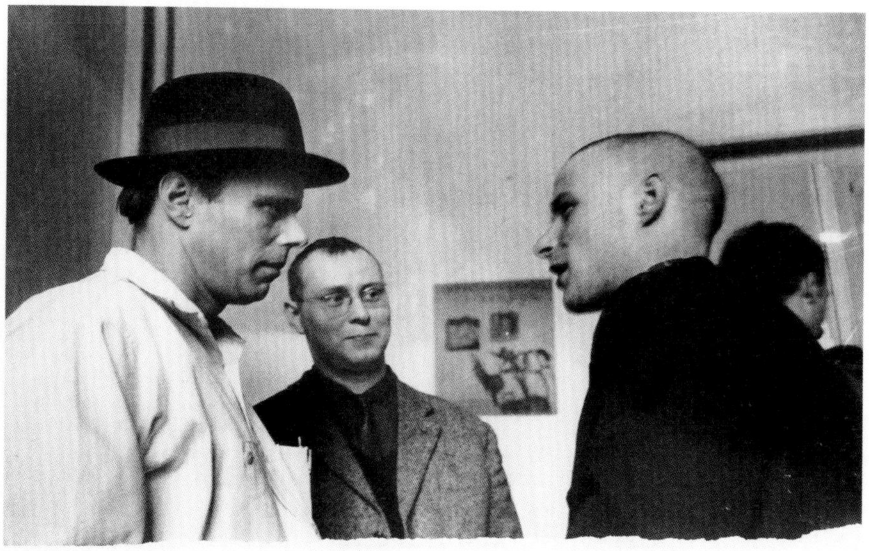

commercial failure – only one work sold, bought by Palermo's father – Heiner Friedrich became one of Palermo's strongest supporters, engaging him on a contract in 1970. Through the gallery Palermo discovered the work of American minimalist and conceptual artists, including Carl Andre (b. 1935), Donald Judd (1928–94) and Robert Ryman (b. 1930), who became important influences. It was during this year that Palermo visited the Stedelijk Museum in Amsterdam, where he encountered the work of Piet Mondrian (1872–1944) and Kazimir Malevich (1879–1935).

In late 1966 Palermo began making his *Stoffbilder*, or 'Fabric paintings', comprising bands of coloured cotton, bought from department stores, sewn together (initially by his first wife, Ingrid, who he married in 1965 and then by Gerhard Richter's first wife, Ema) and mounted on a rectangular stretcher, the size determined by the standardized width of commercially available fabrics. Palermo made over fifty of these works until discontinuing the series in 1972. By presenting the fabrics 'as bought', with minimal intervention, Palermo created a feeling of anonymity that can be likened to the deadpan aesthetic of Gerhard Richter's *Colour Chart* paintings (the two artists began working on their series at roughly the same time, in the autumn of 1966). Both artists were against the notion of art as an

1. *Joseph Beuys, Sigmar Polke and Blinky Palermo at the Kunstakademie Düsseldorf,* 1965
Ute Klophaus, Wuppertal

2. *Untitled,* 1966
Blinky Palermo
Oil on canvas, laid down on wood, 1240 x 160 mm
Formerly Duerckheim collection

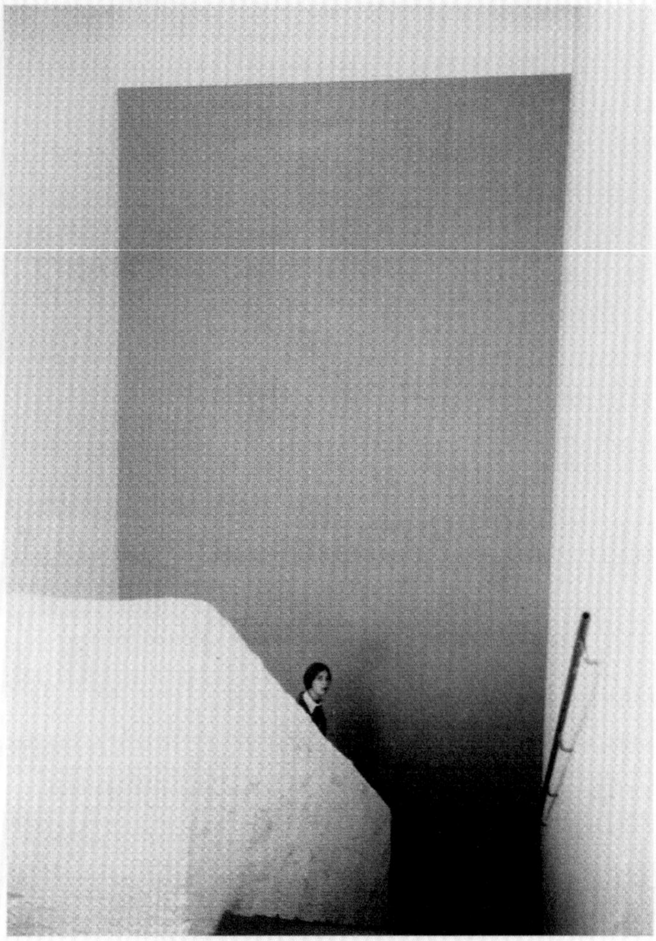

3. *Wall painting,* 1972
Blinky Palermo
Documenta, Kassel

4. *Entwürfe für Objekte* ('Sketches for Object'), 1969
Graphite, watercolour and gouache on paper, 210 x 296 mm
Duerckheim collection

expression of personality, or evidence of virtuoso technique.

After leaving the Kunstakademie in 1967, Palermo shared a studio in Düsseldorf with the artist Imi Knoebel (b. 1940), whom he had met in Beuys's class at the Academy. His emotional life remained unstable, as he separated from his wife, and the following year went to live with Kristin Hanigk, a friend of Sigmar Polke's, who he had met at the famous Düsseldorf nightclub, *Das Creamcheese*, where Palermo worked behind the bar.

At the end of 1968 he made his first work directly onto a wall, a drawing with oil crayon, at Heiner Friedrich's gallery in Munich. He went on to make some thirty such works over the next five years, all for temporary exhibitions. None survive in the original. Palermo referred to them as *Aktivierung des Raums* – 'activation of space' – suggesting the way in which, with very simple means, they brought out the qualities of an architectural setting. For *Wandmalerei auf gegenüberliegenden Wänden* ('Wall Painting on Facing Walls'), one of his most noted wall paintings, created at Heiner Friedrich's gallery in 1971, Palmero painted one wall light ochre, leaving a thin white border, which was then mirrored in reverse by a thick ochre border on the facing wall. The room was otherwise empty.

In other works architectural features were used as the inspiration for a painted form. For *Treppenhaus I* ('Stairway I'), made at the Konrad Fischer Gallery, Düsseldorf, in 1970, Palermo included the profile of an ascending stairway as the basis for a wall painting in a light ochre colour; the 'Treppenhaus' motif reappeared in a number of subsequent wall paintings. For his contribution to the fifth *Documenta* exhibition at Kassel in 1972, Palermo produced a monochrome wall painting on the first floor landing of the staircase in the Museum Fridericianum using *Bleimennige*, an orange rust-preventing undercoat paint, to which he was drawn for its muted colour and understated value as an artistic medium (fig. 3).

One of Palermo's most important friendships forged at the Kunstakademie was with Gerhard Richter. He worked for a short period in Richter's studio before establishing himself, in 1969,

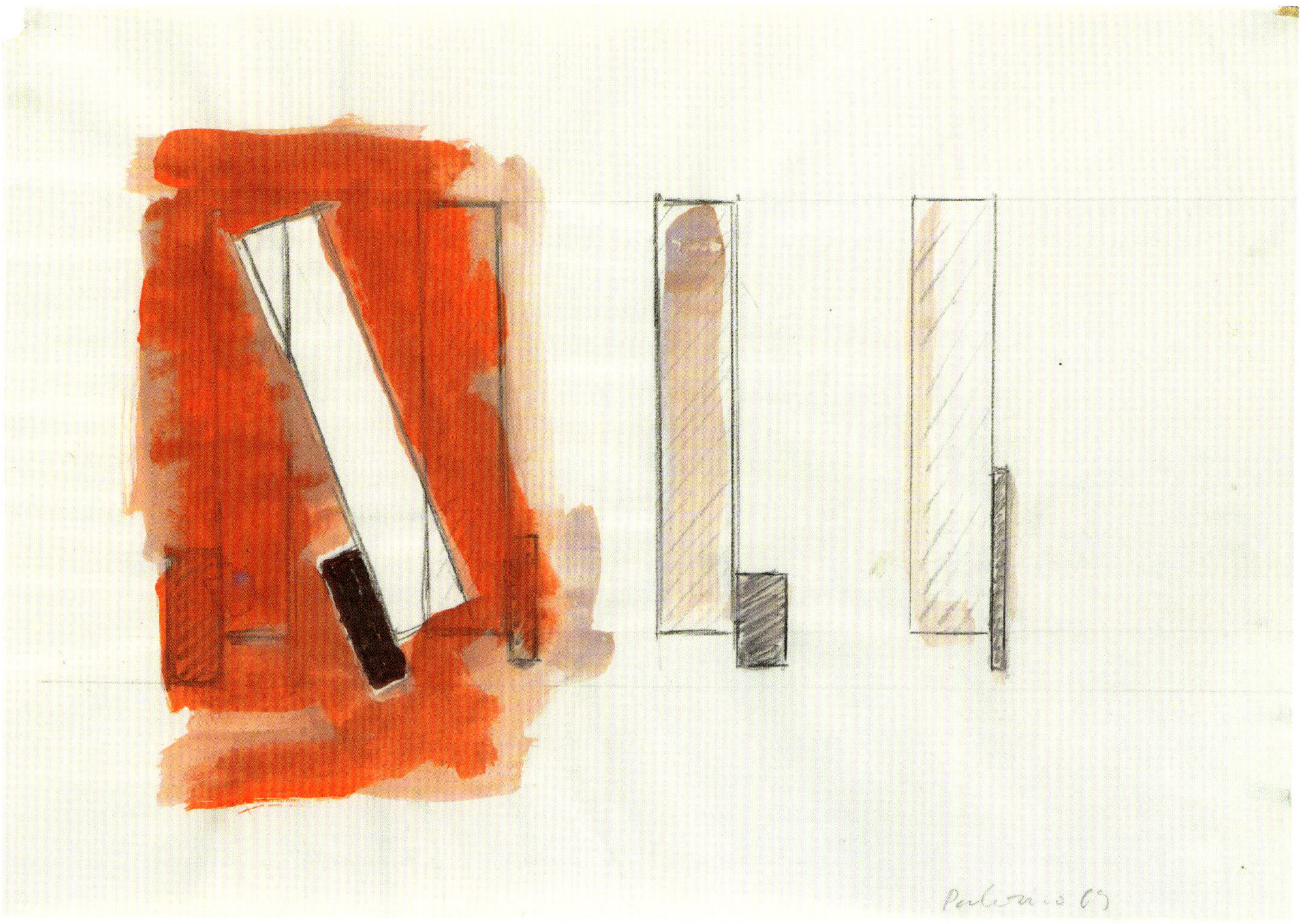

in an old carpenter's shop, shared with the sculptor Ulrich Rückreim (b. 1938), in Mönchengladbach. In November 1970 Palermo and Richter visited New York for the first time. They went on to collaborate on several occasions, most notably in 1971, creating an installation for the Friedrich Gallery in Cologne, comprising a wall painting by Palermo and two portrait busts of the artists by Richter.

First articulated in the *Object* works (figs 4–5), Palermo's enduring interest in shape and colour is encapsulated in *Four Prototypes*, a portfolio of four screenprints published in 1970 (cats 50–53). The four archetypal shapes, contrasting flat, even colour with irregular edges, were also turned into limited edition objects (with the exception of the triangle); they were to be displayed much in the same way as the *Object* works, namely as interventions in and 'activations' of space. Drawings also played an important role for Palermo, both as a way of exploring the possibilities of a reduced pictorial language and as a record of his temporary wall paintings and drawings.

Palermo moved to New York at the end of 1973, without his wife, living and working in two small rooms at the newly opened gallery of Heiner Friedrich, at 141 Wooster Street in SoHo. The move was intended to further his career in the context of the American art market and foster exchange with American artists. From the former point of view it was not a success: Palermo destroyed most of what he made in the first two years of his stay, and there was little critical interest in his work. In the summer of 1974 Palermo and Knoebel travelled around America in a Chevrolet, buying cowboy clothes and visiting the Rothko chapel in Houston, as well as various works of Land Art, including *Las Vegas Piece* (1969) by Walter de Maria (1935–2013) and *Double Negative* (1969) by Michael Heizer (b. 1944). Personal upheavals continued: during a visit to Germany the next year Palermo left his wife, Ingrid, and on his return to New York lived with the painter Robin Bruch (b. 1948), with whom he had been having a long-term affair.

During 1974 Palermo began to paint with acrylic on aluminium, inaugurating a new series of works known as the *Metal Pictures*. These simple works, involving nothing more than three bands of colour on a small rectangular support, constitute the most confident expression of his minimal use of colour and shape. Of the *Metal Pictures*, the series *To the People of New York City* (fig. 6) was the subject of a monograph published in 2009 by the Dia Art Foundation, and is often described as Palermo's major final work. It was made in Germany, in Richter's former studio, after Palermo's return the same year, to live with Babette Polter.

Palermo was preparing a comprehensive exhibition of his *Stoffbilder* and a new series of *Metal Pictures* for the Museum Haus Lang in Krefeld when he died, while on holiday on Kurumba Island in the Maldives archipelago, from heart failure following a heroin overdose. His body was cremated in Sri Lanka. Palermo was a unique figure in post-War German art, whose early death sealed his romantic reputation. The highly simplified coloured shapes and the mysterious objects with which he worked have taken on a magical, even spiritual, quality for many commentators. His reluctance to publish statements about his work, by contrast with the numerous texts and interviews of those such as Richter and Baselitz, has provided a further incentive for interpretation.

The first retrospective of his work after his death took place in 1980 at the Galerie-Verein Munich, organized by the art dealers Heiner Friedrich and Franz Dahlem. The combination of a broad sweep of Palermo's work and the display of memorabilia in this exhibition set the tone for a cult-like reception of his work. Although his reputation steadily increased, writing about his life and work has become more intent on establishing the facts than in reworking myths. The publication in 1995 of a catalogue raisonné by Thordis Moeller of Palermo's paintings, objects and works on paper was followed by the first in-depth study of his work by Pia Gottschaller, *Palermo: Inside his Images*, published in 2004. Christine Mehring's critical monograph published in 2008 placed Palermo's work in the broad historical context of post-War German art.

1. See: Moritz Wesseler, 'Palermo: known facts and new insights into his person', in S. Küper, U. Groos and V.J. Müller (eds), *Palermo*, Cologne, 2007, pp. 179–92.

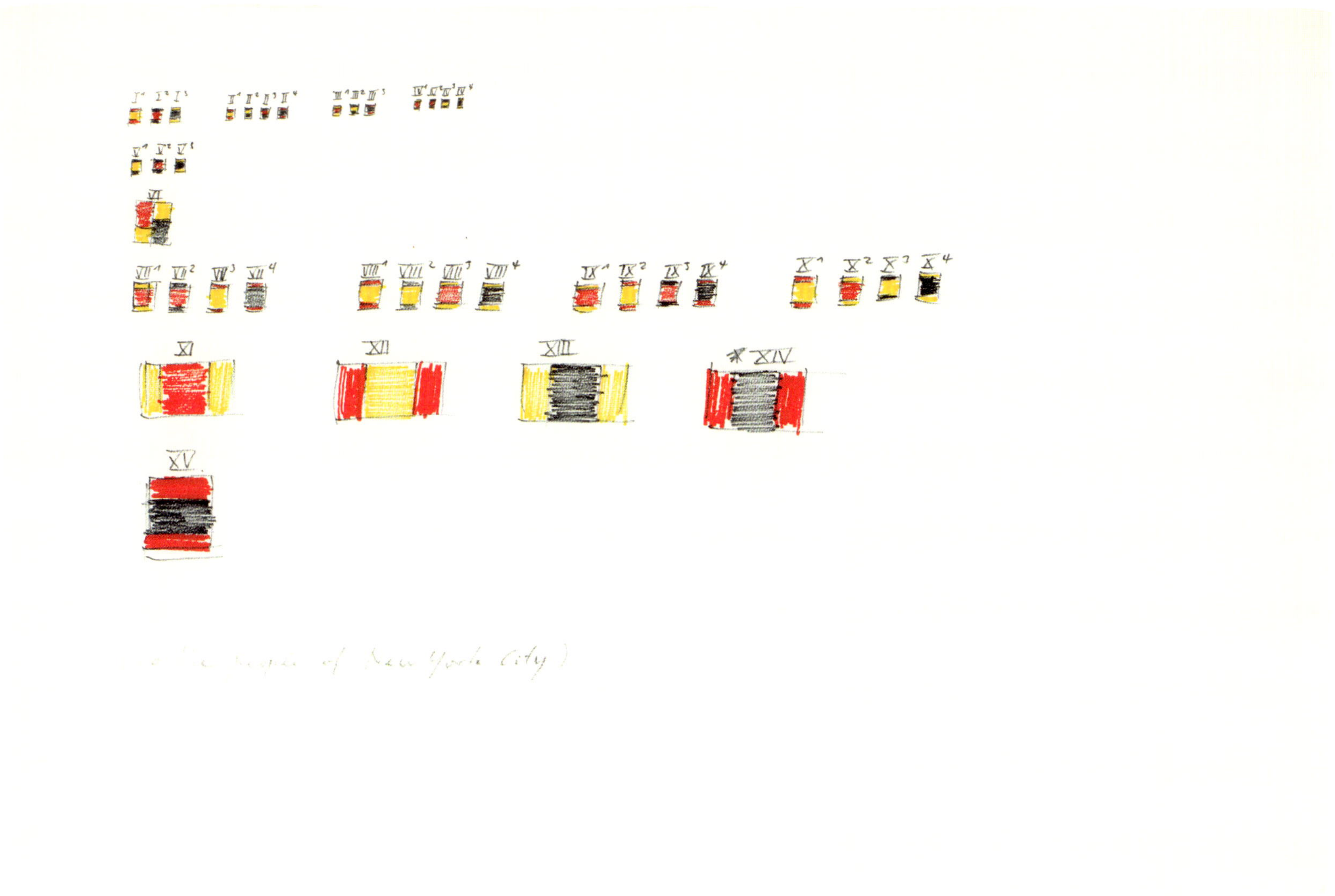

5. *Graue Scheibe ('*Gray Disk'*),* 1970
Blinky Palermo
Oil on canvas laid down on wood,
135 x 260 mm
Formerly Duerckheim collection

6. Study for *To the People of New York City*, 1976
Blinky Palermo
Felt-tip pen on illustration board,
448 x 654 mm
David Zwirner, New York/London

47
Ohne Titel ('Untitled'), 1969
Blinky Palermo
Gouache with pencil under-drawing
479 x 422 mm
Presented by Count Christian
Duerckheim to the British Museum

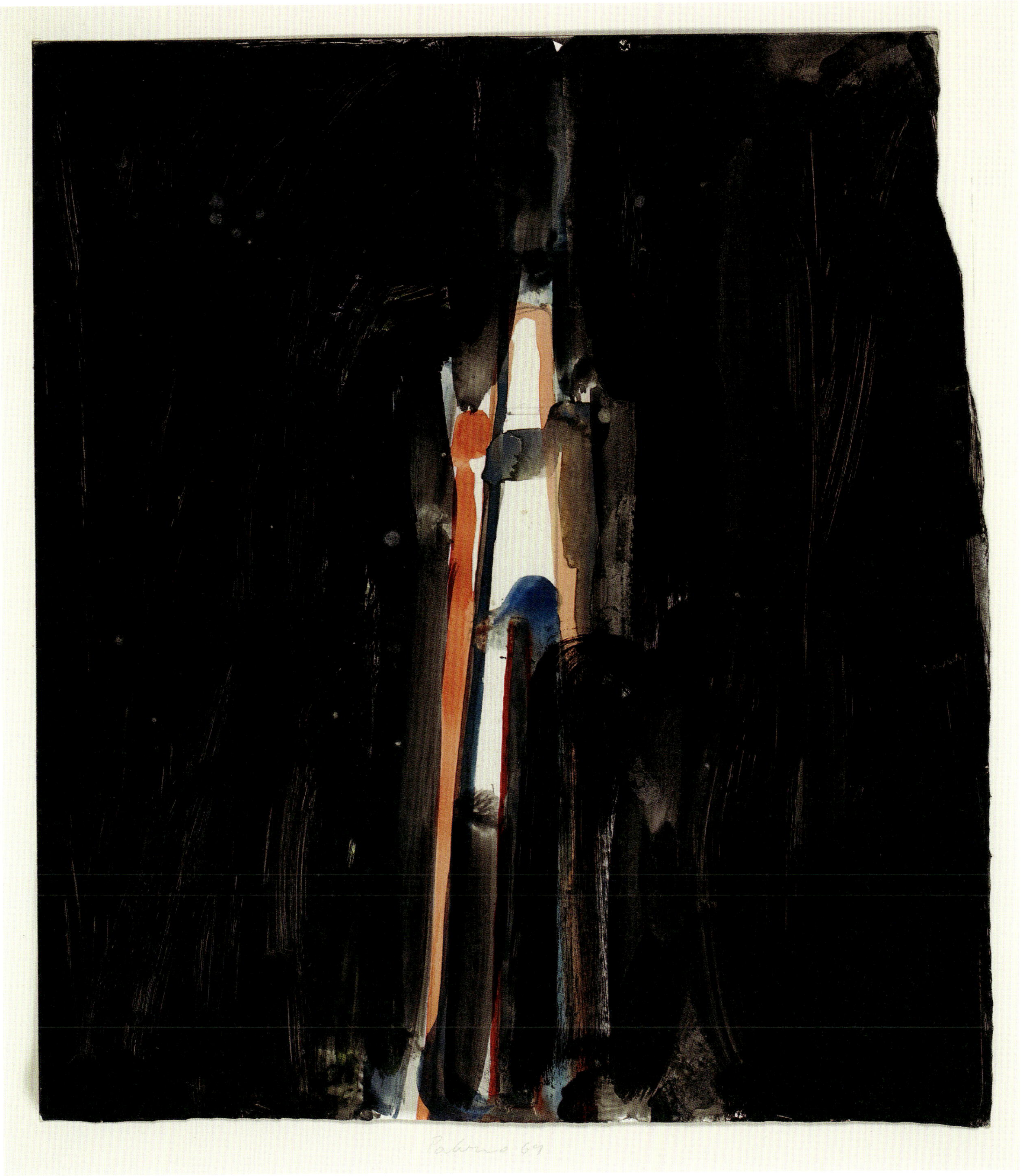
Palermo 69

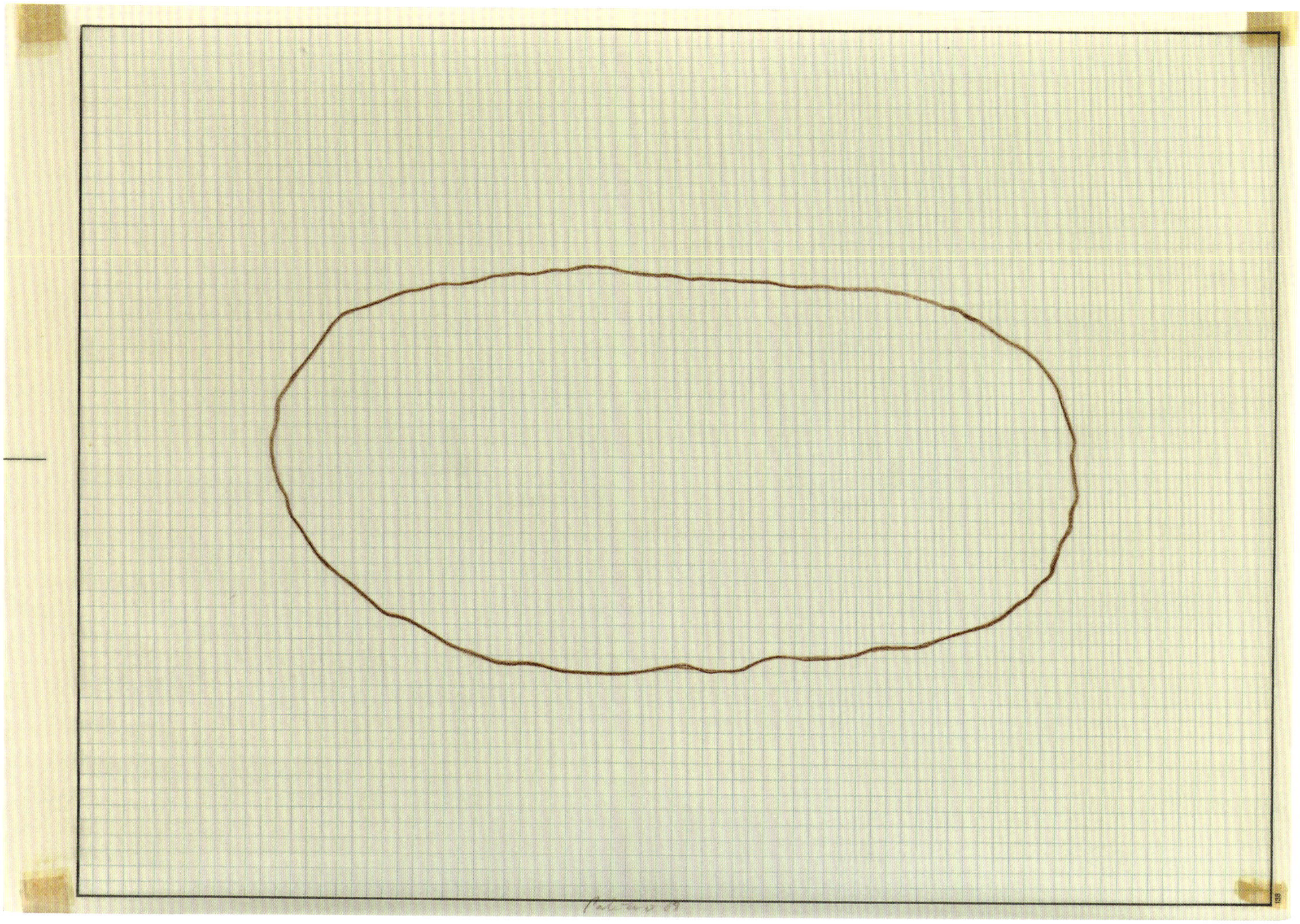

48
Ohne Titel ('Untitled'), 1968
Blinky Palermo
Crayon
295 x 420 mm

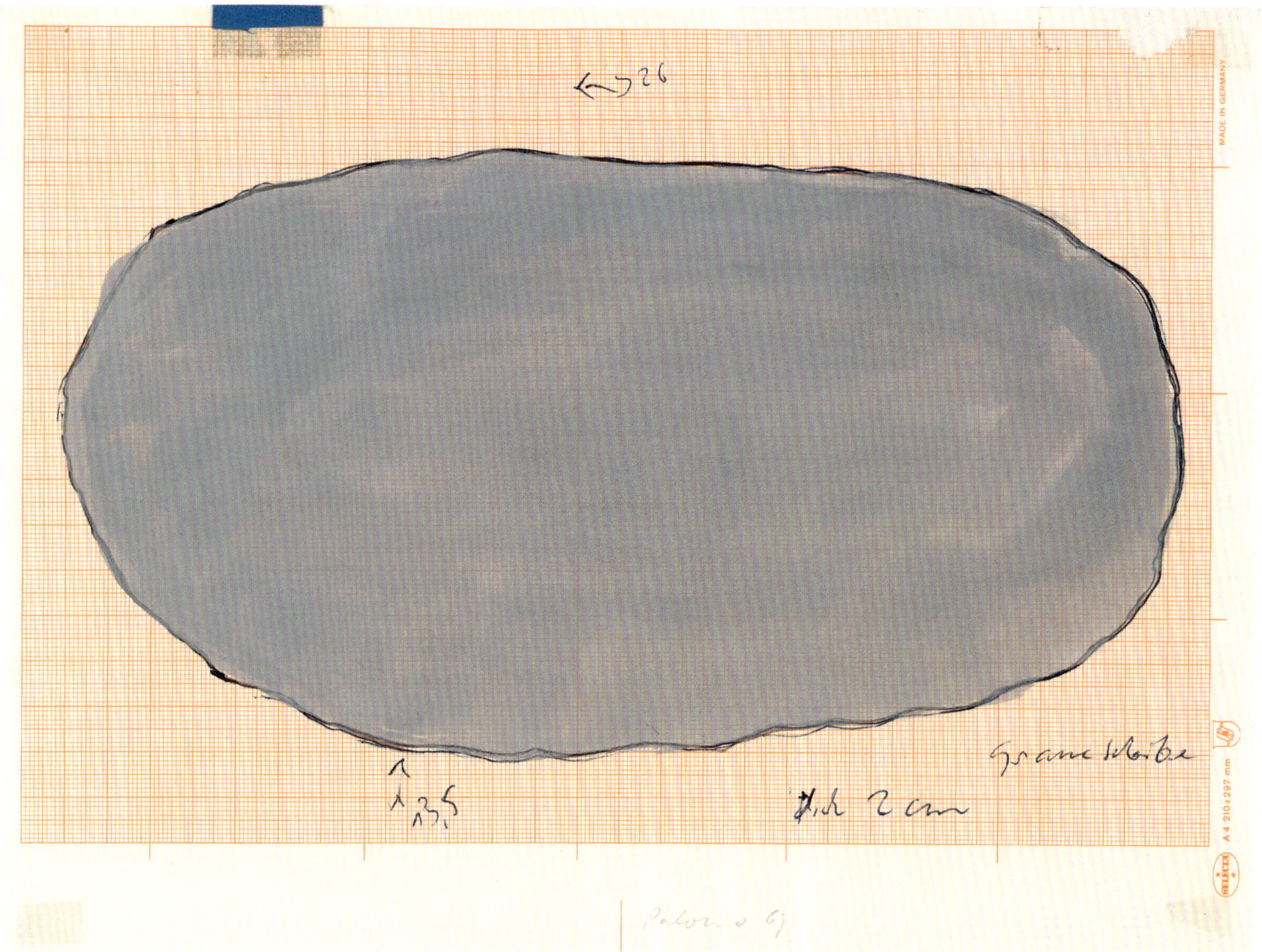

49
Ohne Titel ('Untitled'), 1969
Blinky Palermo
Ballpoint pen and gouache
210 x 296 mm

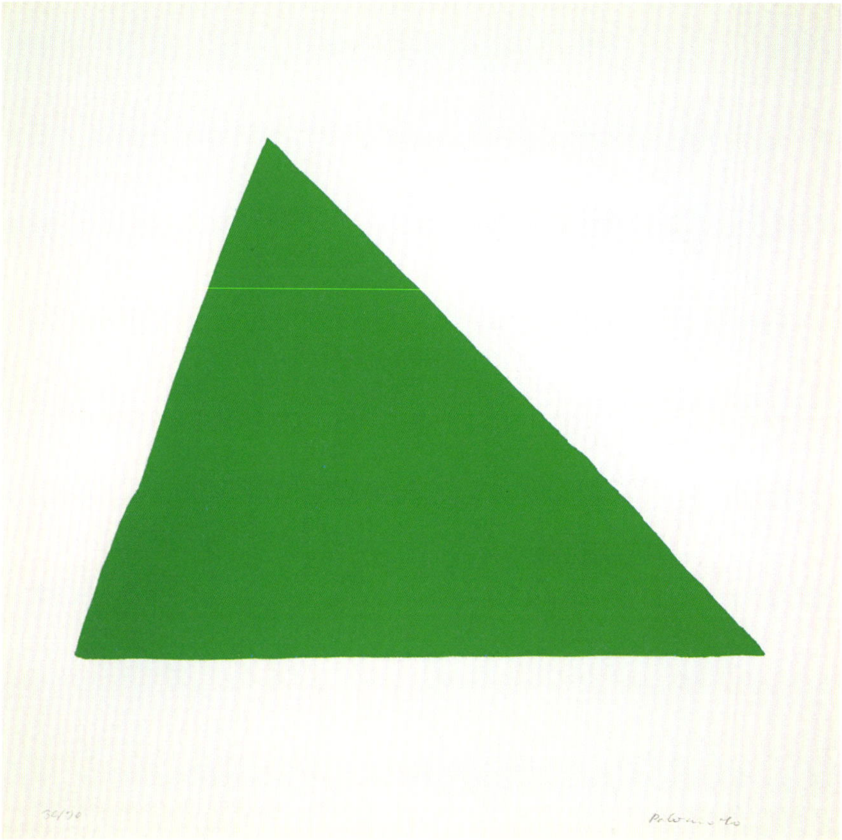

50
Ohne Titel ('Untitled'),
from the portfolio *4 Prototypen*
('4 Prototypes'), 1970
Blinky Palermo
Screenprint in green ink
600 x 600 mm

51
Ohne Titel ('Untitled'),
from the portfolio *4 Prototypen*
('4 Prototypes'), 1970
Blinky Palermo
Screenprint in black ink
600 x 600 mm

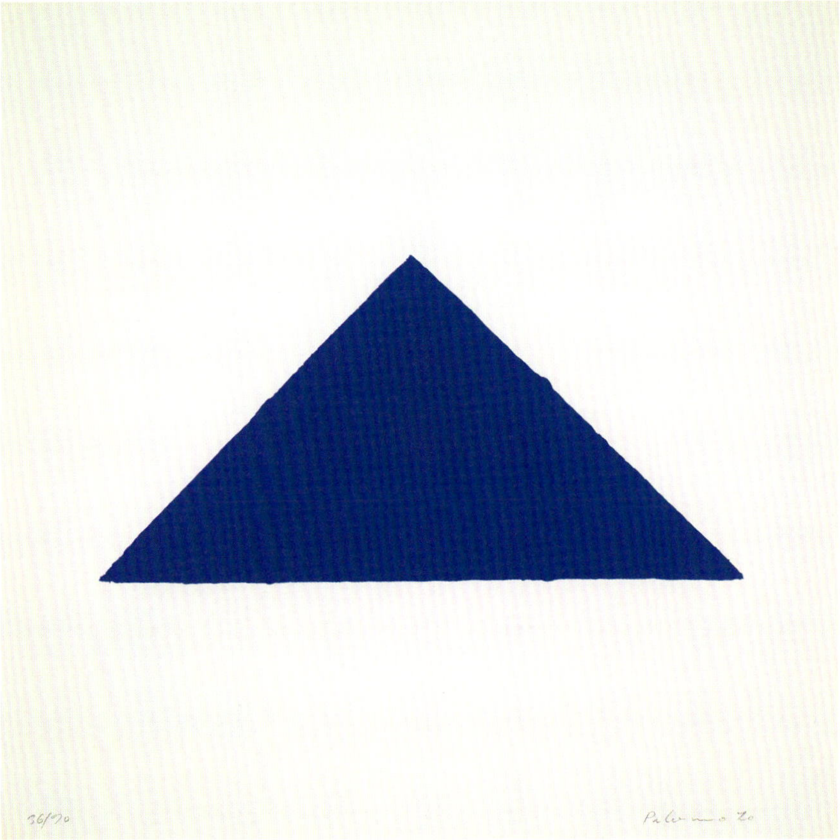

52
Ohne Titel ('Untitled'),
from the portfolio *4 Prototypen*
('4 Prototypes'), 1970
Blinky Palermo
Screenprint in blue ink
600 x 600 mm

53
Ohne Titel ('Untitled'),
from the portfolio *4 Prototypen*
('4 Prototypes'), 1970
Blinky Palermo
Screenprint in grey ink
600 x 600 mm

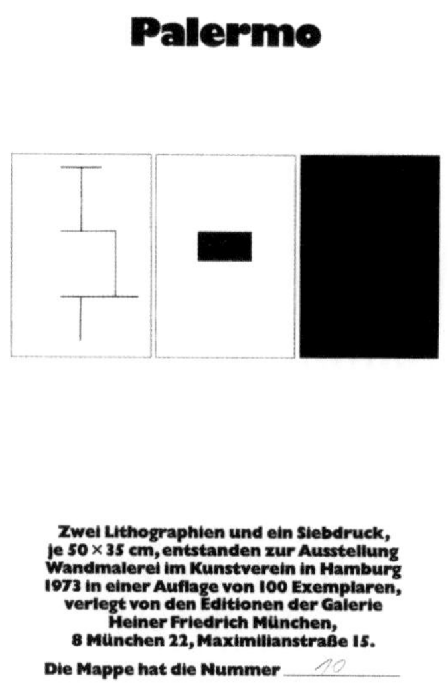

Cover from the portfolio *Zwei Lithographien und ein Siebdruck* ('Two lithographs and one screenprint'), 1973
Offset litho
506 x 354 mm

54
Ohne Titel I ('Untitled I'), from the portfolio *Zwei Lithographien und ein Siebdruck* ('Two lithographs and one screenprint'), 1973
Blinky Palermo
Lithograph
500 x 350 mm

55
Ohne Titel II ('Untitled II'), from the portfolio *Zwei Lithographien und ein Siebdruck* ('Two lithographs and one Screenprint'), 1973
Blinky Palermo
Lithograph
500 x 350 mm

56
Ohne Titel III ('Untitled III'), from the portfolio *Zwei Lithographien und ein Siebdruck* ('Two lithographs and one screenprint'), 1973
Blinky Palermo
Screenprint in brown ink
500 x 350 mm

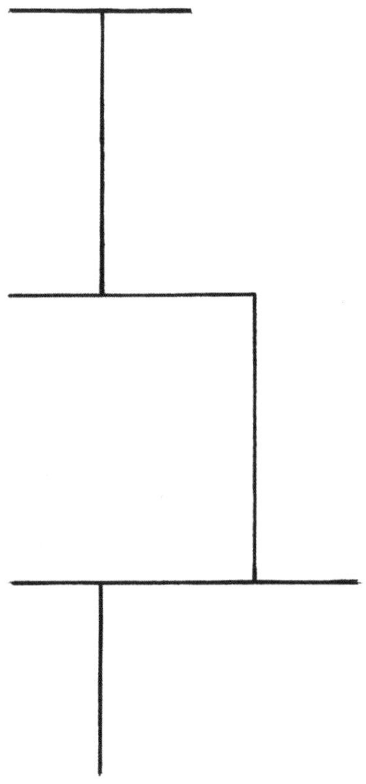

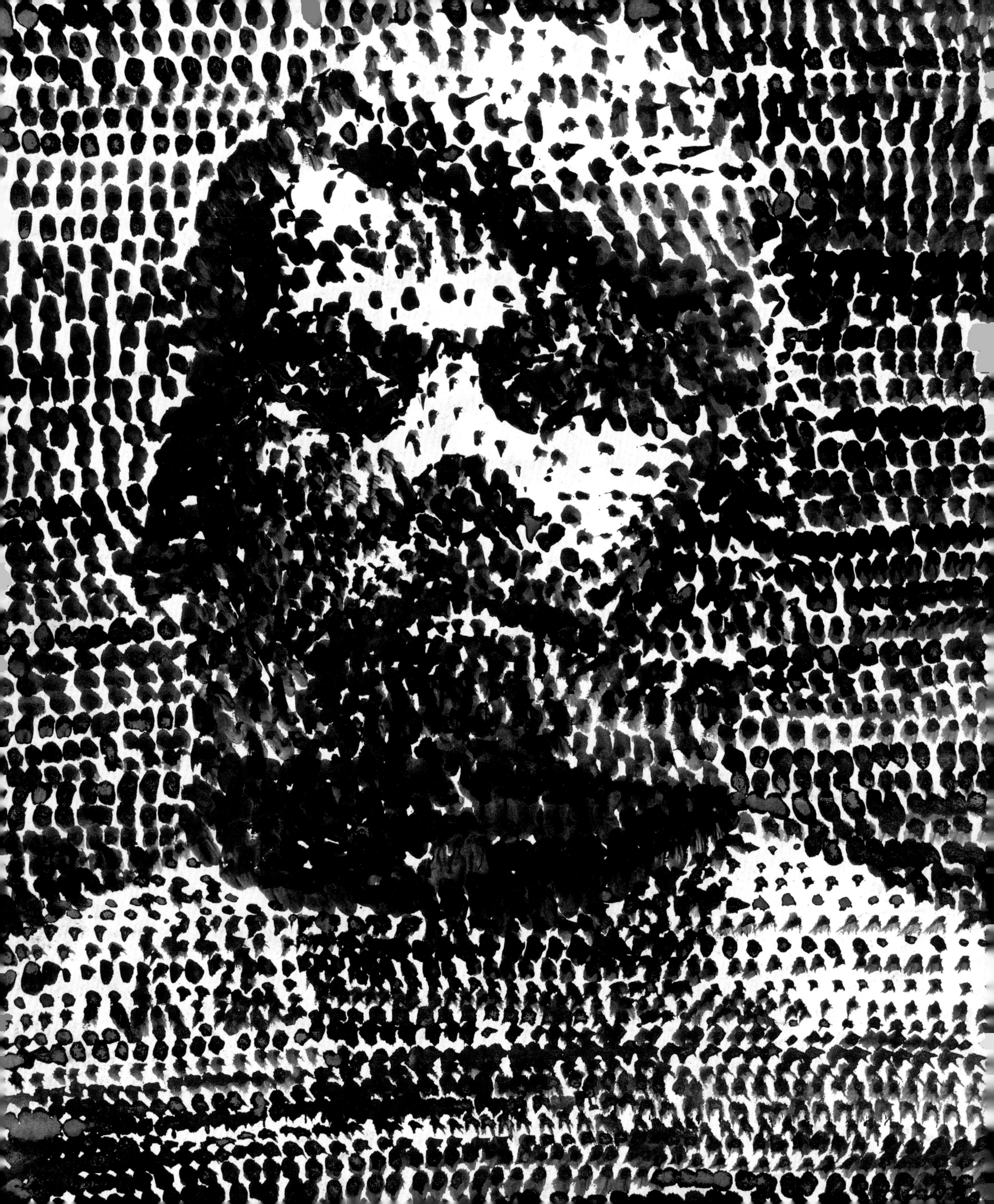

A.R. Penck

Ralf Winkler (who later adopted the pseudonym A.R. Penck) spent the first half of his career working in East Germany as a dissident artist; he created an abstract style of painting using signs and schematic figures through which he explored features of contemporary life, in particular the political division of Germany.

Winkler was born in Dresden in October 1939 and grew up in the working-class district of Nausslitz. He was five years old when Dresden was almost entirely destroyed by Allied planes on the nights of 13 and 14 February 1945, an event he witnessed from the garden of his parents' house, some distance away. He later recalled the strong impression made on him as a child by Arnold Böcklin's (1827–1901) painting *Der Krieg* ('War'; 1896), showing the four horsemen of the apocalypse riding over a burning city.

Although these experiences later found their way into his work, the early years of his career were more immediately marked by his struggle with the East German State, as a dissident who rejected the official style of Socialist Realism. He has traced his ingrained non-conformism to having been brought up during two authoritarian regimes, but also as a result of his parents' early divorce, so that he grew up 'wild, without a father'.[1]

Art was from an early stage a way of negotiating a difficult past. Penck described a childhood drawing of 'Stalin conquering Hitler' as his way of 'putting the whole episode of the War' behind him.[2] His earliest surviving works, made as a teenager – cityscapes and portraits, particularly of his grandfather – combined the pre-War naïve style of *Laienmalerei*, or amateur painting, derived ultimately from Henri Rousseau (1844–1910), with modernist elements taken from Picasso.[3] While still at school he attended painting and drawing classes at the Volkshochschule in Dresden led by Jürgen Böttcher (later known as Strawalde; b. 1931), who became the central figure for a group of younger artists, including Peter Herrmann (b. 1937), Peter Makolies (b. 1936), Winfried Dierske (1934–2006) and Peter Graf (b. 1938).

On leaving school and failing to find a trainee position as a stone-carver, Penck took on an apprenticeship as a draughtsman at a state-run advertising agency, VEB DEWAG. He continued to make art and experimented with different media, including early attempts at making woodcuts. It was for two of these that in 1956 Penck was awarded a prize, after their display in an exhibition of work by apprentices in Dresden. When the display toured to East Berlin, however, Winkler's work was rejected as 'bourgeois decadence'. He nevertheless won a prize for a poem about a quarry worker, for which he received a set of books on literature in the Socialist State of Hungary. Penck described his awareness of the 'manipulation' behind this prize: 'When I realized that, my attitude changed.... I had suddenly developed a hostile image of the State.'[4] From this moment Penck's career was marked by an inability to find official recognition for his status as an artist – repeated applications to study at the Academies in Dresden and Berlin were rejected.

In 1957 Winkler met Hans-Georg Kern (later Georg Baselitz), who became a close friend and associate. Like Baselitz, Winkler remained committed to the idea that art should reflect society and that artists could make a positive contribution to Socialism from an independent position. His friendship with Baselitz ('a self-assured, good-looking type and a great success with women', he later recalled), who by the late 1950s was living

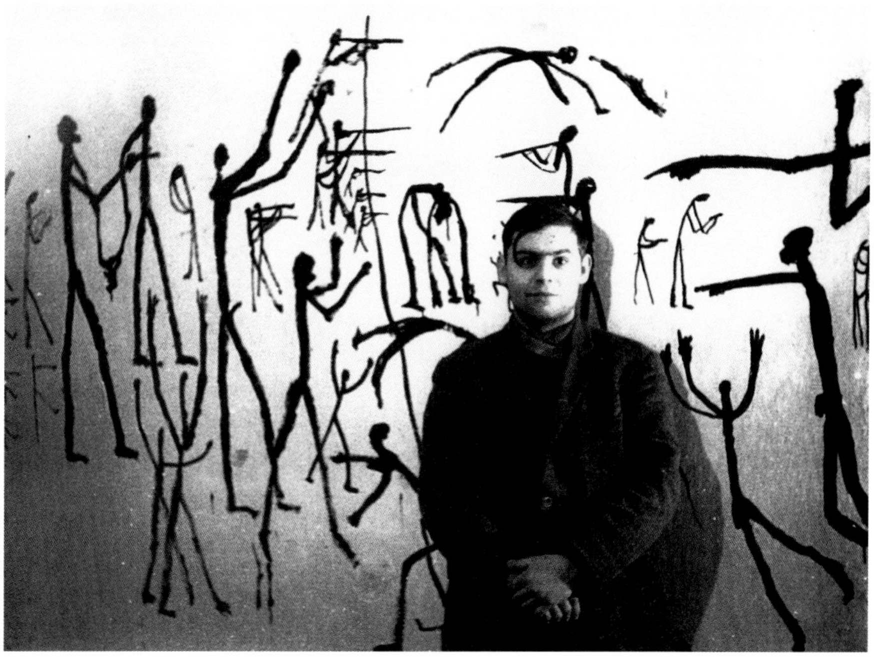

1. A.R. Penck in front of his 1962 painting *Geteiltes Deutschland* ('Divided Germany')

in West Berlin, was an important connection with the West. He visited Baselitz in West Germany on the 12 August 1961, the day before the borders closed and construction began on the 'Anti-Fascist Protection Barrier', later to become the Berlin Wall.

The autumn of 1961 proved a turning point for Penck. Two paintings, a self-portrait and a portrait of a woman, were included in *Junge Künstler* ('Young Artists'), an annual exhibition at the East German Art Academy; but, alongside others, they received particularly harsh criticism from official censors for being too bourgeois and alienated from life in a worker's State.[5] In the winter of that year Penck painted his first *Weltbild* ('World Picture'; 1961), a schematic representation of the social world using simple stick-figures. The same year he made his first *Systembilder* ('System Paintings'), also using minimally graphic figures to construct scenes showing primal human behaviour. These works marked the beginning of his confrontation with the official art of Soviet Germany, a protest that he nevertheless carried out with spirit and humour – his art was increasingly the expression of deeply held personal views and enthusiasms, focused on a positive alternative, rather than cynicism at prevailing conditions.

Two ideas in particular formed Winkler's new direction in the early 1960s: prehistoric art and contemporary theories of communication. His 1962 painting *Geteiltes Deutschland* ('Divided Germany'), later destroyed, showed a wall separating battling stick-figures, referring to the simple forms of Paleolithic cave painting, with escapees fleeing over the barricade (fig. 1). 'It was a modern history painting, a matter of current affairs. The world seen as a system of interrelations', he later said.[6] These paintings were also motivated by theories of information, popularized as 'cybernetics', in the writings of Norbert Wiener, whose *The Human Use of Human Beings: Cybernetics and Society* (1950) was published in German in 1964, as well as in the work of the English pioneer of cybernetics, Ross Ashby.

In 1964 Winkler moved into the first studio of his own, at Lange Straße in Dresden. Here he created the first of his *Standart* works, on the basis of the stick-figure style of his previous work. 'Standart' refers both to a visual model – a 'standard' way of painting – and a standard in the sense of a military ensign or flag (*Standarte* in German), suggesting the strong element of protest in these works. The *Standart* paintings incorporate text and symbols, and often appear as loosely painted diagrams, carrying generally impenetrable theories of social organization, and featuring a variety of schematic figures, most commonly a simple standing figure with raised arms and three large fingers. Penck created images that seem both prehistoric and post-modern, suggesting common qualities of art, on the level of social life, from the distant past to the present day. The series also includes sculptures incorporating everyday materials, such as bottles, tins, books and studio paraphernalia; Penck frequently mounted these assemblages on cardboard-box plinths, naming them *Standart-Modell.* The reduction of Winkler's imagery down to a bare set of signs represented what has been described as a 'Zero Hour' in his own work, and by

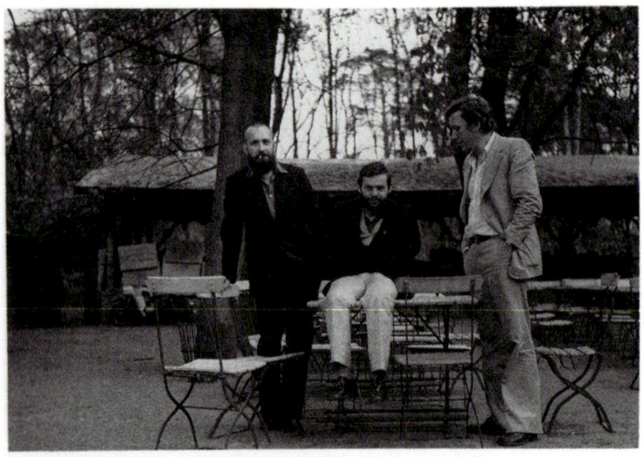

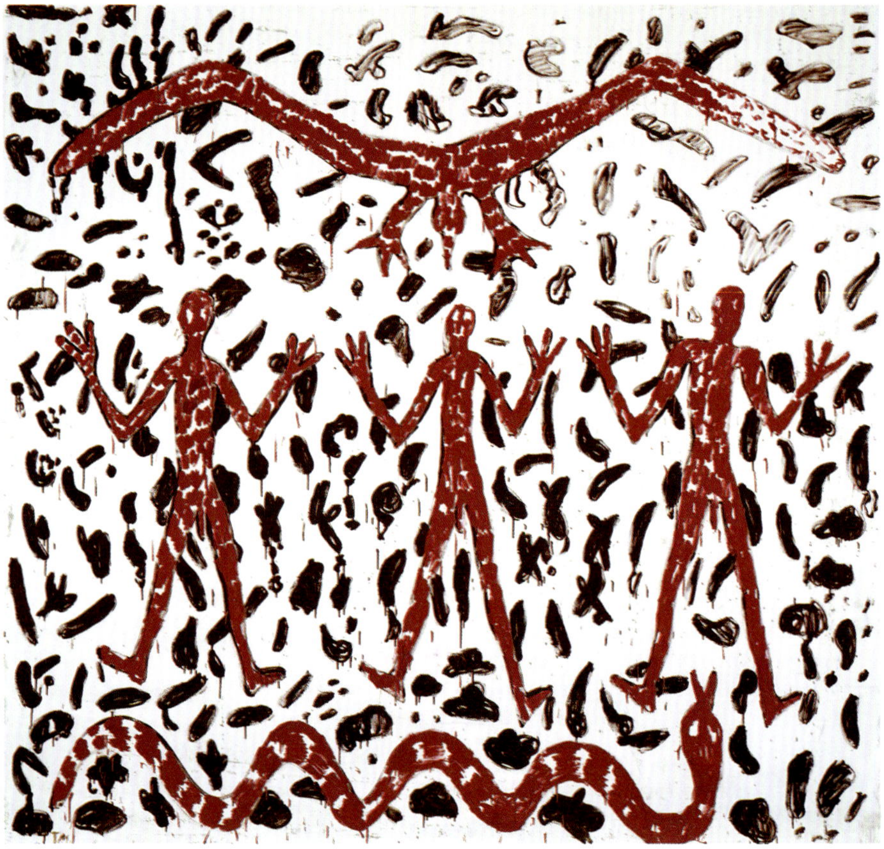

2. Georg Baselitz, A.R. Penck and Michael Werner in Moritzburg, *c.* 1965

3. *Standart 3*, 1974
A.R. Penck
Dispersion on canvas, 272 x 283 cm

extension for art in Germany as a whole in the mid-1960s.[7] His abstract language of signs presented an alternative model to the naturalism of Socialist Realism and belongs to a long tradition of dissent from academic art.

This dissent gathered momentum during the 1960s and led to a friendship with one of the most famous non-conformists, the singer and songwriter Wolf Biermann, a role model for his open criticism of the Socialist government. Winkler also maintained strong connections with West Germany: in 1965, through the intervention of Baselitz, he met the gallerist Michael Werner (fig. 2). Three years later Werner staged the first solo show of his work in West Germany, at the Galerie Hake in Cologne; it was on this occasion that Winkler exhibited for the first time under the name 'A.R. Penck', after the German Ice Age geologist Albrecht Penck. He adopted the pseudonym in part to hide his activities in the West from the East German authorities; but it was also an expression of his sense of split identity and allegiances. He was to exhibit under a number of further pseudonyms – including 'Mike Hammer', 'TM', and also 'Y' – but 'Penck' was the name that prevailed.

By the late 1960s, Penck's relationship with the East German arts establishment had further deteriorated. In 1969 he was denied membership of the *Verband Bildender Künstler*, the official artists' organization of the German Democratic Republic. This isolated him by debarring him from being able to work publicly in East Germany. He survived by sales of his works in the West thanks to Michael Werner, who smuggled paintings out of East Berlin by car. Penck also began to accompany his work with theoretical writings about the nature of symbolism and communication; he published the books *Was ist Standart?* ('What is Standart?') and *Standart Making* to explain the theory underpinning his *Standart* works.

It was thus in the West that Penck first made his name. A solo exhibition of his work at the Museum Haus Lange, Krefeld, in late 1971, was followed the next year by the display of several paintings at the fifth *Documenta* exhibition in Kassel, curated by Harald Szeemann. He was also the subject of an exhibition of drawings at the Kunstmuseum in Basel. Travel restrictions meant that he was unable to visit these exhibitions of his work.

4. *Osten* ('East'), 1980
A.R. Penck
Acrylic on canvas, 2502 x 4000 mm
Tate, London

Artists working in West Germany remained important to Penck as models of an independent mode of making art, particularly Joseph Beuys. Penck admired Beuys's theoretical approach, and his way of combining a scientific approach to making art with a desire to improve society, but he rejected him as a father figure – arguing rather that Beuys was more like a 'big sister'.[8] In East Germany Penck was at the same time making collaborative works with amateur artists, leading in May 1971 to the founding of the artists' collective group *Lücke* ('Void' or 'Hole'), which produced communal paintings and mounted exhibitions in Dresden for the next five years.

In 1972 Penck went to live in the village of Lindenau, outside of Berlin, and worked there for three years, having moved away from what he termed his 'period of working in Dresden as an anonymous political agitator'.[9] He finished making *Standart* works and declared the series a failure, but continued working with a lexicon of signs and graphic symbols, increasingly using colour rather than black and white (fig. 3). Works in various other media appeared, including a series of super-8 films, and also, in 1975, an artist's book, *Ich bin ein Buch, kaufe mich jetzt* ('I am a book, buy me now'), translated into French in 1981, the most successful of his many artist's books.

On his return to Dresden in 1976 Penck met the West German painter Jörg Immendorff, leading to the exhibition *Immendorff mal Penck. Penck mal Immendorff* the following year in Cologne at the Galerie Michael Werner. In 1976 Penck became interested in etching, working with the printmaker Gunter Herrmann at the Dresden Academy of Art, and two years later founded the *Obergrabenpresse* with Peter Herrmann and Eberhard Göschel (b. 1943). This was his first serious work in printmaking, with the exception of a series of woodcuts and linocuts made ten years previously. He went on to work both in lithography and screenprinting.

He also began making sculptures in wood using an axe, later describing the result as an 'act of aggression',[10] and took up playing the drums, following a long-standing interest in jazz music, issuing his first record, *Gostritzer Straße 92*, the first of many experiments with Free Jazz.

Penck's involvement with colleagues in West Germany, and his key role in organizing underground projects and illegal exhibitions, became an increasing problem for the East German authorities. The situation reached a crisis point at the end of the 1970s when State legislation made it illegal to be involved with publications in the West. The forced expatriation of Wolfgang Biermann (b. 1936) led to a wave of protests, and was a turning point for many who felt that it was no longer possible to live and work as dissidents in East Germany. In 1979 Penck had taken part in the large exhibition *Westkunst* in Cologne, a survey of avant-garde art in western Europe and America. By the summer of the following year his position had become untenable: Willi Sitte (1921–2013), the President of the East German artists' organization, refused to exhibit works alongside those of Penck. After completing the series of prints *Ende im Osten* ('End in the East'), and with the financial and legal assistance of Michael Werner, Penck left East Germany on 3 August 1980, crossing the border by foot. He described his *Ausbürgerung*, or 'expatriation', as the result of a long process that stretched back to 1961.

Penck began working immediately in the West (fig. 4), but described the difficulties of making the transition and the 'loss of innocence' that it involved. 'In the East there was no direct

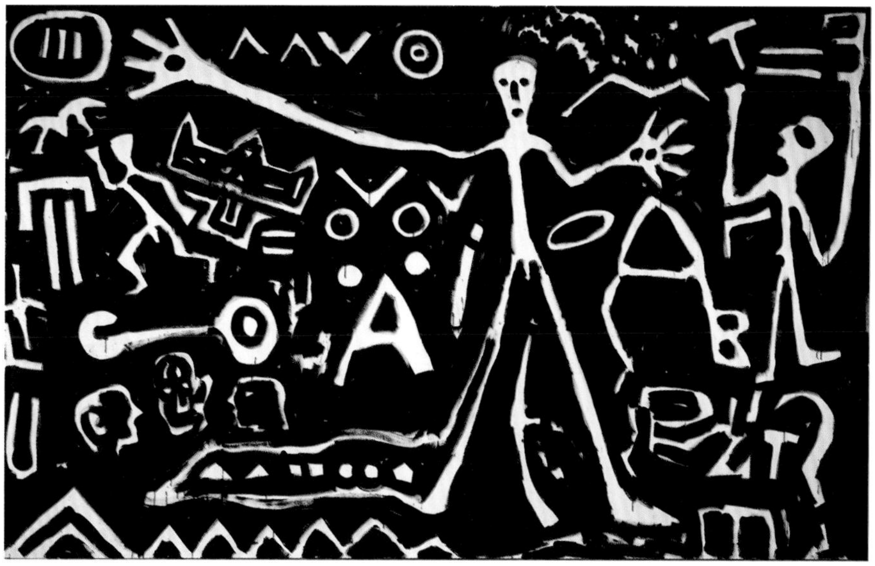

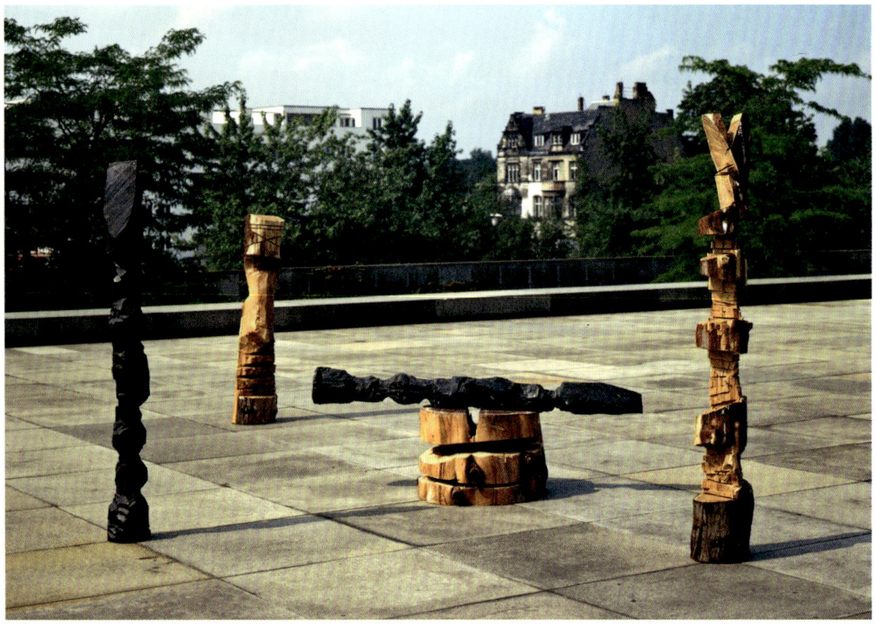

contact to the history of art, but here you get it automatically. Everything you see is in some way an influence, and you have to take a position on it.'[11] He began producing a new series of *Standart* works and also began working with a foundry to cast in bronze from wooden sculptures; at the 1984 Venice Biennale he exhibited his *Denkmal eines unbekannten ostdeutschen Soldaten* ('Monument to unknown East German soldier'; fig. 5), made from a combination of wood and bronze. Sculpture became increasingly important for him, leading to works in a variety of materials, including marble.[12]

After an extended period in Israel, which led to the print series *Reise ins gelobte Land* ('Journey in the Promised Land'), in 1983 Penck moved to the East End of London. Among other activities, he founded the Free Jazz group *Triple Tip Touch* with Frank Woolny, with whom he had previously collaborated in East Germany on the 1979 recording *Afrika Paranoia*. The group performed and made numerous Free Jazz recordings. In 1987 Penck bought a house in Killala, in the west of Ireland. Travelling became an important source of inspiration, an understandable reaction to the restrictions on movement placed by the East German State. In 1988 he began teaching at the Kunstakademie, Düsseldorf.

Penck responded to the fall of the Berlin Wall with the series of paintings *Menschen und Tiere nach der Öffnung* ('Men and Animals after the Opening'; fig. 6), and a cycle of works entitled *Das Jahr 1989*, shown at the Michael Werner Gallery in 1990. He also made a number of prints, including eight colour etchings printed by Kurt Zein in Vienna and a further six printed by Rossi in Rome, and made new editions of eight woodcuts from 1966, printed by Karl Imhof in Munich.[13] After the reunification of Germany, Penck moved back to work in a studio in Berlin. He continued to make bronze sculptures, a large touring exhibition of which was mounted in 1999. Although he was now free to move and exhibit, the habit of living and working underground persisted, and he remains an elusive figure. In 2000 he moved to Dublin to live and work, returning to the Continent some years later to live in Switzerland.

1. Andrea Schlieker, 'The Northern Darkness. An interview with A.R. Penck. 6 December 1986', in *The Northern Darkness. A.R. Penck*, exh. cat., Edinburgh (Fruitmarket Gallery), 1987, unpaginated.
2. Ibid.
3. J. Gachnang, 'Gespräch mit dem Künstler. A.R. Penck alias Ralf Winkler in Dresden', *Kunst-Nachrichten*, September 1975, p. 147.
4. Ibid.
5. See the review by Eberhard Bartke *Junge Kunst. Organ des Zentralrats der Freien Deutschen Jugend*, 5, no. 11, 1961, pp. 34–40.
6. A.R. Penck in conversation with Dieter Koepplin, 10 May 1978. Cited in: *a.r. penck*, exh. cat., Basel (Kunstmuseum), p. 20.
7. K. Lang, 'Expressionism and the two Germanys', in S. Barron and S. Eckmann (eds)., *Art of Two Germanys: Cold War Cultures*, exh. cat., Los Angeles (County Museum of Art); Nuremberg (Germanisches Nationalmuseum), 2009; Berlin (Deutsches Historisches Museum), 2010, pp. 84–100, here p. 91.
8. Cited in: L. Grisebach (ed.), *A.R. Penck*, exh. cat., Berlin (Nationalgalerie), Zürich (Kunsthaus), 1988, p. 38.
9. W. Grasskamp, interview with A.R. Penck, in *Ursprung und Vision. Neue deutsche Malerei*, exh. cat., Madrid (Palacio Velázquez); Barcelona (Centre Cultural de la Caixa de Pensions), 1984.
10. R. Dank, 'Plastisch Situation erlebbar machen', interview with A.R. Penck, *Kunstforum*, no. 86, 1986, p. 246.
11. Grisebach, op. cit. (note 8), p. 57.
12. C. Haenlein (ed.), *A.R. Penck. Skulpturen und Zeichnungen 1971–1987*, exh. cat., Hannover (Kestner-Gesellschaft), 1988.
13. A.R. Penck, *a.r. penck. Editionen 1989*, Munich, 1990.

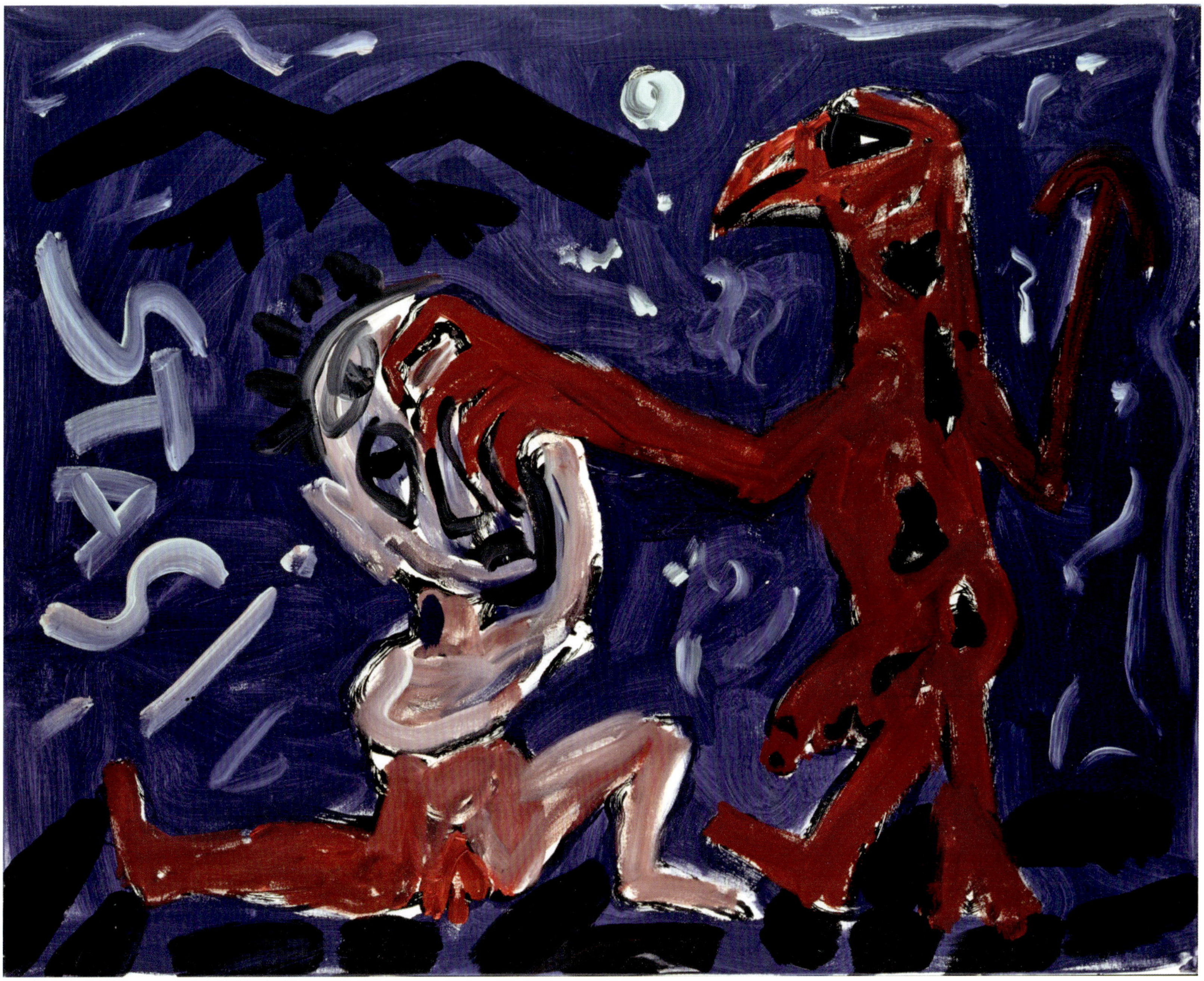

5. *Denkmal eines unbekannten ostdeutschen Soldaten* ('Monument to an unknown East German soldier'), 1984
A.R. Penck
Bronze and wood

6. *Stasi*, 1991
A.R. Penck
Overpainting, silkscreen on canvas, 1300 x 1600 mm

57
Ohne Titel, ('Untitled'), 1967
A.R. Penck
Watercolour, gold and silver paint
419 x 300 mm
Presented by Count Christian
Duerckheim to the British Museum

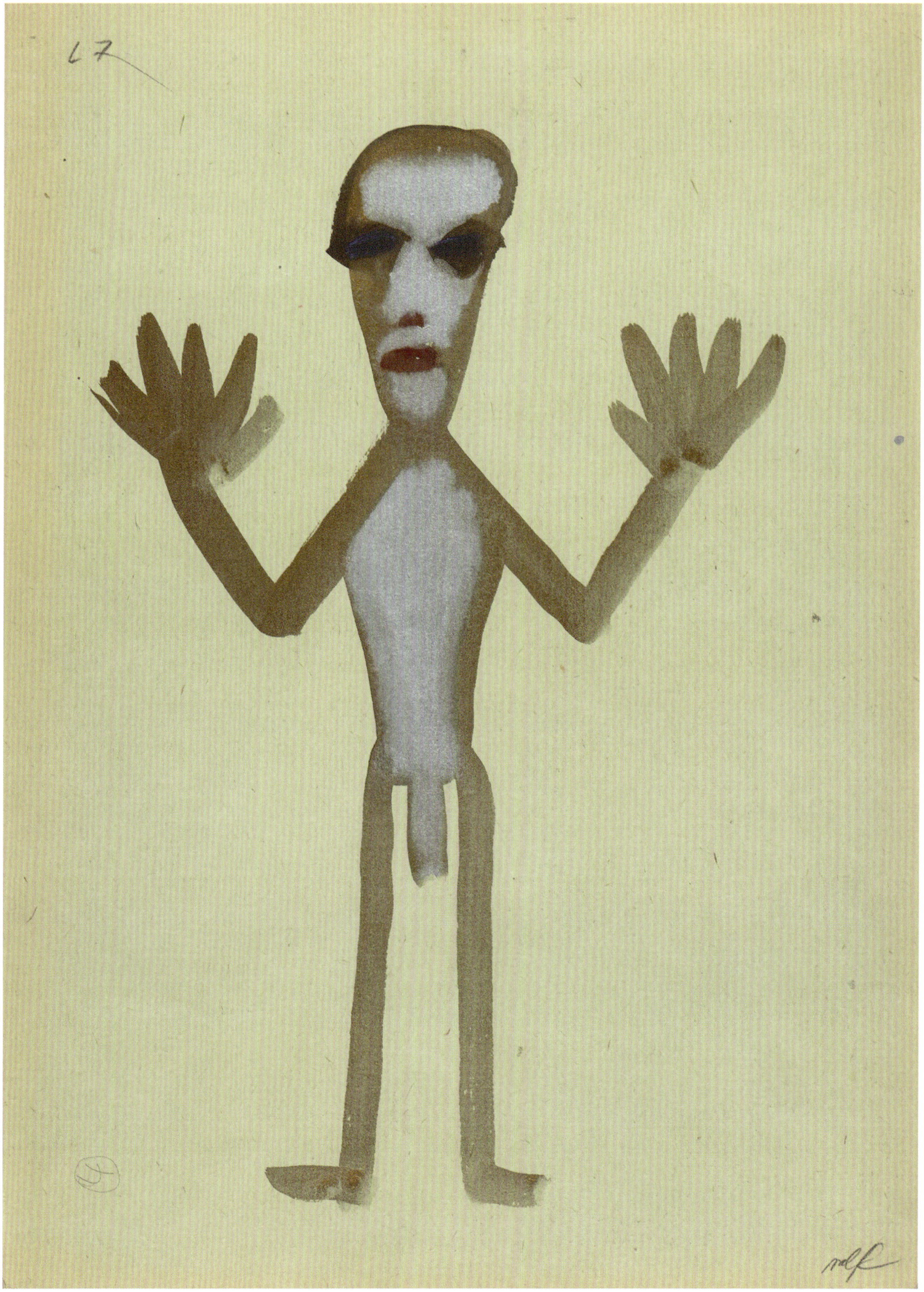

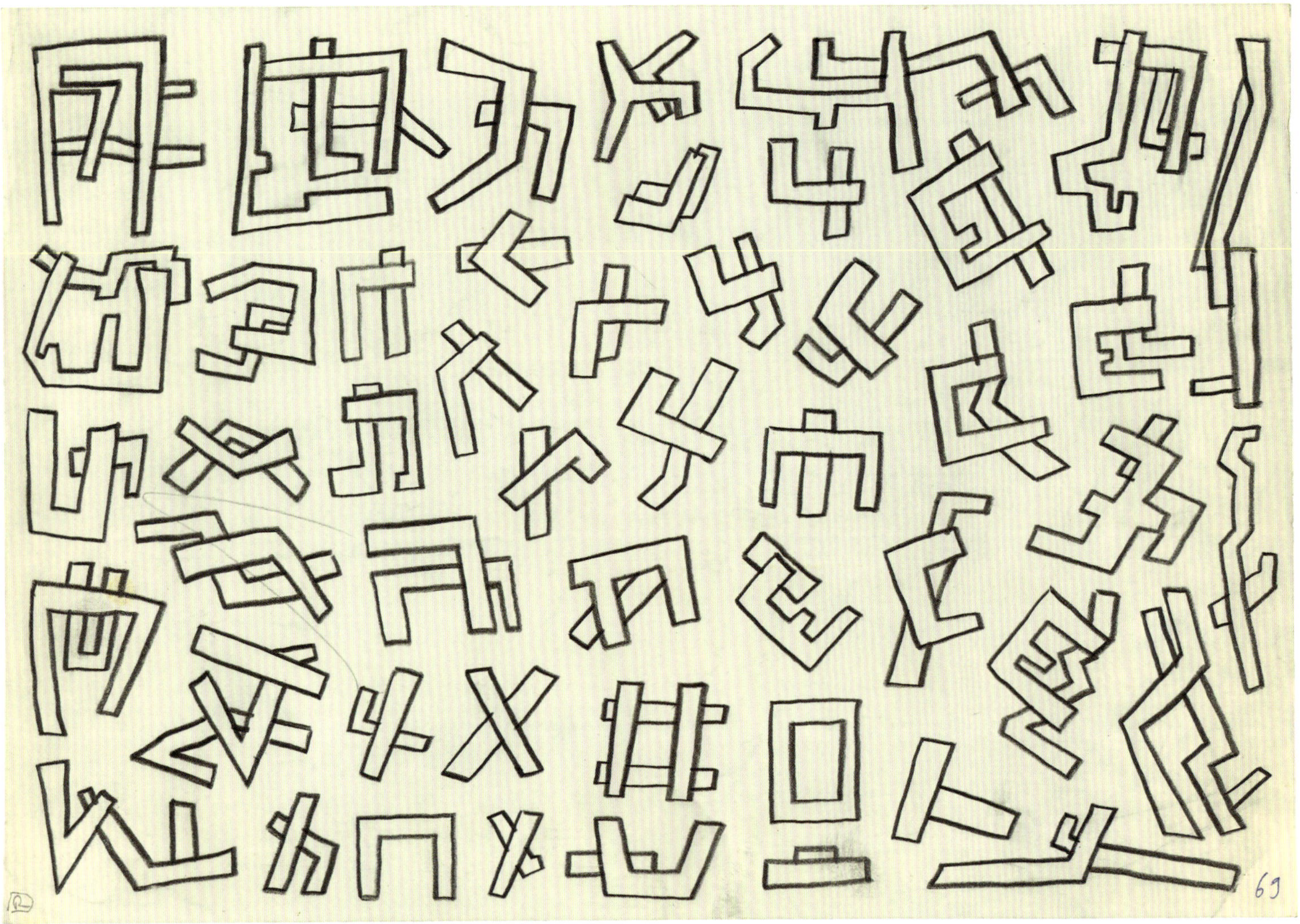

58
Ohne Titel, ('Untitled'), 1969
A.R. Penck
Graphite
297 x 420 mm
Presented by Count Christian
Duerckheim to the British Museum

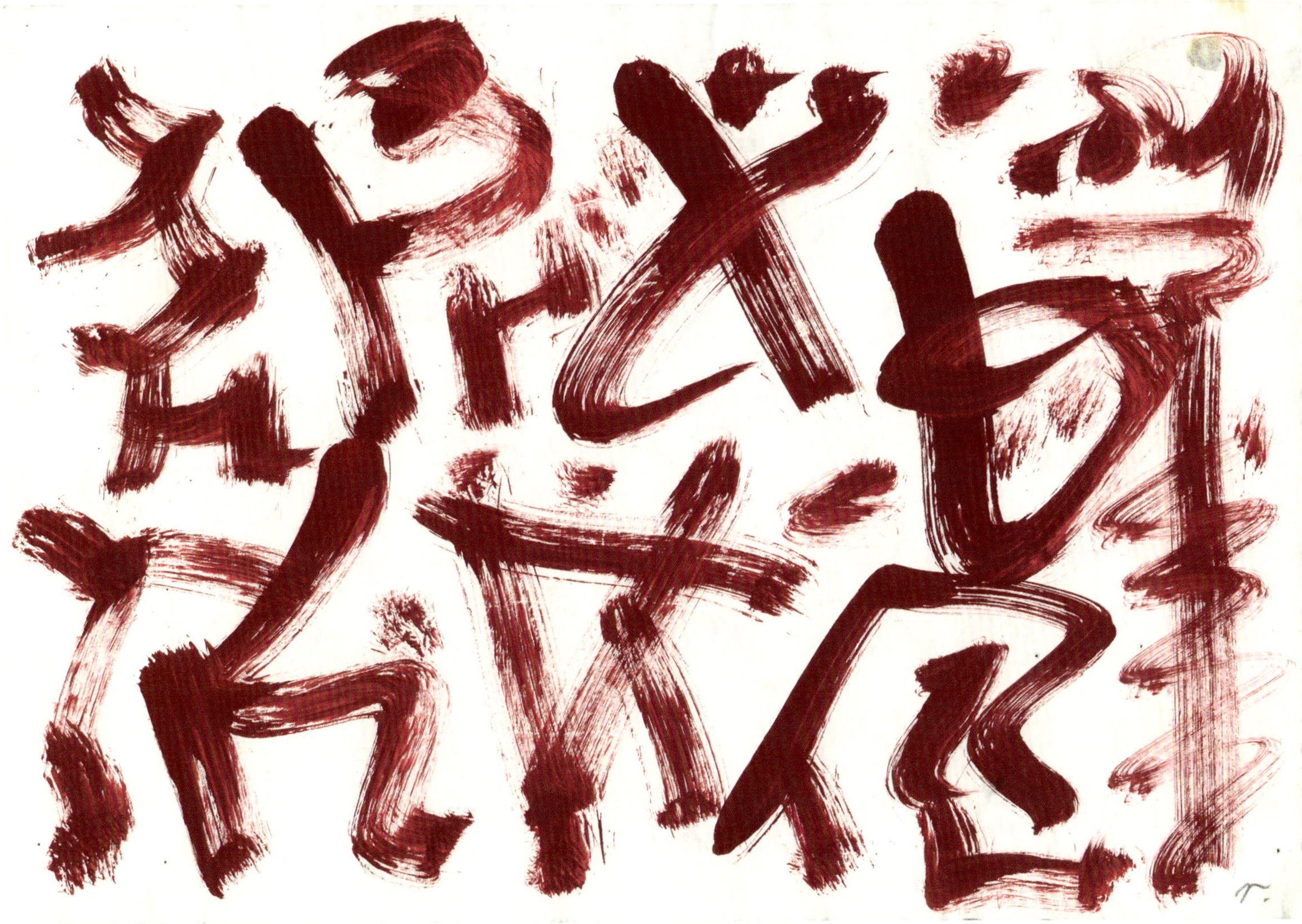

59
Ohne Titel ('Untitled'), *c.* 1981
A.R. Penck
Gouache
295 x 418 mm
Presented by Count Christian Duerckheim
to the British Museum

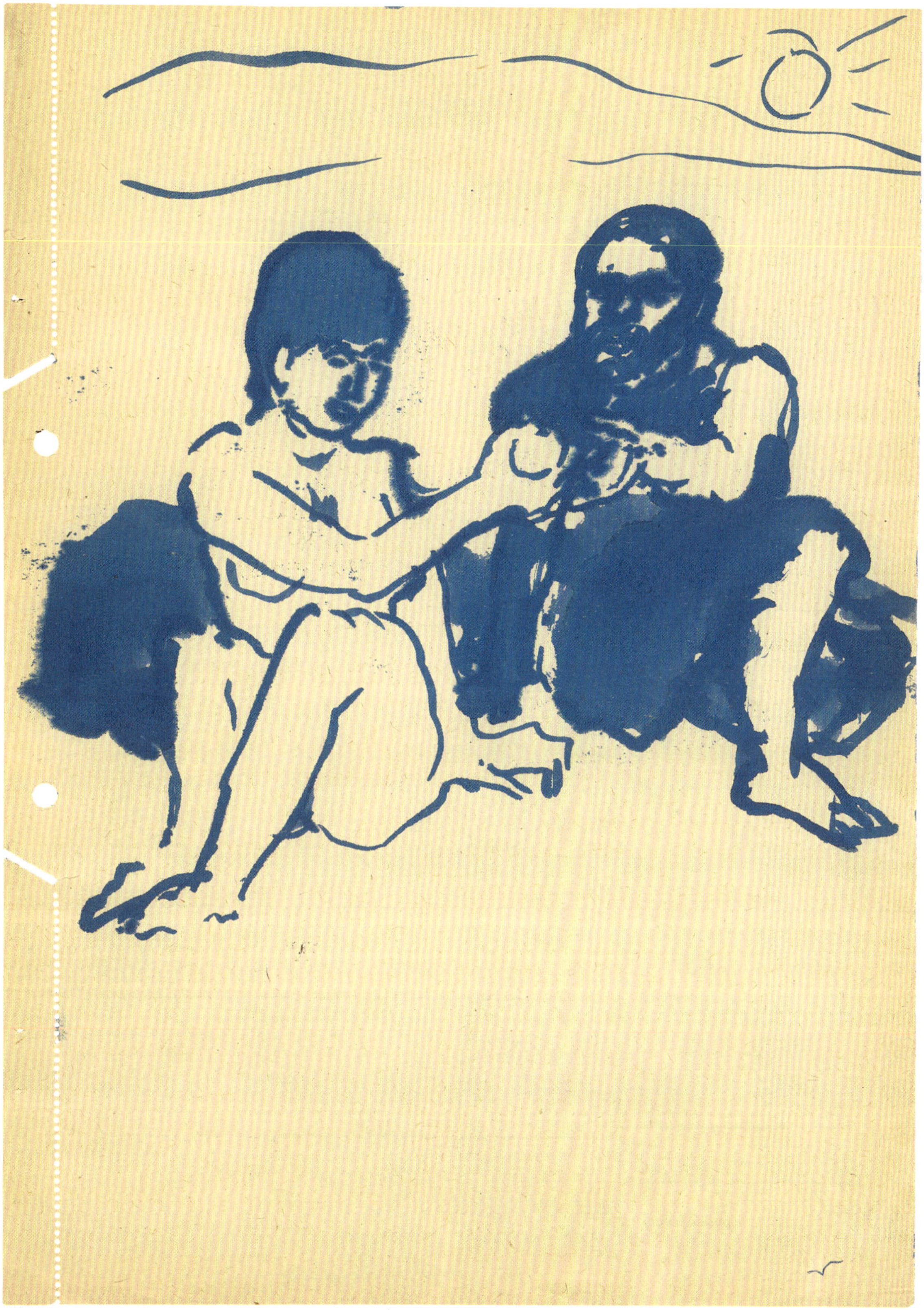

60
Ohne Titel ('Untitled'),
c. 1969
A.R. Penck
Watercolour
293 x 208 mm

61
Ohne Titel ('Untitled'),
c. 1969
A.R. Penck
Watercolour
293 x 208 mm

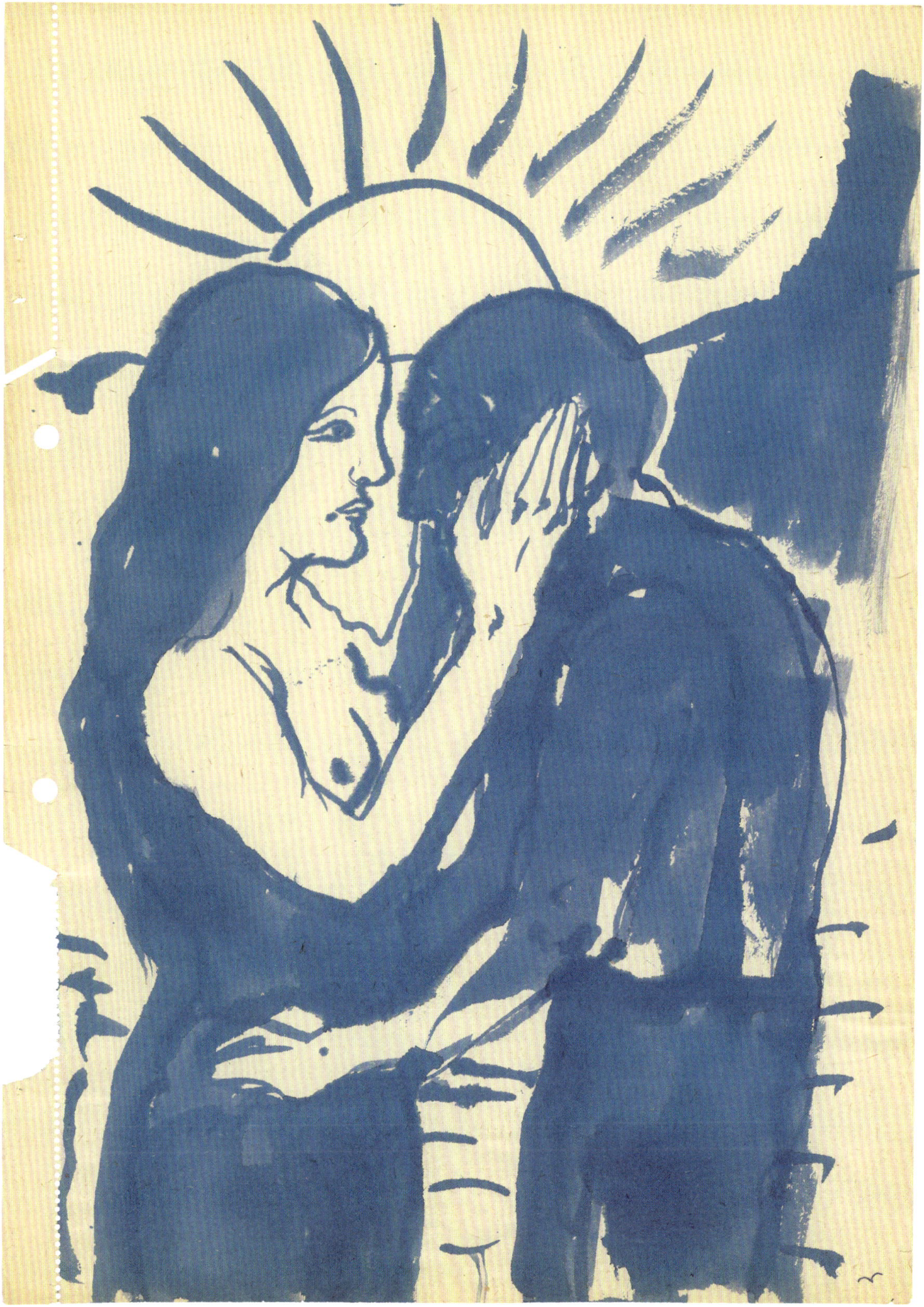

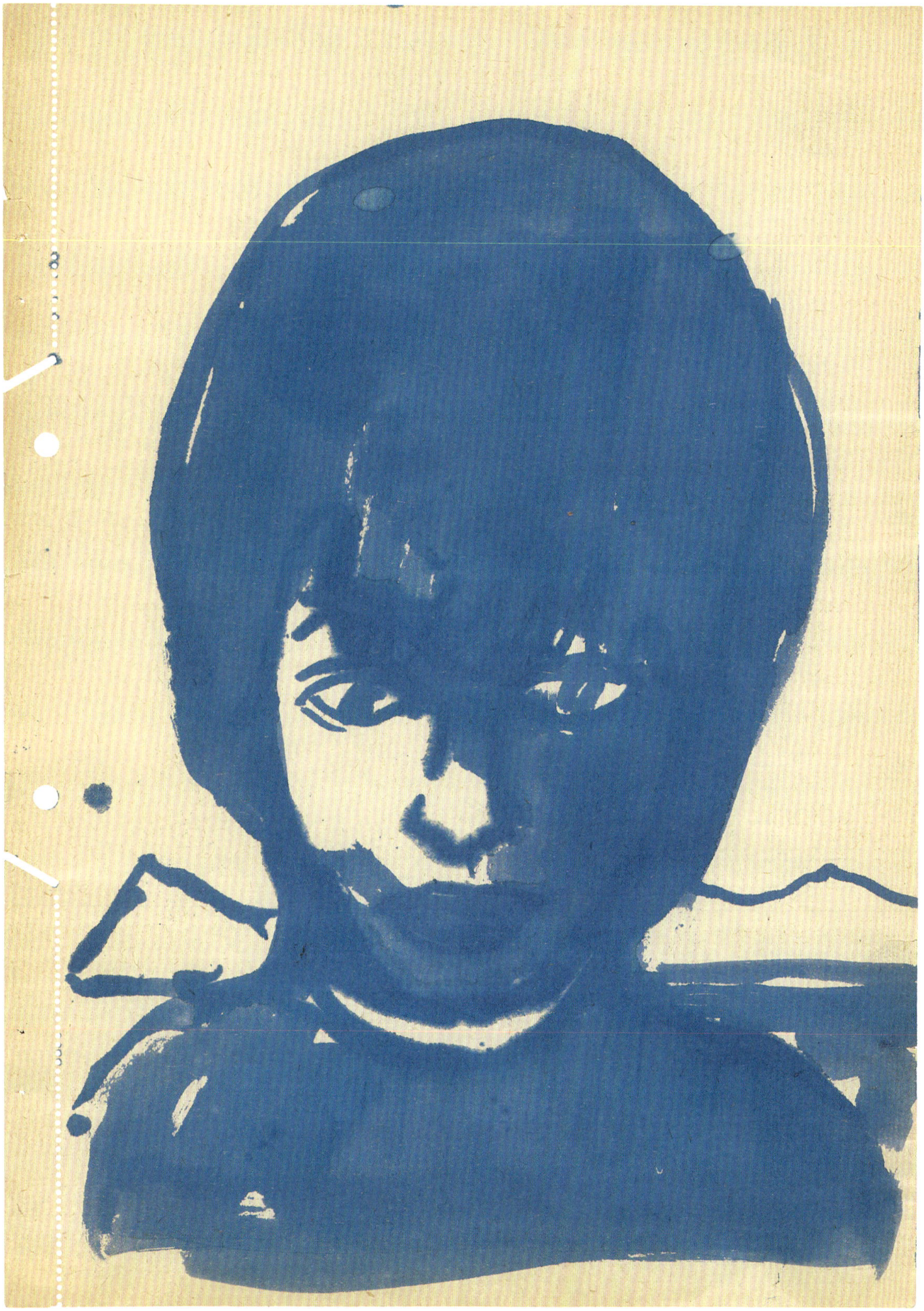

62
Ohne Titel ('Untitled'),
c. 1969
A.R. Penck
Watercolour
293 x 208 mm

63
Ohne Titel ('Untitled'),
c. 1969
A.R. Penck
Watercolour
293 x 208 mm

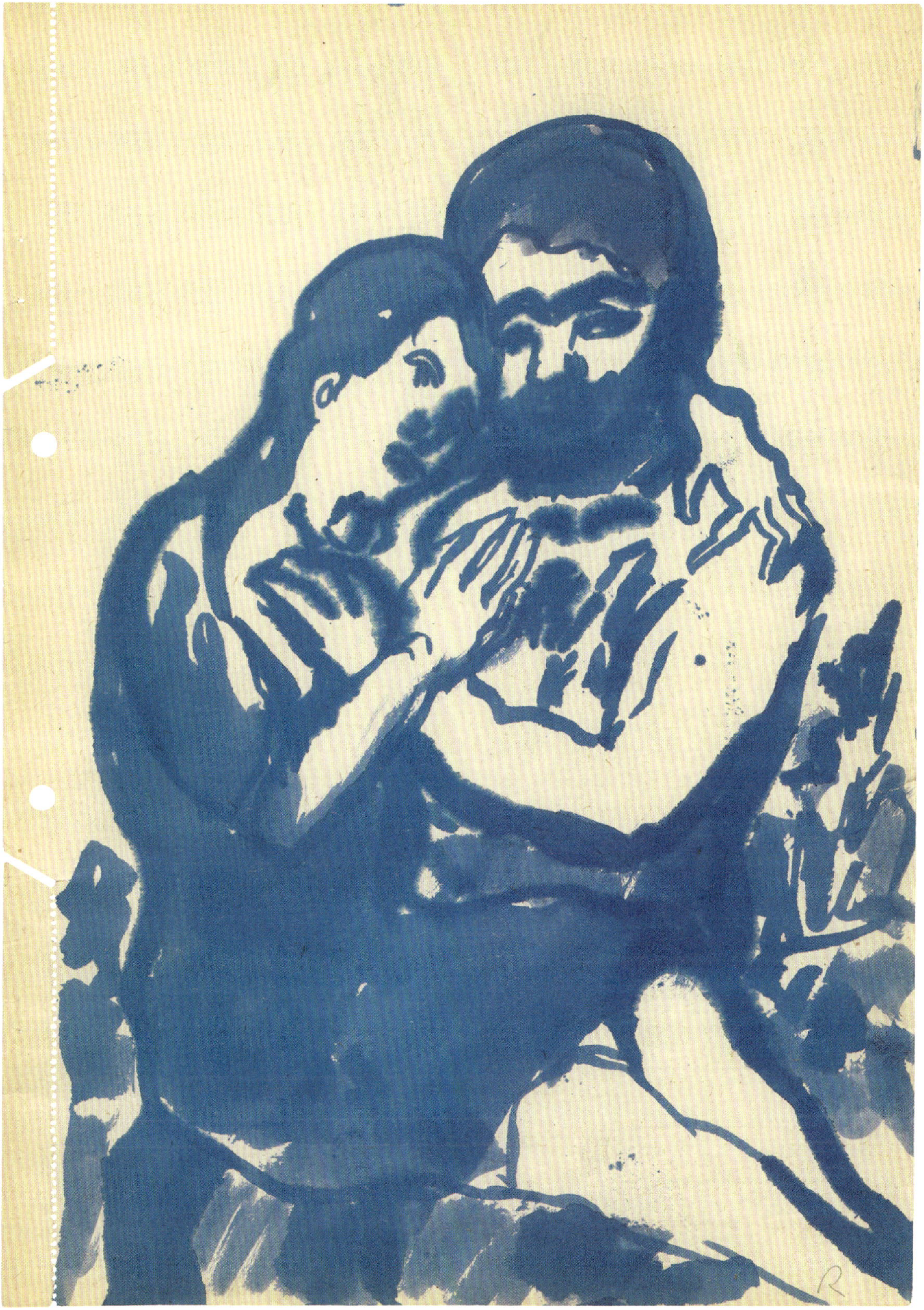

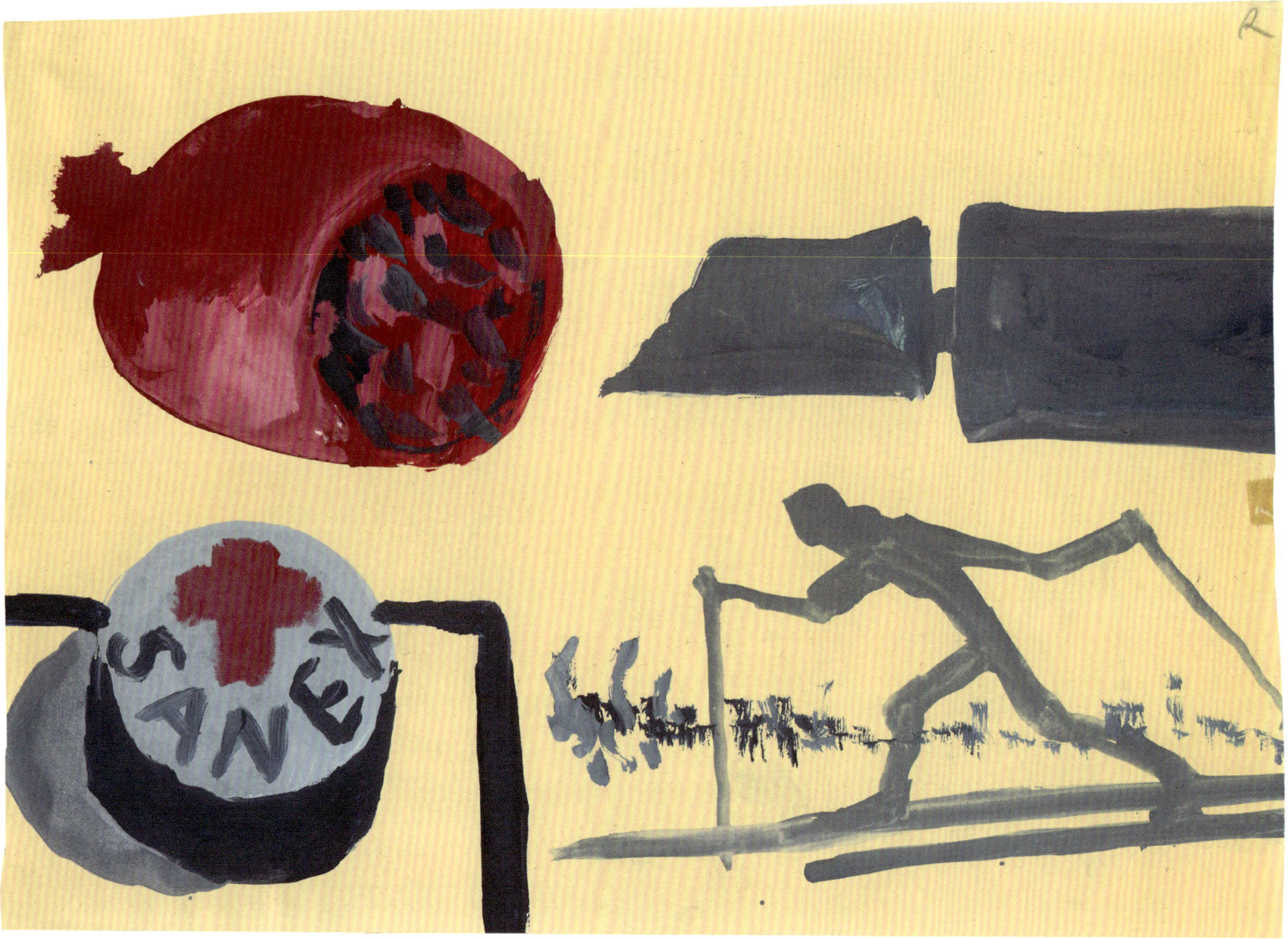

64
Ohne Titel (Sanex), ('Untitled (Sanex)'), *c.* 1975
A.R. Penck
Gouache
205 x 280 mm

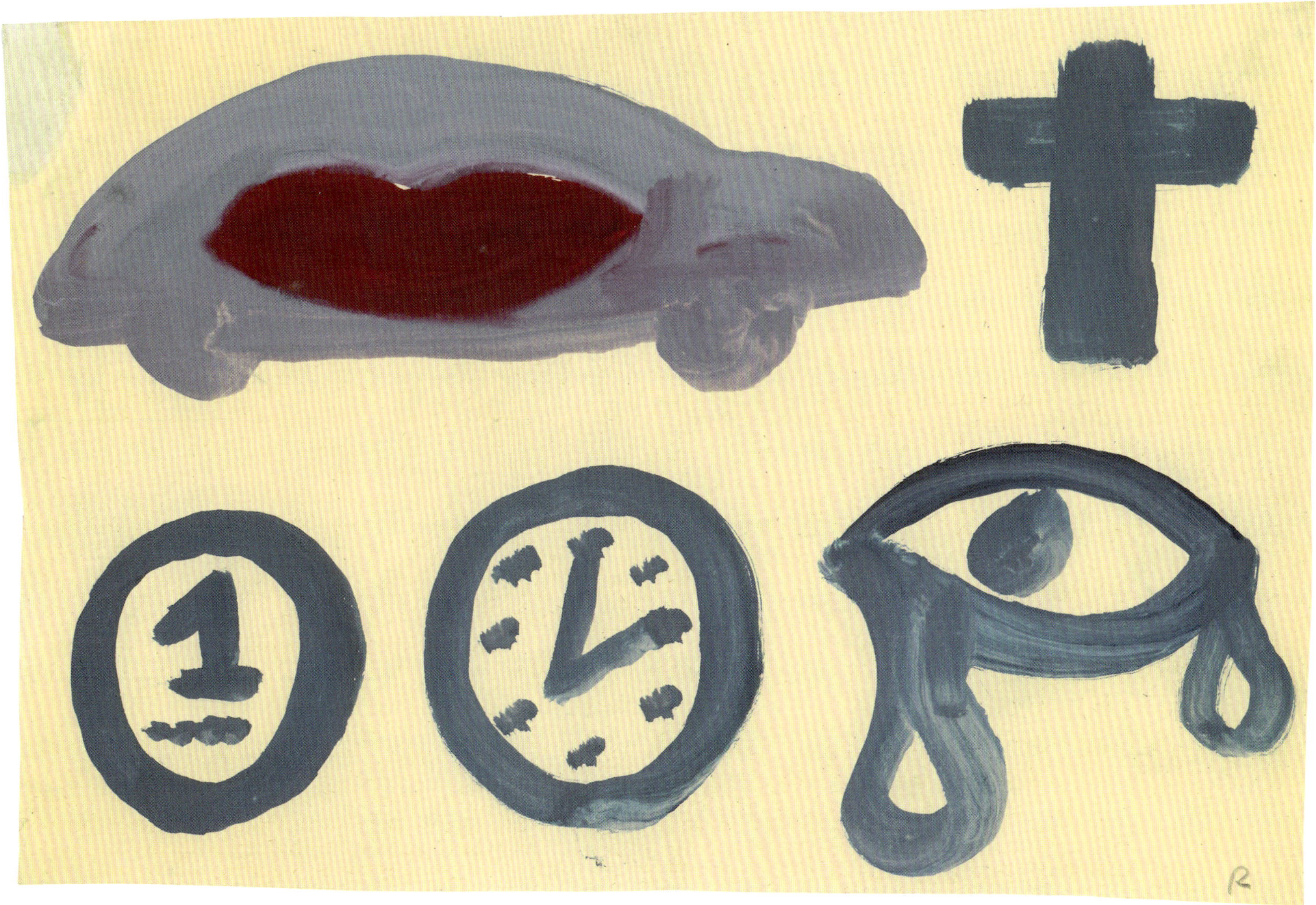

65
Ohne Titel, ('Untitled'), *c.* 1975
A.R. Penck
Gouache
194 x 280 mm

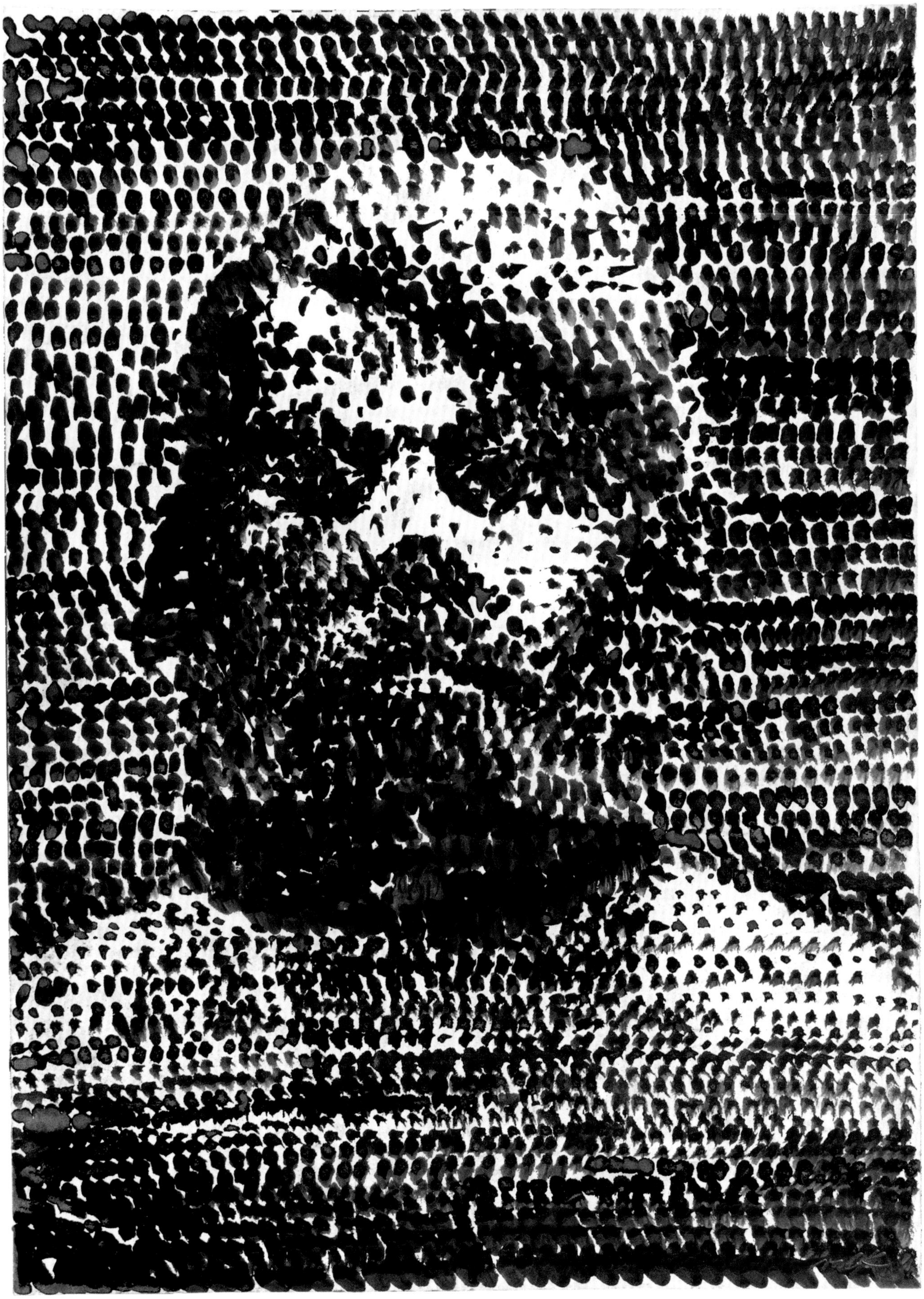

66
Ohne Titel (Selbtsportät), ('Untitled (Self-portrait)'), 1975
A.R. Penck
Grey and black ink wash
592 x 420 mm
Presented by Count Christian Duerckheim to the British Museum

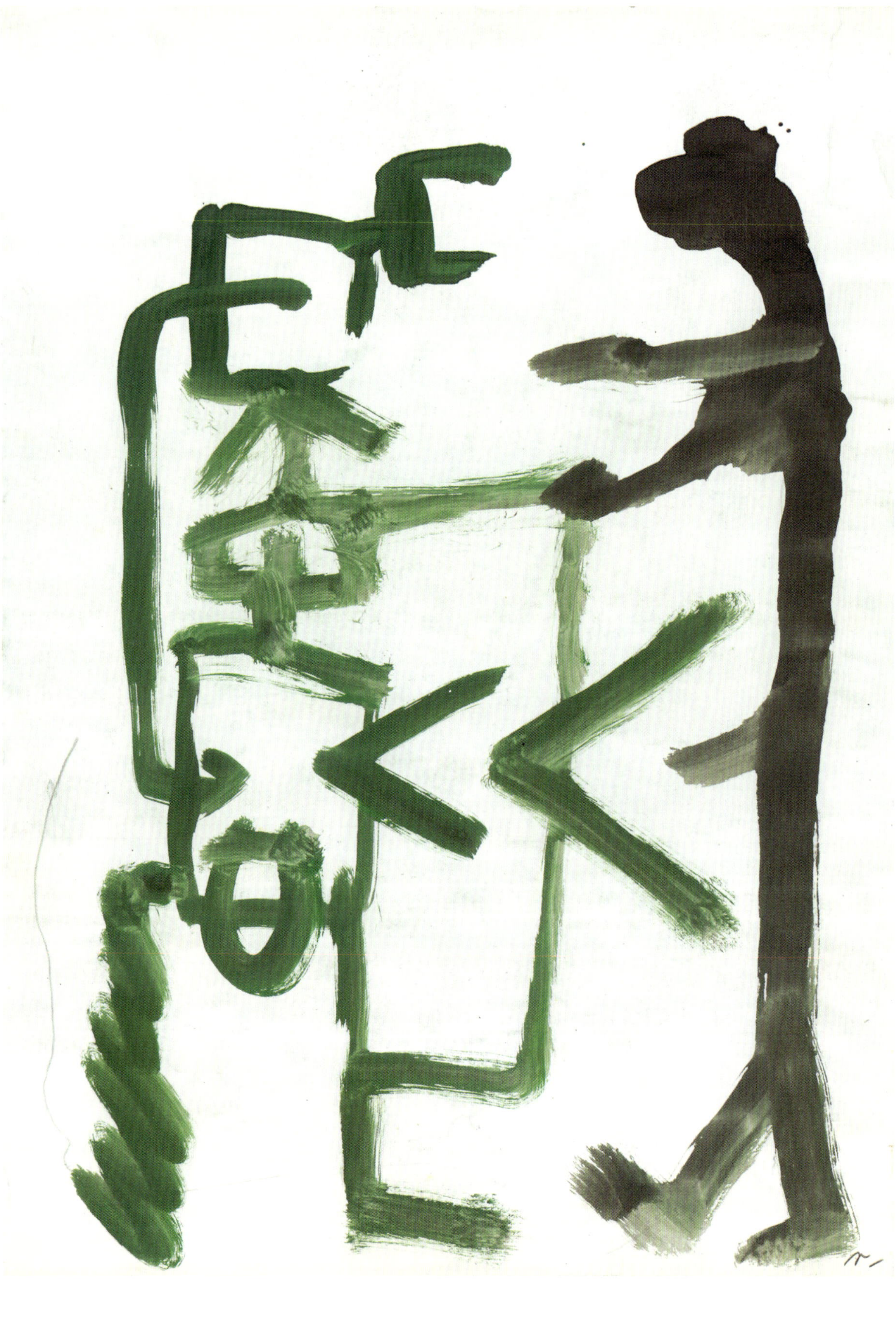

67
Ohne Titel ('Untitled'), *c.* 1982
A.R. Penck
Gouache and pencil
592 x 419 mm
Presented by Count Christian Duerckheim to the British Museum

68
Nachtvision ('Night Vision'), from the portfolio *Erste Konzentration I*, 1982
A.R. Penck
Woodcut
895 x 695 mm

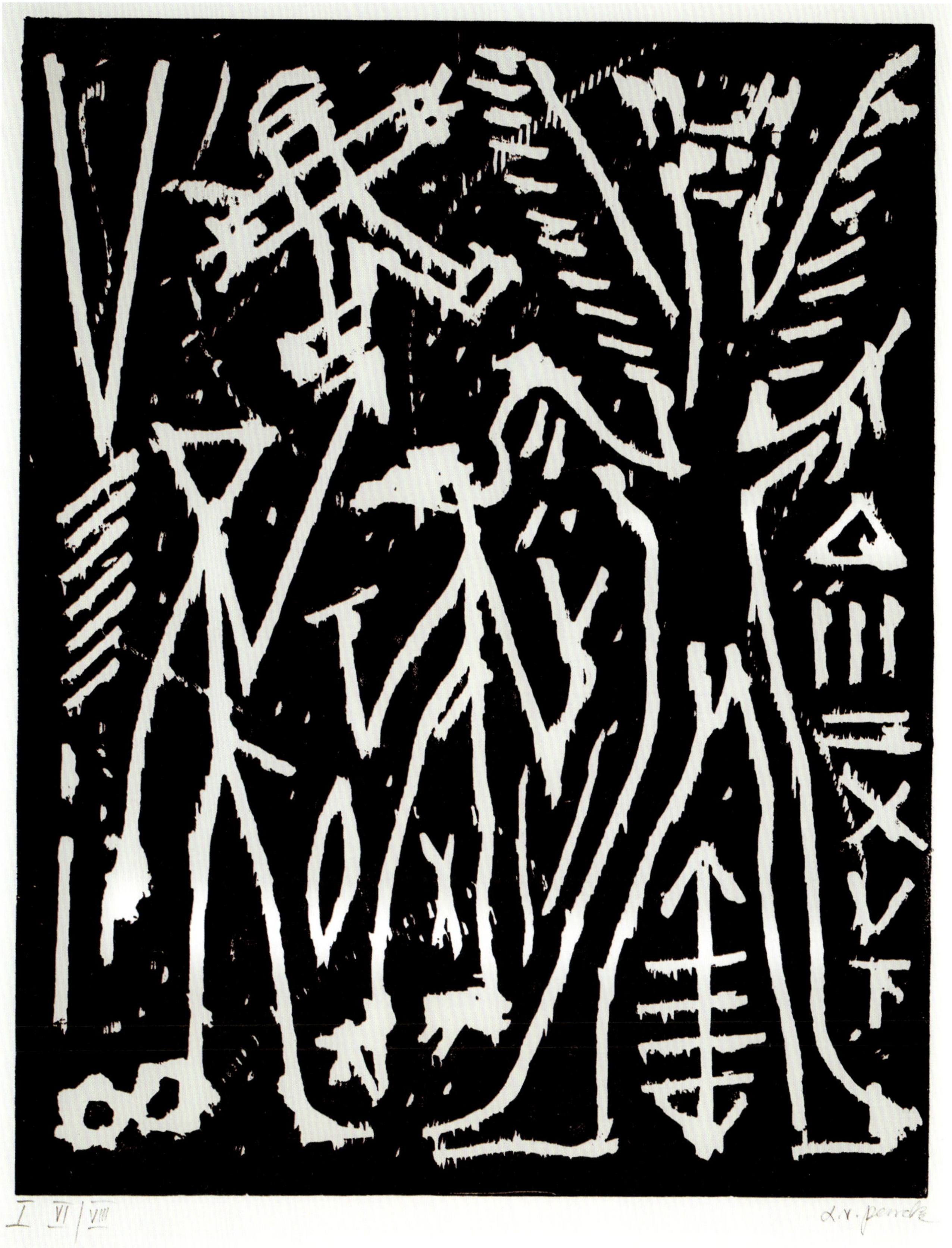

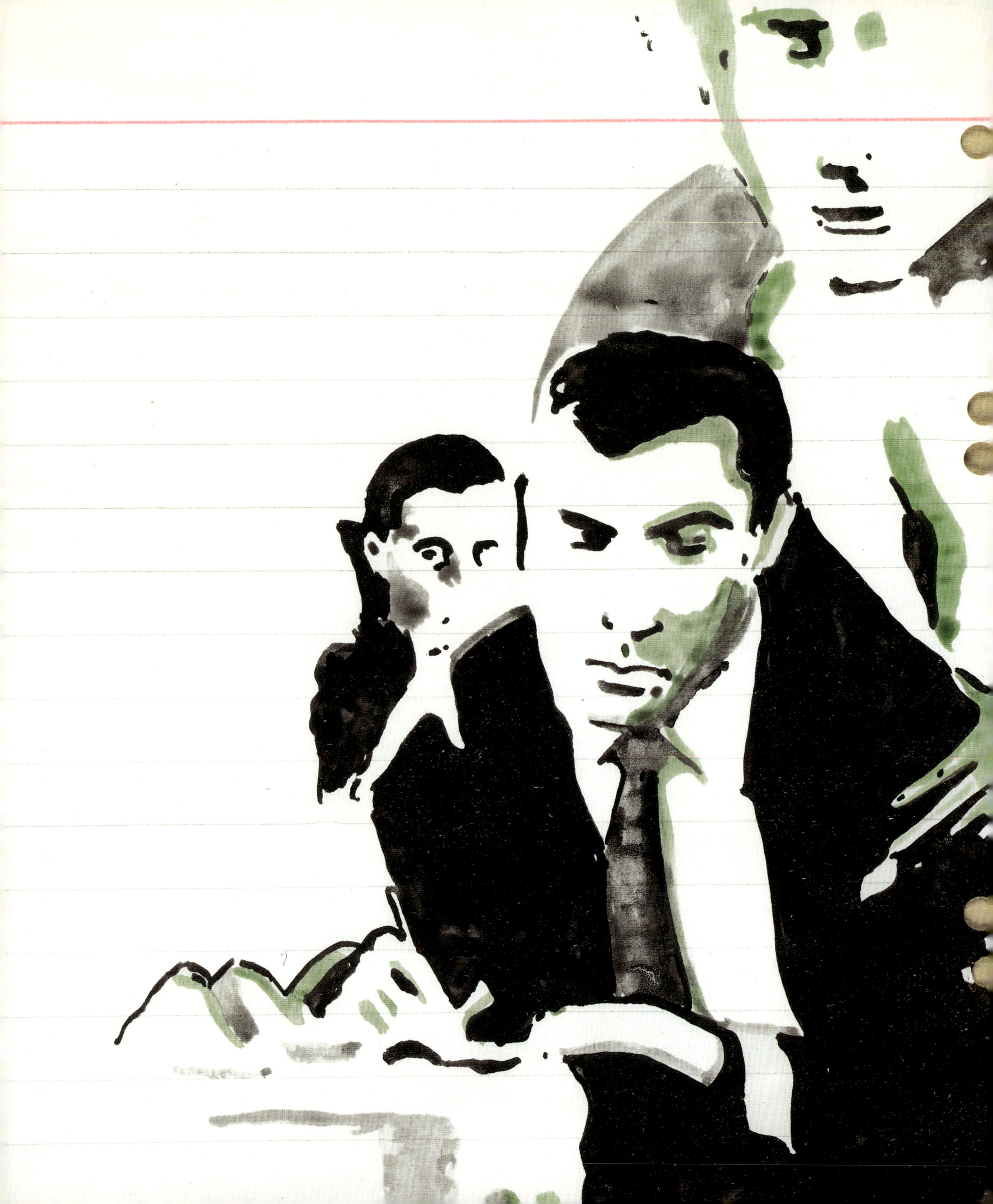

Sigmar Polke

Sigmar Polke was one of the most entertaining yet elusive artists of his generation in Germany. His works range from satires on consumerism in the 1960s, to large abstract paintings exploring a range of themes including alchemy and politics, made from the 1980s until his death in 2010.

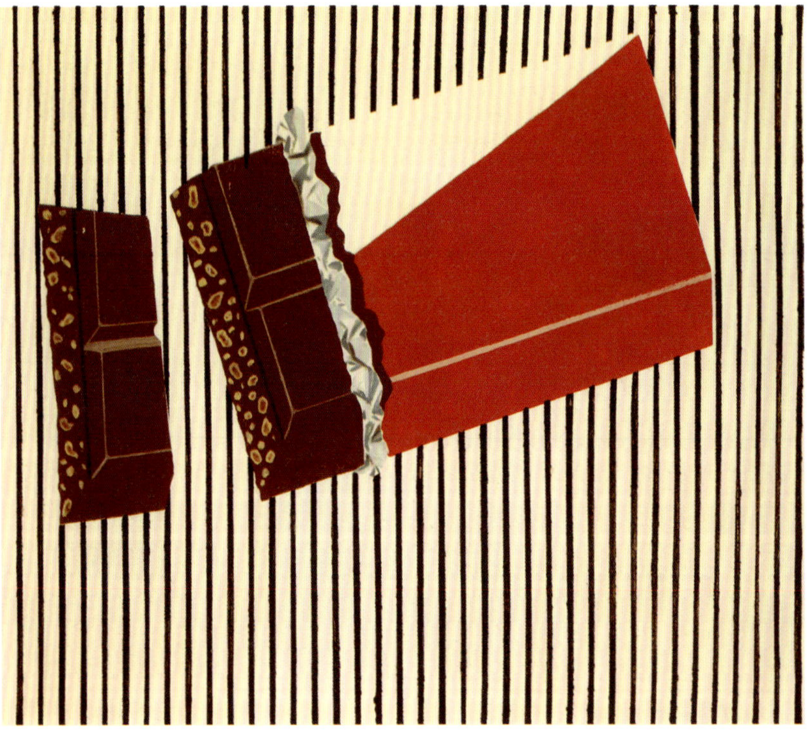

1. *Schokoladenbild* ('Chocolate Painting'), 1964
Sigmar Polke
Lacquer on canvas, 900 x 1000 mm
Private collection

2. *Freundinnen I* ('Girl Friends I'), 1967
Sigmar Polke
Lithograph, 464 x 587 mm
Tate, London

Polke was born in 1941 in the German town of Oels, in Lower Silesia (now Oleśnica, Poland). At the end of the Second World War the town suffered heavy damage with the advance of the Red Army and the German population was expelled. With his parents and seven siblings, Polke went first to Thuringia in the Soviet Zone of Occupation, then to Dingelstädt. In 1953 the family migrated via West Berlin to the West German city of Düsseldorf.

Polke's earliest artistic training was as an apprentice to a glass-painter in Düsseldorf, at the age of eighteen. The translucent, glowing colours and layers of imagery of his later work are often traced to this formative experience. In 1961 Polke enrolled at the Kunstakademie, Düsseldorf, to study under Gerhard Hoehme (1920–89) and Karl Otto Götz (b. 1914); Hoehme's abstract paintings were an important early influence.

Equally significant was his meeting with fellow students Gerhard Richter and Konrad Lueg, both of whom were to become important collaborators, most notoriously on the 1963 exhibition *Kapitalistischer Realismus* ('Capitalist Realism'), including works by Polke, Lueg, Richter and Manfred Kuttner (1937–2007).

Satire was an essential element in the attack that Polke and his fellow students, in particular Richter, were mounting on contemporary trends in painting, especially the consensus surrounding abstract painting as the 'official' style of the free West. The example of conceptual and Fluxus artists, including John Cage (1912–92) and Nam June Paik (1932–2006), was important. Equally inspiring was the advent of American Pop Art, with its emphasis on the commercial language of advertising and

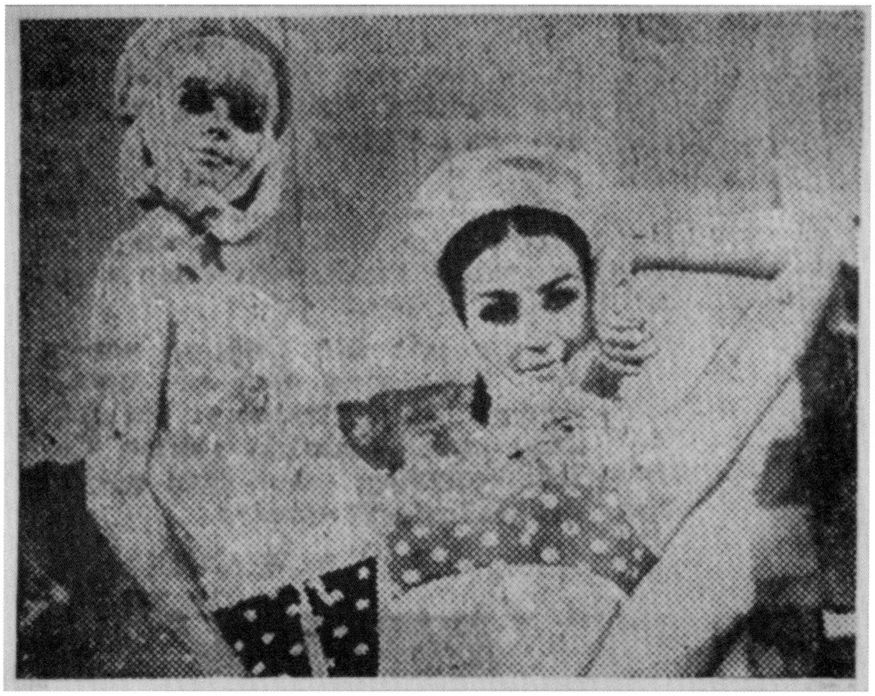

popular culture as a subject for 'high' art. Polke's early paintings show the influence of Pop, but are also marked by his interest in banal subject matter: the 1964 painting *Schokoladenbild* ('Chocolate Painting'; fig. 1), an awkwardly rendered chocolate bar against a striped background, evokes the crude and tentative advertising imagery of the 1950s. Polke's drawings from this time, made while still a student at the Kunstakademie, go even further in their deliberately artless renderings of banal, often humorous, subject matter, such as the ballpoint pen drawing *Ohne Titel* ('Untitled'; 1964), showing a man running in fear from a giant pair of vicious pliers (cat. 69). Polke's satire was also directed towards the official art of East Germany, most notably in his painting *Höhere Wesen befahlen: rechte obere Ecke schwarz malen!* ('The Higher Powers Command: Paint the Right Upper Corner Black!'; 1969), a blank canvas inscribed with the title, the right upper corner painted black.

Polke, like Richter, was fascinated by the possibility of using printed photographic ephemera as a source for painting. The *Rasterbilder* ('Screened Paintings'), begun in 1963, took the dot patterns of enlarged commercial photographic material as their starting point. But whereas Lichtenstein's Ben-Day dots from comic book illustrations were used to clarify subject matter, Polke's 'rasters' obscure and diffuse the image, making it harder to read. At the same time, Polke began using patterned fabric instead of canvas as a support, incorporating the cheap commercial patterns as part of the painting, gently parodying consumer tastes but also the elevation of 'ordinary' materials into art in the early twentieth-century, for example in cubist collage, or in the work of Kurt Schwitters (1887–1948). His appropriation of images from historical art was always underlined by satire, but never reduced to a simple joke. Two paintings from 1968, *Akt mit Geige* ('Nude with Violin') and *Moderne Kunst* ('Modern Art'), both appear as enlarged reproductions from a book of meaningless abstract marks; their ironic titles serve as captions within the paintings.

Polke's first print was an offset lithograph titled *Freundinnen I* ('Girl Friends I'; fig. 2), published in 1967 by Galerie h, Hannover. It was based on a found photograph of two girls posing, previously reproduced in a painting (1965) of the same title. Many of Polke's early prints were made using the process of offset lithography, then more common in commercial printing than for producing fine art. Polke also produced a small number of editioned objects, most famously the 1969 work *Apparat, mit dem eine Kartoffel eine andere umkreisen kann* ('Apparatus, Whereby One Potato Can Orbit Another'), a mechanical device corresponding accurately to the descriptive title, produced by Edition Tangente, run by Klaus Staeck in an edition of thirty. He subsequently published most of his editions with the Heidelberg print publisher and artist Klaus Staeck.

In the early 1970s, Polke moved to Gaspelshof, a large house in the town of Willich, where he kept an open studio. He embarked on collaborations, in particular with the artist Achim

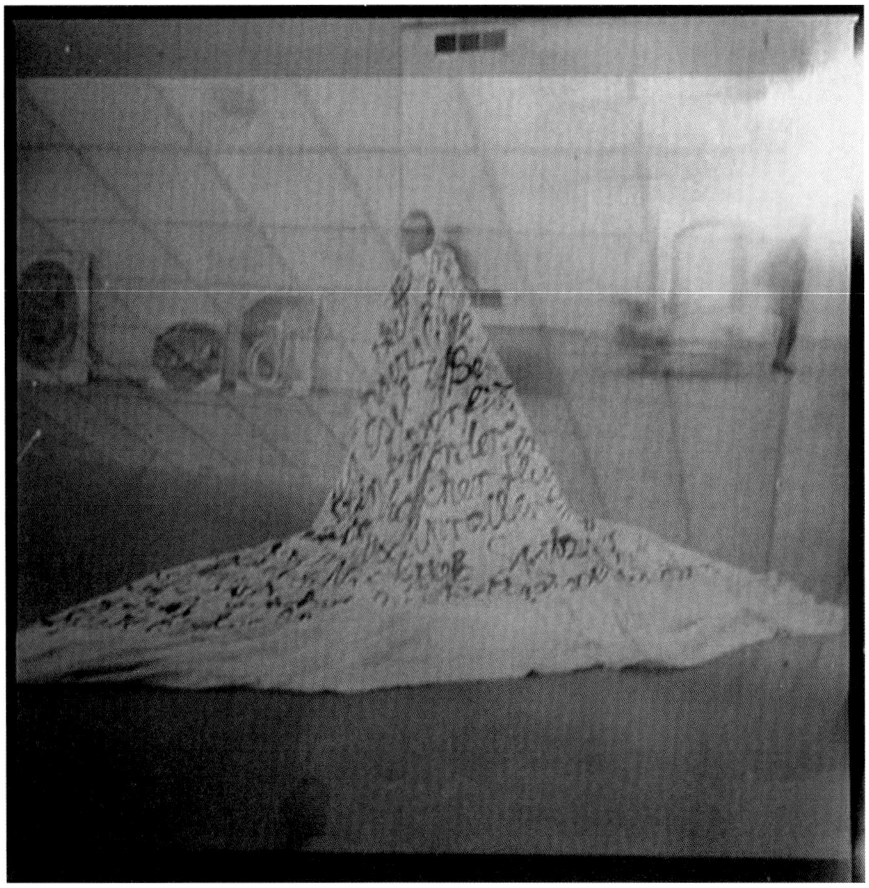

3. Sigmar Polke wearing the *Schimpftuch,* 1976

4. *Druckfehler (Rasterbild)*, 1986
Sigmar Polke
Oil and acrylic on printed fabric,
1270 x 1510 mm
Galerie Neue Meister, Staatliche Kunstsammlungen, Dresden

5. *The Illusionist (Lens Painting)*, 2007
Sigmar Polke
Mixed media on fabric,
2200 x 3000 mm

Duchow (1948–93) – their collaborative works were the subject of exhibitions at the Kunsthalle, Kiel, in 1975, and at the Kunstverein, Kassel, in 1977. Polke also took part in *Documenta 5* held in Kassel in 1972. A further tripartite exhibition, which had been organized by the German art historian Benjamin Buchloh, travelled to Tübingen, Düsseldorf and Eindhoven in 1976; it was marked by controversy over the provocative display at Düsseldorf, where paintings on the gallery floor were arranged in the form of a swastika. Much of the 1970s was, however, spent travelling, gathering material, and working predominantly in film and photography, for example on visits to Afghanistan and Pakistan (1974), and São Paulo (1975), where he took part in the thirteenth São Paulo Bienal. His photographs are marked by a range of experimentation with unconventional darkroom techniques, over- and under-exposure, and deliberate misuse of photographic developing chemicals to create interrupted and degraded images (fig. 3).

In 1977 Polke was appointed Professor at the Hochschule für Bildende Künste in Hamburg, a post he held for over two decades. His pupils included Martin Kippenberger (1953–97), Albert Oehlen (b. 1954), Marcus Oehlen (b. 1956) and Georg Herold (b. 1947), all of whom shared his anarchic and experimental spirit.

From 1980 to 1981, Polke travelled in South-East Asia, Papua New Guinea and Australia, using the trip to move away from his earlier work and to gather new material. On his return to Germany he began to paint in a range of unconventional media, including lacquers and resins, and volatile types of paint, for example hydro-sensitive paint that changed colour according to humidity. The latter featured in a wall painting, *Athanor*, in the German Pavilion, part of Polke's contribution to the 1986 Venice Biennale. For his series *The Spirits that Lend Strength are Visible* (1988), made for the Museum of Modern Art in San Francisco, Polke used a different metal in each of the five paintings: powdered tellurium, meteorite dust, nickel, silver nitrate and silver leaf, combined with resin to create abstract images of translucent layers. Alchemy was a frequent theme in his work, leading to a reflection on the question of materials and value, and the transformative power of art.

During the 1990s representational elements returned to Polke's painting and were combined with his 'raster' patterns to create recognizable, often political, imagery with a seriousness

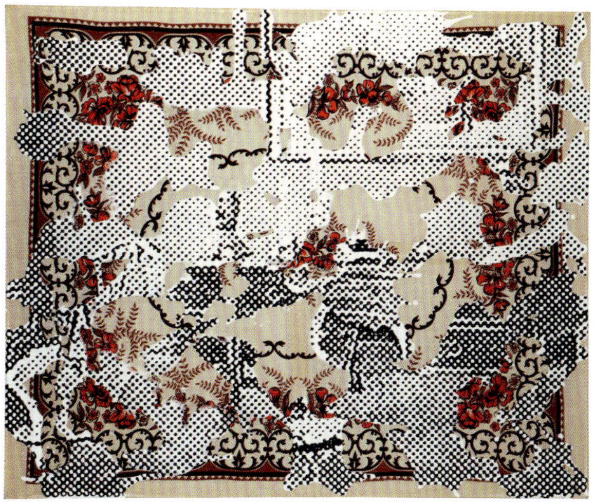

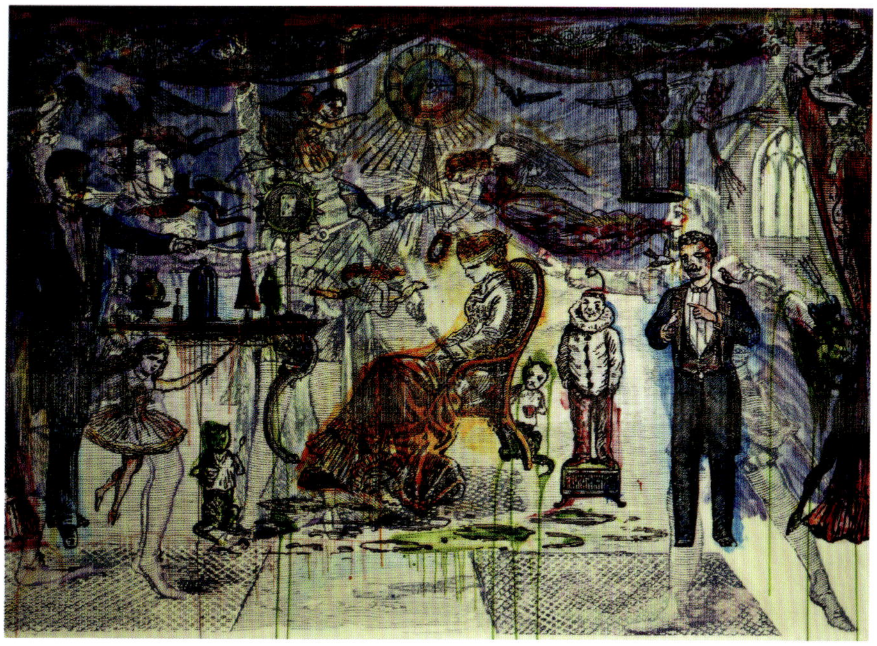

absent from his earlier work. The 1994 painting *Flüchtlingslager* ('Refugee Camp') is based on an image of one of the transit camps in which Polke himself might have stayed as a child. The technique of painting with resin and lacquer on a translucent fabric, showing the wooden support behind, became a defining feature of his work. He remained a tireless innovator throughout his career, ever expanding his range of imagery and repertoire of techniques. He began a series of paintings known as *Druckfehler* ('Printing Mistakes'; fig. 4), based on printing errors in newspapers, enlarged and painted onto a polyester surface, then covered with layers of resin. These followed an earlier series of works made with a photocopier, producing 'disrupted' images by moving the original while being copied, a technique he had first used in the late 1970s. In the early 2000s he continued work on a series of 'Machine Paintings', created by digitally manipulating images and printing them on large sheets of fabric. He also began a series of 'Lens Paintings', based in part on images from the 1685 publication *Oculus Artificialis Teledioptricus Telescopium*, by Johann Zahn, an illustrated treatise on optical devices, in particular the camera obscura, and including Zahn's speculations on the possibility of a portable camera. The largest and most complex of these works, *The Illusionist* (*Lens Painting*; fig. 5), of 2007, shows a range of images from occult and scientific experiments, layering images taken from eighteenth- and nineteenth-century sources. The *Lens Paintings* series remained unfinished at the time of Polke's death.

Polke cultivated an elusive persona, satirical in the spirit of the avant-garde, yet seemingly impossible to classify. A gnomic text by the psychologist and writer on art Friedrich Wolfram Heubach, entitled 'Sigmar Polke. Early influences, later Consequences or: How the Monkey Got Into My Business and Other Icono-biographical Questions', first published in 1976, argues that the name 'Polke' derived from an Egyptian drawing of a man standing under a tree.[1] His work, like this account of his life, appears in many lights as an elaborate, yet profound, and consummately crafted joke. Polke died in June 2010, from cancer.

1. Originally published in: B.H.D. Buchloh (ed.), *Sigmar Polke. Bilder, Tücher, Objekte. Werkauswahl 1962–1971*, exh. cat., Tübingen (Kunsthalle); Düsseldorf (Kunsthalle); Eindhoven (Stedelijk van Abbe-Museum), 1976, pp. 127–34. Reprinted in: *Sigmar Polke: The Three Lies of Painting*, exh. cat., Bonn (Kunst- und Ausstellungshalle der Bundesrepublik Deutschland); Berlin (Hamburger Bahnhof), 1997, pp. 285–94.

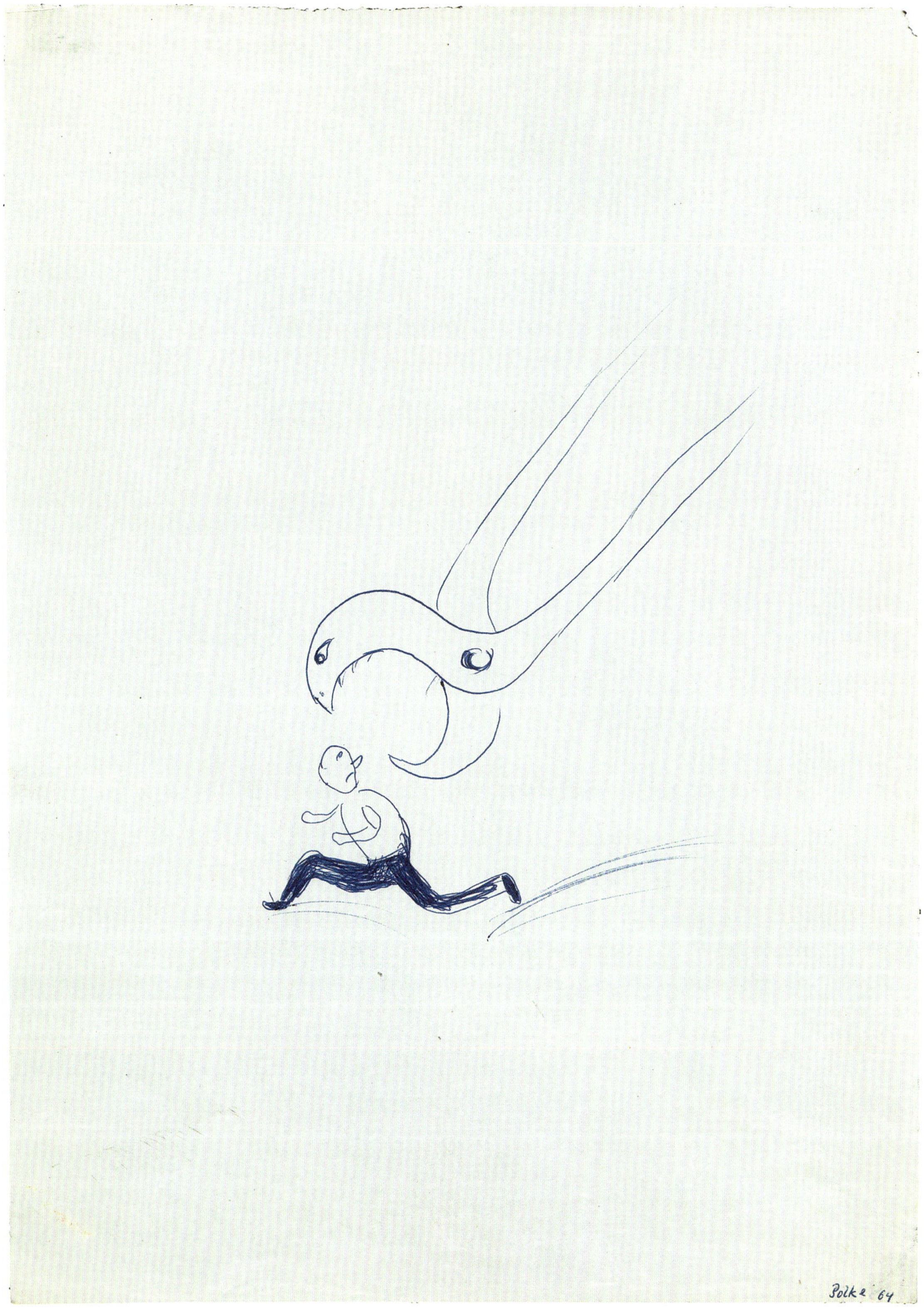

69
Ohne Titel ('Untitled'), 1964
Sigmar Polke
Blue ballpoint pen
295 x 209 mm

70
Empedokles ist in den Berg
('Empedocles is in the Mountain'),
c. 1966
Sigmar Polke
Watercolour
296 x 210 mm

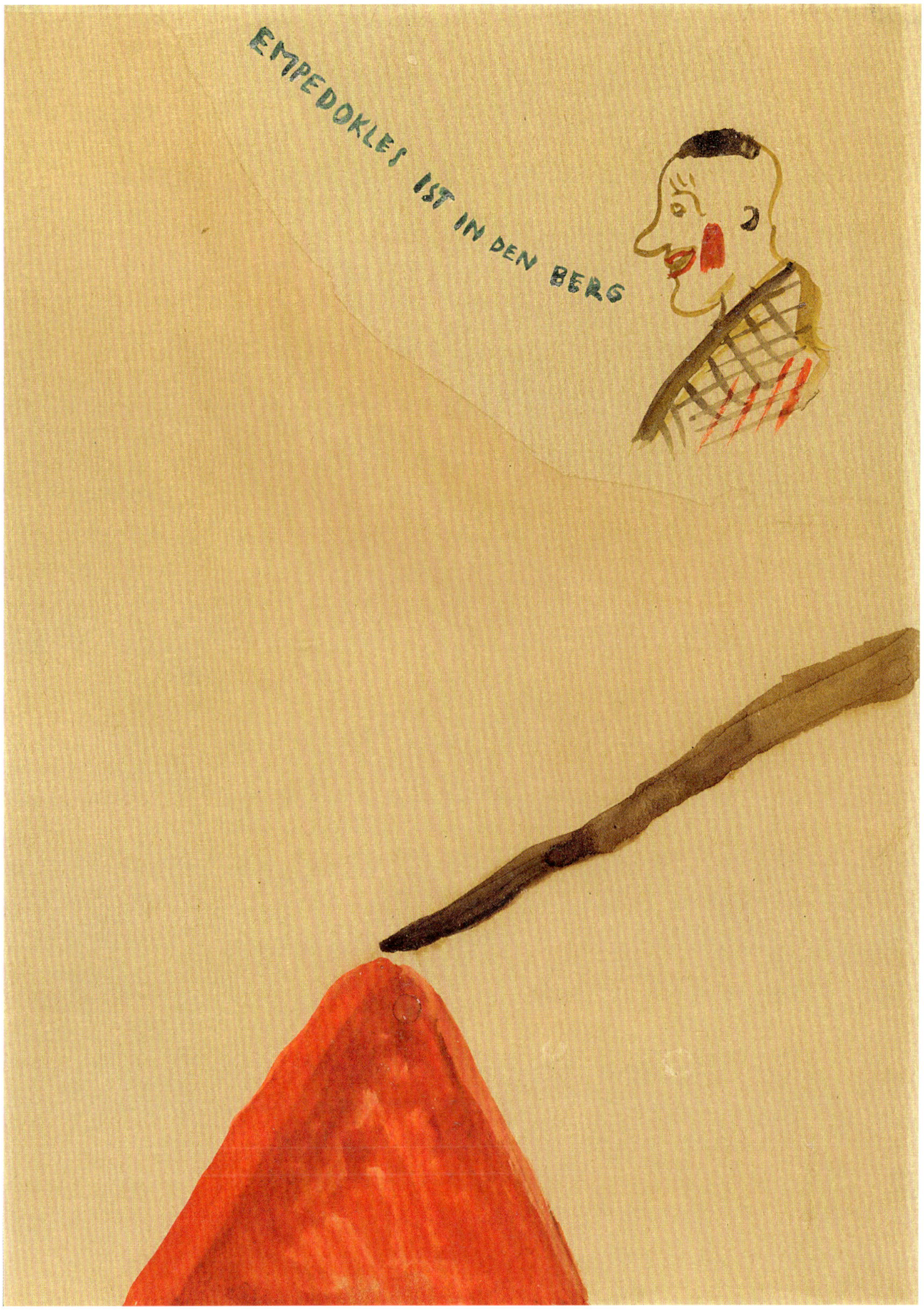

71
Ohne Titel ('Untitled'), 1967
Sigmar Polke
Green and grey watercolour wash
and ink
209 x 148 mm
Presented by Count Christian
Duerckheim to the British Museum

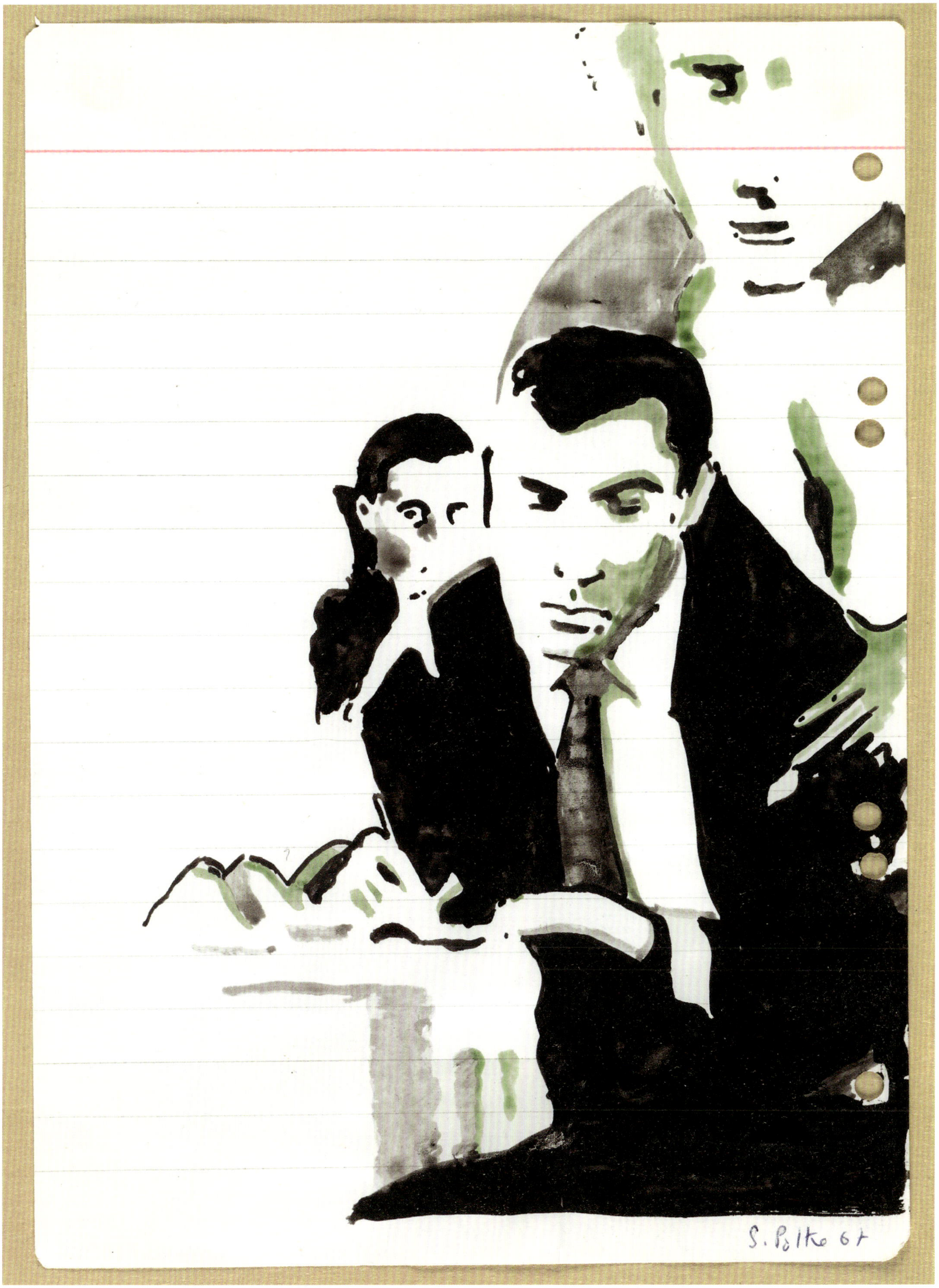
S. Polke 61

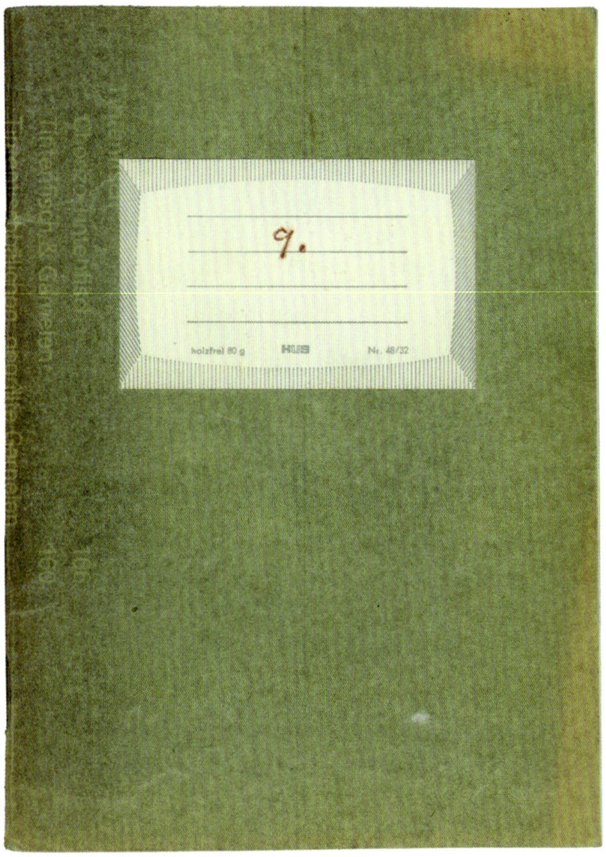

72
Untitled (sketchbook 9), 1969
Sigmar Polke
Twenty-nine watercolour drawings
208 x 147 mm

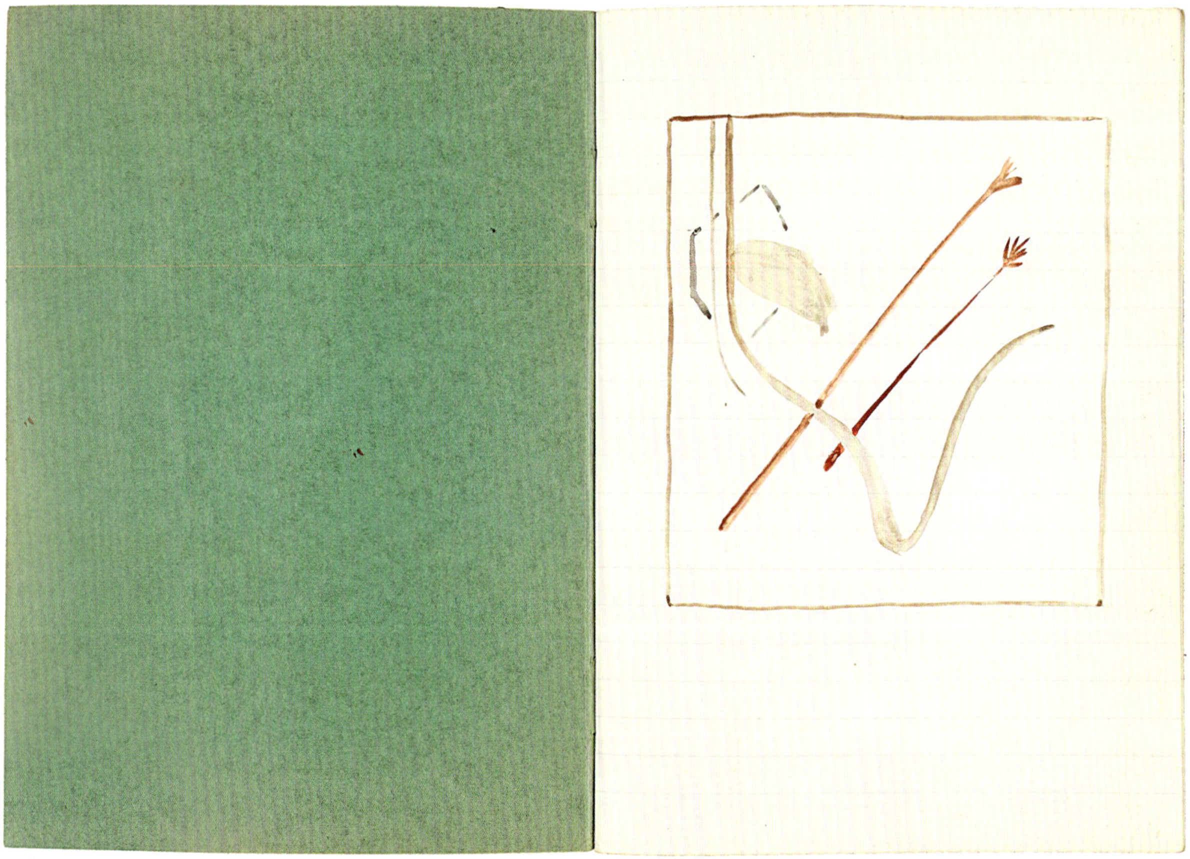

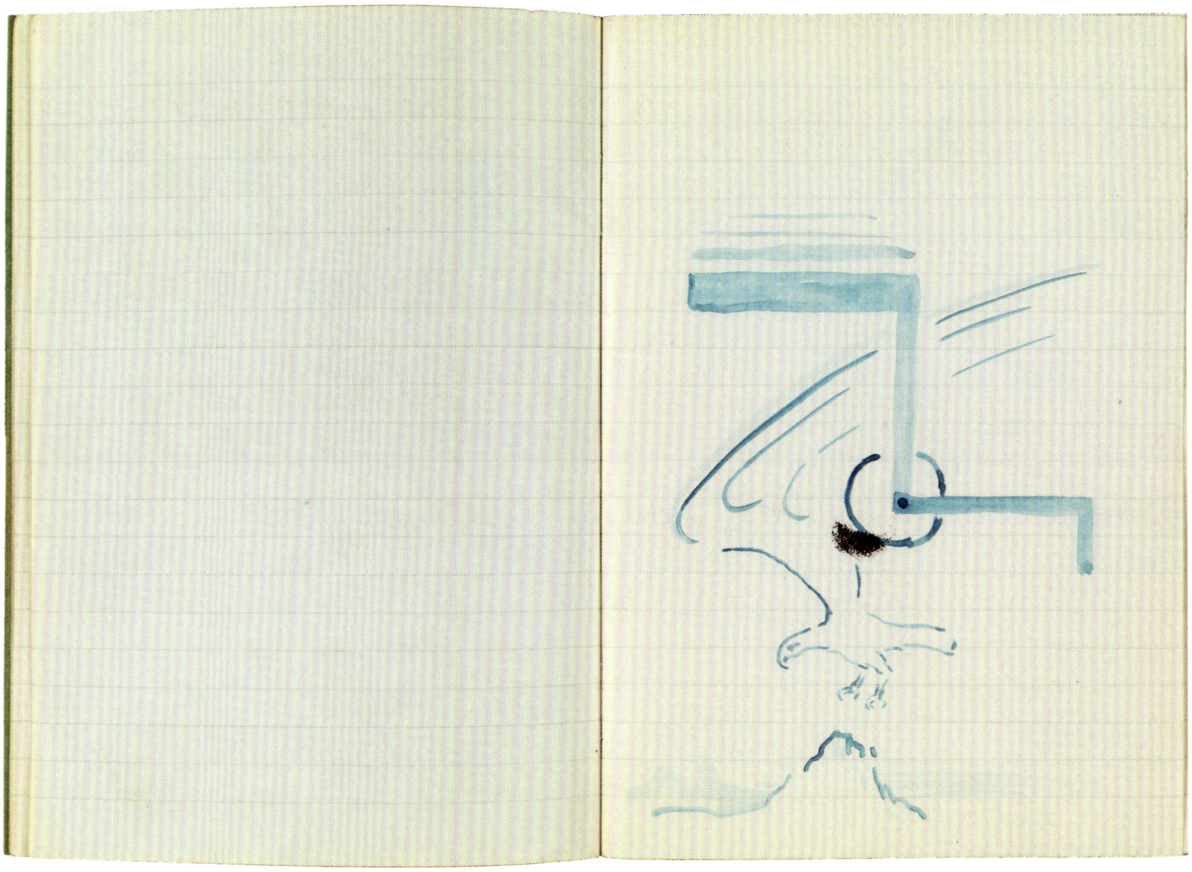

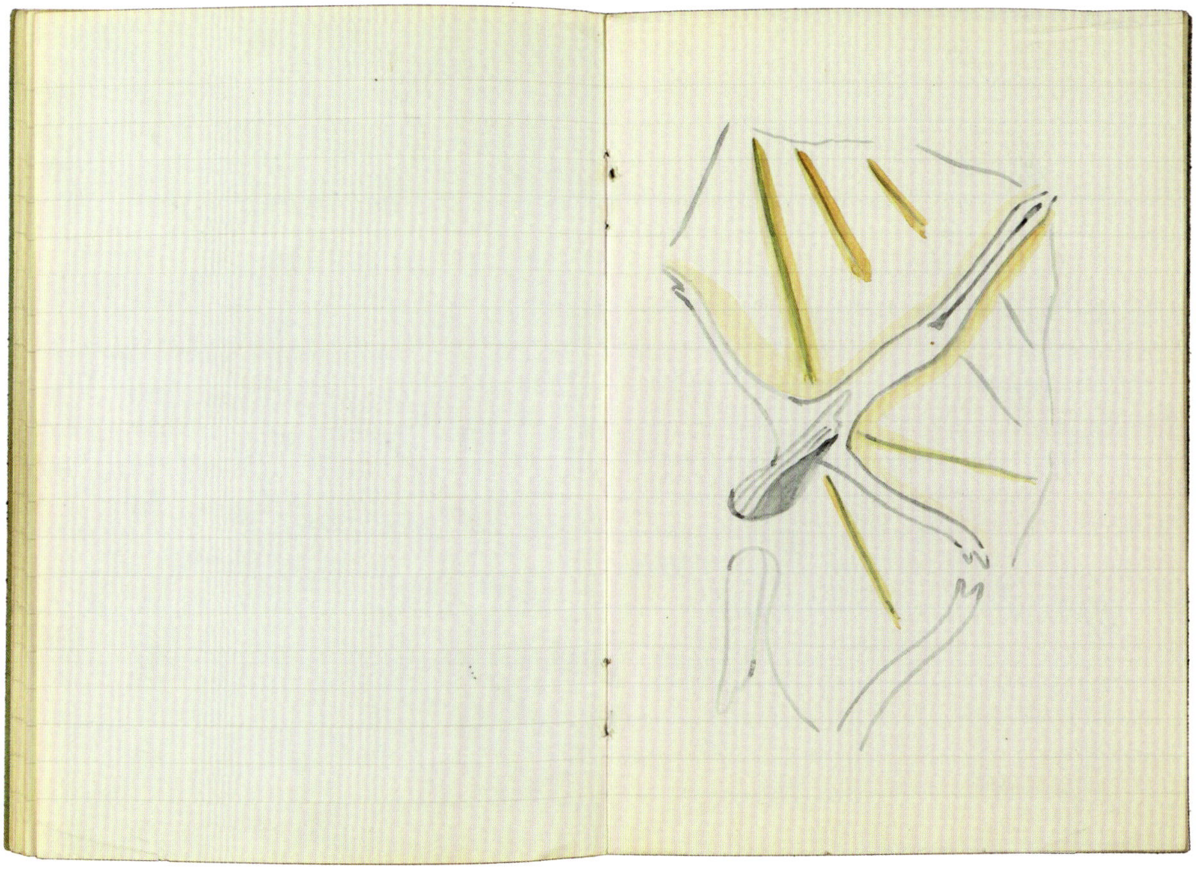

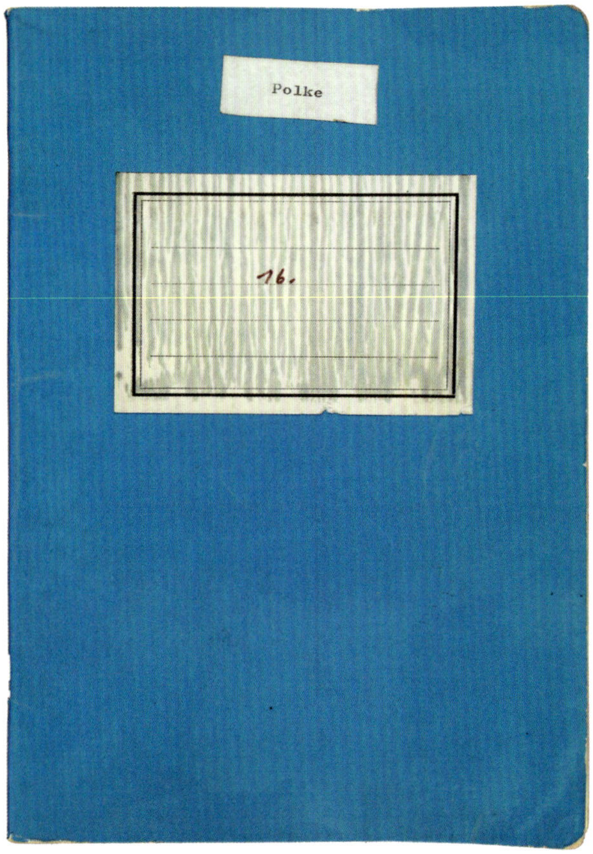

73
Sigmar Polke
Untitled (sketchbook 16), *c.* 1969
Twenty-nine watercolour drawings, seven accompanied by cuttings from illustrated magazines
209 x 145 mm
Presented by Count Christian Duerckheim to the British Museum

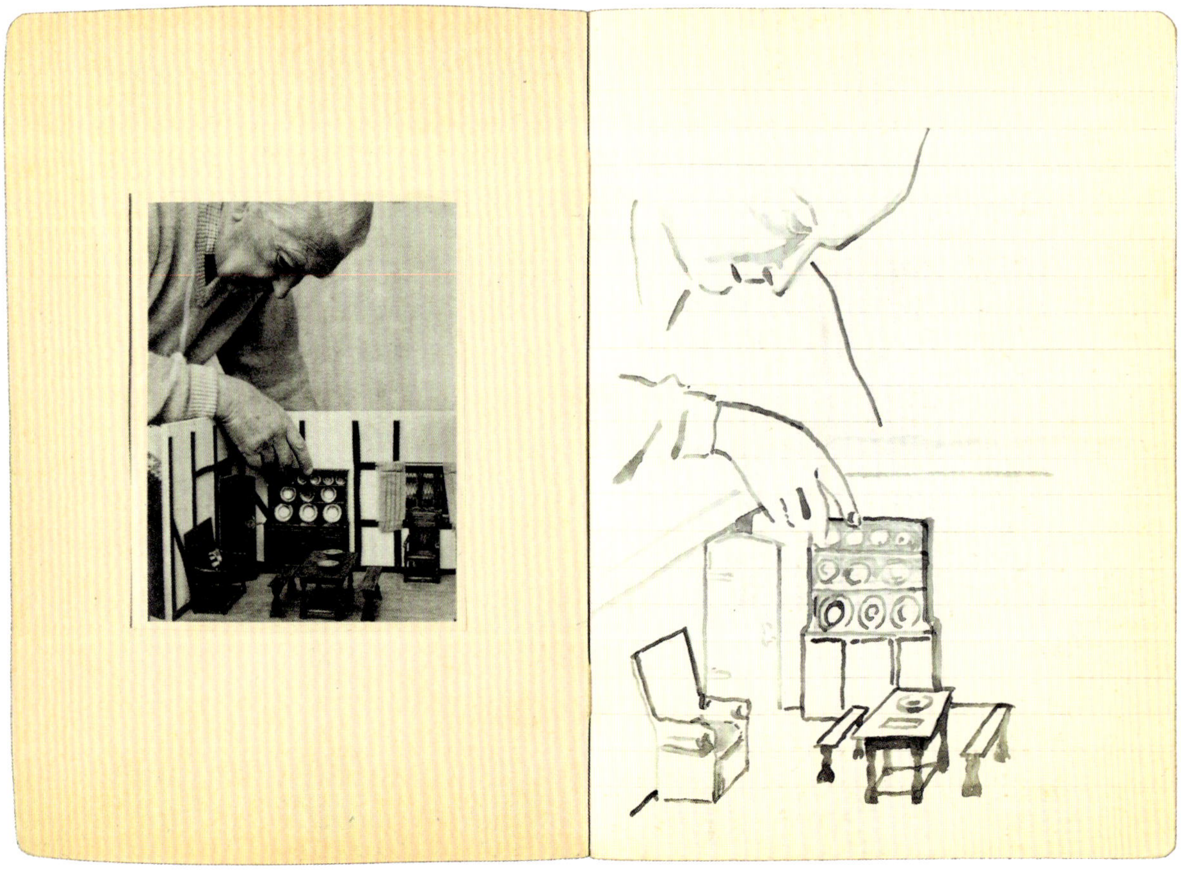

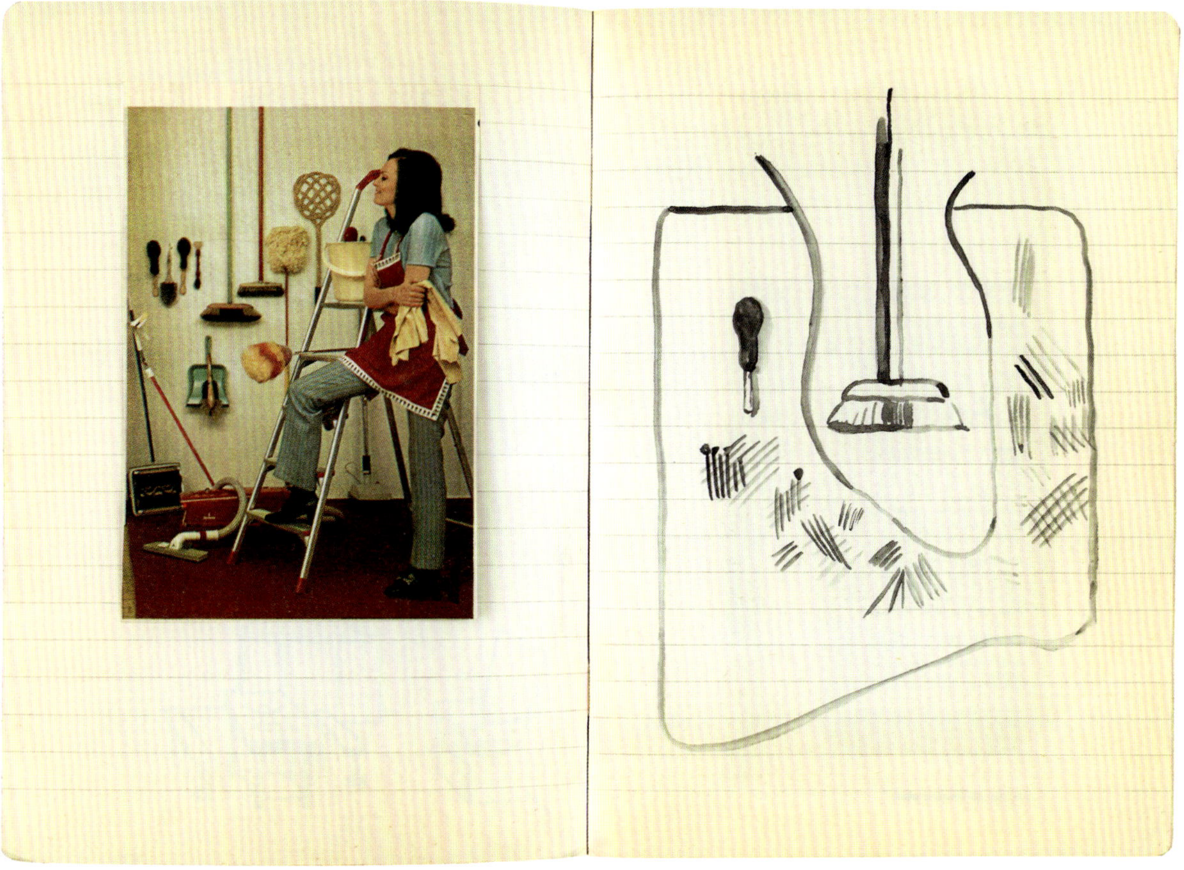

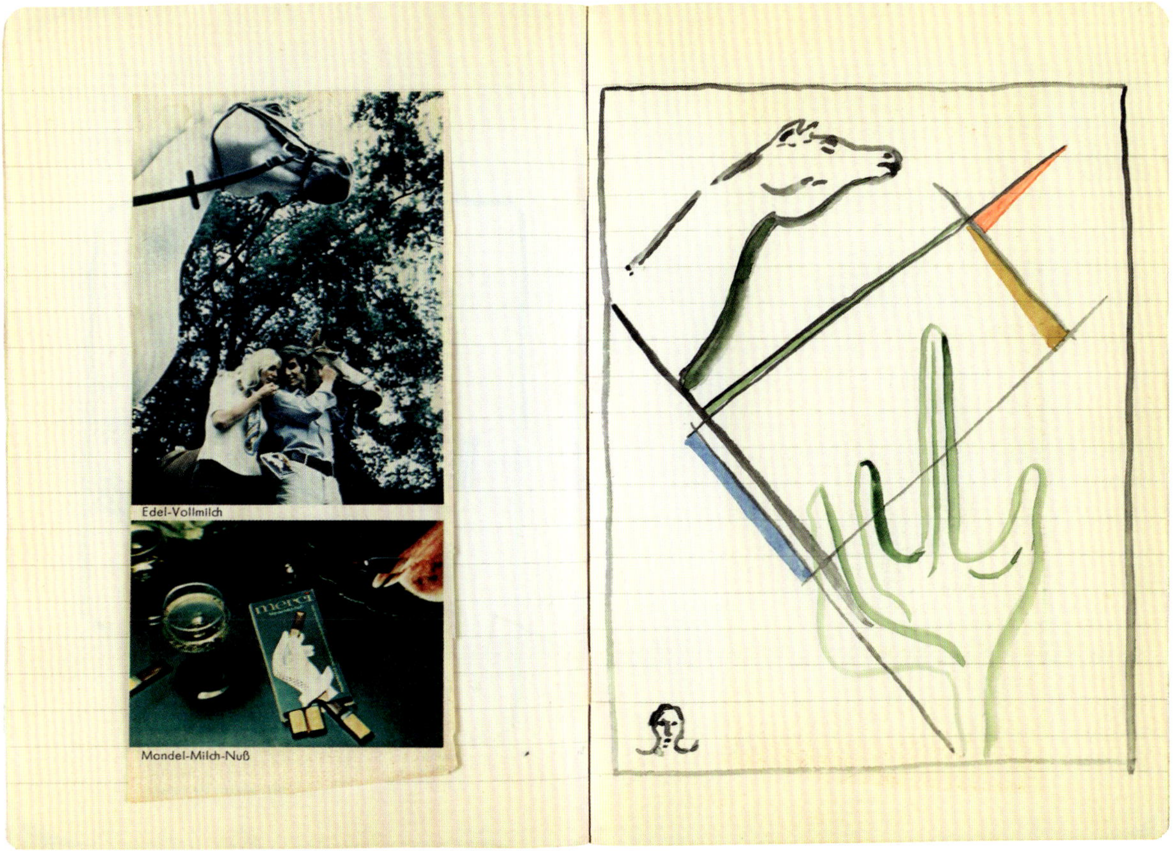
Edel-Vollmilch
Mandel-Milch-Nuß

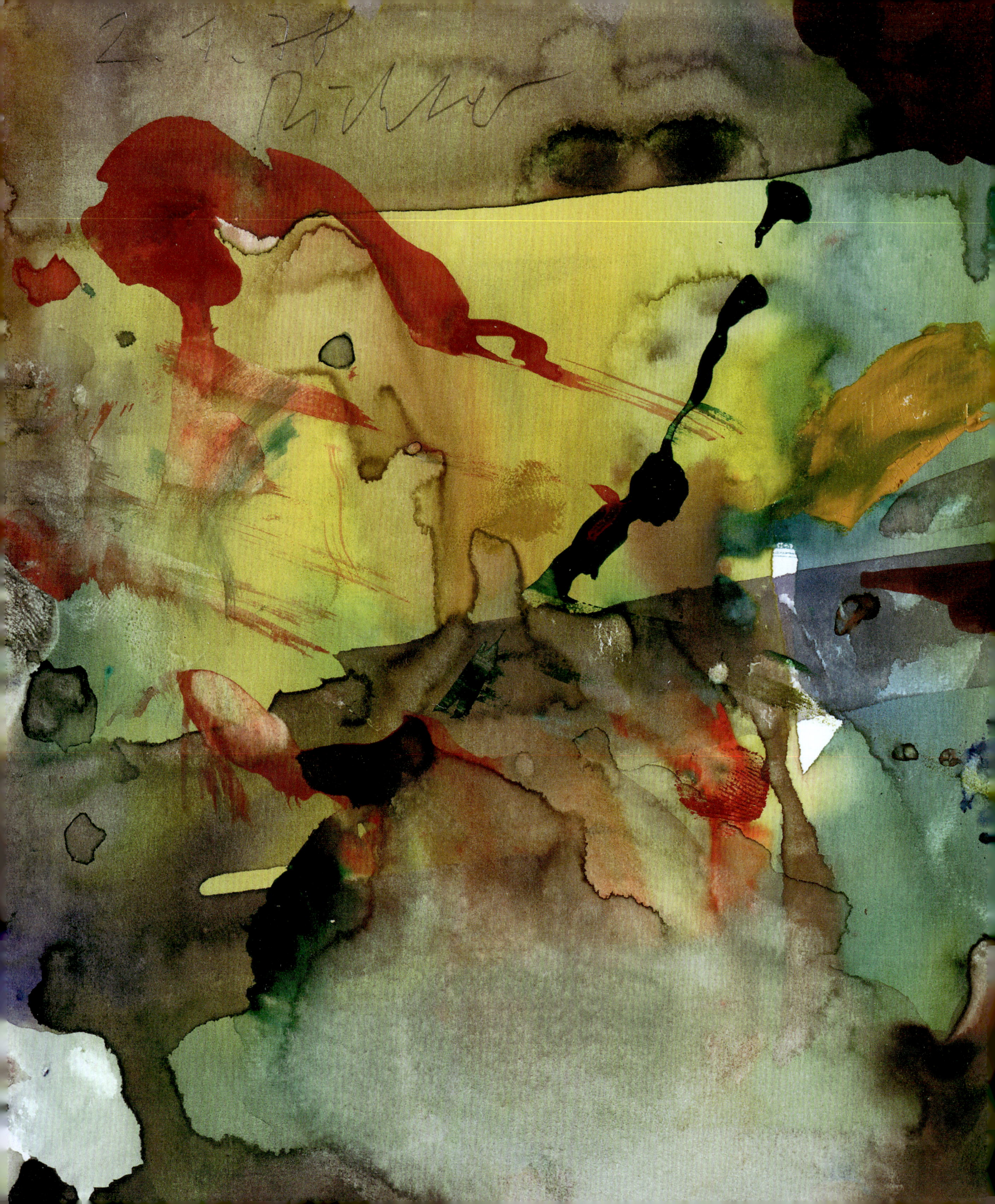
2. 1. 78
Richter

Gerhard Richter

Gerhard Richter has often been described as the most successful artist working in post-War Germany; he is certainly the most prolific. Painting stands at the centre of his work, and he is known for working both in photo-realist and abstract styles of painting, as well as for his flawless technique. Richter's influence on a generation of artists after 1960, who looked both to his technical innovations and his deeply philosophical approach to painting, can be compared to the impact of Picasso during the earlier part of the century.

Richter was born in Dresden in 1932 and grew up in the surrounding countryside. He was too young to be conscripted, but experienced as a child the destruction of the Second World War, the Russian invasion and, from a distance, the firebombing of Dresden. He remained after the war with his family in the Soviet Zone, then East Germany, and in 1951 was accepted, on second application, to the Hochschüle für Bildende Künste (Art Academy), Dresden, to study as a painter. As with all East German academies, studio training was based on the tenets of Socialist Realism, requiring on the one hand a strong technical and academic education in painting, and on the other a study of aesthetics and art history, as well as Marxist theory, economics and the Russian language. Richter chose to study in the mural paintings department under Heinz Lohmar (1900–76), less doctrinaire, as he later described, than other tutors, such as Hans and Lea Grundig (1901–58; 1906–77). He produced figurative, socially oriented works according to the official requirements of Socialist Realism – to show the benign nature of the Worker's State, and to create monuments to Marx and Lenin. At the end of the final year of his study, in December 1955, he was commissioned to paint a mural for the Deutsches Hygienemuseum (German Hygiene Museum) in Dresden, with the title *Lebensfreude* ('Joy of Life'; fig. 1). Having left the Academy he received a number of further commissions for murals in the Socialist Realist style and taught evening classes.

Richter appeared to be embarking on a successful career as an official artist in East Germany. But restrictions on individual freedom, and an increasing awareness of the type of painting being made in the West, led to a growing discontent. 'I was always looking for a third way in which Eastern realism and Western modernism would be resolved into one redeeming construct', he later said.[1] At *Documenta 2* in Kassel, in 1959 (where he could travel before the borders were closed), he saw art from the 'free' world, notably paintings by Jackson Pollock, Jean Fautrier and Lucio Fontana, and the German artist Ernst Wilhelm Nay (1902–68).

After a trip to Moscow and Leningrad in March 1961, Richter became convinced of the necessity of expatriation to the West. Later that same month Richter and his young wife, Marianne Eufinger, left East Germany on a local train travelling

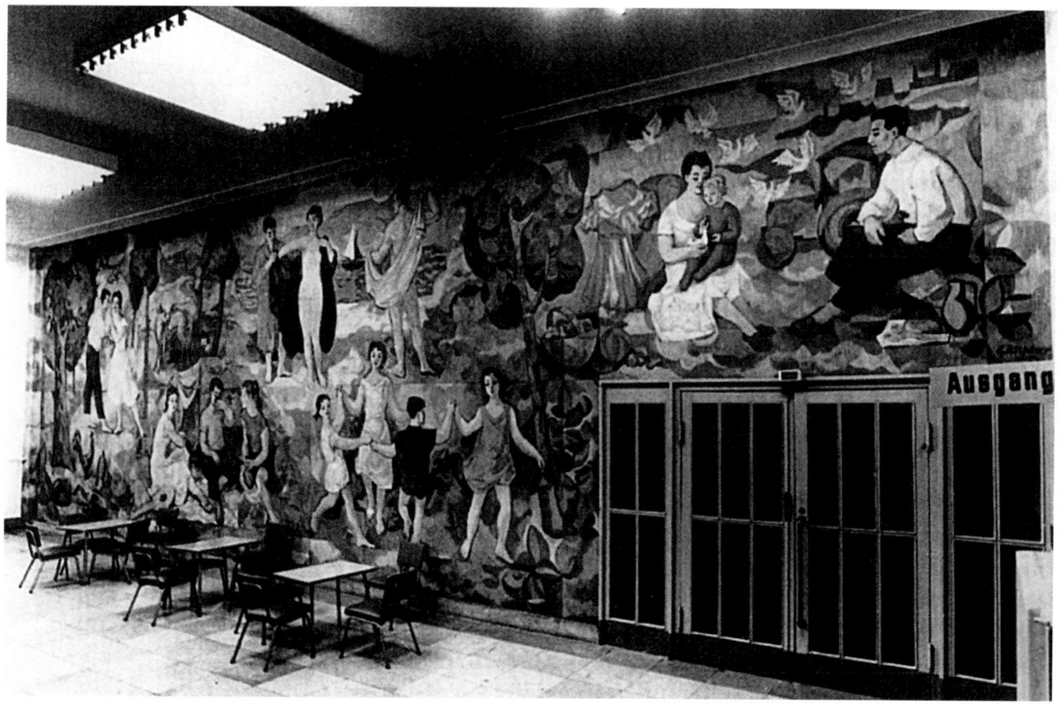

1. *Lebensfreude ('Joy of Life')*, 1956
(painted over in 1979)
Wall painting, Deutsches Hygiene Museum, Dresden
Gerhard Richter

into the Western Sector of Berlin, and declared themselves refugees. They settled in Düsseldorf, where Richter once again embarked on an art school education, enrolling in the famous Kunstakademie, a decade after he had begun his art education in the East.

Richter's new start was symbolized by a painting that he made in his first year as a student, a talismanic work entitled *Tisch* ('Table'; 1962), which became the initial work in the official catalogue of his painting. This simple grey image of a table, obscured by a scumble of brushstrokes, signals many of the themes that have preoccupied Richter since, including the confrontation of photography and painting, and of realist and abstract styles of painting, and of the use of a monochrome palette.

Richter's first works at the Kunstakademie were abstract paintings in the Informel style, inspired, as Richter later suggested, by Dubuffet, Fautrier, Fontana and Francis Bacon (1909–92). Together with his fellow students Lueg and Manfred, in 1962 Richter transferred to the class of the abstract painter Götz, where he met Polke. Rather than abstraction, it was the new spirit of Pop Art, in particular that of Lichtenstein, which was to prove decisive for Richter's work, and for his collaborations with Lueg and Polke. They described themselves as 'German Pop artists' and exhibited works together, most notoriously in the 1963 exhibitions with Lueg, Polke and Kuttner, *Kapitalistischer Realismus* ('Capitalist Realism'), and then with Lueg, *Leben mit Pop – Eine Demonstration für den Kapitalistischen Realismus* ('Living with Pop: A Demonstration for Capitalist Realism'), for which the two artists hung works in a furniture showroom. Richter had developed a style of painting that reproduced images from newspapers and magazines, using a blurring effect, the result of blending and dragging wet paint with a dry brush, creating an astonishing new look for painting, hovering between traditional oil painting and the anonymous naturalism of the photographic image.

The combination of this style with a startling range of subject matter, including advertising imagery, newspaper photographs, American military aircraft, family photographs and even a portrait of Hitler, made in 1963 (later destroyed by Richter), formed the basis for Richter's early success. Among the most striking works

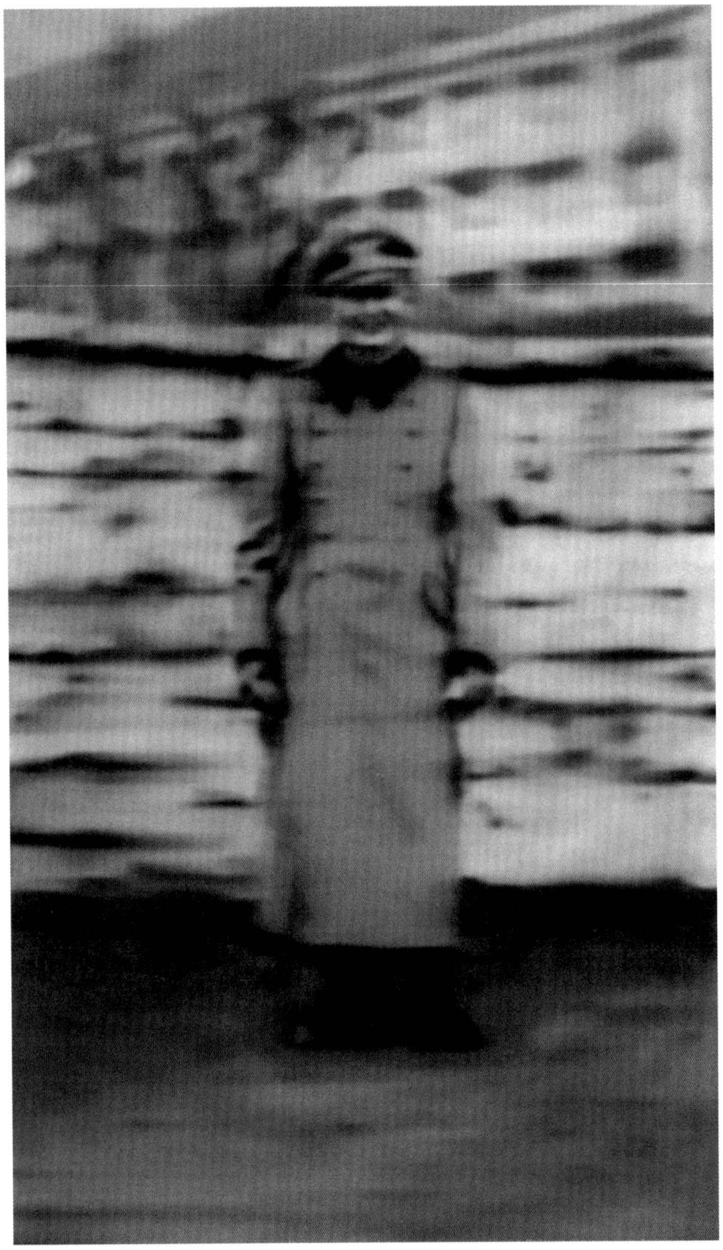

2. *Onkel Rudi* ('Uncle Rudi'), 2000
Gerhard Richter
Cibachrome photograph mounted on Dibond plate, framed, 870 x 500 mm. This is an editioned photograph of Richter's painting of the same title from 1965

3. *Schweizer Alpen II* ('Swiss Alps II'), 1969
From a portfolio of five screenprints of the same motif
Gerhard Richter
Screenprint on lightweight card, 694 x 694 mm

were paintings based on family photographs taken during the Second World War. *Onkel Rudi* ('Uncle Rudi', fig. 2) reproduced a snapshot of a male figure in Nazi uniform, relaxed and smiling for the camera. Rudi was Richter's uncle who had been killed during the war. A further painting from this time *Tante Marianne* ('Aunt Marianne'; 1965) showed Richter's aunt, Marianne, holding him as a baby; she was later a victim of the Nazi euthanasia scheme. *Tante Marianne* and *Onkel Rudi* are among the most powerful works by a German artist to reflect on the private tragedy of Nazism, and the psychological stakes of memory and guilt.

Alongside images of war and everyday life, in 1967 Richter painted a series based on pin-up and pornographic photographs of women, emblems of Western freedom and decadence. A number of related drawings show Richter tracing directly from the source images (cats 75–80). For his photo-paintings Richter used a projector, painting over the image as it appeared directly on the canvas (a method used by many artists since). At the same time he was also developing a contrasting body of work, the *Colour Chart* paintings, his first major departure from the photographic style. The first of these, *192 Farben* ('192 Colours'; 1966), shows a grid of uniform colour squares painted in oils, appearing like a randomized version of a colour swatch chart. Richter developed the series in ever-larger versions, using assistants to complete the work, and in enamel rather than oil paint, to give an entirely impersonal, industrial finish. The result is a work of art devoid of personal expression, a 'deadpan' image.

Richter evolved his work on the basis of contradictions – painting one series of works in direct reaction to what had come before. Accordingly, and following the *Colour Chart* paintings, in 1969 he made the first of his *Seascape* paintings, a series that also includes images of clouds and landscapes. Whereas his early photo-paintings often had a raw, dynamic look, the seascapes are utterly still, perfectly rendered soft-focus images of the photographic source. They bring to mind a Northern tradition of the romantic landscape, particularly the work of Caspar David Friedrich (1774–1840), but with the qualification

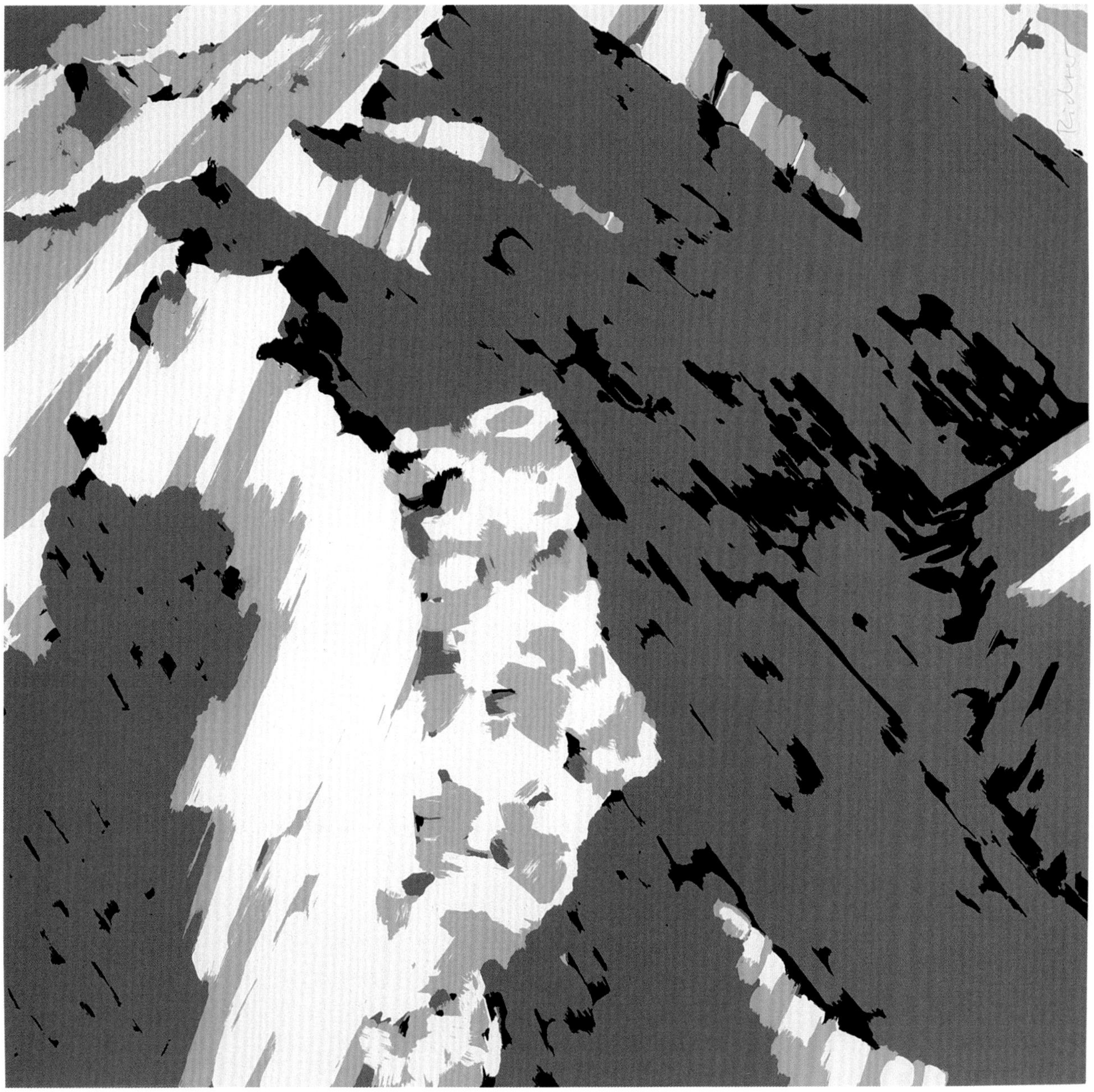

that Richter omits all references to human life – the small details of the human figure or church spire that Friedrich used to give scale and meaning to his vision of nature are entirely absent from Richter's natural scenes.

A further series of 'Grey' paintings arose from Richter's habit of over painting failed canvases, blending the colours to a uniform grey. Richter's exploration of the way in which oil paint can represent natural light also led to a remarkable series of paintings of aerial views of European cities, based on photographs taken during the Second World War for reconnaissance purposes. Thick tonal strokes of paint approximate the light and dark areas that, seen from a distance, resolve themselves into the image of a cityscape, creating uncanny images that switch between expressive abstract painting and photographic realism. Another series of paintings showed the Swiss Alps, using highly simplified tonal schemes to evoke the large masses of light and glowing shadows of snow-covered ascents; these paintings were accompanied by a series of screenprints, *Schweizer Alpen* ('Swiss Alps'; fig. 3).
Richter continued to develop these various series, each one sufficient to substantiate an artist's career, throughout the 1970s. His interest in abstraction, photography and painting as spectacle led to the large colour abstract paintings, for which he is perhaps best known. *Gelbgrün* ('Yellow-green', 1982), first exhibited at

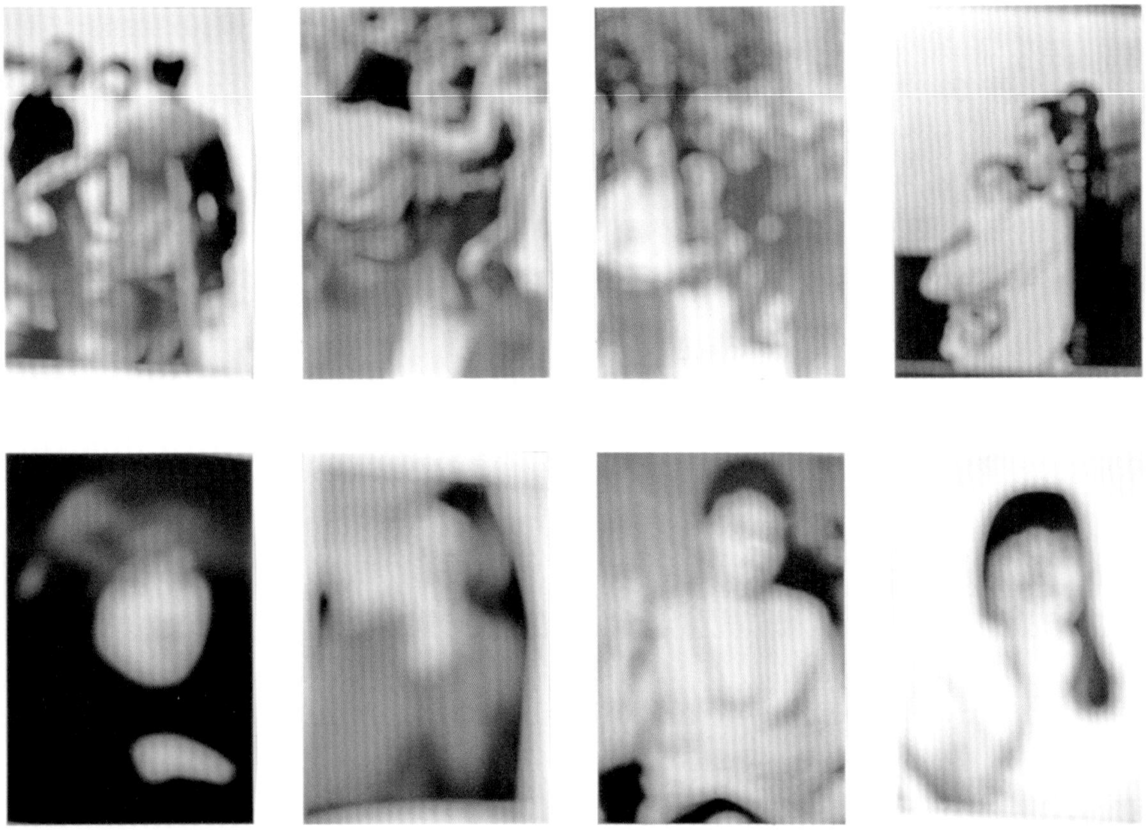

Documenta 7 with four other vast abstract works, was typical of this new type of painting. His dazzling, intensely coloured and textured abstract surfaces were created by various techniques, including the use of a 'doctor blade', a long straight edge drawn across the surface of the wet paint. Technique remained a key element of Richter's work – the evolution and then repeated controlled deployment of a simple method of paint application.

The same was true of his abstract drawings. Drawn in pencil on standard A4 paper, these works explore the range of marks that can be obtained from such a simple medium, and show a similar scale of imaginative possibilities as the large abstract paintings. Drawing for Richter was also an arena for more practical problem solving, and many of his installation sketches and concept diagrams were treated on the same level as these abstract drawings.

Richter's 'democratic' approach to images, drawing from a wide range of sources and avoiding any sense of a hierarchy, is reflected in his image archive, *Atlas*, which he began in 1969. This consists of photographs, drawings and other found images, mounted on numbered panels, in an ever-growing compendium that has undergone various configurations, with panels, for example, removed (see the conversation with Christian Duerckheim in this catalogue, pp. 178–85) and numbering systems changed. The images can often seem nothing more

4. *Baader-Meinhof-Fotos (18. Oktober 1977)* ('Baader-Meinhof photographs (18 October 1977)'), 1989
Gerhard Richter
Atlas sheet: 474 photographs mounted on card, 517 x 667 mm

5. *Selbstportät* ('Self-Portrait'), 1996
Gerhard Richter
Oil on canvas, 510 x 460 mm

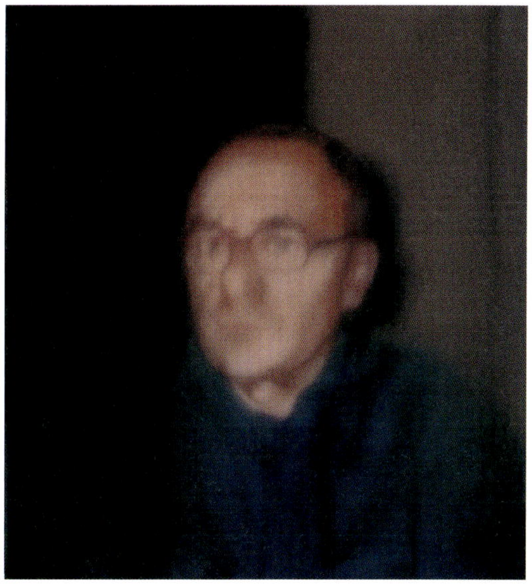

than a collection of family snapshots, such as those of Richter's second wife, the sculptor Isa Genzken (b. 1948), whom he married in 1982; although preserved in *Atlas*, they also become source material and part of the fabric of his working method.

The assembling and archiving of images was crucial for one of Richter's most important groups of work, *Baader-Meinhof-Fotos (18. Oktober 1977)* ('Baader-Meinhof photographs (18 October 1977)'). This cycle of fifteen paintings commemorating the deaths of members of the notorious militant revolutionary Baader-Meinhof group was made by Richter a decade after the event, in 1988 (fig. 4). The title specifies the date on which the bodies of the Red Army Faction members, Andreas Baader and Gudrun Ensslin, were found dead in the high-security prison in Stammheim, near Stuttgart. Two other members had died in suspicious circumstances; many held that it was not suicide but murder by the security services. Richter's images, based on newspaper photographs, show ghostly monochrome scenes, as if viewed on an antique television set; they reflect the dark confusion of the moment, the ambiguity of the official story, and Richter's antipathy to any form of ideology, from right- or left-wing political factions.

18 October 1977 was first shown in Germany in 1989, just as Richter's international reputation was sealed by a major touring retrospective in America. His success might seem like vindication for the 'victory' of the Western European system over Communism, and the destruction of border controls between East and West Germany. Yet during the 1990s Richter's work moved away from political themes and focused increasingly on images of his new family (fig. 5) – he married his third wife, Sabine Moritz, in 1995, and painted a series of her with their first child, Moritz, the same year.

Where Richter made works for public settings, with potential political implications, he invariably used a neutral, abstract style. The large wall-mounted work, *Black Red Gold*, a twenty-metre-high, three-part coloured mirror, was installed in the reconstructed Reichstag building in 1998, one of a number of commissions from contemporary German artists. More ambitious still was the commission for a stained-glass window for the north transept of Cologne cathedral, one of Germany's most important historic buildings. Richter's controversially abstract window developed the look of his colour chart paintings and was unveiled in 2007.

The sense of Richter's own life and work becoming history, after five decades of extraordinary productivity and success, was signalled by the opening of the Gerhard Richter Archive at the Staatliche Kunstsammlung, Dresden, in 2006. A biography by Dietmar Elger, who subsequently became Director of the Dresden Archive, was published in German in 2002, later translated into English. True to form, however, Richter has continued to create new works that challenge views of painting, notably in his series of *Silicate* paintings, based on imaging technologies that can represent the interior of an atom. In 2013 Richter completed a group of large complex digital prints titled *Strip*, and continues to work on a series of paintings using lacquer on glass, notably *Baghdad* (2010) and *Flow* (2013), which recall his first works in watercolour.

1. Cited in: D. Elger, *Gerhard Richter. A Life in Painting*, trans. E.M. Solaro, Chicago 2010, p. 22
2. Ibid., p. 36.

74
Ohne Titel ('Untitled'), 1966
Gerhard Richter
Blue and black ballpoint pen
210 x 296 mm

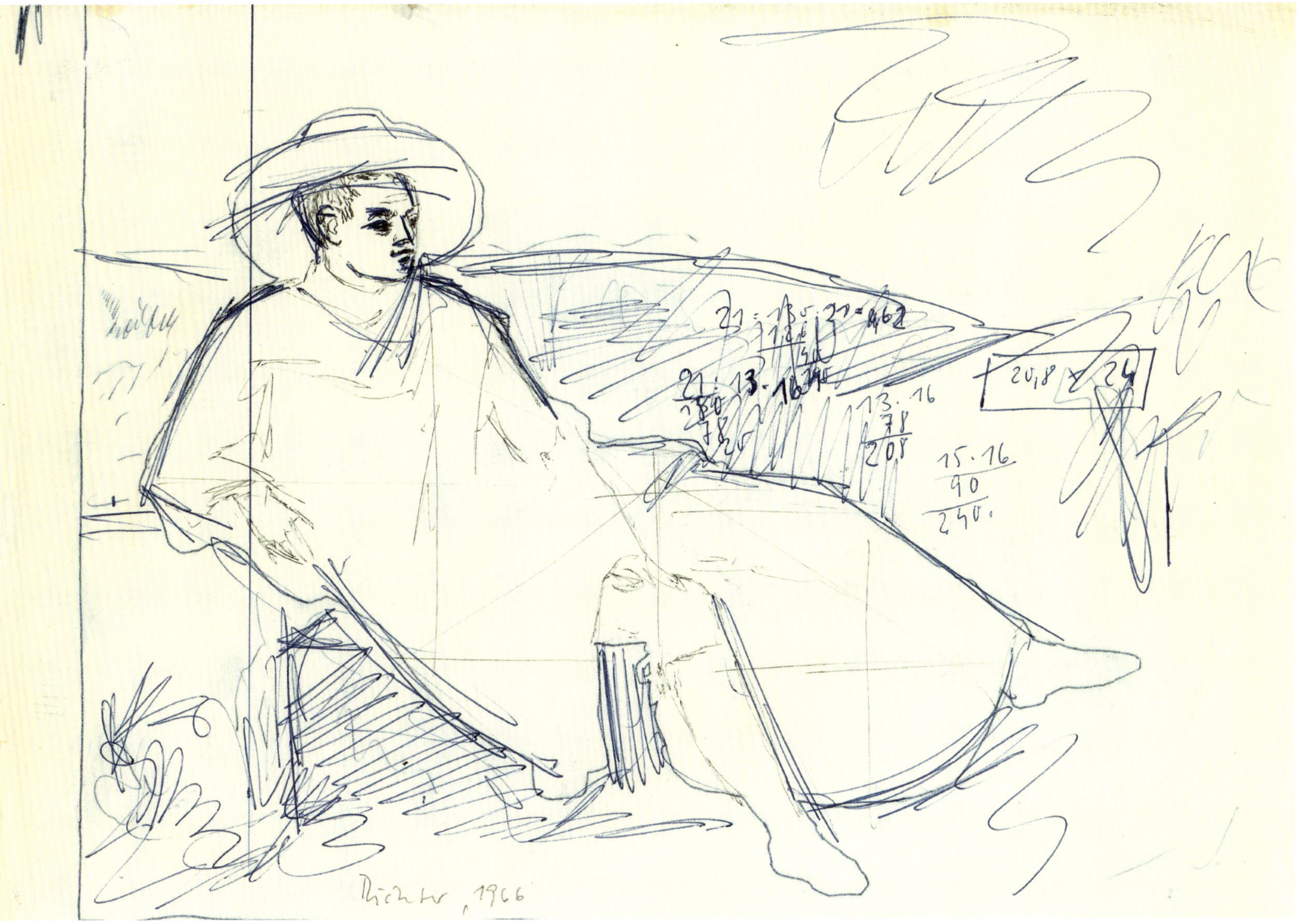

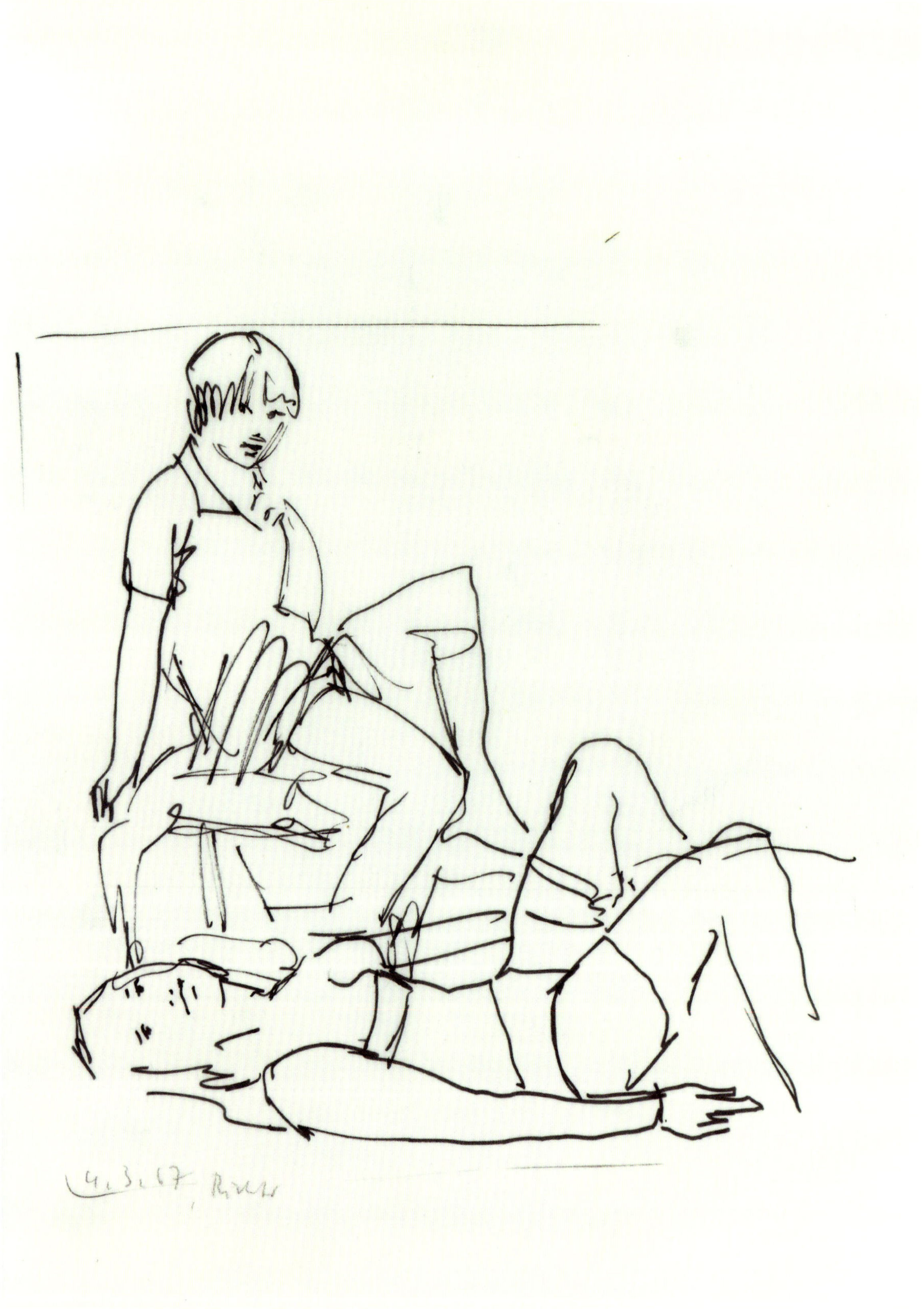

75
Ohne Titel ('Untitled'), 1967
Gerhard Richter
Felt-tip pen
295 x 210 mm
Presented by Count Christian Duerckheim to the British Museum

76
Ohne Titel ('Untitled'), 1967
Gerhard Richter
Graphite and felt-tip pen
295 x 210 mm
Presented by Count Christian
Duerckheim to the British Museum

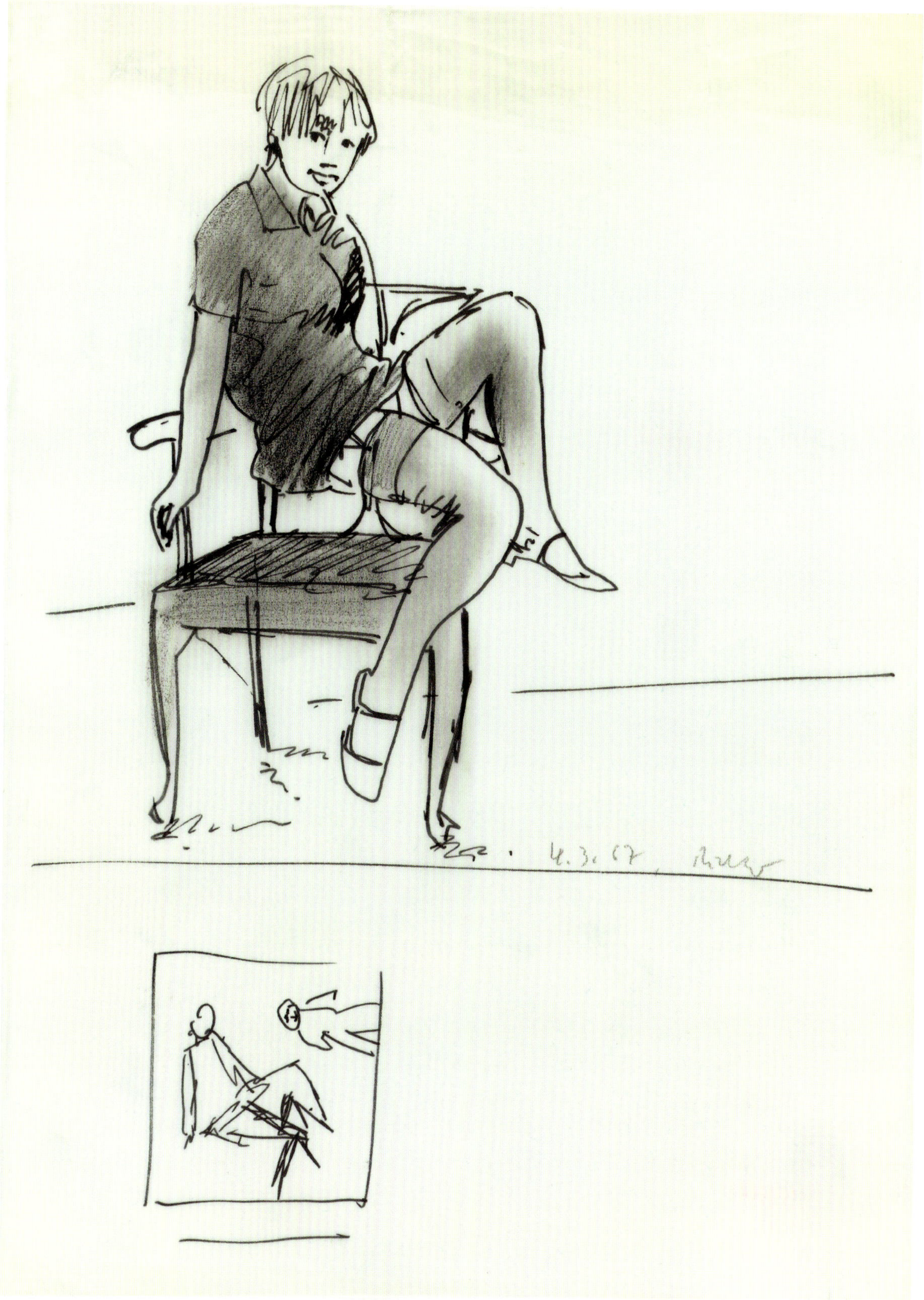

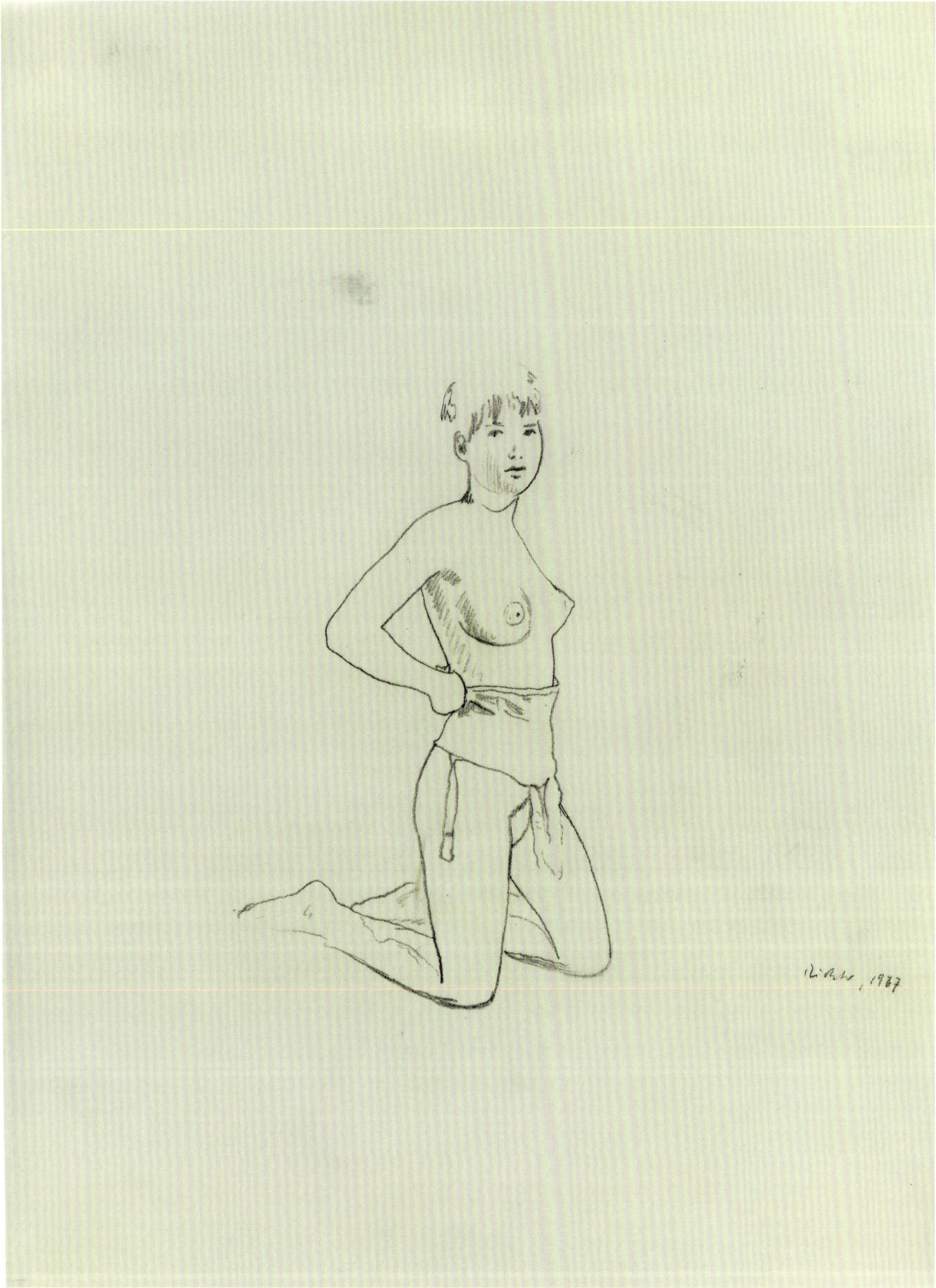

77
Ohne Titel ('Untitled'), 1967
Gerhard Richter
Graphite
295 x 210 mm

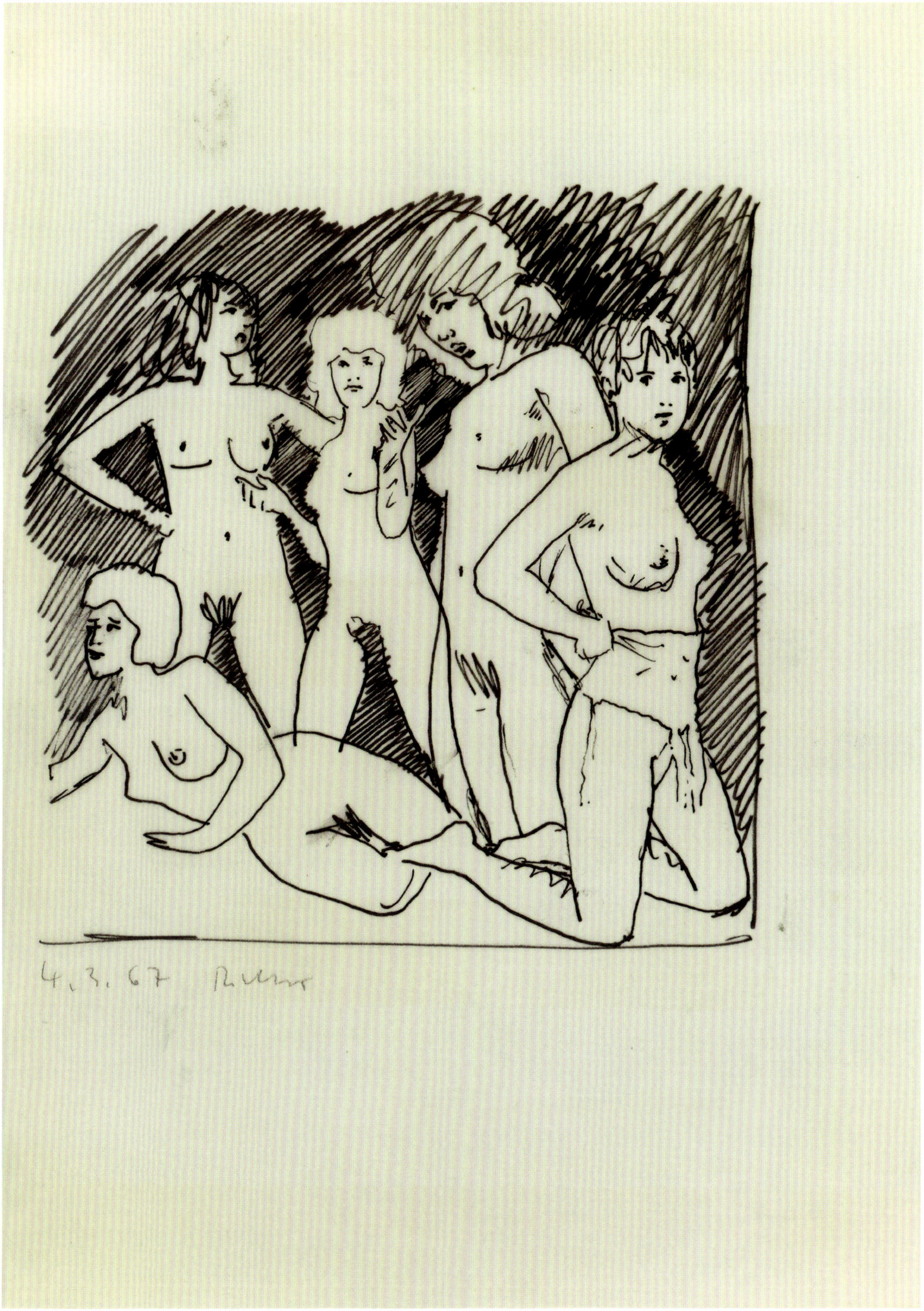

78
Ohne Titel ('Untitled'), 1967
Gerhard Richter
Felt-tip pen
295 x 210 mm

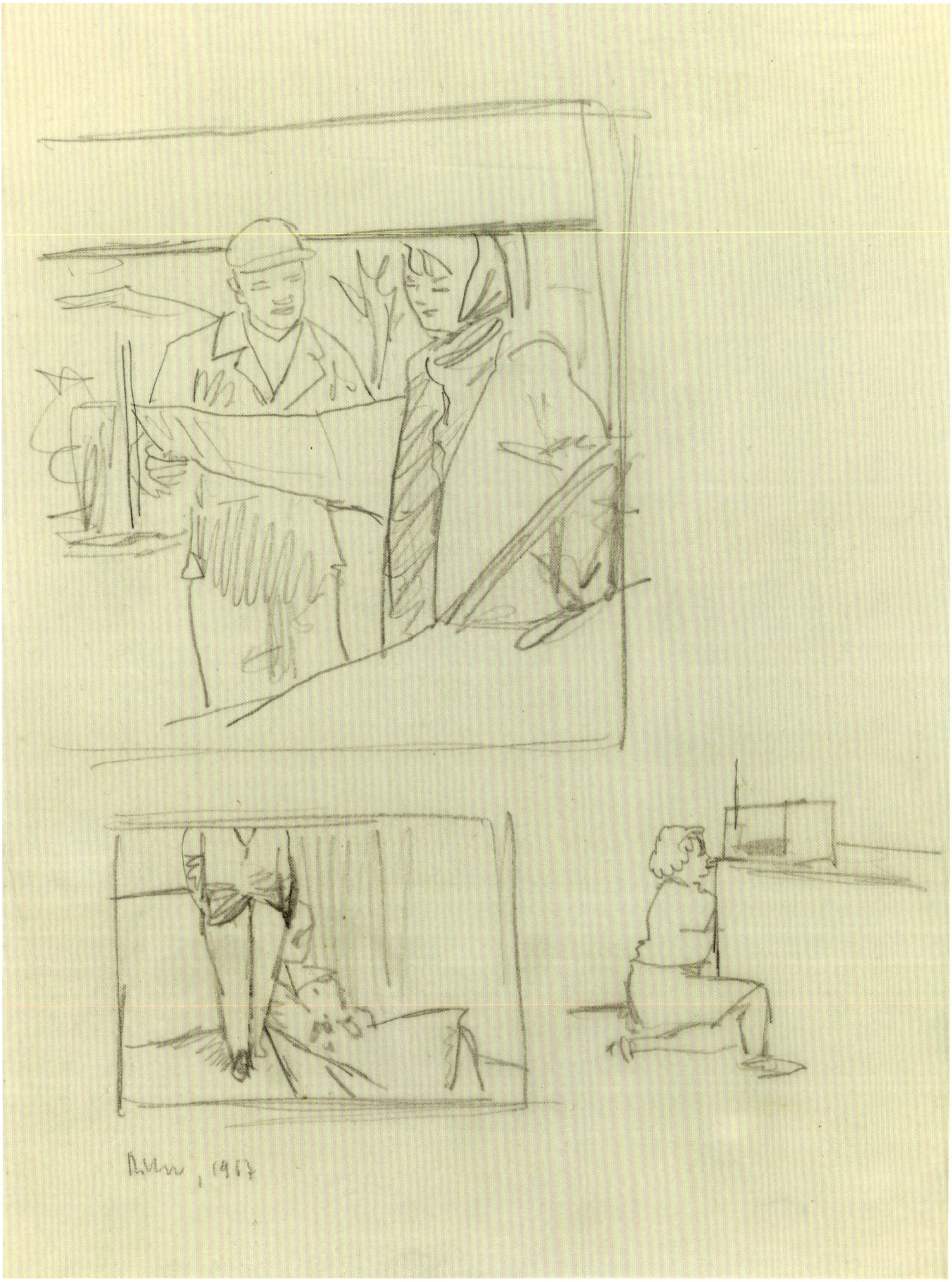

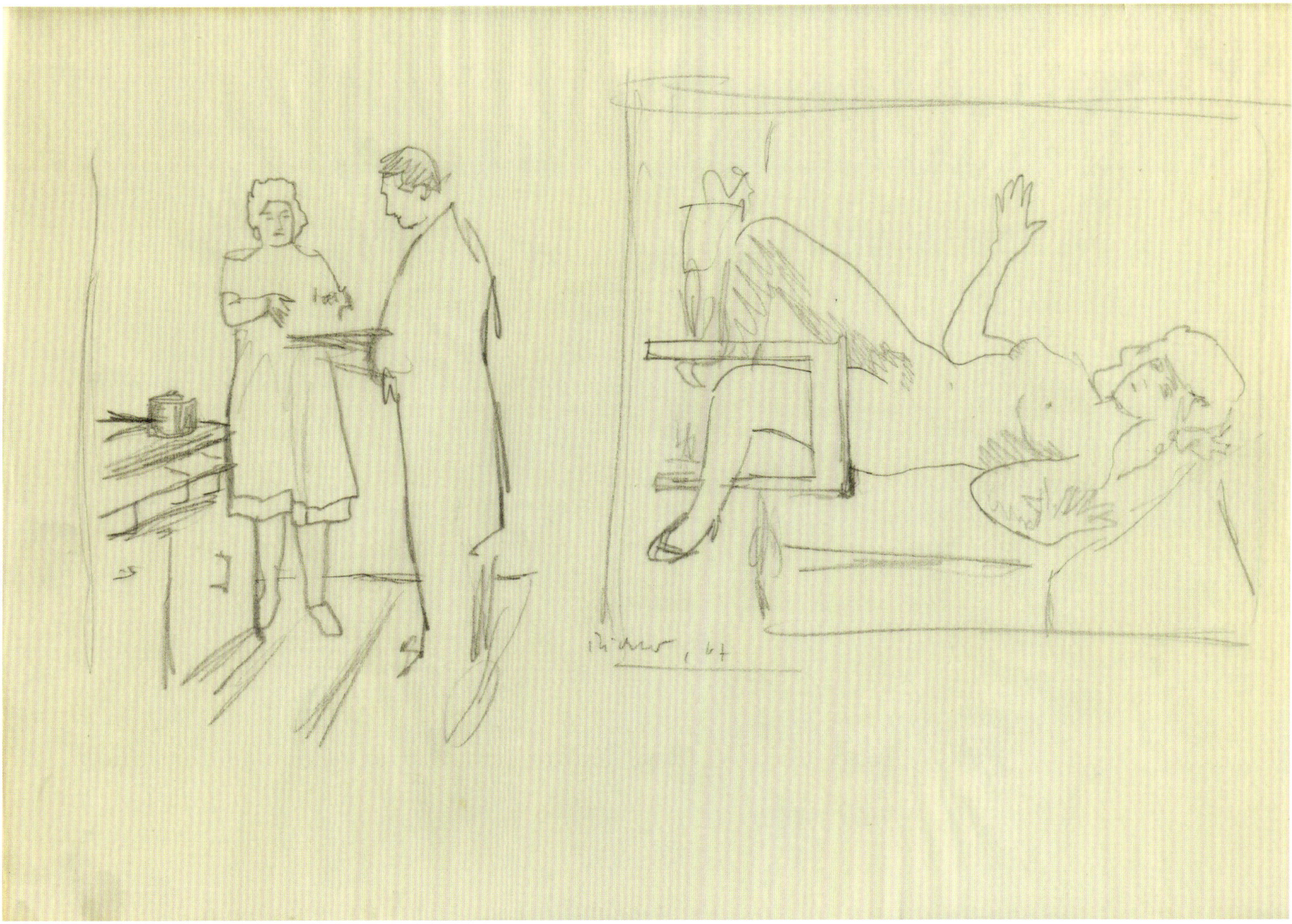

79
Ohne Titel ('Untitled'), 1967
Gerhard Richter
Graphite
295 x 210 mm

80
Ohne Titel ('Untitled'), 1967
Gerhard Richter
Graphite
210 x 295 mm

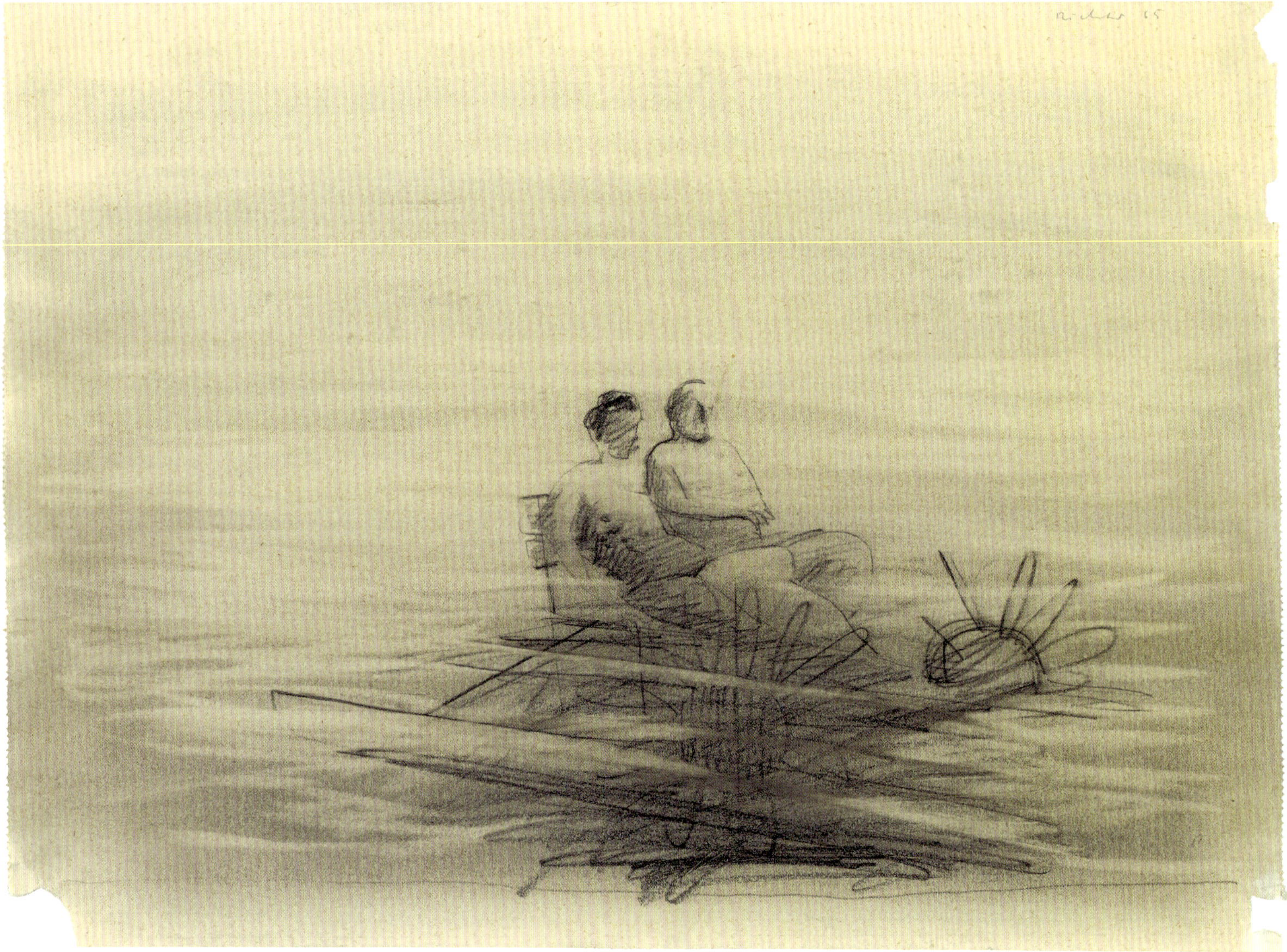

81
Tretbootfahrer ('Pedal Boat Riders'), 1965
Gerhard Richter
Graphite
210 x 295 mm

82
Gerhard Richter
Hotel oder Haus Hutter ('Hotel or Hutter House'), 1965
Graphite
295 x 236 mm

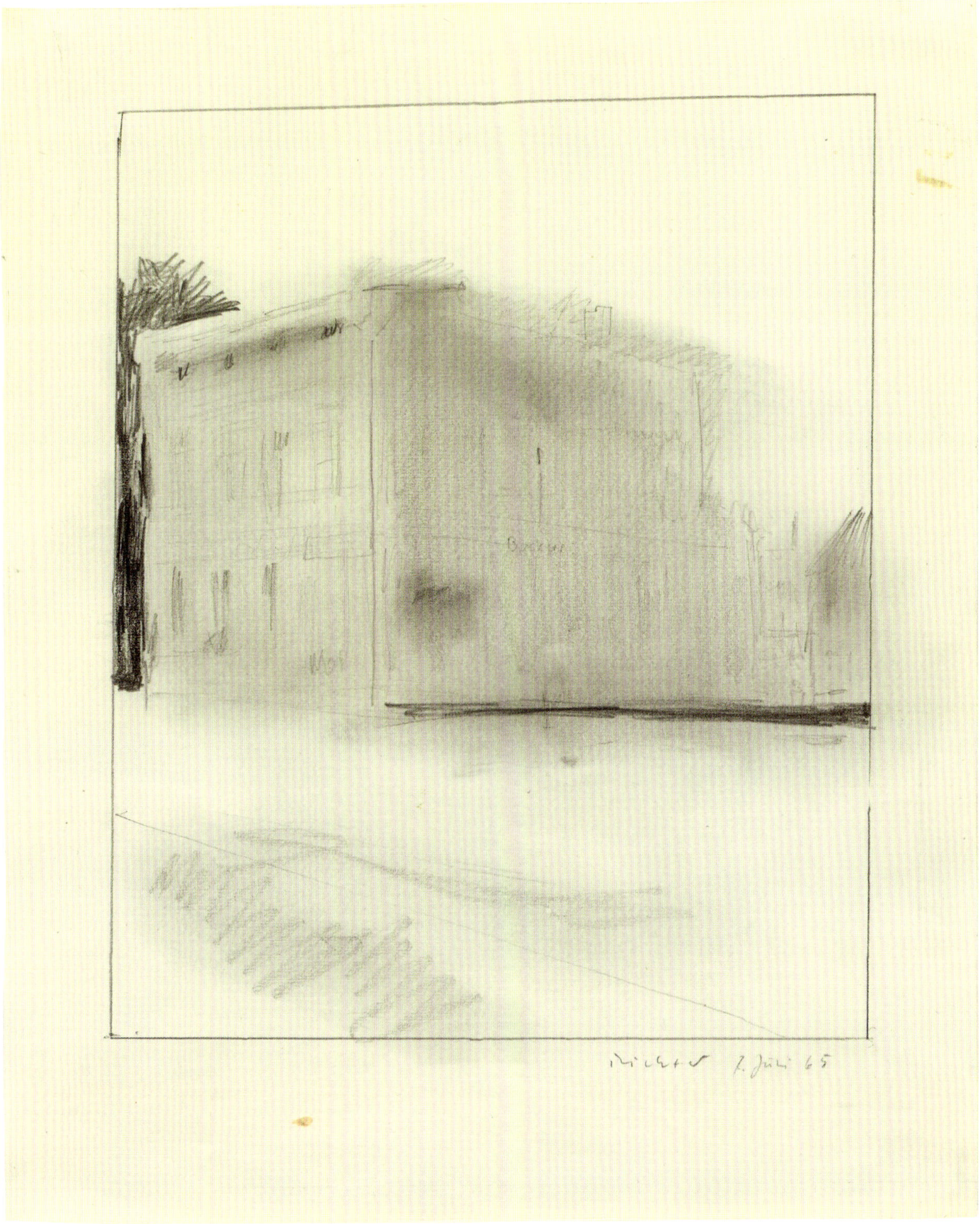

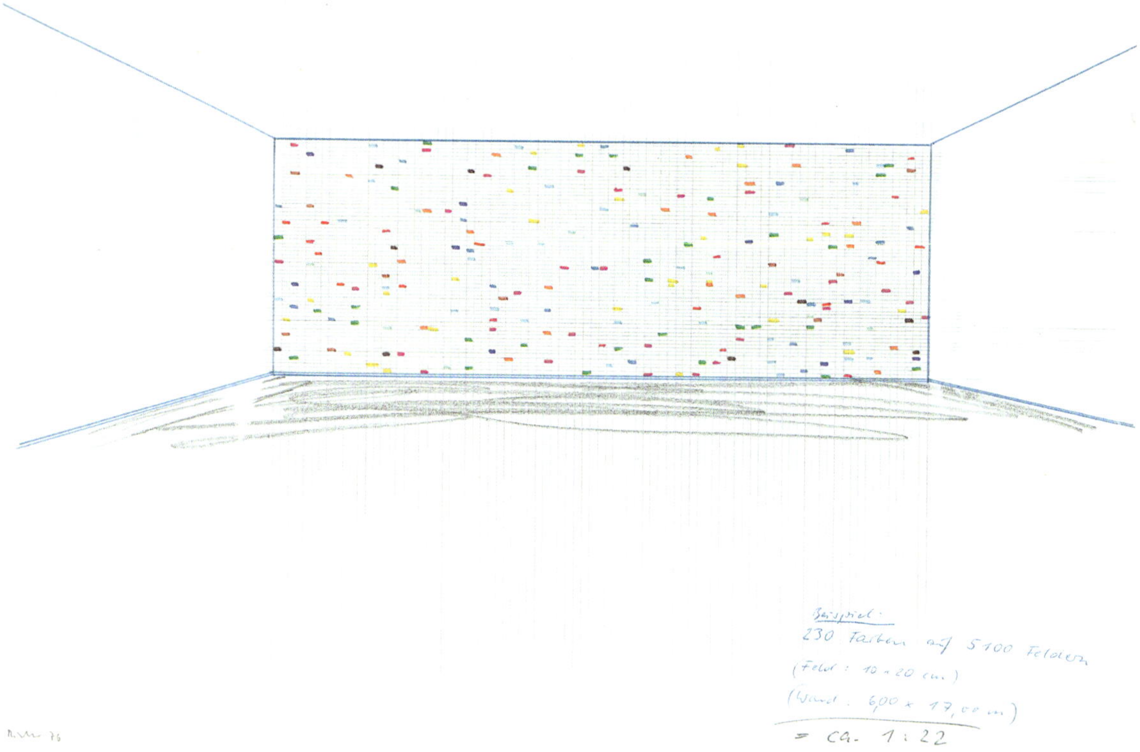
Beispiel:
230 Farben auf 5100 Feldern
(Feld: 10 x 20 cm)
(Wand: 6,00 x 17,00 m)
= ca. 1:22

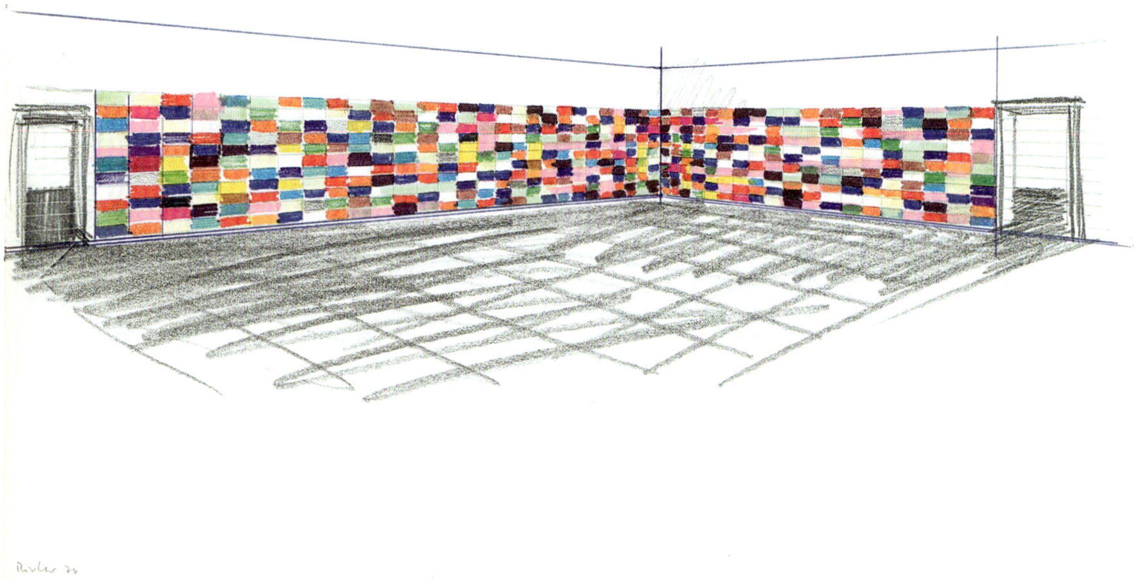

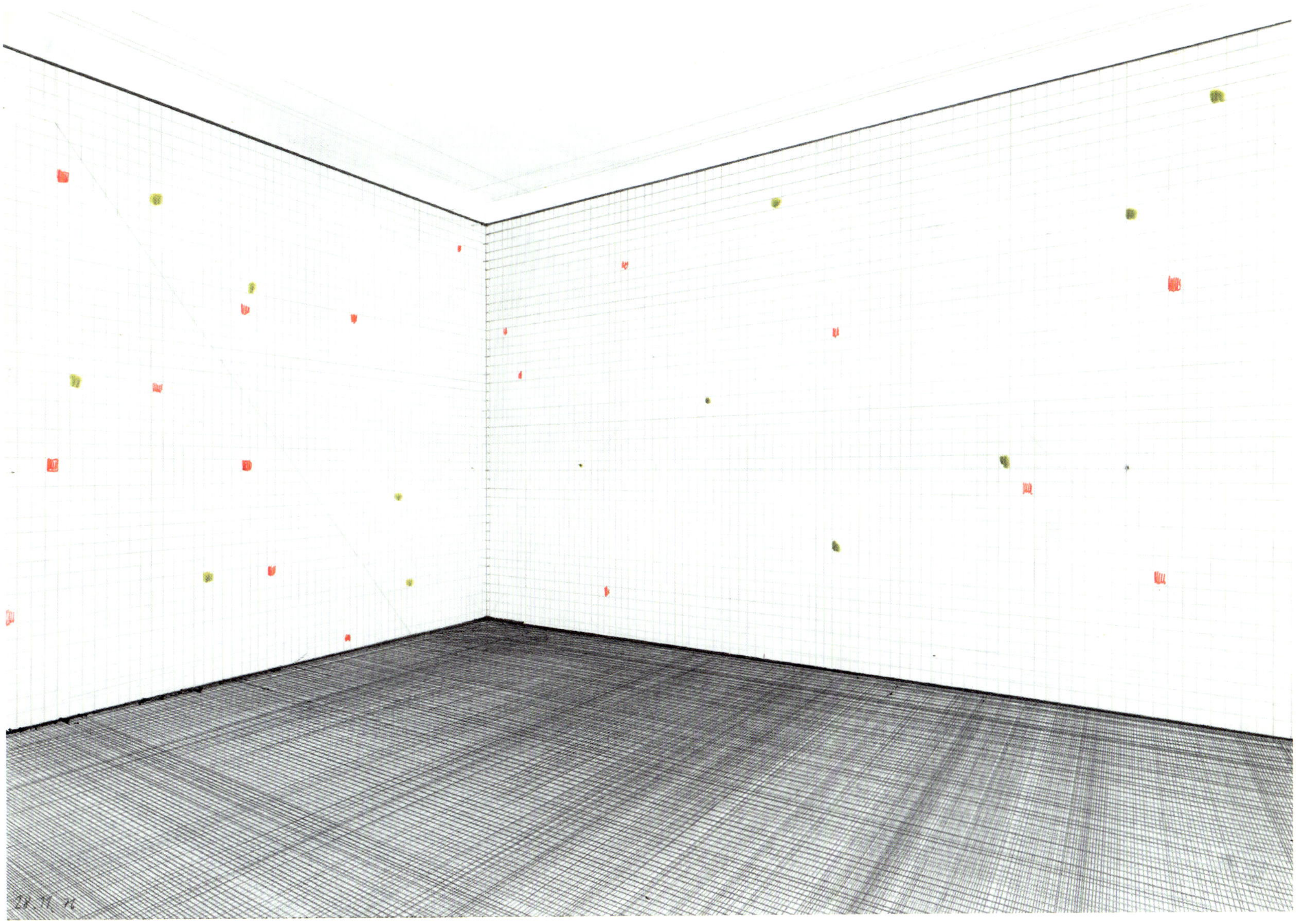

83
Ohne Titel ('Untitled'), 1976
Gerhard Richter
Felt-tip pen, ballpoint pen and graphite
210 x 295 mm

84
Ohne Titel ('Untitled'),
28 November 1976
Gerhard Richter
Felt-tip pen, ballpoint pen and graphite
210 x 295 mm

85
Ohne Titel ('Untitled'),
28 November 1976
Gerhard Richter
Felt-tip pen, ballpoint pen and graphite
210 x 295 mm
Presented by Count Christian Duerckheim to the British Museum

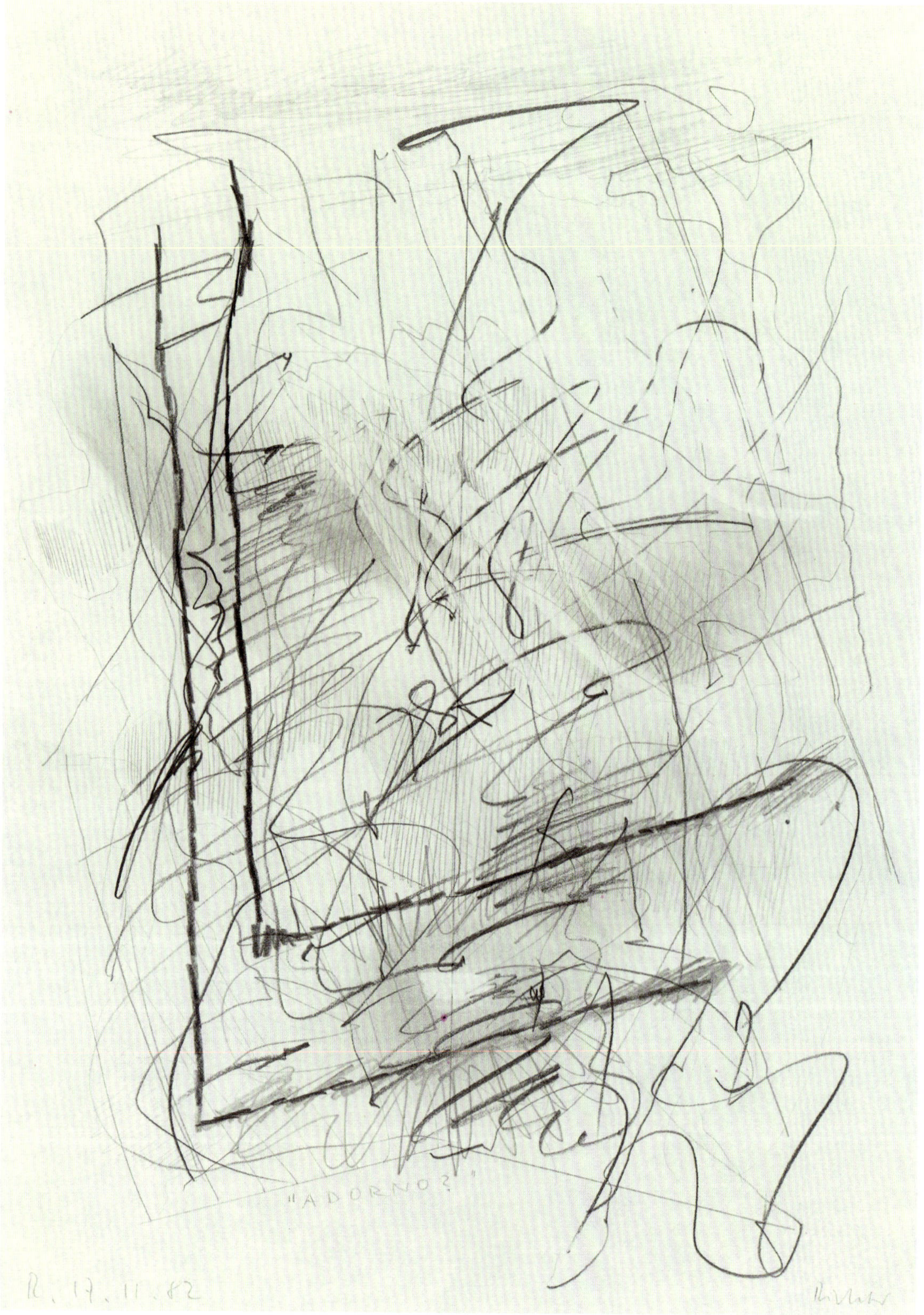

86
Adorno?, 17 November 1982
Gerhard Richter
Graphite
297 x 210 mm

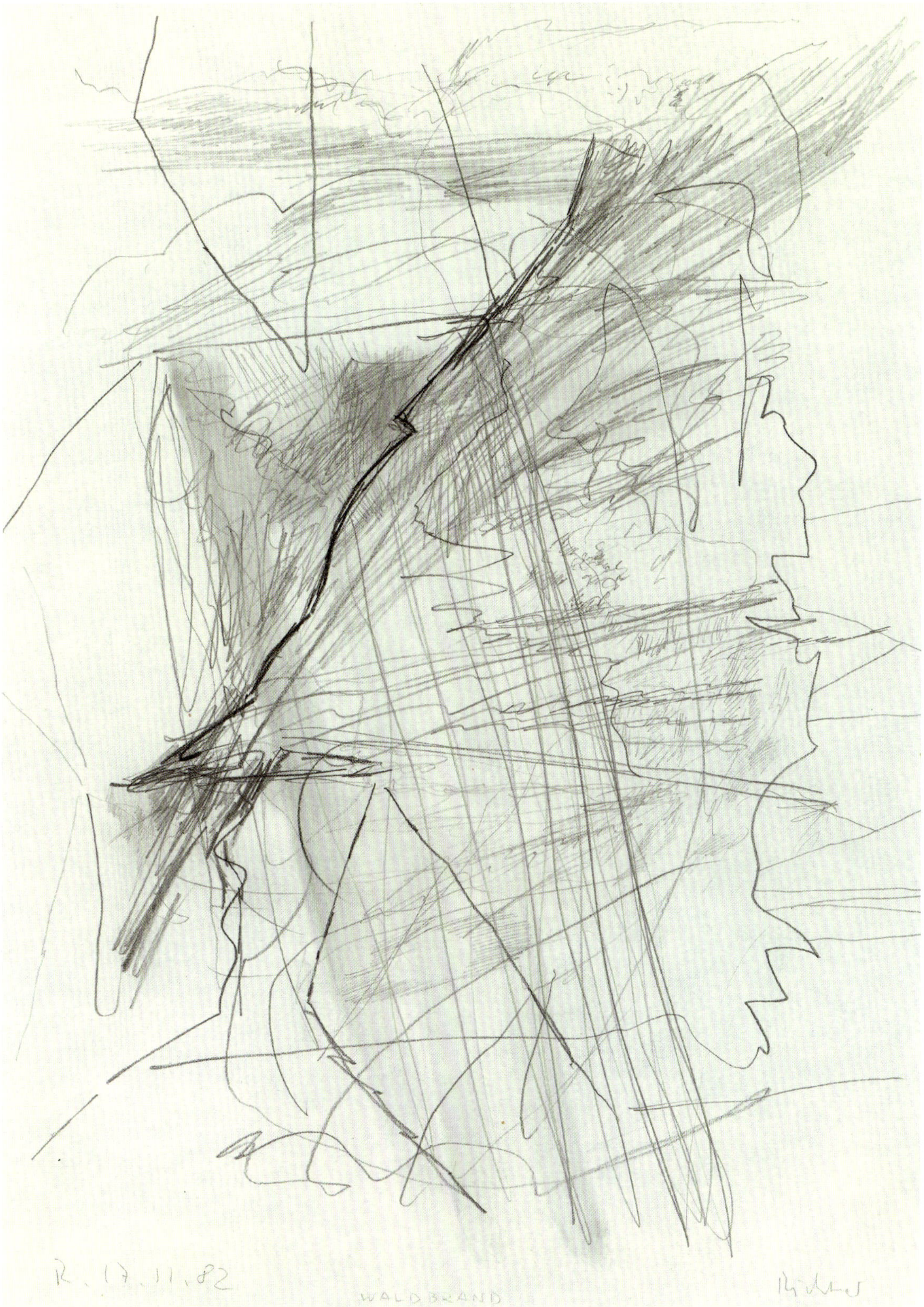

87
Waldbrand ('Forest Fire'),
17 November 1982
Gerhard Richter
Graphite
297 x 210 mm

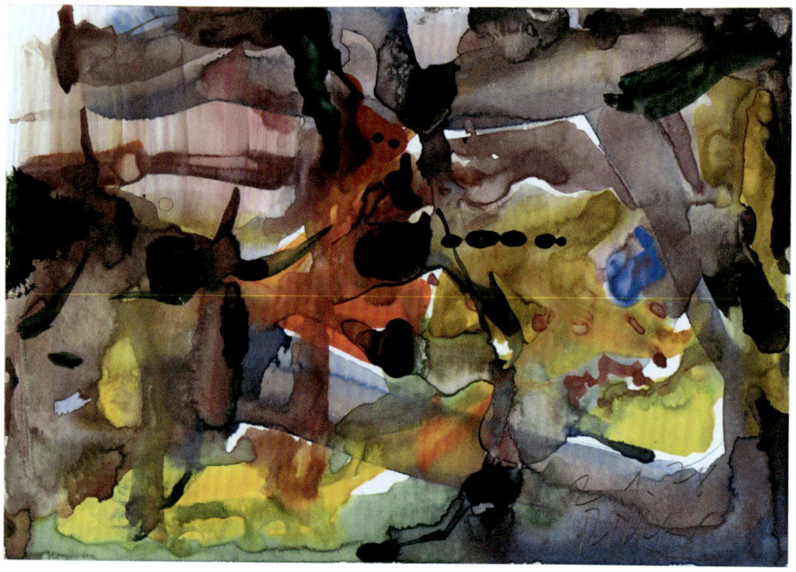

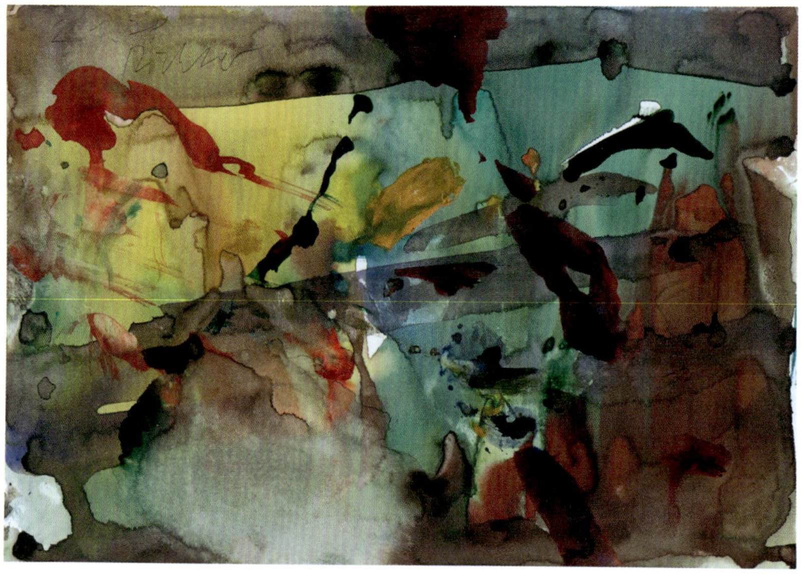

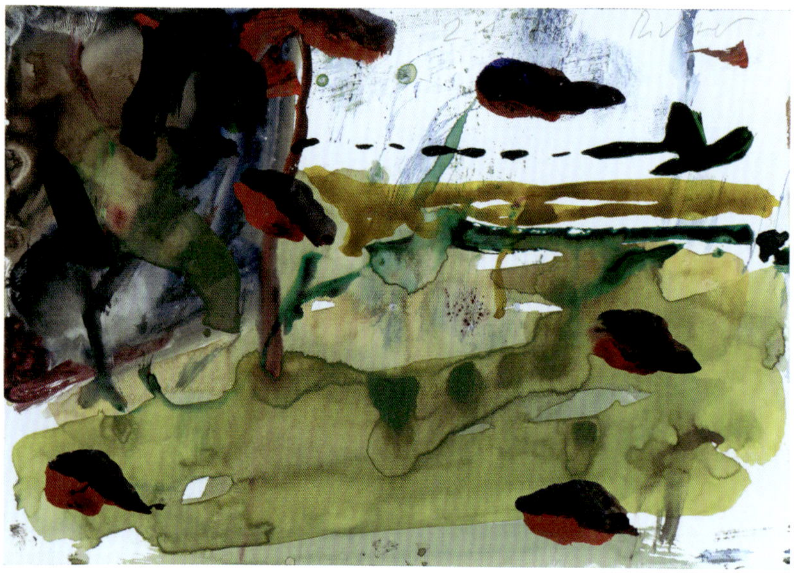

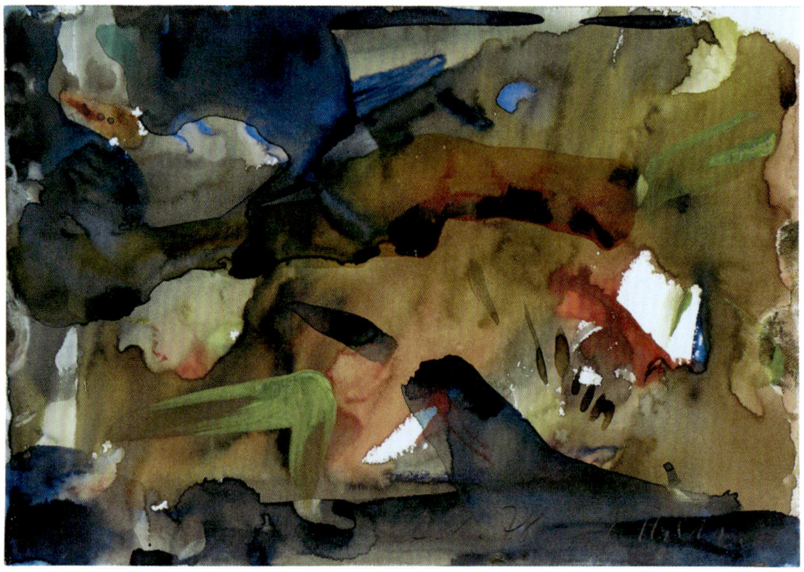

88
Ohne Titel (2.1.1978) ('Untitled (2.1.1978)'), 2 January 1978
Gerhard Richter
Watercolour
148 x 209 mm

89
Ohne Titel (2.1.1978) ('Untitled (2.1.1978)'), 2 January 1978
Gerhard Richter
Watercolour
148 x 209 mm

90
Ohne Titel (2.1.1978) ('Untitled (2.1.1978)'), 2 January 1978
Gerhard Richter
Watercolour
148 x 209 mm

91
Ohne Titel (2.1.1978) ('Untitled (2.1.1978)'), 2 January 1978
Gerhard Richter
Watercolour
148 x 209 mm

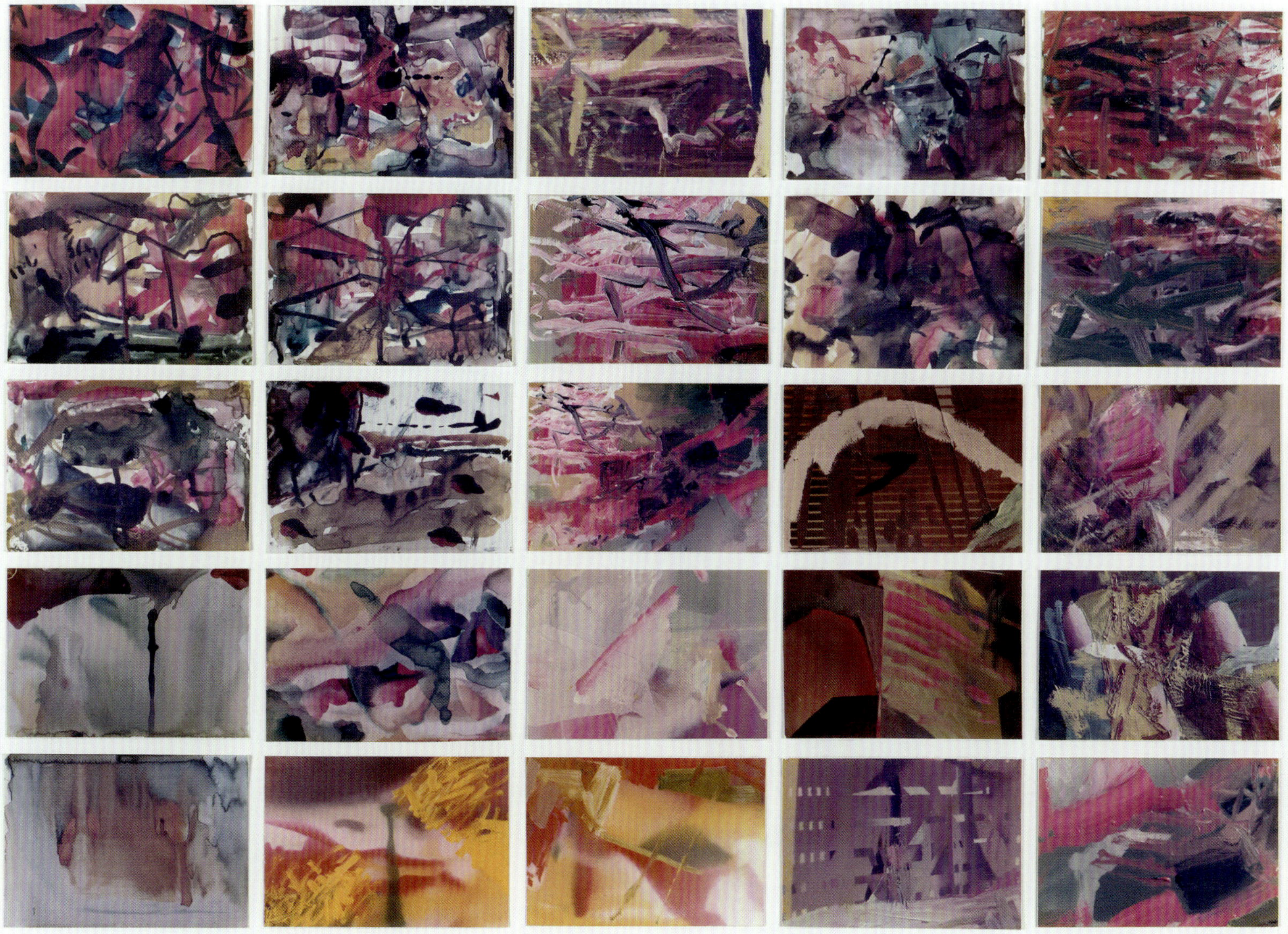

92
Sheet from *Atlas*, 1962–89
Gerhard Richter
Twenty-five colour photographs of abstract
paintings in watercolour and oil
499 x 649 mm

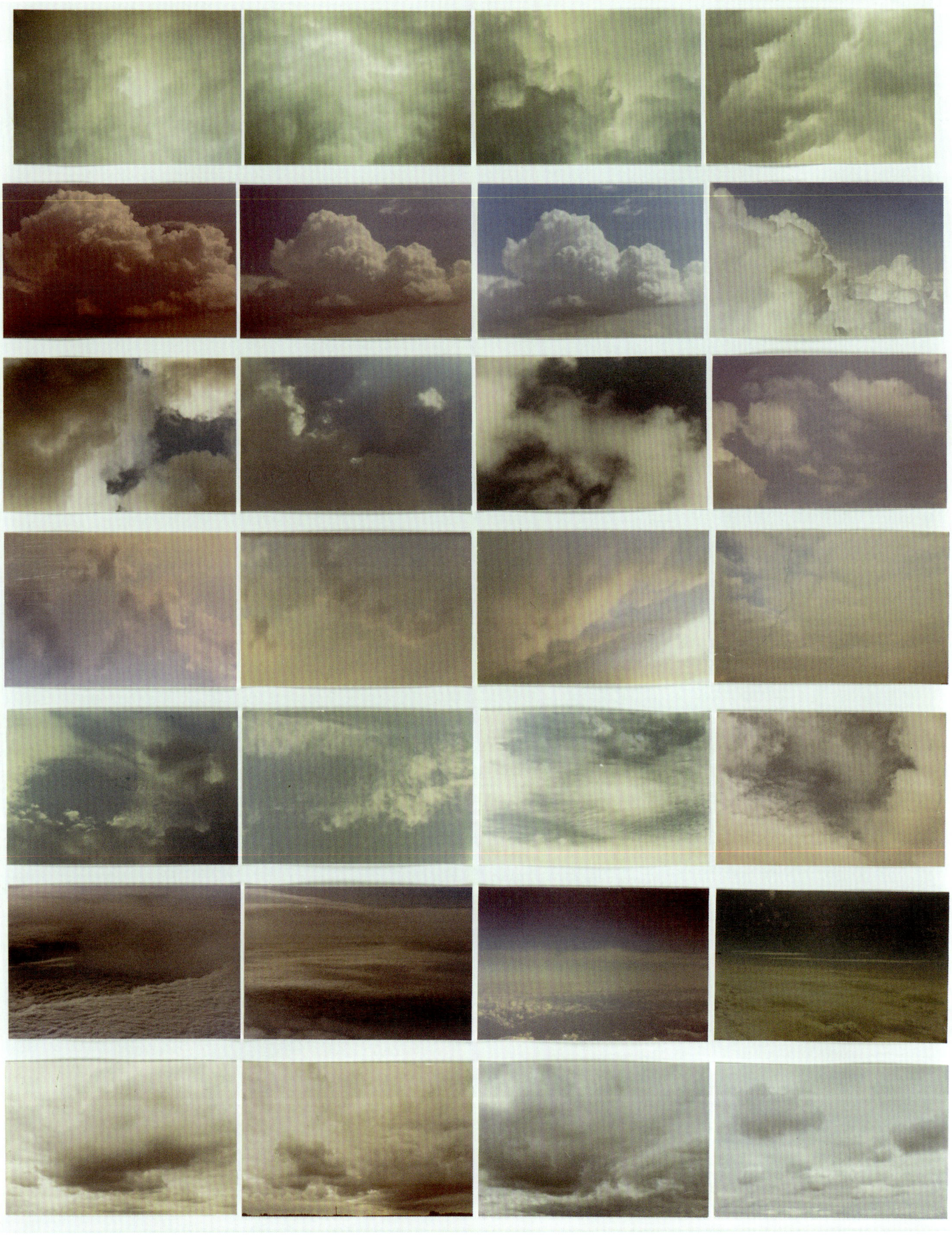

93
Sheet from *Atlas*, 1962–89
Gerhard Richter
Twenty-eight colour photographs
667 x 517 mm
Presented by Count Christian Duerckheim to the British Museum

94
Sheet from *Atlas*, 1962–89
Gerhard Richter
Fourteen black and white photographs and a newspaper clipping
667 x 517 mm

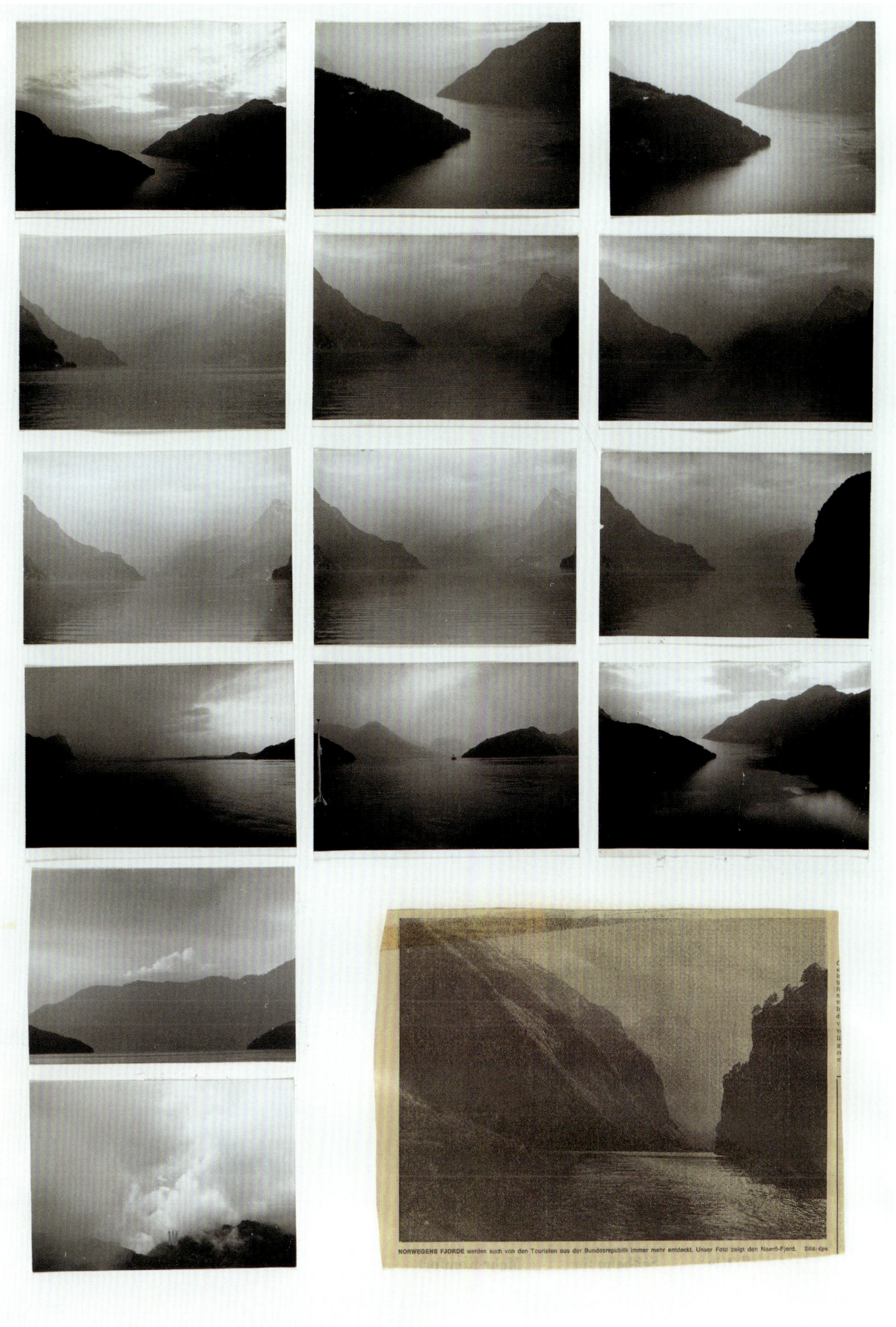

Catalogue

Unless otherwise stated, all works are from the Duerckheim collection.

Measurements refer to sheet size for drawings and to plate and image size for prints.

1 Georg Baselitz
Der Acker ('Field'), 1960
Ink and wash on thin wove paper
Dated lower right '6.7.60' in pencil. Verso: inscribed in pencil top right with title 'Acker' and top left '1960/69'. Various other markings in different hands, including lower left in pencil '[?] Graf Dürckheim'
295 x 207 mm
Duerckheim BG163
British Museum, London 2013,7043.1
Presented by Count Christian Duerckheim

Der Acker was one of the many early drawings Baselitz made of dismembered, disfigured bodies in landscape settings. Outsize feet were a recurrent motif and were partly inspired by an image in the *Nuremberg Chronicle* (1493) of a figure lying on the ground raising his one giant leg in the air. From 1960 to 1963 Baselitz made a series of paintings titled *P.D. Feet* (P.D. is an abbreviation for 'Pandemonium') showing a series of monumental feet, some clearly severed, on murky-grey grounds. The feet appear to be rotting and suggest a morbid relationship between the body and the landscape. This drawing relates in particular to the 1962 painting *Der Acker* ('The Field', ill. Rosenthal 2007, p. 53) showing two dismembered corpses, indistinct, but one with an erect penis, in a similarly barren field, with insect-like forms in the foreground and blades of grass marking the horizon.

2 Georg Baselitz
Ohne Titel ('Untitled'), 1961
Pen and ink and wash on thin wove paper
Signed lower right in pencil 'GB.61'. Verso: inscribed in pencil top right 'Ades 1961' and unidentified number markings in pencil
210 x 296 mm
Duerckheim BG147

3 Georg Baselitz and Eugen Schönebeck
Pandämonisches Manifest II ('Pandemonium Manifesto II'), 1962
Blueprint
Signed in pencil: 'G. Baselitz' below blueprint signature
Multiple blueprint signatures by both artists
Edition, this numbered in red biro pen '8'
901 x 1278 mm
Duerckheim BG278
Literature: Calvocoressi 1983, translation of text into English, pp. 23–9; Sotheby's 2011, ill. on pp. 78–9

Baselitz and Schönebeck wrote the first Pandemonium Manifesto in Berlin in November 1961. A handwritten version, accompanied by drawings, was printed using the cheap reproductive method of blueprint as the poster advertising an exhibition of works by the two artists held in Wilmersdorf that month. The two artists produced a further manifesto, *Pandämonisches Manifest II* ('Pandemonium Manifesto II') the following February, again printed as an editioned poster, comprising a text and drawings by each artist. The combination of youthful euphoria, eroticism and an expressive stream of language continues in Baselitz's text from the first manifesto: 'With solemn obsessiveness, autocratic elegance, with warm hands, pointed fingers, rhythmic love, radical gestures – we want to excavate ourselves, abandon ourselves irrevocably…'. References to Antonin Artaud and to the 'great Mannerist de-monstrance' are combined with descriptions that relate to the imagery of works from the 1960s, for example: 'Standing barefoot on suppurating stumps of felled trees, shouting into madness'. This might be taken as a description of the etching *Hirte* ('Herdsman'), 1966 (cat. 11). English translations of Baselitz's contributions to both Manifestos were published in the catalogue of the exhibition of his work held at the Whitechapel Gallery in 1983 (Calvocoressi 1983, pp. 23–9).

4 Georg Baselitz
Hunde ('Dogs'), 1964
Graphite and crayon on laid paper, cockerel and shield watermark. Direct transfer drawing in brown ink on verso
Signed lower right in pencil 'G.B. 64'. Verso: unidentified number markings in pencil
253 x 317 mm
Duerckheim BG156
British Museum, London 2013,7043.2
Presented by Count Christian Duerckheim
Literature: Munich 1972, cat. no. 20 (listed on sheet separate to bound catalogue), ill., unpaginated

A group of semi-featureless creatures, identified by the title as dogs, huddle together in what might be interpreted as a nest or a burrow. *Hunde* is in fact a drawing used to create a soft-ground etching, or *Vernis mou*, made by placing the sheet directly over an etching plate, a prepared ground recording the drawn marks. Baselitz began making soft-ground etchings in 1964, while on a scholarship to use the print studio at Schloss Wolfsburg. Reinhardt 1989 lists twenty-four etchings made using this method. This drawing was used to make the 1964 etching *Heulende Hunde*, which exists in three states. See Leverkusen 1974, pp. 16–17; Reinhardt 1989, cat. no. 16, ill. on p. 179.

5 Georg Baselitz
Ohne Titel ('Untitled'), *c.* 1965
Pen and ink and wash on laid Ingres Canson Paper
Signed below figure in pen and ink 'GB'
649 x 500 mm
Duerckheim BG076
Literature: Sotheby's 2011, ill. on p. 134

A stout, duck-like creature stands alone in a bare setting, suggesting a stage and backdrop, defined by quickly drawn horizontal and vertical strokes.

6 Georg Baselitz
Ohne Titel ('Untitled'), 1964
Pen and ink, brush and wash on wove paper
Signed lower right pen and ink 'Baselitz 64'. Verso: inscribed in pencil '65' in triangle
498 x 345 mm
Duerckheim BG056
British Museum, London 2013,7043.3
Presented by Count Christian Duerckheim
Literature: Dietrich-Boorsch 1982, cat. no. 6; ill. on p. 15

A winged figure appears to be tethered between two trees, with a large spherical form in the foreground. Vigorous drawn lines incise the paper and suggest Baselitz's knowledge of the destructive drawing technique of Antonin Artaud, whose work he had seen in Paris in 1959. This drawing can be compared to the 1964 ink drawing *Beatrice*, showing a similar figure suspended against a tree surrounded by indistinct creatures, and the painting *Das Kreuz II* ('The Cross II'), from the same year.

7 Georg Baselitz
Ohne Titel ('Untitled'), 1965
Charcoal on wove paper
Signed lower right of centre in pencil 'G.B. 65'
495 x 376 mm
British Museum, London 2013,7043.4
Presented by Count Christian Duerckheim
Duerckheim BG042
Literature: Hofmann and Joachimides 1988, ill. on p. 22

A lumpy humanoid figure is shown walking. The figure wears trousers and shoes, but its upper body is an indistinct agglomeration of corpulent shapes and, in place of a head, there is a bulging fleshy form with a long lizard's tongue. It can be compared with other drawings made in the same year, for example *Tierstück* ('Animal Piece').

Baselitz made this drawing while on a scholarship year in Florence, as a photograph taken of drawings pinned to the wall of his studio at the time demonstrates (reproduced by Hofmann and Joachimides 1988, p. 22). The motif of the full-length standing figure was developed in the *Heroes* series, for which this drawing may be taken as a precursor.

8 Georg Baselitz
Die Falle ('Trap'), 1965

Etching and drypoint with plate-tone on zinc plate, printed on wove paper
Signed on plate lower right 'GB'. Signed in pencil on sheet, lower right 'Baselitz 65'. Numbered lower left in pencil '3/10'.
Plate size 315 x 235 mm
Paper size 430 x 323 mm
Jahn 24; declared edition of ten, six of which printed in 1965
Duerckheim BG257
British Museum, London 2013,7043.5
Presented by Count Christian Duerckheim
Literature: Gercken 1973, cat. no. 6, ill., unpaginated; Friedrich 1974, ill. on. p. 39; Jahn 1983, cat. no. 24, ill. on p. 38; Gohr 1984, cat. no. 16, ill. on p. 80; Reinhardt 1989, cat. no. 37, ill. on p. 185; Semff 2008, cat. no. 15, ill. on p. 89

A monumental figure sits in a landscape, his bare feet caught in strange traps, his fingers jammed and apparently caught in crevices in the earth. His clothes are bulky and torn, his hair long and he carries a large knapsack from which three paint brushes protrude. He wears a mourning band around his arm; a miniature wheelbarrow and high-heeled shoe on the ground before him emphasize his grand size.

The gesture of the rigid hand appears in a number of the *Helden* ('Heroes') prints and paintings and is often accompanied by a wound, providing a direct reference to the crucifixion, for example in *Versperrter Maler* ('Blocked Painter'; 1965) (Rosenthal 2007, cat. no. 26), and *Ein moderner Maler* ('A Modern Painter'; 1966). The foot trap in *Die Falle* reappears in the 1966 painting of the same name (Rosenthal 2007, cat. no. 29), showing a similar crouching figure. Baselitz's hero-painters are allegorical figures of the situation in which many artists found themselves in the wake of the Third Reich, but they are also more generalized figures indicating the 'existential' plight of man in the ruins of Europe.

9 Georg Baselitz
Ohne Titel ('Untitled'), 1965
Etching and drypoint on zinc plate, printed on Richard-de-Bas wove paper
Signed in pencil on sheet lower right 'Baselitz 65'; numbered lower left '4/5'
Plate size 338 x 243 mm
Paper size 435 x 325 mm
Jahn 20
Duerckheim BG258
Literature: Gercken 1973, cat. no. 1, ill., unpaginated; Friedrich 1974, ill. on p. 31; Jahn 1983, cat. no. 20, earlier state ill. on p. 34; Reinhardt 1989, cat. no. 34, ill on p. 97; Rosenthal 2007, cat. no. 56, ill. on p. 110; Semff 2008, cat. no. 185, ill. on p. 82

The barefoot heroic figure in this print holds a house in his outstretched oversized hand, and is accompanied by a dog. What appears to be a pile of excrement blocks the figure's path. A makeshift wooden structure in the background and an empty porter's trolley suggest the theme of *dépaysement*, the sense of physical as well as psychic displacement.

10 Georg Baselitz
Der Hirte ('Herdsman'), 1965
Etching, drypoint and aquatint on zinc plate, printed on wove paper
Signed on plate lower right 'Baselitz'. Signed in pencil lower right 'Baselitz 65'; numbered lower left '6/60'
Plate size 313 x 237 mm
Paper size 423 x 325 mm
Jahn 28.II
Duerckheim BG256
Literature: Friedrich 1974, ill. on p. 47; Jahn 1983, cat. no. 28, ill. on p. 47; Gohr 1984, cat. no. 20, ill. on p. 76; Reinhardt 1989, cat. no. 45, ill. on p. 101; Semff 2008, cat. no. 18.2, ill. on p. 99

Der Hirte, along with the print *Rebel*, made the same year, are Baselitz's first successful attempts to create tonal values with an intaglio process (cf: Gohr, 1984, p. 21).

The format of an elongated figure against a low horizon recurs in the *Heroes* series, giving the figures a monumental, symbolic appearance. Their unnaturally small heads have been linked to the figure types common in the Mannerist prints admired and collected by Baselitz (Gohr 1984, p. 21), but might equally be connected with the diminutive heads featured on the large sculptural figures of Henry Moore.

The herdsman's right foot is caught in a simple trap – like a miniature goalpost – a recurrent theme of frustrated ambition in the *Heroes* series. An open standing structure behind the figure suggests the remains of a gateway – the indistinct morass of the landscape evokes the way in which bombardment destroyed all sense of identity and place, reducing everything to uniform piles of bricks and rubble. This print relates to the 1966 painting *Der Hirte* ('The Herdsman'; collection Frieder Burda).

11 Georg Baselitz
Hirte ('Herdsman'), 1966
Etching and drypoint on zinc plate, printed on wove paper
Signed on plate, lower centre left 'GB'. Signed lower right in pencil 'Baselitz 66'; numbered in pencil lower left '2/10'
Plate size 319 x 235 mm
Paper size 432 x 323 mm
Jahn 42.III
Duerckheim BG259
British Museum, London 2013,7043.6
Presented by Count Christian Duerckheim
Literature: Gercken 1973, cat. no. 2, ill., unpaginated; Friedrich 1974, ill. on p. 75; Jahn 1983, cat. no. 42.3, ill. on p. 63; Gohr 1984, cat. no. 29, ill. on p. 84; Reinhardt 1989, cat. no. 84, ill. on p. 201; Semff 2008, cat. no. 24.1, ill. on p. 122

The tragic demeanour of many of Baselitz's *Heroes* is undercut by a comic-grotesque mood, which runs throughout his work. Here the herdsman raises a whip to herd two large duck-billed creatures, a species that appeared in earlier works, such as the 1965 painting *Die Banane* ('The Banana'; Rosenthal 2012, ill. p. 43) showing two grotesque duck-headed creatures guarding a green banana.

12 Georg Baselitz
Ohne Titel ('Untitled'), 1966
Single block woodcut on wove paper
Signed lower right in pencil 'Baselitz 66'.
Verso: failed print of *Drei auf einer Bank* ('Three on a Bench')
Block size 418 x 325 mm
Paper size 515 x 390 mm
Jahn 50.III (third version)
Duerckheim BG100
Literature: Jahn 1983, cat. no. 50, two-block version ill. on p. 63; Gohr 1984, cat. no. 3a, two-block version ill. on p. 56; Semff 2008, cat. no. 30, two-block versions ill. on p. 136

This is a single-block version using the drawing block of Jahn 50.

13 Georg Baselitz
Ohne Titel ('Untitled'), 1966
Chiaroscuro woodcut printed from one drawn block in black and one tone block in dark grey, cut for highlights
Inscribed on verso in pencil 'Baselitz 66'
Block size 420 x 330 mm
Paper size (unevenly cut along lower edge) 425 x 388 mm
Jahn 50
Duerckheim BG099
British Museum, 2013,7043.7
Presented by Count Christian Duerckheim
Literature: Friedrich 1974; ill. on p. 225; Jahn 1983, cat. no. 50; ill. on p. 63; Gohr 1984, cat. no. 3a, ill. on p. 56; Semff 2008, cat. no. 30, ill. on p. 136

Ohne Titel (1966) was one of the first prints made by Baselitz on moving to Osthofen, in south-west Germany. The image of a crouching figure with his fingers trapped in the earth is developed from the etching *Die Falle*, made the previous year. A mid-grey tone block with white highlights is overlaid by a black drawn block, defining the figure and the surrounding landscape. Compared to the *Helden* etchings, the figure is larger and pushed further forward; yet stylistically the billowing lines and complex, interlaced structure is common to works in both media.

14 Georg Baselitz
Ohne Titel ('Untitled'), 1967
Chiaroscuro woodcut printed from three blocks on laid Canson paper
Signed lower right in pencil 'Baselitz 67'.
Verso blank
Block size 360 x 300 mm (line block)
Paper size 410 x 325 mm
Jahn 55.I (first state of four, probably seventh version of variant proof described by Jahn)
Duerckheim BG102
Literature: Friedrich 1974, ill. on p. 235; Jahn 1983, cat. no. 55, later state ill. on p. 82; Reinhardt 1989, cat. no. 121–6, ill. in different states on pp. 46–50; Rosenthal 2007, cat nos. 62–5, showing four variants, ill. on p. 115; Semff 2008, cat. nos. 35-2, ill. on p. 149. Semff also shows three other states.

Ohne Titel (1967) is one of a series of prints showing hunters and woodsmen with their dogs and prey. The figure is shown in black over an olive-green background tone, with the tree and ground overlaid by a thin, light reddish-brown. The olive-green tone block is larger than the black drawn block, creating a green border around the image.

The figure, whose facial features connect him with the *Heroes* series, appears to hold a large wooden plate on which a dead dog-like animal has been laid. The hunter stands in front of a tree and is horizontally bisected at the waist, the parts pulled apart so that the tree is visible through him. This fracturing of the motif came to define Baselitz's work over the next couple of years, developing the theme of the broken, disconnected body.

Jahn describes ten variant proofs of the first edition, leading to an edition of twenty, itself containing different combinations of two and three blocks with various colour schemes. Four further states show modifications of the image, particularly the background, with an edition of twenty variants of the fourth state (and none for the second, third and fifth). Such an extensive exploration of this image in some sixty-one variant prints indicates the importance of the woodsman motif for Baselitz.

15 Georg Baselitz
Ohne Titel ('Untitled'), 1966
Chiaroscuro woodcut printed from one drawn block in black and one tone block in reddish-brown, cut for highlights, on prepared paper.
Inscribed lower right 'Probedrücke II Zust. Baselitz 66' (Artist's proof, second state). Verso: inscribed in pencil 'CD' in circle
Block size 360 x 300 mm
Paper size 433 x 330 mm
Jahn 55.II (seventh variant proof described by Jahn)
Duerckheim BG108
Literature: Jahn 1983, cat. no. 55.2, later state ill. on p. 82; Gohr 1984, cat. no. 37a, ill. on p. 60; Rosenthal 2007, cat. nos 62–5, showing four variants, ill. on p. 115; Semff 2008, cat. nos 35-3, ill. on p. 150

The second state of this woodcut is printed in reddish-brown and black on paper prepared with an off-white coating, providing mute highlights. Compared to the first state, the drawn block for this state has been cut more, to show a tree on the upper right and an area of light textural strokes on the left. Highlights in the tone block indicate that Baselitz cut a new block for this version, the same size as the drawn block, unlike for the first state.

16 Georg Baselitz
LR, 1966
Chiaroscuro woodcut from one drawn block in black and two tone blocks in green and ochre
Signed lower right 'Baselitz 66'. Verso: inscribed lower centre in pencil 'CD' in circle
Block size 420 x 330 mm
Paper size 450 x 340 mm
Jahn 49.II (edition)
Duerckheim BG109
Literature: Friedrich 1974, ill on p. 223; Jahn 1983, cat. no. 49.II, edition, ill. on p. 72; Gohr 1984, cat. no. 32; artist's proof of second state ill. on p. 59; Semff 2008, cat. no. 29-1, version ill. on p. 134

LR is a reference to the nineteenth-century Saxon painter Ludwig Richter (1803–84) who painted landscapes and mountain scenes in the Elbe Valley and Bohemian mountains. He later became famous for woodcut illustrations of fairy tales and stories of country life. A fellow Saxon, he features a number of times in Baselitz's *Heroes* series, for example in the 1965 *Ludwig Richter auf dem Weg zur Arbeit* ('Ludwig Richter on the Way to Work') in which he seems shell-shocked and wounded, sleep-walking through a war-blackened landscape, his arms held rigid before him.

In the woodcut *LR*, the figure of Ludwig Richter stands in a landscape, cradling in his hands a wheelbarrow and a miniature house, symbols of displacement that often appear in the *Heroes* series. Objects are scattered, including a walking stick and a knapsack, attributes perhaps of the itinerant painter Ludwig Richter.

As with other chiaroscuro woodcut prints from the *Heroes* series, Baselitz produced an edition comprising variants using two to three blocks with different colour combinations, on different paper types.

17 Georg Baselitz
LR, 1966
Chiraoscuro woodcut from one drawn block in black and one tone block in purplish grey on smooth wove paper
Signed in pencil lower right 'Baselitz 66'. Verso: inscribed in pencil 'C.D' lower edge centre
Block size 420 x 328 mm
Paper size 450 x 348 mm
Jahn 49.II (edition)
Duerckheim BG110
Literature: Jahn 1983, cat. no. 49.II, edition, ill. on p. 72. Jahn illustrates five versions of the edition, made from the second state, each using different colour and block combinations; Gohr 1984, cat. no. 32, artist's proof of second state ill. on p. 59; Semff 2008, cat. no. 29-1, version ill. on p. 134

A two-block version of cat. 16.

18 Georg Baselitz
Partisan ('Partisan'), 1965
Yellow ochre gouache, grey wash, charcoal, graphite, white and pink pastel on laid paper
Signed in pencil lower centre 'G.B. 65'. Verso: inscribed in pencil top left: 'Baselitz/65/'Partisan''. Various other pencil markings
520 x 390 mm
British Museum, London 2013,7043.10
Presented by Count Christian Duerckheim
Duerckheim BG132
Literature: Sotheby's 2011, illustrated in photograph of artist's studio, p. 131

A figure stands in a landscape, legs apart and arms wide, his clothes tattered and torn; yet his expression seems optimistic, and his cavalier appearance is emphasized by what appears to be a pointed 'English' moustache. The emotional register of the figures in Baselitz's *Heroes* series is not always one conditioned by the pathos of defeat: they are 'caught in a kind of comic extremis; their faces look heavenward, but it is not clear if they're about to say "Ecce Homo" or start singing "Oh, What a Beautiful Morning"' (R. Smith, 'The Burden of Isolation in Baselitz's "Hero" paintings', *New York Times*, 30 March 1990).

19 Georg Baselitz
Ein neuer Typ ('A New Type'), 1965
Yellow ochre gouache, grey wash, charcoal, graphite, white and pink pastel on paper
Signed in pencil lower centre 'G.B. 65'. Verso: inscribed in pencil along lower right side 'Galerie M. Werner'. Various other markings in pencil
523 x 421 mm
Duerckheim BG131
British Museum, London 2013,7043.9
Presented by Count Christian Duerckheim
Literature: Koepplin 1984, cat. no. 106, ill., unpaginated; Sotheby's 2011, ill. on p. 130

The surrendering pose of the figure can be compared with the gesture of the hero in the painting *Spekulatius* (1965) (Sotheby's 2011, no. 24, ill. on p. 129), and the figure in the 1966 etching *Grün-Roter* ('Green-Red One'). Baselitz's *Heroes* often appear surrounded by a halo-like border, suggestive of a further protective layering; the figure is otherwise exposed, his trousers open at the front, alluding to an attitude of surrender. The pose of the figure suggests either falling, or having fallen, and indicates that this might be a paratrooper wearing a jump suit.

20 Georg Baselitz
Ein neuer Typ ('A New Type'), 1965
Grey and yellow ochre watercolour, charcoal, graphite and white pastel on laid paper
Signed in pencil lower left 'G.B.'. Verso: inscribed top left in pencil 'G.Baselitz/65/'Ein neuer Typ'. Various other pencil markings, including lower left 'Dahlem'
485 x 314 mm
Duerckheim BG130
British Museum, London 2013,7043.8
Presented by Count Christian Duerckheim

The 'New Type' in Baselitz's hero iconography is a figure symbolizing youthful regeneration and brings to mind the idea of the 'New Man', prevalent in Weimar Germany. The loose-fitting, baggy clothes, suggestive of battle-worn military outfit, are rendered with loosely-drawn marks over an ochre wash and evoke ragged, threadbare clothes. Swirling marks of grey wash and charcoal suggest a muddy battleground. The title might be read as ironic – if this is the 'New Type' then he appears tired and defeated, his head inclined to one side, a mourning band on his arm, his shoes lost in the muddy, ruined landscape through which he has been walking.

In the aftermath of the Second World War the question of the 'Menschenbild', or the 'Image of Man', was frequently raised in relation to art. When human rationality and morality had been put so much into question and when human life itself appeared to have been evacuated of all value, on what basis could one construct a meaningful image of the human body? For Baselitz the human body was bound to register the pathos of defeat.

21 Georg Baselitz
Zweigeteilter, mit ausgebreiteten Armen ('Divided Figure with Outstretched Arms'), 1966
Ink wash and graphite on heavy wove paper
Signed in pencil lower right 'G Baselitz 66'. Verso: various markings in pencil
502 x 341 mm
Duerckheim BG069
Literature: Werner 1974, cat. no. 6, ill., unpaginated; Friedrich 1976, ill., unpaginated

In 1966 Baselitz began dividing, or

fracturing, his full-length figures. The earliest of these are divided by a horizontal line, bisecting the image. Here the effect is like a game of consequences: the upper half of the drawing shows a figure wearing a bicorne hat, with a knapsack and outstretched arms; the lower shows a different figure. The stark division of the sheet suggests a different pictorial space. The perhaps unintended effect is of a figure standing waist-deep in water, emphasized by his raised arms.

Other drawings made at this time show a similar horizontal division of the image into two separate fields, such as *Geteilter Held* (1966) Private collection (Gohr 1992, cat. no. 53, unpaginated).

22 Georg Baselitz
L(udwig) R(ichter) auf dem Wege zur Arbeit (Halt suchend) ('L(udwig) R(ichter) on the Way to Work (Getting a Grip)'), 1965
Graphite, ink and wash on cartridge paper
Signed in ink lower right 'G.B.' Verso: inscribed in pencil 'G. Baselitz 65/– sucht Halt [?]. Other pencil markings and dark ink/printing marks on lower left
430 x 304 mm
Duerckheim BG134
Literature: Koepplin 1984, cat. no. 120, ill., unpaginated

This drawing relates to the painting *Ludwig Richter auf dem weg zur Arbeit* (1965), showing a similar figure leaning forward with straight arms and outstretched hands. Here the long-haired, ragged figure appears to drift through the messy landscape, over a pair of severed frozen hands with fingers jammed into the earth.

The drawing relates to depictions of soldiers rigid and prostrate with their fingers trapped in the ground, particularly the etching *Schubkarre mit Tornister* ('Wheelbarrow with Knapsack'), 1966 (Jahn 40), and the drawing *Am Boden* ('Being Down'), 1966, Ludwig Collection (Rosenthal 2007, cat. no. 51, ill. on p. 106).

23 Georg Baselitz
Fünf Streifen – Der Hirte ('Five Stripes – The Herdsman'), 1966/67
Ink wash and graphite on thin smooth wove paper
Signed in pencil lower right 'G Baselitz 66 '67'. Verso date inscribed in pencil '1967'
430 x 266 mm
Duerckheim BG068
Literature: Sotheby's 2011, ill. on p. 158

In this drawing of a herdsman with a wooden leg and a bandaged foot, Baselitz highlights the rough division of the picture into five horizontal bands by different strokes on the background. The figure relates to an untitled print from 1966 showing a figure holding a dead animal (Jahn 53) – possibly a lamb – against a background with similar linear divisions. On the basis of this print the indistinct mass in place of the midriff of the figure can be read as a dead animal, the hunter's prey.

24 Georg Baselitz
Ein neuer Typ ('A New Type', *c.* 1965)
Charcoal, grey wash, ink, white paint and graphite on textured wove Fabriano paper
Signed lower right 'G.B.'. Verso: faint pencil inscription upper left, '[?] am 3 Mai 66'
656 x 483 cm
Duerckheim BG043

A monumental figure stands in a ruined landscape, a flag on the ground behind him and a wheelbarrow to his right. The rigid gesture of his upper body, one arm set at an awkward right angle, recalls the highly-mannered poses of figures in the paintings of Egon Schiele, evoking extreme psychological states. Here the suggestion is of a frozen gesture of defeat. The figure type relates directly to the right-hand figure in the 1965 painting *Die großen Freunde* (Museum Ludwig, Cologne), who is in a similar pose with a flag and wheelbarrow. The pose was also repeated in the print *Ohne Titel* ('Untitled'), 1965/66.

25 Georg Baselitz
Zwei Streifen ('Two Stripes'), 1966
Charcoal, watercolour and graphite on thin laid paper
Signed lower left in pencil 'G Baselitz 66'. Verso: inscribed at foot of page 'Zwei Streifen/1966 G Baselitz'
500 x 295 mm
Duerckheim BG066
British Museum, London 2013,7043.11
Presented by Count Christian Duerckheim

Baselitz constructs his figure with a mass of marks that spill out from the body and occupy the surrounding space. The picture is bisected horizontally, a murky lower register giving the impression of a figure standing in water, although this is not the explicit subject matter. The gender of the figure is ambiguous, and it might be read as a female upper and a male lower body.

Baselitz began working on his *Frakturbilder*, or 'Fracture Paintings', in 1966. The division both of the subject, often a single standing figure, and the pictorial space into different zones of 'reality', emphasizes the artificial, abstract nature of the images. Baselitz was countering the naturalism and refined technique of Socialist Realism as well as the media-saturated world of Pop and commercial art. The earthy colour palette, the depiction of figures and animals in landscape settings, and the absence of any overt abstract elements, show the importance to Baselitz of nature and the imagery of the natural world.

Baselitz has related the *Frakturbilder* to cubism, with the difference that he worked by a method of 'patchwork': 'I simply paint patches, I do not sew them together but leave them free, in pieces' ('Outcomes, Prospects, Bounces. Georg Baselitz talks to Rainer Michael Mason', Mason 2007, pp. 150–67; here p. 165). Contemporary American painting was also a strong point of reference, particularly that of Willem de Kooning; Diane Waldman has compared the *Frakturbilder* with de Kooning's 'Women' painting, and noted the way in which both artists combine the figure and ground (D. Waldman, 'Georg Baselitz Kunst auf der Kipper', in: Waldman 1996, pp.1–178, here p. 52). Waldman draws further connections with Mark Rothko's divided pictorial field, and the painterly realism of Jasper Johns. As Shulamith Behr has noted, alongside further associations with the Surrealist game of *cadaver exquis* and an undeniable pictorial violence, the *Frakturbilder* also show how Baselitz absorbed the influence of Artaud's 'Theatre of Cruelty' and the implications of Prinzhorn's study of psychotic art (S. Behr, 'Fracture', in Rosenthal 2007, pp.121–2, here p. 121).

26 Georg Baselitz
Ohne Titel ('Untitled'), 1968
Charcoal and graphite on cream laid paper
Signed in pencil lower right 'G.B. 68 VI'. Verso inscribed in pencil with various numbers
353 x 500 mm
Duerckheim BG128

This drawing shows a single standing cow, probably a bull, divided into four sections.

27 Georg Baselitz
Ohne Titel ('Untitled'), 1968
Green watercolour, grey wash and graphite on Ingres Canson watermarked laid paper
Signed in pencil upper left 'Baselitz 68 VII'. Verso: inscribed in pencil upper left 'Baselitz 68'; various other pencil markings
325 x 498 mm
Duerckheim BG129
British Museum, London 2013,7043.12
Presented by Count Christian Duerckheim

Two yoked cows are shown standing, apparently divided in two. The vigorous drawing and shading are an exercise in dynamic mark-making, obscuring the subject in lines, forms and gestures that are difficult to read. Where the subject of Baselitz's series of etchings of the cow motif is, as Siegfried Gohr has suggested, not an actual cow but a drawing of a cow, the subject here appears more as the possibilities of drawing when the common sense rules of naturalism are dispensed with (Gohr 1984, p. 35).

The motif of the cow entered Baselitz's work in 1966 as part of the series of *Frakturbilder* and often appears as a segmented yet still living creature. Diane Waldman has related the 1968 painting *Die Kühe*, showing two cows in separate, collaged pictorial spaces, to Jacob Jordaens and Vincent van Gogh, particularly Van Gogh's 1890 painting of cows after Jordaens, held in the Musée des Beaux-Arts in Lille (Waldman 1996, p. 50). Yoked half-cows reappear in two etchings made the following year: *Zwei halbe Kühe mit Leine* (Jahn 68) and *Zwei Kühe im Joch* (Jahn 73).

28 Georg Baselitz
Drei Streifen Kühe ('Three Strips Cows'), 1966
Ink, graphite and grey wash on coarse laid paper
Signed in pencil lower left 'G Baselitz 66'. Verso: inscribed in pencil upper left 'G. Baselitz 66/drei Streifen Kühe'; in pencil 'Dahlem' in lower half of sheet
368 x 370 mm
Duerckheim BG126

The drawing is divided into three bands, the topmost a separately attached sheet.

The upper two bands show two cows, while in the lower section a dog growls at a pair of shoes. This drawing relates directly to the painting *Muh-Kühe* ('Moo-Cows'; 1966).

Baselitz's technique of drawing with short calligraphic lines fluidly defining the animal forms, hatched shading, and linear hatching of the background recalls the draughtsmanship of Mannerist artists, in particular Hendrik Goltzius, works by whom Baselitz collected.

29 Georg Baselitz
Zwei Hunde abwärts ('Two Dogs Downwards'), 1967
Ink and wash on brown paper
Signed top right in ink 'Baselitz' [G Baselitz?]. Verso: inscribed in pencil at top of page 'Zwei Hunde abwärts/1967/ Baselitz Osth'
520 x 380 mm
Duerckheim BG071
Literature: Sotheby's 2011, ill. on p. 162 (as *Ohne Titel*)

Two dogs hang pointing downwards in a landscape setting. They appear to be alive, but somehow magically rotated through ninety degrees.

Dogs often appear accompanying woodsmen in paintings of this period and carry both rural and military connotations; in the 1967 painting *Zwei Meißener Waldarbeiter* ('The Woodsmen from Meissen', Staatsgalerie moderner Kunst, Munich), the two woodsmen are dressed in green greatcoats and the fragmented dogs, depicted hovering in mid-air, have an air of violence.

This drawing relates to the painting *Drei Hunde abwärts* (1967) (Sotheby's 2011, cat. no. 33, ill. on p. 162); and also *Ein Hund abwärts* (1968) (Mason 2007, cat. no. 23, unpaginated).

Although not technically upside down, the inverted, hanging orientation of the two dogs looks forward to the full inversion of Baselitz's subject matter two years later. Elsewhere a dog is shown pointing upwards, rather than downwards: see *Ein Hund aufwärts* ('One Dog Upwards'; 1967, charcoal) (Burckhardt-Koechlin-Fonds, Koepplin 1989, cat. no. 21, ill. on p. 28).

30 Georg Baselitz
Landstraße ('Country Road'), 1969
Ink, watercolour and pencil on laid paper
Unsigned, undated. Verso: Unavailable to view, attached to mount
246 x 303 mm
Duerckheim BG001
Literature: Werner 1974, cat. no. 7, ill., unpaginated; Groningen 1979, cat. no. 13, ill. on p. 21

Baselitz's first upside-down painting was a landscape from 1969, *The Wood on its Head* (Museum Ludwig, Cologne). He has described the origins of this painting as being a landscape by the nineteenth-century Saxon artist Ferdinand von Rayski, *Pause During a Hunt in the Wermsdorf Woods* (Georg Baselitz in conversation with Jean-Louis Froment and Jean-Marc Poinsot, reprinted in Gretenkort 2010, pp. 61–9; here p. 67).

This small landscape drawing is among the first to show the inverted motif that was to dominate Baselitz's work over the coming decades. It shows a straight path receeding into a woodland, a motif deployed by Paul Cézanne in depictions of the *Jas de Bouffon* and before him Poussin in his painting *A Roman Road* (Dulwich Picture Gallery).

31 Georg Baselitz
Birken (Paysage) ('Birch Trees (Paysage)'), 1972
Ink and watercolour on printed page
Signed in ink lower right 'GB. 72'; preceeded by pencil inscription 'XI'. Verso: minor pencil inscription
577 x 435 mm
Duerckheim BG025
British Museum, London 2013,7043.13
Presented by Count Christian Duerckheim

An inverted drawing of tree motifs on a page torn from an antiquarian book. Baselitz used a sheet (page 92) from the third volume of *Le Musée Français. Recueil complet des tableaux, statues at bas-reliefs qui composent le collection nationale*, Paris, 1807, part of a series of volumes cataloguing and illustrating with engraved plates the art treasures of France under Napoleon and subsequently under the restored Bourbon monarchy. The series is divided by subject, the third volume covering *Paysage, marines et vues* ('Landscapes, seascapes and views'). Baselitz made numerous drawings on sheets from *Le Musée Français*, the earliest dating to 1969 and the most recent 1989.

The page for *Birken (Paysage)* is headed 'Paysage' and describes a painting by the Flemish artist Willem de Heusch: *Paysage avec Paysans Conduisant un Troupeau*, Musée du Louvre. The reverse of the sheet shows the first page of the chapter on landscape and the beginning of the description of Heusch's work. Baselitz develops his natural images from photographs or memories, rather than working directly from nature. Drawing on a page from an art historical text evokes this distance from the subject matter and the sense in which Baselitz's subjects are filtered not only by the technique of inversion, but also by their origins in literature.

32 Georg Baselitz
Apfelbäume ('Apple Trees'), 1975
Oil, watercolour and charcoal on smooth brown paper
Signed in pencil lower right 'G Baselitz Nov 75'. Verso: inscription lower right of number calculation
613 x 429 mm
Duerckheim BG045

In 1975 Baselitz moved to live and work in Derneburg Castle near Hildesheim. During this year he made paintings of figures, often himself and his wife, Elke, and of landscape motifs around his home and studio. These landscape and figure paintings signal a move away from the often allegorical and symbolic imagery of his work of the 1960s, introducing subject matter from his immediate surroundings and daily life. The drawing is related to the painting *Apfelbäume* ('Apple Trees'; 1973, coll. Museum Brandhorst, Munich).

33 Georg Baselitz
Mann am Baum abwärts ('Man on a Tree Downwards'), 1968/69
Charcoal on laid paper
Signed in pencil lower right 'Baselitz 1969'. Verso: inscribed in pencil lower right 'Mann aus Baum abwärts /68/69'
500 x 324 mm
Duerckheim BG124
British Museum, London 2013,7043.14
Presented by Count Christian Duerckheim

This rapid sketch shows the bare description of a figure upside down on, or against, a tree. A related, more complete drawing made the same year, also titled *Mann am Baum abwärts* (Koepplin 1989, cat. no. 23, ill. on p. 30) shows that the figure holds the tree with his left arm while his right arm is extended and reaches out into a clutter of unidentified objects. This drawing relates to the painting *Der Mann am Baum* ('Man by a Tree'; 1969, coll. Pinakothek der Moderne, Munich).

34 Georg Baselitz
Am Baum abwärts ('Downwards by a Tree'), 1969
Graphite and watercolour on laid paper
Signed in pencil lower right 'G.B. IV 69'. Verso: inscription in pencil on lower edge 'am Baum abwärts/G. Baselitz 69'. In different hand in pencil 'KATZ 284'
499 x 330 mm
Duerckheim BG067

This drawings relates directly to the painting *Waldarbeiter* ('Woodmen'; 1967/68, coll. Museum of Modern Art, New York). See also *Der Mann am Baum* ('The Man by the Tree'; 1969, Pinakothek der Moderner, Munich; Rosenthal 2007, cat. no. 78, ill. on p. 133). The motif of a figure standing next to a tree appears frequently in the *Heroes* series, for example in the 1966 drypoint *Einer am Baum* (Jahn 32).

35 Georg Baselitz
Akt mit Flügel ('Nude with Wings'), 1975
Oil on smooth light brown paper
Signed lower right 'G Baselitz Dez 75'. Verso blank
558 x 407 mm
Duerckheim BG048
Literature: Sotheby's 2011, ill. on p. 132

This inverted self-portrait relates to a number of paintings and drawings Baselitz made of himself and his wife in 1975. The painting *Dreieck Zwischen Arm und Rumpf* ('Triangle between Arm and Torso'; Rosenthal 2007, cat. no. 84, ill. on p. 143) made two years earlier presents the figure in the same pose, the title emphasizing the formal, abstract qualities of the work, influenced in particular by the painting of Edvard Munch.

Baselitz was focusing on his self-image at a time when he was becoming internationally successful as an artist. The nude portraits of himself and his wife are remarkable for their frank exposure. The outstretched arm of the figure suggests an artist at work, but also connects with the pose of certain of the figures in the *Heroes* series. The blue halo, the 'wing' of the title, surrounding the figure in the self-portait recalls the protective halo around many of the *Heroes* figures. A further drawing from this series was used as the poster for an exhibition of Baselitz's works at the Kunsthalle, Bern, in 1976.

The outstretched arm pose was to be repeated most notoriously in Baselitz's first sculpture *Model for a sculpture* (1979–80) showing a recumbent figure lifting itself from the ground and saluting with an outstretched arm.

36 Georg Baselitz
Sitzender männlicher Akt ('Seated Male Nude'), 1976
Charcoal with grey, green and black wash on off-white laid paper
Signed and dated in pencil lower right, 'Baselitz 14.II.76'
487 x 300 mm
Duerckheim BG123

This drawing relates directly to the paintings *Männlicher Akt – sitzend* ('Male nude – seated'; 1979, Private collection) and *Sitzender männlicher Akt – Marokko* ('Seated Male Nude – Morocco'; 1976 coll. St Louis Art Museum, St Louis).

A series of similar drawings, dated 25.2.1976, is documented in Groningen 1979, cat. nos 31–3, ill. on p. 27.

37 Georg Baselitz
Sitzender männlicher Akt ('Seated Male Nude'), 1973
Graphite and red watercolour on page torn from antique register with blind stamp.
Signed in pencil lower left 'VI 1973 GB.'; inscribed in ink, lower right, upside down in older hand '400'. Verso: Unavailable to view, attached to mount
427 x 290 mm
Duerckheim BG013

This is one of a number of works from mid-1970s showing a seated nude figure, inverted, often identified as a self-portrait. The pose relates to the painting *Männlicher Akt* ('Male Nude'; 1975, coll. North Carolina Museum of Art, Raleigh).

38 Georg Baselitz
Adler im Gebirge ('Eagle in the Mountains'), 1977
Linocut, printed in black oil-based ink, over painted with grey oil paint, on paper
Inscribed and signed in pencil on verso, lower right: 'No. 4/Jun 77/G Baselitz'
612 x 270 mm
Duerckheim BG211
Literature: Jahn 1987, 211.IV (erroneously illustrated on p. 65 as the fifth state and reproduced upside down); Gohr 1979, cat. no. 27 (d), ill. on p. 68

An eagle is shown in flight against a backdrop of mountain ridges, the image inverted and further obscured by a covering of translucent brushed grey paint. Baselitz frequently used a narrow vertical format for his images of standing or sitting figures; this is one of a small group of prints in which the format is used to show an eagle in a landscape.

39 Georg Baselitz
Fliegender Adler ('Flying Eagle'), 1977
Linocut printed in black oil-based ink with additions in grey, red and yellow oil paint on thin smooth paper
Inscribed and signed in pencil on verso, lower edge, 'No 4 Jan 77/G Baselitz'
308 x 276 mm
British Museum, London 2013,7043.15
Presented by Count Christian Duerckheim
Duerckheim BG221
Literature: Jahn 1987, cat. no. 207.IV, ill. on p. 60

Eagles appear frequently as a motif in Baselitz's paintings, beginning in the 1970s. This linocut shows an eagle flying upside down, alongside three patches of paint that suggest the colours of a flag. Although Baselitz has stated that his technique of inversion was a way of emptying his paintings of content, so that we might not read meaning into the symbols he paints, it also allows him to use highly charged symbols such as the eagle and the flag, both emblems of national history.

40 Georg Baselitz
Adler ('Eagle') 1977
Linocut with oil paint on paper
Signed in pencil lower right 'GB 77'
300 x 270 mm
British Museum, London 2013,7043.16
Presented by Count Christian Duerckheim
Duerckheim BG192

The forms of an inverted eagle are obscured in a mass of lines, and further covered by three broad strokes of oil paint, evoking the colours of the German flag.

41 Georg Baselitz
Adler ('Eagle'), 1981/82
Woodcut with oil-based ink on 'offset' litho paper
From the portfolio *Erste Konzentration I*, published by Maximilian Verlag, Sabine Knust, Munich, 1982
Signed lower left on block 'B'; signed in pencil on sheet lower right 'G Baselitz'.
Verso: numbered in pencil lower left 'I/ VI/VIII'
997 x 794 mm
British Museum, London 2013,7043.32.1
Presented by Count Christian Duerckheim
Duerckheim BG289
Literature: Dückers 1982, cat. no. 1, ill., unpaginated; Geneva 1983, cat. no. 59, ill. on p. 54; Gohr 1984, cat. no. 139, ill. on p. 153; Jahn 1987, cat. no. 419, from second listed edition, number six of declared edition of eight, ill. on p. 241; Adriani 1994, cat. no. 50, ill. on p. 89; Chávez 2003, cat. no. 34, ill. on p. 202

Adler, one of Baselitz's most unambiguous uses of the eagle motif, was included in the first part of the *Erste Konzentration* tripartite print portfolio, published by Sabine Knust, Munich, in 1982. Each of the three portfolios contained twelve prints collated by size, made by one of the six contributing artists: Georg Baselitz, Antonius Höckelmann, Jörg Immendorff, Per Kirkeby, Markus Lüpertz and A.R. Penck (see Dückers 1982; and S. Knust, 'Über Meine Verlegerische Tätigkeit', in Geneva, 1983 pp. 131–2). As Alexander Dückers writes in the foreword to the catalogue of the Erste Konzentration, the term 'concentration' refers both to the act of collecting thirty-six prints together in three portfolios, but also to the sense of reflection on recent history. All six contributing artists were born during the Third Reich and made work that in some way reflected on the experience of war, defeat and then the political division of the country. Baselitz's raptor is shown perched, upside down, and given the appearance of falling, inevitably evoking a political downfall.

42 Markus Lüpertz
Ohne Titel ('Untitled'), 1972
Graphite and coloured pencil on smooth white paper
Signed with monogram in pencil lower left 'M' and 'L' combined. Verso: various inscriptions in pencil including, lower left, date '1972' and lower right pricing and inventory numbers
150 x 205 mm
Duerckheim LM032

Lüpertz began using military regalia in his paintings around 1970. The helmet shown can be compared with the *Stahlhelm*-type helmets depicted in paintings such as *Schwarze Rot Gold I* ('Black Red Gold I'; 1974, Kunstmuseum Stuttgart), and also to articulated armour incorporating a visor, as well as *Kabuto*, the head pieces of traditional Japanese armoured suits.

A similar drawing is illustrated in Pforzheim 1994, cat. no. 105, p. 134.

43 Markus Lüpertz
Ohne Titel ('Untitled'), 1972
Graphite and coloured pencil on smooth white paper
Signed in pencil with monogram lower left 'M' combined with 'L'. Verso: various inscriptions in pencil including, lower left, date '1972', and lower right pricing and inventory numbers
150 x 205 mm
Duerckheim LM035

44 Markus Lüpertz
MONUMENT – dithyrambisch ('MONUMENT – dithyrambic'), 1976
Gouache and ink on brown packing paper
Signed in pencil lower left 'Markus'[?].
Verso: signed in black pastel along upper right edge: 'Markus'. Inscribed in pencil along lower right edge 'CD', in circle
447 x 626 mm
Duerckheim LM014
British Museum, London 2013,7043.25
Presented by Count Christian Duerckheim
Literature: Hofmann 1977, cat. no. 139, ill. on p. 50

Entry as with cat. 45.

45 Markus Lüpertz
MONUMENT – dithyrambisch ('MONUMENT – dithyrambic'), 1976
Gouache, ink and oil pastel on brown packing paper
Signed in pencil lower right 'Markus'.
Inscribed in pencil lower right, 'CD' in circle
447 x 625 mm
Duerckheim LM013
British Museum, London 2013,7043.24
Presented by Count Christian Duerckheim
Literature: Hofmann 1977, cat. no. 136, ill. on p. 50

MONUMENT – dithyrambisch is one of a series of drawings by Lüpertz relating to the 'Style' paintings of the same moment and directly to three monumental compositions *Bilder zur Erschaffung der Erde* ('Pictures for the Creation of the Earth'), all 1976. Of these, Siegfried Gohr wrote: 'The first picture [in the series] establishes the vocabulary and framework. The linear construction of the left half of the painting is related to the more fixed, superficial arrangement of the right half. The colour is restricted to black and blue with an admixture of white. A reddish-brown swathe is the only violation of this palette. The surface of the picture is enlivened with gestural brush-work which gives the impression of an unceasing process of change in the pigment' (S. Gohr, 'Remarks on the paintings of Markus Lüpertz', in Gohr 1981, unpaginated).

Further drawings from the same series are in the Ludwig Collection (see: Aachen 1999, cat. nos. 98–101, ills. on pp. 114–17). Hofmann 1977 illustrates eight similar drawings, developing the motif, including this and LM013 (Hofmann, 1977, cat. nos 132–9, p. 50).

46 Markus Lüpertz
Ohne Titel ('Untitled'), *c.* 1977
Ink wash and coloured crayon on smooth off-white paper
Signed in pencil lower right 'Markus'
652 x 499 mm
Duerckheim LM016
British Museum, London 2013, 7043.26
Presented by Count Christian Duerckheim

This drawing relates to paintings made by Lüpertz around 1977 as part of the 'Style' paintings series, for example, *Stil: Eins – Zehn/VII. Große form mit Linie 2* (1977), which shows a comparable kite-like structure on the left.

A series of 43 drawings made in 1977 develops the motif of the parallelogram, referring to architectural structures that began appearing in Lüpertz's paintings in the mid-1970s, for example in the series *Babylon* (1975) and *Kathedrale* ('Cathedral'; 1976). See: Kneubühler 1977.

47 Blinky Palermo
Ohne Titel ('Untitled'), 1969
Gouache with pencil under-drawing on smooth white paper, mounted on off-white card
Signed and dated on mount, below image, 'Palermo 69'
Image: 479 x 422 mm
Mount: 832 x 674 mm
British Museum, London 2013,7043.23
Presented by Count Christian Duerckheim
Duerckheim PB005
Literature: Dietrich-Boorsch 1982, cat. no. 65, ill. on p. 63; Moeller 1995 (1), cat. no. 367, ill., unpaginated

This large drawing suggests a view through a dark curtain to an illuminated architectural interior. Like many of Palermo's works, it is presented as a mysterious fragment.

48 Blinky Palermo
Ohne Titel ('Untitled'), 1968
Crayon on squared tracing paper, attached to off-white card mount, above cat. 49
Signed in pencil lower edge centre, 'Palermo 68'. Verso of card mount inscribed in pencil 'Friedrich'
Drawing: 295 x 420 mm
Card mount: 683 x 480 mm
Duerckheim PB013.01
Literature: Moeller 1995 (2), cat. no. 345, ill., unpaginated; Cooke 2010, ill. on. p. 89; Sotheby's 2011, ill. on p. 174

Palermo frequently produced drawings for his personal archive as a way of recording both his sculptural works and wall paintings, the latter being always temporary installations. *Ohne Titel* ('Untitled'; 1968) relates to the sculpture *Graue Scheibe* ('Gray Disk'; 1970). The use of graph paper suggests that this is a working drawing for a sculpture or an architectural installation.

Catalogued by Moeller with Duerckheim cat. 49 as a single item.

49 Blinky Palermo
Ohne Titel ('Untitled'), 1969
Ballpoint pen and gouache on graph paper, mounted on off-white card, below cat. 48
Signed and dated in pencil lower edge centre 'Palermo 69'; various ballpoint pen inscriptions on sheet, including words 'Graue Scheibe' ('Gray Disk'). Verso of card mount inscribed in pencil 'Friedrich'
Drawing: 210 x 296 mm
Card Mount: 683 x 480 mm
Duerckheim PB013.02
Literature: Moeller 1995 (2), cat. no. 345, ill., unpaginated; Cooke, 2010, ill. on p. 89; Sotheby's 2011, ill. on p. 174

50 Blinky Palermo
Ohne Titel ('Untitled'), from the portfolio *4 Prototypen* ('4 Prototypes'), 1970
Screenprint in green ink on white card
Signed in pencil lower right 'Palermo 70'; edition number inscribed in pencil lower left '36/90'. Verso blank
600 x 600 mm
Duerckheim PB011.01
Literature: Leverkusen 1975, ill. on p. 27; Jahn 1983, cat. no. 7, ill. on pp. 26–7; Dahlem 1989, ill. on p. 128; Leipzig 1993, ill. on p. 153; Mehring 2008, ill. on p. 28; Cooke 2010, ill. on. p. 94

The series *4 Prototypen* ('4 Prototypes') was published by Galerie H. Friedrich, Munich, through the Verlag G. v. Pape, Munich, March 1970. It was printed by Serigraphisches Atelier Laube, Munich.

This series of four screenprints relates to Palermo's *Objects*, coloured sculptural works, usually simple monochrome shapes displayed on a wall like paintings. The strong, vibrant colour contrasts with the ragged, uncertain edges of the shapes.

51 Blinky Palermo
Ohne Titel ('Untitled'), from the portfolio *4 Prototypen* ('4 Prototypes'), 1970
Screenprint in black ink on white card
Signed in pencil lower right 'Palermo 70'; edition number inscribed in pencil lower left '36/90'. Verso blank
600 x 600 mm
Duerckheim PB011.02

52 Blinky Palermo
Ohne Titel ('Untitled'), from the portfolio *4 Prototypen* ('4 Prototypes'), 1970
Screenprint in blue ink on white card
Signed in pencil lower right 'Palermo 70'; edition number inscribed in pencil lower left '36/90'. Verso blank
600 x 600 mm
Duerckheim PB011.04

53 Blinky Palermo
Ohne Titel ('Untitled'), from the portfolio *4 Prototypen* ('4 Prototypes'), 1970
Screenprint in grey ink on white card
Signed in pencil lower right 'Palermo 70'; edition number inscribed in pencil lower left '36/90'. Verso blank
600 x 600 mm
Duerckheim PB011.03

54 Blinky Palermo
Ohne Titel I ('Untitled I'), from the portfolio *Zwei Lithographien und ein Siebdruck* ('Two lithographs and one screenprint'), 1973
Lithograph on white wove paper
Numbered, signed and dated in pencil on verso, lower edge, 'I 10/100 Palermo 73'
500 x 350 mm
Duerckheim PB010.01
Literature; Jahn 1983, cat. no. 33, ill. on pp. 78–9; Leverkusen 1975, ill. on p. 73; Leipzig 1993, ill. on pp. 184–5

The portfolio *Ohne Titel – Zwei Lithographen und ein Siebdruck*, otherwise known as *Mappe zur Wandmalerei Hamburger Kunstverein* ('Portfolio for the wall painting at the Hamburg Kunstverein'), was published by the Galerie Heiner Friedrich in 1973, in an edition of 100, alongside an exhibition of a wall painting executed by Palermo at the Kunstverein, Hamburg.

The portfolio was printed by Tünn Konerding, Essen.

55 Blinky Palermo
Ohne Titel II ('Untitled II'), from the portfolio *Zwei Lithographien und ein Siebdruck* ('Two lithographs and one screenprint'), 1973
Lithograph on white wove paper
Numbered, signed and dated in pencil on verso, lower edge, 'II 10/100 Palermo 73'
500 x 350 mm
Duerckheim PB010.02

56. Blinky Palermo
Ohne Titel III ('Untitled III'), from the portfolio *Zwei Lithographien und ein Siebdruck* ('Two lithographs and one screenprint'), 1973
Screenprint in brown ink on white wove paper
Numbered, signed and dated in pencil on verso, lower edge, 'III 10/100 Palermo 73'
500 x 350 mm
Duerckheim PB010.03

57 A.R. Penck
Ohne Titel ('Untitled'), 1967
Watercolour, gold and silver paint on coarse light-green wove paper
Signed in pencil lower right 'ralf', dated '67' in pencil upper left. Verso: abstract ink drawing
419 x 300 mm
Duerckheim PA085
British Museum, London 2013,7043.28
Presented by Count Christian Duerckheim
Literature: Sotheby's 2011, ill. on. p. 188

A single stick-figure is drawn with gold and silver paint, arms upraised and with prominent genitals. The use of metallic paint adds to his extraterrestrial appearance. Penck used this figure frequently in his *Standart* works as an archetypal symbol of human life. The figure is similar, for example, to that in a drawing from 1968, *Figur* ('Figure'), watercolour, 295 x 207 mm (Gachnang 1986, no. 46, ill., unpaginated.

The verso shows an abstract ink drawing (Sotheby's 2011, ill on p. 190) very similar to two drawings illustrated by Koepplin 1987, cat. nos 46 and 47, both dated *c.* 1969.

58 A.R. Penck
Ohne Titel, ('Untitled'), 1969
Graphite on smooth off-white paper
Signed in pencil lower left 'R' in square; dated in pen lower right '69'. Verso inscribed in pencil lower right 'CD'
297 x 420 mm
Duerckheim PA064
British Museum, London 2013,7043.30
Presented by Count Christian Duerckheim

59 A.R. Penck
Ohne Titel ('Untitled'), *c.* 1981
Gouache on smooth off-white wove paper
Signed in pencil lower right 'r'. Verso: inscribed in pencil lower left 'CD'
295 x 418 mm
Duerckheim PA065
British Museum, London 2013,7043.31
Presented by Count Christian Duerckheim

A rapid improvisation of crimson marks covers the surface with animated forms, perhaps stick-figures in motion. Penck was a prolific draughtsman and, where undated, his drawings can often be difficult to ascribe to a particular period. A date from the early 1980s can be suggested on the basis of a comparison with a similar drawing included in the 1988 exhibition of Penck's drawings organized by Rudi Fuchs at the Gemeentemuseum, Den Haag (*Untitled*, 1981, in Gemeentemuseum 1988, cat. no. 218, ill. on p. 105).

60 A.R. Penck
Ohne Titel ('Untitled'), *c.* 1969
Watercolour on blank reverse side of a commercial order form in German; light brown paper
Signed in pen lower right 'r'. Verso: printed order form; inscribed in pencil lower right 'CD'
293 x 208 mm
Duerckheim PA095

A series of drawings, made in a commercial order book, are presented without explanation, but implying a narrative – a story of love in an exotic location, perhaps. Similar drawings made on the same paper type are held in the Kupferstichkabinett, Basel, and are illustrated in Koepplin 1987, cat. nos 53–59, unpaginated.

61 A.R. Penck
Ohne Titel ('Untitled'), *c.* 1969
Watercolour on blank reverse side of a commercial order form in German
Signed in pen lower right 'r'. Verso: printed order form; inscribed in pencil lower right 'CD'
293 x 208 mm
Duerckheim PA101

62 A.R. Penck
Ohne Titel ('Untitled'), *c.* 1969
Watercolour on blank reverse side of a commercial order form in German; light brown paper
Not signed or dated. Verso: printed order form; inscribed in pencil lower right 'CD'
293 x 208 mm
Duerckheim PA093

63 A.R. Penck
Ohne Titel ('Untitled'), *c.* 1969
Watercolour on blank reverse side of a commercial order form in German; light brown paper
Signed in pencil lower right 'R'. Verso: printed order form; faintly inscribed in pencil lower right 'CD'
293 x 208 mm
Duerckheim PA096

64 A.R. Penck
Ohne Titel (Sanex), ('Untitled (Sanex)'), *c.* 1975
Gouache on light brown paper
Signed in pencil upper right 'R'. Verso: inscribed in pencil lower right '14'
205 x 280 mm
Duerckheim PA091

65 A.R. Penck
Ohne Titel, ('Untitled'), *c.* 1975
Gouache on light brown paper
Signed in pencil lower right 'R'. Verso: inscribed in pencil lower right '15'
194 x 280 mm
Duerckheim PA092

A group of five symbols – a car, a cross, a one mark coin, a clock showing two o'clock, and a tearful eye – taken together suggest a narrative, perhaps that of a fatal car crash. The assemblage of symbolic motifs, suggesting a personal narrative, relate to paintings made in the mid-1970s, for example *A Dream by D.G.* (1975) which also features the one mark coin, in the bottom left of the image.

66 A.R. Penck
Ohne Titel (Selbstportät), ('Untitled (Self-portrait)'), 1975
Grey and black ink wash on laid paper
Signed in pencil lower right 'ralf'. Verso: inscribed in pencil lower right 'CD'
592 x 420 mm
Duerckheim PA063
British Museum, London 2013,7043.29
Presented by Count Christian Duerckheim

According to the art dealer Michael Werner, this was one of the many drawings that he collected from Penck on his visits to East Germany and that Penck had made directly in response to a catalogue of Pop Art from the Stroher collection, which Werner had given him on a previous visit (*Sammlung 1968 Karl Ströher*, exh. cat., Berlin (Kunstverein; Nationalgalerie); Düsseldorf (Städtischen Kunsthalle), 1969). Penck made a series of self-portraits using dabs of black ink as a response to the statement by Andy Warhol, reprinted in this catalogue, that he wanted to be like a machine. Responding to Werner's question about what he meant by this, Penck explained that he had started in the top left corner, working his way along and down, as if the drawing was being produced mechanically. The quote from Warhol begins the essay 'Pop Art oder die Realität als Kunstwerk', by Jürgen Wissman, pp. 1–16, here p. 1).

Three similar portraits are illustrated in: Gemeentemuseum 1988, cat. nos 121, 122, 123, ill. on p. 67

67 A.R. Penck
Ohne Titel ('Untitled'), *c.* 1982
Gouache and pencil markings on wove paper
Signed in pencil lower right, 'r /'. Verso: inscribed lower right in blue ink 'R' in square
592 x 419 mm
Duerckheim PA061
British Museum, London 2013,7043.27
Presented by Count Christian Duerckheim
Literature: Sotheby's 2011, ill. on p. 62

Many of Penck's paintings during the 1980s showed two figures confronting one another, suggesting both an elemental opposition, such as the hunter and the hunted, but also evoking the confrontation of East and West Germany. This drawing suggests an animal form attacking an abstract, machine-like configuration; the confrontation of Western consumerism with the Eastern political system is implied.

68 A.R. Penck
Nachtvision ('Night Vision'), 1982
Woodcut on Hahnemühle wove paper
From the portfolio *Erste Konzentration I*, published by Maximilian Verlag, Sabine Knust, Munich, 1982
Signed in pencil lower right 'a.r. penck', numbered in pencil lower right, 'I VI / VIII'
Image size: 895 x 695 mm
Sheet size: 1002 x 784 mm
British Museum, London 2013,7043.32.3
Presented by Count Christian Duerckheim
Duerckheim
PA002
Literature: Knust 1982, cat. no 32, ill., unpaginated; Geneva 1983, cat. no. 84, ill. on p. 77; Reutlingen 2003, cat. no. 11, ill. on p. 15

See commentary under cat. 41.

69 Sigmar Polke
Ohne Titel ('Untitled'), 1964
Blue ballpoint pen drawing on smooth white paper
Signed and dated in blue pen lower right 'Polke 64'. Verso: inscribed in blue pen lower right '8'
295 x 209 mm
Duerckheim PS009

A giant pair of pliers with eyes threatens a running cartoon man. Polke's drawings using a ballpoint pen, made from 1963 until the end of the decade, are his best-known early graphic works. They are his first essays in the profane satire that he was to develop over the next fifty years.

They were exhibited as a group for the first time in an exhibition organized in 1972 by Johannes Gachnang in the gallery of the Goethe Institute in Amsterdam (see Gachnang 1991, p. 9).

70 Sigmar Polke
Empedokles ist in den Berg ('Empedocles is in the Mountain'), *c.* 1966
Watercolour on thin smooth light brown paper
Unsigned, undated. Verso: inscribed in pencil on upper edge, 'oben 1. links'
296 x 210 mm
Duerckheim PS023

A clown-like figure with red cheeks emits the words 'Empedokles ist in den Berg' (Empedocles is in the Mountain); beneath him schematic shapes suggest a smoking volcano.

The pre-Socratic philosopher Empedocles was best known for his writings on the four elements: fire, air, water and earth. His verse work *On Nature* (some still survives) presented an explanation of the nature and history of the universe and also had theories on causation, perception, thought, and natural and biological phenomena. Classical authors gave various accounts of his death, allegedly by throwing himself into a Mount Etna volcano to prove that he was immortal. Polke may have come to Empedocles through Friedrich Hölderlin's tragic poem *Tod des Empedokles* ('The Death of Empedocles'), 1798–1800.

Polke had first used the motif in a 1963 'raster drawing', made using poster paint and a rubber stamp.

71 Sigmar Polke
Ohne Titel ('Untitled'), 1967
Green and grey watercolour wash and ink on lined white paper with holes punched on right-hand edge, originally tipped to card mount
Signed and dated in blue ballpoint pen lower right 'S. Polke 67'. Verso blank
209 x 148 mm
Duerckheim PS001
British Museum, London 2013,7043.21
Presented by Count Christian Duerckheim

Polke frequently copied images from illustrated magazines and other sources. This watercolour shows a suited man, who appears to be in a restaurant, with two other figures behind him, one looming over him their hands on his shoulders. The pallid green wash conveys a feeling of unease, increasing the sense of mystery around this small unexplained scene.

72 Sigmar Polke
Untitled (sketchbook 9), 1969
Twenty-nine drawings in watercolour on unnumbered pages, three final pages blank, of a lined exercise book with green card covers
Signed in pencil on lower right of final page, 'Sigmar Polke 69'. Label on cover inscribed in brown ink '9.'
Single page 208 x 147 mm
Duerckheim PS032.01-28 [nb 29 rather than 28 drawings]
Literature: Bonn 1988, cat. no. 9.9, not illustrated

Twenty-nine drawings in brush and watercolour are presented without notes or explanation; the imagery is mysterious, dreamlike and abstract, often showing lightly-sketched figures negotiating abstract forms, floating or in meditative postures.

73 Sigmar Polke
Untitled (sketchbook 16), *c.* 1969
Twenty-nine drawings in watercolour on unnumbered pages of a lined exercise book with blue cover, seven accompanied on opposite page by image cuttings taken from illustrated magazines
Unsigned, undated; typed label with word 'Polke' on cover of notebook; larger label below inscribed in brown ink '16.'
Single page 209 x 145 mm
Duerckheim PS033. 01-29
British Museum, London 2013,7043.22.1–29
Presented by Count Christian Duerckheim
Literature: Bonn 1988, cat. no. 9.16, not illustrated

Twenty-nine watercolour line drawings show a range of strange abstract and figurative imagery. Certain drawings are placed alongside source material – advertisements and images from magazines, although they are transformed and made mysterious. As Katherine Schmidt has described: 'In the period from 1965 to 1970 [Polke] filled well over thirty stenographer's notebooks and exercise books with drawings and watercolours of all kinds, which, despite the variety among the individual sheets, are seen today as a significant component of his oeuvre…. Studies done in the evening, sketches for ideas, first jottings, musings on specific plans for exhibitions, word games, and excerpts – these things fill the flimsy sheets of graph paper. […] Other, perfectly worked-through books contain in the sum of their rhythmic pages the Polke universe in a nutshell. […] Numerous themes and motifs, which are familiar in Polke's paintings, are found in their first formulation here' (K. Schmidt, 'Arrows into the storm: observations on the drawings, watercolours and sketchbooks of Sigmar Polke', in San Francisco 1990, pp. 35–43).

Thirty-nine sketchbooks, including cats 72 and 73, were exhibited at the 1988 retrospective of Polke's work at the Kunstmuseum, Bonn.

74 Gerhard Richter
Ohne Titel ('Untitled'), 1966
Blue and black ballpoint pen on smooth off-white paper
Signed and dated in pencil lower edge, 'Richter, 1966'. Verso blank
210 x 296 mm
Duerckheim RG001
Literature: Sotheby's 2011, ill. on p. 88

A sketch, probably traced from a reproduction, based on Johann Tischbein's famous portrait of Goethe in the Roman Campagna, *Goethe in der Campagna*, painted in 1787, in the collection of the Städel Museum, Frankfurt am Main. The landscape is indicated by loosely executed marks. The sheet has been used for numerical calculations, the arithmetic jottings overlaid by scribbles, surrounding and seemingly undermining the figure.

75 Gerhard Richter
Ohne Titel ('Untitled'), 1967
Felt-tip pen on tracing paper
Signed and dated in pencil lower left '4.3.67, Richter'
295 x 210 mm
Duerckheim RG009
British Museum, London 2013,7043.18
Presented by Count Christian Duerckheim

The two figures appear in the painting *Schwestern* ('Sisters' (1967); Elger 2011, no. 153; Formerly Duerckheim collection), where they sit alongside each other.

76 Gerhard Richter
Ohne Titel ('Untitled'), 1967
Graphite and felt-tip pen on tracing paper
Signed and dated in pencil centre right, '4.3.67, Richter'
295 x 210 mm
British Museum, London 2013,7043.17
Presented by Count Christian Duerckheim
Duerckheim RG008

The large finished figure relates directly to the left-hand figure in the painting *Schwestern* ('Sisters'; 1967), (Elger 2011, no. 153)

77 Gerhard Richter
Ohne Titel ('Untitled'), 1967
Graphite on tracing paper
Signed in pencil left edge, 'Richter, 1967'
295 x 210 mm
Duerckheim RG011

This drawing relates to one of the two female figures in the painting *Osterakte* ('Easter Nudes'; 1967), (Elger 2011, no. 148). Richter's drawings of nude females are traced from photographs in pin-up magazines.

78 Gerhard Richter
Ohne Titel ('Untitled'), 1967
Felt-tip pen on tracing paper
Signed and dated in pencil lower left '4.3.67, Richter'
295 x 210 mm
Duerckheim RG010

The figure at the far right relates to one of the two female figures in the painting *Osterakte* ('Easter Nudes'; 1967), (Elger 2011 no. 148); the other figures do not relate to any known painting from this period.

79 Gerhard Richter
Ohne Titel ('Untitled'), 1967
Graphite on tracing paper
Signed and dated in pencil lower left 'Richter 1967'
295 x 210 mm
Duerckheim RG019

A man in a cap shows a map, or plan, to a woman wearing a headscarf standing by a car. A male figure is shown in an interior, his hands in his pocket, his head cut off by the frame of the drawing. A woman sits on the ground, reaching behind an identified object. Richter appears to be gathering images for use in painting, although the drawings relate to no particular work in oil.

80 Gerhard Richter
Ohne Titel ('Untitled'), 1967
Graphite on tracing paper
Signed and dated in pencil lower centre 'Richter, 67'
210 x 295 mm
Duerckheim RG003

Two drawings at different orientations on the sheet; a couple standing in a kitchen; and a naked female model, kneeling, her leg interlinked with a small table.

81 Gerhard Richter
Tretbootfahrer ('Pedal Boat Riders'), 1965
Graphite on light brown paper with serrated sides
Signed and dated in pencil upper right 'Richter 65'. Attached to mount
210 x 295 mm
Duerckheim RG056
Richter Catalogue Raisonné: 65/9
Literature: Wedewer 1970, ill. unnumbered, unpaginated; Dietrich-Boorsch 1982, cat. no. 103, ill. on p. 85

This drawing, showing a couple in a paddle boat, suggests the effects of motion and blur that Richter was using in his larger oil paintings. Richter has used an eraser to work into the drawing and create a sense of the reflection of light on water. It relates to no known painting.

82 Gerhard Richter
Hotel oder Haus Hutter ('Hotel or Hutter House'), 1965

Graphite on smooth off-white paper
Signed and dated in pencil lower right 'Richter 2 Juni 65'
295 x 236 mm
Richter Drawings CR 65/10
Duerckheim RG058
Literature: Dietrich-Boorsch 1982, cat. no. 101, ill. on p. 82

A large square villa is shown at an angle, standing against trees. Richter uses a fine pencil and smudges the graphite in way that evokes the blurred effect of his oil paintings – both a way of suggesting movement and of obscuring the image by approximating the look of an unfocused photograph. The drawing is based on an image from *Atlas* Sheet no. 4, from 1962, of a photograph of a house, and was repeated again in the painting *Grau Haus* ('Grey House'; 1966).

83 Gerhard Richter
Ohne Titel ('Untitled'), 1976
Felt-tip pen, ballpoint pen and graphite on smooth off-white paper
Signed and dated lower left, 'Richter 76'; inscribed lower right, 'Beispiel/230 Farben auf 5100 Feldern/(Feld: 10 x 20 cm)/(Wand: 6,00 x 17,00 m)/= ca. 1:22'
210 x 295 mm
Duerckheim RG049

84 Gerhard Richter
Ohne Titel ('Untitled'), 28 November 1976
Felt-tip pen, ballpoint pen and graphite on smooth off-white paper with double 'Zero' watermark, two holes punched at top of page
Signed and dated lower left, 'Richter 76'. Verso blank
210 x 295 mm
Duerckheim RG047

85 Gerhard Richter
Ohne Titel ('Untitled'), 28 November 1976
Felt-tip pen, ballpoint pen and graphite on smooth off-white paper
Dated lower left, '28.11.76'. Verso blank
210 x 295 mm
Duerckheim RG048
British Museum, London 2013,7043.19
Presented by Count Christian Duerckheim

86 Gerhard Richter
Adorno?, 17 November 1982
Graphite on smooth off-white paper
Inscribed beneath drawing: 'ADORNO?'; dated and signed on lower edge, 'R. 17.11.82 Richter'. Verso blank
297 x 210 mm
Duerckheim RG033
Literature: Schwarz 2000, cat. no. 82/12

Theodor W. Adorno was one of the key thinkers and writers in post-War Germany, who played an important role in forging a critical response to society. The reference to Adorno in Richter's abstract drawing is allusive and indirect, although his sense of an aesthetic position arising out of the 'damaged life' of post-War Germany, the subtitle for his 1951 book, *Minima Moralia*, might be compared with the erasure and cancelling-out with which Richter builds up his abstract drawing.

87 Gerhard Richter
Waldbrand ('Forest Fire'), 17 November 1982
Graphite on smooth off-white paper
Dated, inscribed and signed lower edge: 'R 17.11.82 WALDBRAND Richter'.
Verso blank
297 x 210 mm
Duerckheim RG029
Literature: Schwarz 2000, cat. no. 82/25

Richter began making abstract drawings in 1978, using pencil on a single sheet of A4 'typing' paper. The modest, everyday medium and support are set in contrast to the highly dramatic imagery of these drawings, occasionally given context by the use of inscribed titles.

88 Gerhard Richter
Ohne Titel (2.1.1978), ('Untitled (2.1.1978)'), 2 January 1978
Watercolour on smooth white paper
Signed and dated lower right '2.1.78/ Richter'
148 x 209 mm
Duerckheim RG041
Literature: Schwarz 1999, cat. no. 18, ill. on p. 42

Richter uses layers of translucent and opaque pigment to create small jewel-like watercolours that echo the dramatic use of colour and space in his larger abstract oil paintings. *Ohne Titel (2.1.1978)* is one of a group of eight watercolours made on 2 January 1978. Although Richter has worked sporadically in watercolour throughout his life, these are the earliest works made as part of a series, all in the same format, exploring the same pictorial idea. They were made, as Richter has said, in Davos, during a two week holiday: 'Small watercolours are easy to do in a hotel room' (Schwarz 1999, p. 19). Watercolour was an unfashionable medium at the time, and it was only a number of years later that they were exhibited, at the Galerie Thomas Borgmann in Cologne, in 1984 (*Gerhard Richter: Aquarelle – Zeichnungen*, Cologne (Galerie Thomas Borgmann), 14 January to 2 March 1984). As Dieter Schwarz has noted, this first group of eight watercolours was unique in Richter's work at the time, and it was six years before Richter returned to the medium, with a series of seventy-five watercolours made in 1984. He has described the process of making abstract watercolours as similar to that involved in larger abstract oil paintings – 'the same sort of problem, but with different means'.

89 Gerhard Richter
Ohne Titel (2.1.1978) ('Untitled (2.1.1978)')), 2 January 1978
Watercolour on smooth white paper.
Signed and dated upper left '2.1.78/ Richter'
148 x 209 mm
Duerckheim RG042
Literature: Schwarz 1999, cat. no. 16, ill. on p. 41

90 Gerhard Richter
Ohne Titel (2.1.1978) ('Untitled (2.1.1978)'), 2 January 1978
Watercolour on smooth white paper.
Signed and dated upper right '2.1.78/ Richter'
148 x 209 mm
Duerckheim RG040
Literature: Schwarz 1999, cat. no. 17, ill. on p. 42

91 Gerhard Richter
Ohne Titel (2.1.1978), ('Untitled (2.1.1978)'), 2 January 1978
Watercolour on smooth white paper
Signed and dated lower right '2.1.78/ Richter'
148 x 209 mm
Duerckheim RG043
Literature: Schwarz 1999, cat. no. 15, ill. on p. 41

92 Gerhard Richter
Sheet from *Atlas*, 1962–89
Twenty-five colour photographs of abstract paintings in watercolour and oil by Gerhard Richter, mounted on a sheet of white card
Unsigned, undated
Sheet size: 499 x 649 mm
Duerckheim RG072

Eight of the twenty-five photographs of Richter's paintings shown on this sheet can be identified as the series of watercolours that he made on 2 January 1978 (cats 88–91).

93 Gerhard Richter
Sheet from *Atlas*, 1962–89
Twenty-eight colour photographs of clouds, each approximately 78 x 116 mm, grouped according to vantage point, mounted in a grid on a sheet of white card
Unsigned, undated, inscribed in pencil upper right '203'
Frame size: 667 x 517 mm
Duerckheim RG070
British Museum, London 2013,7043.20
Presented by Count Christian Duerckheim
Literature: Utrecht 1972, ill. unnumbered, unpaginated

94. Gerhard Richter
Sheet from *Atlas*, 1962–89
Fourteen black and white photographs of irregular size and a newspaper clipping showing the Naerö-fjord, Norway, mounted on a sheet of white card
Unsigned, undated, inscribed in pencil upper right '129'
Frame size: 667 x 517 mm
Duerckheim RG090

In 1969 Richter began arranging clippings on scrapbook-like pages, creating an archive that he named *Atlas*. Early panels show images taken from West German illustrated magazines and from personal photograph albums, and were often used as the basis for Richter's paintings. Later panels include drawings (see conversation with Count Duerckheim in this volume), architectural studies and a range of personal photographs, including many of Richter's own works.

Atlas continues to be updated, if intermittently, and has also been exhibited as an independent work of art, sometimes alongside paintings. The combination of photographs and a press clipping showing a Norwegian fjord in this panel, not included in Richter's official catalogue of the *Atlas* sheets, suggests a comparison of personal and public memory.

Conversation with Count Christian Duerckheim

by John-Paul Stonard, 18 June 2013

JPS Christian Duerckheim, can we begin by talking about your childhood and upbringing: where were you born?

CD I was born in Saxony in 1944. One year later the Soviets invaded and so my parents had to leave immediately. The story is that my mother boarded a train near Dresden, but the train was stopped because of the firebombing of the city. So I had the chance to see, although I do not remember it, the burning city in February 1945. The train was held for a couple of days; then was able to move to the West. We were refugees who had left home with no money. My mother had a suitcase with just what you need to look after two small children – nothing else. We went to Bavaria, not knowing anybody. My father was a soldier somewhere in Germany – we had no contact with him then. And that was our lives for the next few years, being refugees, having left everything behind. It took quite a while for the family to recover financially. My parents got divorced – another problem – my sister and I stayed with our mother. It is hard to understand now, perhaps, but from one day to the next you had to leave your home. Everything – jewels, pictures, prints, letters, whatever you can think of – left behind.

JPS Where was your family home?

CD It was a castle in a small village called Milkel near Dresden. You can go there still today. After Reunification in 1990 the old families didn't get back what they had before the (Second World) War. But that's life. I would say that when you want to succeed, you should not start, then lose, a war! We were the losers in the war, which was right to our victims. Then in the years of the *Wirtschaftswunder* (the 'Economic Miracle'), my family was successful in business. I had the chance to have a good education and to start anew. I felt free to look to the future.

JPS I'm interested in what it was like being in Germany as a child. What are your first memories?

CD I was brought up in ruins. Wherever we moved, in every town, we found the same: they had been bombed. I remember playing after school in the ruins. It was forbidden because they could have collapsed, or there could have been an unexploded bomb inside, but that made it even more thrilling for a child.

JPS This was while you were in Bavaria, in Munich?

CD Yes, but I moved again when I was six years old and went to boarding schools in the so-called Rhine-Ruhr area. All these towns were completely bombed, but I enjoyed it. It was fascinating in the ruins, finding things – you would suddenly come across a fully equipped kitchen, and we found guns and other such things. At one time I constructed my own little house in a tree in a garden and then, without warning, bulldozers came along and destroyed it. At the time I didn't know why, but of course they were rebuilding Germany. And for the first time I realized that you can really lose something; since then I have been careful not to become too attached to anything, or at least to keep my possessions small and portable.

I didn't start collecting at that time, but the important thing is that I eventually felt that the surroundings were not inspiring, with all these very boring German songs – *Schlager* ('easy listening') music. And all of a sudden, and this was in 1955, I heard the music, not of Frankie Lane or Frank Sinatra, who are good but old-fashioned for a young teenager, but of Elvis Presley. Music was a sort of relief from the boredom of life, but also the harshness of life at school, which was very strict; so I realized that music is important. The family didn't like Elvis, so to listen to his music I had to go to an ice skating hall, where it was played publicly. I paid my fifty Pfennigs to get in and could listen to the music. A little later a couple of friends and I decided we had to get some jeans – American jeans, Wranglers. I was in a boarding school near Hanover at that time and had to order them from a US military store in Munich. These things – rock music, jeans, parka coats – were either forbidden or hard to get hold of, that made them attractive.

Another memory: when I was about fourteen, I remember a very modern, contemporary painting hanging at school – today I would say it is in the Informel style –

and I realized, here is something interesting. At the time I knew oil paintings through the work of the Impressionists and also portraits of my ancestors – not always pleasant to look at – but here was something that was interesting, just because it was possible.

JPS You told me before that it was a painting by Ulrich Knispel (1911–78).

CD Knispel, yes. It was the first time I realized that art is something completely different from everything else – it is for recreation, for freedom of the brain. That can only really be achieved through art, not through learning. It was also something new, looking forward, not back. Many were trying to do this for different reasons. In 1963 I had a clash with a teacher at my school, who I tried to interview for a school magazine. All the other teachers were happy to be interviewed, but not him – he was clearly hiding something that had happened in the war. I published his refusal to be interviewed in the school magazine – there was an uproar and I was almost expelled. But in the event, he left, and not me.

JPS These influences and experiences were happening in the mid-1950s, but it was only later that you began to collect art.

CD Well, I started by making art myself – little pieces of art at school. The first, in the late-1950s or early 1960s, was made by pulling all the tape out of an 8 mm cassette and nailing it to the wall! It was nailing the chaos on the wall to give it a lasting shape. My first personal piece of art. I made various things, because this was the only chance to do something different in art lessons. Collecting art started later.

JPS Did you want to be an artist?

CD No, never. I realized that I wasn't very good and there would always be someone better.

JPS When did the collecting begin in earnest?

CD It was when I left school. I took my Abitur (A-levels) in 1964 and got the certificate at the age of twenty-one. Then I went to Hamburg as an apprentice in a merchant bank and stayed there for two and a half years. The first works I bought were prints by Horst Janssen (1929–95). I saw them in the window of the famous Laatzen Bookshop in Warburgstraße in Hamburg, as part of their advertising display. One week they had books by Gottfried Benn, so showed Janssen's portrait of Benn, then the next week Heinrich Mann, and so on. And I realized for the first time that you can show more in such drawings than simply by doing a physical likeness. Janssen took the idea of Franz Kafka, of James Joyce, and so on, and I found that great. It was particularly interesting for me, as I was heavily involved with literature at school, but it was at this time that I switched my interest from writers such as Günter Grass or Albert Camus, to art, and asked myself the question: what does a picture say to me? After two and half years the bank sent me to London, but here I was less interested in buying works of art than in the way of life.

JPS This must have been around 1967. What was it about life in London around that time that you liked?

CD Well by comparison in the mid-1960s, Hamburg was a small world for a young man. For entertainment you either went to Star-Club or Top Ten to dance, which I had already done when still at school, by escaping and driving over the night, or you had a private party. But it was stuffy and provincial, although I took all chances to explore Hamburg and its countryside. In Hamburg I had to be at the bank at 8 o'clock. In London it was half past nine and the first major event of the day was the tea trolley coming around at ten o'clock. And when I took an English girl out, we went to Wheeler's (the seafood restaurant), where the Dover sole cost one pound, the bottle of wine cost one pound, so the whole evening was just three pounds – and she admired me for being so generous! I wasn't rich at that time, but had enough to get by. In London, even with not much money, I had a marvellous time. I lived in Campden Hill Road, Notting Hill. One of my friends was Ned Ryan. He ran a couple of stalls on Portobello Road, and I worked with him there on Saturdays and during the week very early in

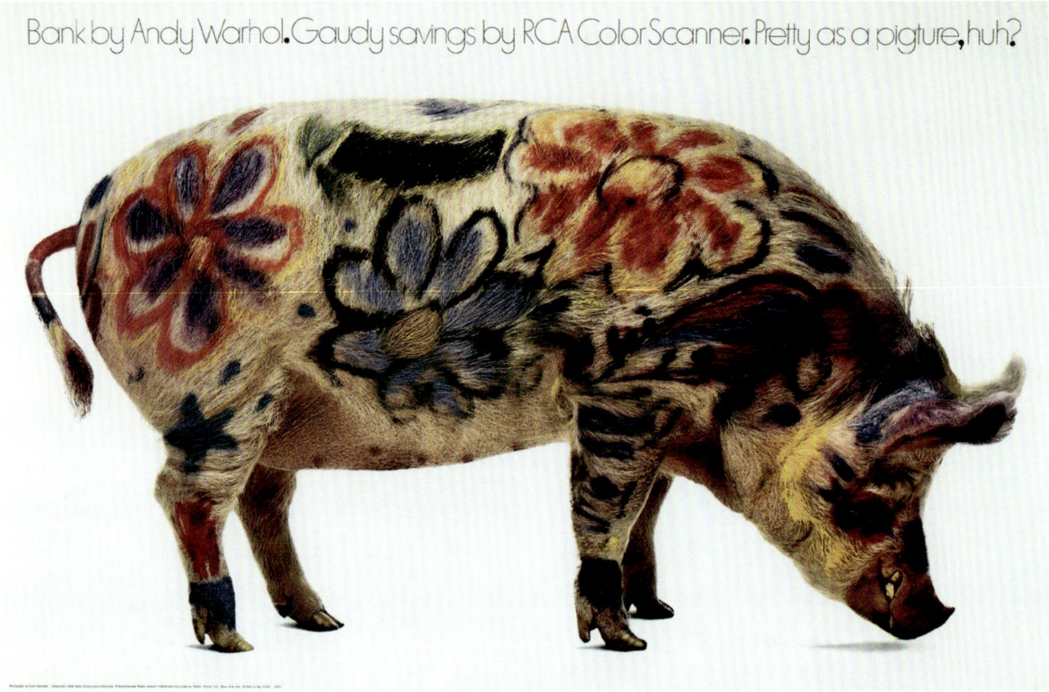

1. Poster for *Bank by Andy Warhol. Gaudy Savings by RCA Color Scanner. Pretty as a pigture, huh?*, 1968
Offset lithograph, 759 x 1150 mm
Museum of Modern Art, New York

2. Cover of *ZET 1* featuring a drawing by Georg Baselitz, January 1973

the morning we would go out together buying bits and pieces.

JPS What kind of antiques?

CD Silver. The stall was on the street, not inside. During the winter it got very cold, so one of us would go into the pub nearby and get hot whiskey or hot rum. So I learned the English way of life. And the people in Portobello were very nice, although still in the 1960s I was careful speaking German. Not everybody was happy to see a German. It didn't happen often, but you would hear 'You are German! My father died in the War!' or 'My grandfather lost an arm!' It was understandable.

JPS What happened next?

CD Next was New York, the year before Woodstock – 1968. I didn't take drugs, but was interested in them. I realized that Timothy Leary was a very interesting man. I wasn't sure – do drugs help or not? My education said no – but I was still interested, also in the Flower Power movement and hippies. In London I had the funny experience of working in the City and living in Notting Hill (at that time run-down and bohemian). In New York I was working on Wall Street and living in the Chelsea Hotel, West 23rd Street, where I stayed for half a year. I didn't talk about living in the Chelsea Hotel while I worked on Wall Street – that was out. Only a couple of friends knew. I met a few people, but not the really Pop people. I can't say that I was directly influenced by Andy Warhol, or that type of people, but the atmosphere was clear – this was today.

JPS Were you visiting galleries or museums at this time?

CD A few galleries, but not many, and of course all the main museums. But my interests were elsewhere – I was collecting posters from the Flower Power movement, from Dave Schiller, Sparta Graphics. I still have them. The Museum of Modern Art has a good collection of these posters. One of them was *Bank* (1968; fig. 1) by Andy Warhol – that was on my wall in the Chelsea Hotel. It is a real pig painted to look like a piggy bank. But at the time I hardly had any money to buy anything. I realized that it might be better to go back to Germany, to study at university. I was twenty-five years old, but this is no problem in Germany. And it was when I went back to study at university that the collecting started seriously.

JPS Where did you go to study?

CD I went to Mannheim, near Heidelberg. Mannheim was in the 1960s, alongside Cologne, the best place to study economics. So I decided to go there. And we spent a lot of time in Heidelberg, which is just a short car journey away. And it was at this time that I began collecting various artists.

JPS These were works by German artists that you were buying?

CD Yes, German artists. And this happened through the Galerie Rothe, which is still going.[1] I met the husband of the gallery owner, Dr Wolfgang Rothe (his wife managed the gallery), and he showed me his new idea, which was a magazine about writers and poets entitled *ZET*, which on the cover always featured a picture by a contemporary artist. He showed me the first issue and the front cover had a drawing by

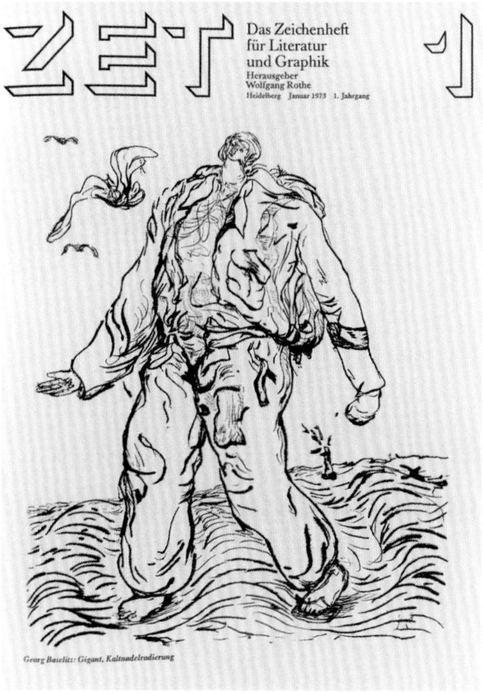

Georg Baselitz (fig. 2). This was the first time I remember being confronted with a work by Baselitz.

JPS What was that like?

CD It was great! It was a drawing from the *Heroes* series. And I realized, this is something new, different from Pop Art, and utterly different from what I had seen in Germany so far. I subscribed to the magazine and now have them all. In the meantime I left Mannheim and went to Munich – you can do this as an undergraduate in Germany. But in between I had made another collection, of prints by what I call German academic artists, from about 1890 to 1950. I bought these works from two or three little collections, because I was interested to see how artists work. I didn't study art, so I had to learn about it by looking at it.

JPS Which artists?

CD Alfred Kubin (1877–1959), for example, Max Klinger (1857–1920), Franz von Stuck (1863–1928), Heinrich Vogeler (1872–1942) and Friedrich August von Kaulbach (1850–1920). All prints and drawings, hundreds of them. And also various collections of ex-libris (bookplates). It is very interesting to see what the academic world was doing around 1900 in Germany, especially in Munich. This collection I formed from 1971 until 1974.

The next step was American artists. I started collecting through the Galerie Art in Progress, run by Ingvild Goetz. From 1974 on, that was my favourite gallery. I realized what I had missed in the States – they were showing artists I could have seen five years previously in New York.

JPS Which artists?

CD Andy Warhol, Cy Twombly (1928–2011), Ed Moses (b. 1926), Alfano, Shusaku Arakawa (1936–2010). But I soon realized that I couldn't afford them – I was after all still operating with a low budget. So I decided – let's go for the German artists. And I went to the Galerie Heiner Friedrich, run by Six Friedrich, Heiner's ex-wife, with her business partner Sabine Knust. And in early 1976, I started buying Baselitz from both galleries.

JPS Which works by Baselitz?

CD Well, they admired me because I bought the early works by Baselitz – nobody else wanted to buy them.

JPS The *Pandemonium* drawings?

CD Yes, drawings from 1959 to 1963. Nobody else was interested in them. And I bought around forty of them in a very short time. And – much more interestingly – I paid cash! That was possible then – not today of course. And I was very much helped by the two ladies who provided me with information about the artist. So by the end of 1976 I had about forty to fifty drawings by Baselitz, three smaller oils and some others – some by Imi Knoebel, two by A.R. Penck – so I had started. And at the end of 1976 – I can recall these details, which are written in my diary for that year – I started talking to Fred Jahn. He was at that time a manager in the Galerie Heiner Friedrich. I asked him: are there any other promising younger artists like Baselitz and Gerhard Richter, and he said yes, there is Franz Hitzler (b. 1946). We went to Hitzler's studio, and our first business together was the purchase of a painting by Hitzler. Then I asked him, what else can I do, and he said: 'Christian, if you want to do something clever, carry on collecting Baselitz and Richter, and add a few others.' So this was his idea, to bring in Antonius Höckelmann, Norbert Tadeusz (1940–2011) – not Blinky Palermo, he was not in the Gallery – and others to create a German group. The next year he became a dealer on his own. At that time I was number three on his list of old clients – first there was Franz, Herzog von Bayern, then Walter Bareiss, then me.[2] My advantage was that when he showed me a picture I could say yes straight away and pay at short notice. All the others needed a bit more time. I decided what to buy. The simple point is that I am a businessman – so when you have one million and buy from ten dealers, it is less effective than having one million and buying from one dealer. Then he loves you, he will do everything for you. That is how it was with Fred Jahn. I concentrated quite a lot of money on what he could offer – so he became a very important person because most of the paintings and drawings I bought through him. With one exception – Baselitz. Most of the works by Baselitz I bought from dealers in Cologne.

JPS At the time, in the 1970s, there was only a very small group of people supporting these artists – Baselitz, Penck, Richter – there was no international market. They relied on dealers such as Fred Jahn, Franz Dahlem and Michael Werner and an equally small group of collectors, and those working in museums, such as Johannes Gachnang and Rudi Fuchs.

CD I bought from Dahlem, Hans Neuendorf, Thomas Borgmann and Werner, and from various dealers in Munich, including Fred Jahn, who went on offering art to me and other collectors.

JPS When was the first time you met Baselitz?

CD In Munich, when he had his large exhibition at the Pinakothek (1976). He realized that I was born very near to him – Deutschbaselitz is very near to where I come from.

JPS You are both from Saxony.

CD I'm not really a Saxon – my family is from the West. So we don't have old Saxon roots. In 1908, a great-grand aunt bought the estate and moved there. By adoption, I inherited the title and the estate. However, becoming a Baselitz collector, and being from the same part of the world, and probably a person he likes – that made it more special.

JPS What was your impression when you met him?

CD He painted very aggressively and he looked at that time very aggressive. He is such a nice person when he likes you, but can also be tough and unfriendly. He is twice my size! And very sensitive.

JPS He puts his aggression into his art as a provocation – he is a provocateur.

CD Yes, he loves that. We always got on very well, even if we didn't meet often. I never really had the need to be friends with artists in my collection. It was enough to see them once, to hear the tone of their voices, to see how they walk and talk.

JPS As a figurative painter from Saxony, who then worked in Berlin, and after that in the countryside in West Germany – most famously at Schloss Derneburg – Baselitz is very different from those artists who came out of the Kunstakademie in Düsseldorf, for example Richter and Sigmar Polke, who were pioneering a different kind of painting during the 1960s.

CD Polke I met once, in a gallery. Richter I've met several times and we did not get on very well, for various reasons. When you get together with artists, they expect you to behave in a certain way. They are today's princes.

JPS *Malerfürsten* (painter-princes).

CD Yes. And of course I fulfil their expectations – but not too often. But the problem with Richter was a different one. I bought the *Atlas* from him, and the deal was that he would re-create and add to it every year, and I would pay for it. What I realized too late is that he was not only adding, but taking things out. Most of the things he took out were original drawings. One day I asked, where are they? And he said – I've thrown them away. But I don't know what happened. So every year I had more photographs and less drawings. And every month there was a loan request from somewhere in the world and I had to employ someone simply to deal with this. And one day there was an exhibition at the Lenbachhaus, and I said, OK – let's sell it to them. Big mistake. Because half the amount for which I sold it was paid as a tax credit – so then I had to earn the money to get this credit! I learned too late.

JPS All the artists in this exhibition of works from your collection were born in the East and moved to the West. You made this journey yourself. It seems almost the formula for success as an artist in post-War Germany; to be somehow suspended between the two halves.

CD You left something behind you – especially tradition. You have to start from inception –

when you have to leave everything behind you, why should you have to start with the old things again? You realize that the world has changed – especially after a war. The new world was really dictated by America – Coca-Cola, chewing gum, jeans, ketchup, Elvis Presley – so why should you start with the old stuff again?

JPS But still you have the memory of the past and that other place – the 'names that are no longer named', in the words of Marion Gräfin Dönhoff.[3] These memories and sense of a shared past have a strong impact on how the new world is received. The Pop Art that Polke was making in the 1960s, for example, was a very German Pop Art. It gives a direct sense of what it was like to live between two opposing economic systems.

CD Of course you cannot forget history. History is in the brain. But you realize, I can't copy the old ideas, I must find another way. Polke did it; Baselitz found a new way; Richter developed a new style. It was about a new combination of history and the present, and also not being a copy of what was happening in France – don't forget Paris was still very important at that time.

JPS Were you aware of art being made in East Germany?

CD Socialist Art in East Germany?

JPS Yes. Socialist Realism, but also the art being made by dissidents and underground artists.

CD Concerning Socialist Realism, I considered going for Willi Sitte, Wolfgang Mattheuer (1927–2004), and Bernhard Heisig (1925–2011). I looked at it, and of course it is one way of painting – it is a form of modern academicism. It is quite interesting, and then more recently there are the painters from Leipzig; but in the end I decided, no. I don't have money to collect everywhere, and it is much better to have fifty good paintings, than 200 that are not so good. Concentration is the important thing: you only need sixty paintings to constitute a good collection. As for dissidents: Penck was the only one. When I started collecting Penck he was in the East. It was always a problem to get a canvas over. Michael Werner would tell us that in half a year, or in three months' time, there would be another lot of works. But we never knew exactly when.

JPS This must have given a sense of mystery and allure to his work.

CD Yes. And the connection to Jörg Immendorff was very important. The two were close, obviously, and painted together, shared their ideas, even though they came from completely different worlds. But Immendorff, always a sort of revolutionary – was always more interested in the message. He was fascinated by Penck, and his way of life – the fact of being in such a claustrophobic situation as an artist.

JPS Penck was such a mystery in the West that there was even the suggestion that he did not exist – that he was the creation of Michael Werner!

CD I believed in his existence! I never had any doubt about that.

JPS The works by Penck and Immendorff that were used in *Immendorff besucht Y* come from your collection. What was your involvement in the creation of this book? You are credited as 'Duerckheim Art Promotion'.

CD As the book seemed too large a financial risk, the publishers Rogner & Bernhard were looking for a sponsor to print the gouaches, which I had already bought. Although I did not agree with their political direction, I was interested in showing the bipolar situation, and the ideas of Penck and Immendorff, so I financed the book. At that time Duerckheim Art Promotion was involved in producing films about artists. The company had only a short lifetime due to financial problems.

JPS When Penck moved west in 1980 he went to live and work in Cologne, in a studio prepared for him by Michael Werner.

CD Yes, I met him several times in Werner's gallery, and in Derneburg, on the invitation of Baselitz. He was not particularly outspoken, but polite enough to answer all my questions.

JPS Penck moved west at a time when West German artists were for the first time achieving international success. This was due, at least in part, to the important exhibition *A New Spirit in Painting*, held at the Royal Academy in London in 1981, organized by Norman Rosenthal, and the exhibition *Zeitgeist* held in West Berlin in the following year, 1982. Reputations took off, canvases got bigger and bigger, and prices increased.

CD I was very happy that my artists went international, but very unhappy about the rise in prices. But in 1981 my collection was nearly formed. Of course I carried on buying, but the major works were already in place. So I was proud that I had done the right thing. It was at that time that Charles Saatchi began to buy German artists. That meant that the prices went right up, and I realized – I'm out. He bought bigger pieces of art than I had bought – so he and this exhibition, *A New Spirit in Painting*, changed the market more than anything else. So in the mid-1980s I stopped collecting Baselitz, and was for a time very much interested in artists such as Rupprecht Geiger (1908–2009), Rémy Zaugg (1943–2005) and Raimer Jochims (b. 1935). But I was also very keen on the Austrian artist Hermann Nitsch (b. 1938). I was introduced to his work at that time by Fred Jahn and thought that he might become one of my major interests. So he almost – but not entirely – came to take the place of Baselitz. But with Nitsch it was not the blood on canvas works, but the drawings and other early works, as well as the slaughtering he does from time to time, that is of importance from my point of view. I like his ideas, about what is religion, what is ritual, what is tradition – that is the message conveyed by his work. Everybody goes for these spilled canvases – they are less important for me. So Nitsch became an important person in my life as a collector. And the group of German-speaking artists I used to collect became less important – because I realized that I had in fact made a little mistake. You see, the idea was to one day show them in a museum.

JPS You mean to show all your German artists together as a group?

CD Yes. And nobody had warned me – not even Fred Jahn – that this was a bad idea! Because the big German museum directors say – we decide who is an important German artist from the 1960s, not you. And of course I didn't have Joseph Beuys, or Bernd Köberling (b. 1938) or Karl-Horst Hödicke. So I realized quite late – but not too late – that it was to some extent wrong to say that this was a representative German collection, although it was also a great, but very personal collection. That made me decide one day to sell it. And so there was an exhibition, at Sotheby's (in June 2011), which was a wonderful show, but of course only on display for one week, and they made a fantastic auction. I accepted my mistake, and from the 1990s on I started again with films and photography. And then from the mid-1990s with the Young British Artists, mostly through the White Cube Gallery. So you see I changed my interests completely.

JPS What photography were you collecting?

CD Political photography, but all blown up to one or two metres. And also, for example, the series of photographs made by the Chapman Brothers (Dinos, b. 1962; Jake, b. 1966), of their work *Hell* (2000), or Rauf Mamedov's (b.1956) *Last Supper* (1998). You see my taste changed in the 1990s, I became much more interested in what the work said, in the message, and the message had to be a political message, or a social critical message. Of course I still had some works by Baselitz that fitted into this scheme, but all the others didn't – not even Richter. My collection today is more interesting, as it is based on an idea. I bring the idea and that helps understand the message of the work. Picasso's *Guernica* (1937) may not mean much until you know that it is a response to an atrocity committed by the German Air Force during the Spanish Civil War.

JPS Knowledge illuminates the work.

CD And that's what I do with the works that I have, by combining them and showing them in a certain way. Be aware of dictators! And behind even the nicest bourgeois exterior you can find evil. Take Hitler on the Berghof, living with Eva Braun, inviting children and behaving as a civilized host; and at the same moment, countless Jews were being killed somewhere in Europe.

JPS It seems that your attitude to art has become more political since the fall of the Berlin Wall and the end of the Soviet Union. What did the fall of the Wall mean to you?

CD Beside happiness, all I was thinking was – should I buy a piece of the Wall! In the end I didn't. We had a chance to buy back the family estate in Saxony, but we decided not to. We preferred to keep our money in the West.

JPS Is there one work in your collection that you prize beyond all others?

CD Yes, I can tell you who it is – my old friend the philosopher and artist Carl-Heinz Wegert (1926–2007; fig. 3), who I met in 1972. He is only known to a few friends. His work is in only four collections – mine, those of Walter Bareiss and Franz, Herzog von Bayern, and the collection of the Lenbachhaus, Munich. I have admired him since the day I met him. One day in the early 1970s, I bought one of his rare oil paintings and looked at this picture while listening to Pink Floyd's *Dark Side of the Moon*. It all just seemed to click! It was at the same time that I started going for Twombly. And Wegert he worked in the same way all his life, drawing every day, for fifty years – unbelievable!

JPS Christian Duerckheim, thank you.

1. Now based in Frankfurt.
2. Franz, Herzog von Bayern, formerly known as Franz, Prinz von Bayern (b. 1933), is the head of the Wittelsbach family, former rulers of Bavaria, and known for his patronage of the arts; Walter Bareiss (1919–2007) was a German–American businessman known for his collection of classical, African and contemporary art.
3. M.G. Dönhoff, *Namen die keiner mehr nennt. Ostpreussen-Menschen und Geschichte,* Köla, 1985.

3. *Untitled*, 1972
Carl-Heinz Wegert
Watercolour and pencil,
150 x 130 mm
Duerckheim collection

Select Bibliography

General titles

Wedewer 1970
R. Wedewer and F. Jahn, *Zeichnungen. Baselitz, Beuys, Buthe, Darboven, Erber, Palermo, Polke, Richter, Rot*, exh. cat., Leverkusen (Städtisches Museum Schloß Morsbroich); Hamburg (Kunsthaus), Munich (Kunstverein), 1970

Dietrich-Boorsch 1982
D. Dietrich-Boorsch, *German Drawings of the 1960s*, exh. cat., New Haven (Yale University Art Gallery); Toronto (Art Gallery of Ontario), 1982

Knust 1982
S. Knust, *Erste Konzentration. Georg Baselitz, Antonious Höckelmann, Jörg Immendorff, Per Kirkeby, Markus Lüpertz, A. R. Penck*, Munich (Maximilian Verlag), 1982

Joachimides 1985
C.M. Joachimides, N. Rosenthal and W. Schmied, *German Art in the 20th Century: Painting and Sculpture, 1905–1985*, exh. cat., London (Royal Academy), 1985

Düsseldorf 1987
Brennpunkt Düsseldorf 1962–1987, exh. cat., Düsseldorf (Kunstmuseum), 1987

Schmidt 1990
W. Schmidt (ed.), *Ausgebürgert. Künstler aus der DDR und aus dem Sowjetischen Sektor Berlins 1949–1989*, exh. cat., Dresden (Albertinum), 1990; Hamburg (Kleine Deichtorhalle), 1991

Chávez and Heller 2003
A. Chávez and R. Heller, *Two and One. Printmaking in Germany 1945–1990*, exh. cat., Wellesley (Davis Museum and Cultural Center), 2003; Kiel (University Art Museum), 2004

Stonard 2007
J.P. Stonard, Fault Lines. Art in Germany 1945–1955, London, 2007

Mesch 2008
C. Mesch, *Modern Art at the Berlin Wall. Demarcating Culture in the Cold War Germanys*, London and New York, 2008

Barron and Eckmann 2009
S. Barron and S. Eckmann (eds), *Art of Two Germanys: Cold War Cultures*, exh. cat., Los Angeles (County Museum of Art); Nuremberg (Germanisches Nationalmuseum), 2009; Berlin (Deutsches Historisches Museum), 2010

Sotheby's 2011
The Duerckeim Collection, Sotheby's evening and day auctions catalogue, 29 and 30 June 2011

Georg Baselitz

Werner & Katz 1963
Georg Baselitz, exh. cat., with texts by Herbert Read and Martin G. Buttig, Berlin (Galerie Werner & Katz), 1963

Munich 1972
Georg Baselitz. Zeichnungen und Radierungen, 1960–1970, exh. cat., Munich (Staatliche Graphische Sammlung), 1972

Gercken 1973
G. Gercken, *Georg Baselitz. Ein neuer Typ. Bilder 1965–66*, exh. cat., Hamburg (Galerie Neuendorf), 1973

Friedrich 1974
S. Friedrich, *Georg Baselitz, Radierungen 1963–1974, Holzschnitte 1966–1967*, catalogue raisonné of prints, Leverkusen (Städtisches Museum Schloß Morsbroich), 1974

Leverkusen 1974
Georg Baselitz Radierungen 1963–1974, Holzschnitte 1966–1967, exh. cat., Leverkusen (Städtisches Museum), 1974

Werner 1974
Georg Baselitz. Zeichnungen 1960–1974, exh. cat., Cologne (Galerie Michael Werner), 1974

Friedrich 1976
Georg Baselitz, 'Der neue Typ', exh. cat., Munich (Galerie Heiner Friedrich), 1976

Gohr 1979
S. Gohr, *Georg Baselitz. 32 Linolschnitte aus den Jahren 1976–1979*, catalogue raisonné of large linocuts, Cologne (Josef-Haubrich-Kunsthalle), 1979

Groningen 1979
Georg Baselitz Tekeningen/Zeichnungen, exh. cat., Groningen (Groninger Museum), 1979

Calvocoressi 1983
R. Calvocoressi (ed.), *Georg Baselitz*, exh. cat., London (Whitechapel Gallery), 1983

Geneva 1983
L'Italie & L'Allemagne. Nouvelles Sensibilités, Nouveaux Marchés, exh. cat., with texts by M. Besset, P. Blum, J. Gachnang, N. Gillespie, S. Knust, R. M. Mason, C. Ritschard, F. Salvadori; Geneva (Cabinet des estampes, Musée d'art et d'histoire), 1983

Jahn 1983
F. Jahn, *Baselitz Peintre-Graveur*, Bd.I, catalogue raisonné of prints, 1963–1974, Bern (Berlin, Verlag Gachnang & Springer), 1983

Gohr 1984
S. Gohr, *Georg Baselitz. Druckgraphik, Prints, Estampes 1963–1983*, exh. cat., Munich (Staatliche Graphische Sammlung); Geneva (Cabinet des estampes du Musée d'art et d'histoire), 1984; Trier (Städtisches Museum Simeonstift); Paris (Bibliothèque Nationale); London (Tate Gallery), 1985

Koepplin 1984
Georg Baselitz: Zeichnungen, 1958–1983, exh. cat., with texts by Dieter Koepplin and Rudi Fuchs, Basel (Kunstmuseum); Eindhoven (Van Abbemuseum), 1984

Jahn 1987
F. Jahn, *Baselitz Peintre-Graveur*, Bd. II, catalogue raisonné of prints, 1974–1982, Bern (Berlin, Verlag Gachnang & Springer), 1987

Hofmann and Joachimedes 1988
W. Hofmann and C. M. Joachimides (eds), *Georg Baselitz. Bilder 1965–1987*, exh. cat., Florence (Sala d'Arme di Palazzo Vecchio), Hamburg (Kunsthalle), 1988

Koepplin 1989
Georg Baselitz, Zeichnungen und druckgraphische Werke aus dem Kupferstichkabinett Basel, Basel (Kunstmuseum), 1989

Reinhardt 1989
Georg Baselitz. Druckgraphik 1963–1988. Radierungen, Holzschnitte, Linolschnitte, Leverkusen (Museum Morsbroich), 1989–90

Gohr 1992
S. Gohr (ed.), *Georg Baselitz. Retrospektive 1964–1991*, exh. cat., Munich (Kunsthalle der Hypo-Kulturstiftung); Edinburgh (Scottish National Gallery of Modern Art); Vienna (Museum moderner Kunst Stiftung Ludwig), 1992

Adriani 1994
G. Adriani, *Georg Baselitz Druckgraphik 1965–1992*, exh. cat., Stuttgart (Instituts für Auslansbeziehungen), 1994

Waldman 1996
D. Waldman, *Georg Baselitz*, exh. cat., with contributions by D. Hönisch, P.-K. Schuster and A. Schneider, New York (Solomon R. Guggenheim Museum), 1995; Washington (Hirshhorn Museum and Sculpture Garden); Berlin (Nationalgalerie); Los Angeles (County Museum of Art), 1996

Mason 2007
R.M. Mason, *Georg Baselitz*, exh. cat., Lugano (Museo d'Arte Moderna), 2007

Rosenthal 2007
N. Rosenthal, *Georg Baselitz*, London (Royal Academy), 2007

Semff 2008
M. Semff, *Georg Baselitz. Druckgraphik von 1964–1983. Aus der Sammlung Herzog Franz von Bayern*, exh. cat., Dresden (Staatliche Kunstsammlungen); Munich (Pinakothek der Moderne), 2008

Gretenkort 2010
D. Gretenkort (ed.), *Georg Baselitz. Collected Writings and Interviews*, London, 2010

Rosenthal 2012
Georg Baselitz – Berliner Jahre/Bilder aus der Sammlung Baselitz, exh. cat., Potsdam (Villa Schöningen), 2012

Lupertz

Hofmann 1977
W. Hofmann and S. Holsten, *Markus Lüpertz*, exh. cat., Hamburg (Kunsthalle), 1977

Kneubühler 1977
T. Kneubühler, *Markus Lüpertz Zeichnungen*, Dortmund 1977

Gohr 1981
S. Gohr, *'Stil' Paintings*, exh. cat., London (Whitechapel), 1981

Pforzheim 1994
'Homo homini lupus'. Markus Lüpertz – Krieg, exh. cat., Pforzheim (Reuchlinhaus), 1994; Stuttgart (Galerie der Stadt), 1995

Aachen 1999
Markus Lüpertz. Zeichnungen 1963–1977. Sammlung Ludwig, Aachen, 1999

Bonn 2009
Markus Lüpertz. Highways and Byways. A Retrospective. Paintings and Sculptures from 1963 until 2009, exh. cat., Bonn (Kunst- und Ausstellungshalle der Bundesrepublik Deutschland), 2009

Palermo

Leverkusen 1975
Palermo Druckgraphik 1970–1974, exh. cat., Leverkusen (Städtisches Museum Schloß Morsbroich), 1975

Dahlem 1989
F. Dahlem, E. Weiss and M. Weschler, *Blinky Palermo 1943–1977*, New York, 1989

Leipzig 1993
Blinky Palermo, exh. cat. Leipzig (Museum der Bildenden Künste); Munich (Kunstraum), 1993

Moeller 1995 (1)
T. Moeller (ed.), *Palermo: Bilder und Objekte. Werkverzeichnis Band I*, with a text by K. Schrenk, Bonn 1995

Moeller 1995 (2)
T. Moeller (ed.), *Palermo: Zeichnungen. Werkverzeichnis Band II*, with a text by C. Schreier, Bonn 1995

Küper, Groos and Müller 2007
S. Küper, U. Groos and V. J. Müller (eds), *Palermo*, Düsseldorf (Kunsthalle; Kunstverein für die Rheinlande und Westfalen), 2007

Mehring 2008
C. Mehring, *Blinky Palermo. Abstraction of an Era*, New Haven and London, 2008

Cooke 2010
L. Cooke, K. Kelly, B. Schröder, *Blinky Palermo. Retrospective 1964–1977*, with essays by B.H.D. Buchloh, L. Cooke. S. Hudson, S. Küper, J. Lawrence, exh. cat., Los Angeles (County Museum of Art), 2010; Washington (Hirshhorn Museum and Sculpture Garden), 2011; New York (Dia: Beacon; CCS Bard), 2011

Penck

Penck and Immendorff 1979
A.R. Penck and J. Immendorff, *Immendorff besucht Y*, Munich, 1979

Geneva 1983
L'Italie & L'Allemagne. Nouvelles Sensibilités, Nouveaux Marchés, exh. cat., with texts by M. Besset, P. Blum, J. Gachnang, N. Gillespie, S. Knust, R.M. Mason, C. Ritschard, F. Salvadori; Geneva (Cabinet des estampes, Musée d'art et d'histoire), 1983

Edinburgh 1987
The Northern Darkness. A.R. Penck, exh. cat., Edinburgh (Fruitmarket Gallery), 1987

Koepplin 1987
D. Koepplin, *a.r.penck: Zeichnungen und druckgraphische Werke im Basler Kupferstichkabinett*, exh. cat., Geneva (Cabinet des estampes), 1986; Mönchengladbach (Städtisches Museum Abteiberg); Ulm (Ulmer Museum), Strassburg (Musées de Strasbourg); Eindhoven (Stedelijk Van Abbemuseum), 1987

Gemeentemuseum 1988
Tekeningen: A.R. Penck, exh. cat, The Hague (Gemeentemuseum), 1988

Grisebach 1988
L. Grisebach (ed.), *A.R. Penck*, exh. cat., Berlin (Nationalgalerie); Zürich (Kunsthaus), 1988

Haenlein 1988
C. Haenlein (ed.), *A.R. Penck. Skulpturen und Zeichnungen 1971–1987*, exh. cat., Hannover (Kestner-Gesellschaft), 1988

Graw 2000
I. Graw, *Immendorff X Penck, Penck X Immendorff. Rekonstruktion einer Ausstellung*, exh. cat., Cologne, New York (Michael Werner), 2000

Reutlingen 2003
A.R. Penck. Holzschnitte 1966–1995, exh. cat., Reutlingen (Städtische Galerie), 2003

Polke

Buchloh 1976
B.H.D. Buchloh (ed.), *Sigmar Polke. Bilder, Tücher, Objekte. Werkauswahl 1962–1971*, exh. cat., Tübingen (Kunsthalle); Düsseldorf (Kunsthalle); Eindhoven (Stedelijk van Abbe-Museum), 1976

Werner 1983
Sigmar Polke, exh. cat., with a text by A.R. Penck, Cologne (Michael Werner), 1983

Bonn 1988
Sigmar Polke: Zeichnungen, Aquarelle, Skizzenbücher 1962–1988, exh. cat., with texts by K. Schmidt and G. Schweikhart, Bonn (Kunstmuseum), 1988

San Francisco 1990
Sigmar Polke, exh. cat., with texts by J. Caldwell, P. Schjeldahl, J. Baldessari and R. Speck, San Francisco (Museum of Modern Art), 1990
Gachnang 1991

J. Gachnang, *Sigmar Polke. The Early Drawings 1963–1969*, Bern and Berlin, 1991

Bonn 1997
Sigmar Polke: The Three Lies of Painting, exh. cat., Bonn (Kunst- und Ausstellungshalle der Bundesrepublik Deutschland); Berlin (Hamburger Bahnhof), 1997

Richter

Utrecht 1972
Atlas van de foto's en schetsen, exh. cat., Utrecht (Hedendaagse Kunst), 1972

Schwarz 1999
D. Schwarz, *Gerhard Richter. Aquarelle = Watercolours 1964–1997*, Düsseldorf, 1999

Schwarz 2000
D. Schwarz and B. Pelzer, *Gerhard Richter. Drawings 1964–1999. Catalogue Raisonné*, Düsseldorf, 2000

Elger 2009
D. Elger, *Gerhard Richter. A Life in Painting*, trans. E.M. Solaro, Chicago, 2009

Elger 2011
D. Elger (ed.), *Gerhard Richter, Catalogue Raisonné, Volume 1*, Ostfildern, 2011

Acknowledgements

This publication was supported by a grant from Count Christian Duerckheim, who also agreed to be interviewed; I am very grateful to him for his kind involvement and inspired support.

I am grateful to Stephen Coppel for inviting me to write this catalogue; Hugo Chapman, Monica Sidhu, Giulia Bartrum, Barbara Canepa and the staff of the Prints and Drawings Department at the British Museum offered crucial suggestions and support for which I am much obliged. At The British Museum Press a debt of gratitude is owed to Claudia Bloch, Senior Development Editor, for her adept editing and production of this book, and to Katherine Anderson, Picture Researcher and Kate Oliver, Senior Production Controller. Thanks also to the Department of Photography and Imaging at the British Museum, and to Andy Wilke of Thomas Manss & Company for the design and layout of this publication.

A number of others provided information and ideas at various stages in the research and I am pleased to acknowledge: Jeffrey Allford, Tobias Bäumer, Georg Baselitz, Shulamith Behr, Katherine Graham, Detlev Gretenkort, Fred Jahn, Benjamin Katz, Wolf Meier-Ewart, Norman Rosenthal, Karsten Schubert, Nina Sturm, Julia Westner and Michael Trier. A special thanks is owed to Michael Werner, who opened up his library and archive, and enabled a study trip to Germany, which was essential for the completion of this catalogue.

Illustration Credits

The publishers would like to thank the copyright holders for granting permission to reproduce the images illustrated. Every attempt has been made to trace accurate ownership of copyrighted images in this book. Errors and omissions will be corrected in subsequent editions provided notification is sent to the publisher.

All photographs of British Museum objects are © The Trustees of the British Museum, courtesy of the Department of Photography and Imaging.

Introduction
Fig. 1: David Hoxley
Fig. 2: Foto 7105 © www.bilderbuch-koeln.de
Fig. 3: © Heinz Löffler Estate. Photo. Stiftung Stadtmuseum Berlin
Fig. 4: © DACS, London 2014. Photo © Tate, London 2014
Fig. 5: Photographer Günther Becker/ © Documenta Archive
Fig. 6: © Georg Baselitz. Photo courtesy of Galerie Michael Werner Märkisch Wilmersdorf, Cologne & New York
Fig. 7: © Georg Baselitz
Fig. 8: British Museum 1845,0809.1731
Fig. 9: British Museum I,7.102
Fig. 10: British Museum 1895,0607.83
Fig. 11: British Museum 1982,0724.28.23 © DACS, London 2014
Fig. 12: British Museum 1980,1011.45 © Nolde Stiftung Seebüll
Fig. 13: © Anselm Kiefer. Photo courtesy of Guggenheim Bilbao
Fig. 14: © DACS, London 2014. Photo courtesy of Albertina, Vienna
Fig. 15: © DACS, London 2014. Photo courtesy of Kunsthaus Zürich, Vereinigung Zürcher Kunstfreunde
Fig. 16: © DACS, London 2014
Fig. 17: Rogner & Bernhard / Duerckheim Art Promotion
Fig. 18: © Jörg Immendorf Photo © Tate, London 2014
Fig. 19: British Museum 2013,7043.32.2 © DACS, London 2014
Fig. 20: © DACS, London 2014 © Tate, London 2014
Fig. 21: © BPK/Angelika Platen
Fig. 22: © Gerhard Richter, 2014. Photo courtesy of Kunstmuseum Bonn, permanent loan from Jürgen Hall
Fig. 23: © The Estate of Sigmar Polke, Cologne, DACS, London 2014
Fig. 24: © Gerhard Richter, 2014

Georg Baselitz
Fig. 1: © Georg Baselitz. Photo courtesy of Farbanalyse
Fig. 2: © Georg Baselitz. Photo Archive Rhine Cologne: rolling, Sabrina, 2007
Fig. 3: British Museum E,4.87
Fig. 4: © Georg Baselitz
Fig. 5: © Georg Baselitz. Photo © Tate, London 2014
Fig. 6: © Georg Baselitz. Photo courtesy of Farbanalyse
Fig. 7: © Daniel Blau
Fig. 8: © Georg Baselitz. Photo courtesy of Farbanalyse
Fig. 9: © Georg Baselitz. Photo courtesy of Farbanalyse
Cats 1–41: All British Museum or Duerckheim collection images by Georg Baselitz are © Georg Baselitz. Images courtesy of the British Museum Department of Photography and Imaging.

Markus Lüpertz
Fig. 1: Photo courtesy of Galerie Michael Werner Märkisch Wilmersdorf, Cologne & New York
Fig. 2: © DACS, London 2014. Photo courtesy of Galerie Michael Werner Märkisch Wilmersdorf, Cologne & New York
Fig. 3: © DACS, London 2014. Photo courtesy of Galerie Michael Werner Märkisch Wilmersdorf, Cologne & New York
Fig. 4: © DACS, London 2014. Photo courtesy of Galerie Michael Werner Märkisch Wilmersdorf, Cologne & New York
Fig. 5: © DACS, London 2014. Photo courtesy of Galerie Michael Werner Märkisch Wilmersdorf, Cologne & New York
Fig. 6: Photo © Andrea Stappert, Berlin. Photo courtesy of Galerie Michael Werner Märkisch Wilmersdorf, Cologne & New York
Cats 42–46: All British Museum or Duerckheim collection images by Markus Lüpertz are © DACS, London 2014. Images courtesy of the British Museum Department of Photography and Imaging.

Blinky Palermo
Fig. 1: Ute Klophaus
Fig. 2: © DACS, London 2014. Courtesy of Sotheby's Picture Library
Fig. 3: © DACS, London 2014. Photo courtesy of (Blinky) Palermo Archive, Millerton, NY
Fig. 4: © DACS, London 2014
Fig. 5: © DACS, London 2014. Courtesy of Sotheby's Picture Library
Fig. 6: © DACS, London 2014. David Zwirner, New York/London
Cats 47–56: All British Museum or Duerckheim collection images by Blinky Palermo are © DACS, London 2014. Images courtesy of the British Museum Department of Photography and Imaging.

A.R. Penck
Fig. 1: Photo courtesy of Galerie Michael Werner Märkisch Wilmersdorf, Cologne & New York
Fig. 2: Rights reserved
Fig. 3: © DACS, London 2014. Photo courtesy of Galerie Michael Werner Märkisch Wilmersdorf, Cologne & New York
Fig. 4: © DACS, London 2014. Photo courtesy of Galerie Michael Werner Märkisch Wilmersdorf, Cologne & New York
Fig. 5: © DACS, London 2014. Photo courtesy of Galerie Michael Werner Märkisch Wilmersdorf, Cologne & New York
Fig. 6: © DACS, London 2014. Photo courtesy of Galerie Michael Werner Märkisch Wilmersdorf, Cologne & New York
Cats: 57–68: All British Museum or Duerckheim collection images by A.R. Penck are © DACS, London 2014. Images courtesy of the British Museum Department of Photography and Imaging.

Sigmar Polke
Fig. 1: © The Estate of Sigmar Polke, Cologne, DACS, London 2014
Fig. 2: © The Estate of Sigmar Polke, Cologne, DACS, London 2014. Photo © Tate, London 2014
Fig. 3: © The Estate of Sigmar Polke, Cologne, DACS, London 2014
Fig. 4: © The Estate of Sigmar Polke, Cologne, DACS, London 2014. Photo © Scala, Florence/BPK, Bildagentur fuer Kunst, Kultur und Geschichte, Berlin
Fig. 5: © The Estate of Sigmar Polke, Cologne, DACS, London 2014. Photo courtesy of Galerie Michael Werner Märkisch Wilmersdorf, Cologne & New York
Cats: 69–73: All British Museum or Duerckheim collection images by Sigmar Polke are © The Estate of Sigmar Polke, Cologne, DACS, London 2014. Images courtesy of the British Museum Department of Photography and Imaging.

Gerhard Richter
Fig. 1: © Gerhard Richter 2014, Foto: courtesy Gerhard Richter Archive.
Fig. 2: © Gerhard Richter 2014, Foto: courtesy Gerhard Richter Archive.
Fig. 3: © Gerhard Richter 2014, Foto: courtesy Gerhard Richter Archive.
Fig. 4: © Gerhard Richter 2014, Foto: courtesy Gerhard Richter Archive.
Fig. 5: © Gerhard Richter 2014, Foto: courtesy Gerhard Richter Archive.
Cats 74–94: All British Museum or Duerckheim collection images by Gerhard Richter are © Gerhard Richter 2014. Images courtesy of the British Museum Department of Photography and Imaging.

Conversation with Count Christian Duerckheim
Fig. 1: © 2013 The Andy Warhol Foundation for the Visual Arts, Inc./Artists Rights Society (ARS), New York
Fig. 2: © Georg Baselitz
Fig. 3: © DACS, London 2014

Index

Note: page numbers in **bold** refer to information contained in captions.